THE MAKING
OF AMERICAN
EXCEPTIONALISM

THE MAKING
OF AMERICAN
EXCEPTIONALISM

*The Knights of Labor
and Class Formation in the
Nineteenth Century*

KIM VOSS

Cornell University Press

ITHACA AND LONDON

First published 1993 by Cornell University Press.

Library of Congress Cataloging-in-Publication Data

Voss, Kim.
    The making of American exceptionalism : the Knights of Labor
and class formation in the nineteenth century / Kim Voss.
        p.   cm.
    Includes bibliographical references and index.
    ISBN 0-8014-2882-3 (acid-free paper). — ISBN 0-8014-8119-8 (acid-free
paper : pbk.)
    1. Knights of Labor—History.   2. Working class—United States—History
—19th century.   3. Trade-unions—United States—History—19th century.
    4. Labor movement—United States—History—19th century.   5. Trade-
unions—New Jersey—History—19th century.   6. Labor movement—New
Jersey—History—19th century.   I. Title.
HD8055.K7V67   1993   93-28073
331.88'33'0973—dc20

Printed in the United States of America

FOR RICK

Contents

PART THREE
Conclusion

Tables

Preface

I began this book because my reading of the new labor history of the 1970s and early 1980s suggested that the traditional explanations offered for America's weak and conservative labor movement had been discredited. No longer was it tenable to argue that workers in the United States have historically been incapable of or felt no need for class-based collective action. Instead, labor historians published study after study demonstrating instances of class-conscious activity in nineteenth-century America that rivaled that of working-class movements in Europe.

At the same time, it was clear to me that the new labor history was not itself producing a compelling alternative account of the distinctive evolution of the American labor movement. Many scholars felt they had accomplished their task when they uncovered new examples of American workers behaving in class-conscious ways while others issued appeals that we simply banish the question of exceptionalism altogether. I found both of these approaches unsatisfying: the intellectual return on each community study seemed to grow progressively smaller over time, and I thought it premature to dismiss the question of exceptionalism before we had dealt convincingly with the puzzle of how radical attitudes and actions on the part of American workers were eventually transformed into a weak and conservative labor movement.

Thus, I set out to construct a new explanation of the development of the American labor movement, one that would integrate workers' radical rhetoric and behavior with the singularly narrow organizational forms and conservative politics adopted by unions at the turn of the century.

The intellectual tools and tastes I brought to this task were profoundly shaped by my training and experiences as a historical sociologist. Most important, I believed that making sense of the American labor movement required systematic comparison both with other countries and with different types of situations and communities in the United States. I used international comparisons to understand the nature of critical junctures and to make sense of the actual range of variation that existed in workers' actions and discourses at key moments in the development of labor movements. Too often, it seemed to me, analysts of the American working class had fallen into the trap of judging workers' behavior and rhetoric by some preconceived notion of how workers ought to have behaved and thought in key moments, without evaluating the actual ways that workers in similar situations elsewhere acted and spoke of themselves.

It was my exploration of the history of the French and English labor movements that led me to focus on the Noble and Holy Order of the Knights of Labor. Several of the new labor historians had written of the Order, highlighting its radicalism. From a comparative vantage point, however, it became clear that the Knights of Labor was important not only because it represented an oppositional ideology and engaged in militant strike activity but also because it represented a major watershed in the history of the American working class. Knights activists tried to organize the American working class broadly for the first time in roughly the same period when labor leaders in England and France were first beginning to incorporate less-skilled wage earners into their labor movements. However, while activists' efforts in these other countries led to permanent successes, similar efforts by the Knights ended in failure. In the aftermath of the Order's collapse, the American labor movement looked increasingly different from its French and English counterparts. Because students of American exceptionalism have rarely attempted to historicize its emergence, conceptualizing "exceptionalism" instead as an invariant feature of American society, they had missed the remarkable similarities in the American, English, and French labor movements earlier in the nineteenth century. My comparative appraisal suggested that by examining the rise and demise of the Knights, I stood a good chance of shedding new light on the puzzle of American exceptionalism.

My approach to investigating the Knights of Labor also made use of systematic comparisons, this time of a statistical nature. My goal was to identify the general interplay of forces behind both the success of the Knights in organizing broad sectors of the American working class and the organization's ultimate inability to endure. Others had impressionistically gauged the relative importance of the various causes of the national achievements and defeats of the Knights, or had done a careful assessment of the growth and decline of the Knights in a few communities. But no one had examined the creation and collapse of the organization's sponsored alliances between skilled and less-skilled workers in a wide range of communities and industries. By doing so, I hoped to distinguish the general conditions that explained the Knights' rise and demise.

Statistical analysis is invaluable for identifying general patterns and refuting arguments; it is much less useful for uncovering the nuances of historical processes or breathing life into the relationships it reveals. Thus, I also incorporate case studies in my investigation of the Knights' growth and collapse.

In combining comparative history, statistical analysis, and case studies, I move throughout the text from the global to the local and back again in a manner that some historians will no doubt find a bit dizzying. This is the nature of historical sociology. What it offers to offset the discomfort is an account of the American labor movement that weighs and uses the contributions of historians while developing fresh arguments and raising new questions for future exploration. Sociologists will find the interplay of theory and history, global and local, more familiar, although those of a less historical bent than my own will perhaps encounter more of the particular than they are accustomed to. What I offer in compensation is not only a new interpretation of the American labor movement, one that builds on the best recent work in labor history, but also a new theoretical argument about the consequences of the ways that participants in social movements frame defeats. I hope that both the interpretation and the argument will inspire further investigation.

While writing this book, I have sometimes glimpsed an exquisite vision in which the lofty realm of comparative history, the elegant cosmos of statistical equations, and the gritty, vital universe of my nineteenth-century subjects all come together with perfect clarity. Reality is inevitably messier than our mental constructs, but to the extent that I have achieved anything approximating the lucidity revealed in those rare moments, it is due in part to the intellectual stimulation and personal support I have received from several people.

I owe particular thanks to my colleagues in the sociology department at the University of California, Berkeley. They are an extraordinary group of scholars whose respect for "big" books allowed me to pursue the puzzle of "American exceptionalism" even though it meant my book would be several years in the making. Mike Hout deserves special thanks; he read and provided thoughtful advice on significant portions of the manuscript. Jorge Arditi, Michael Burawoy, and Neil Smelser offered valuable suggestions for improving individual chapters.

In my graduate school days, Seymour Martin Lipset offered significant comparative insight and, although I did not know it at the time, passed on to me his continuing fascination with American exceptionalism. Carol Conell's enormous critical abilities helped me at every turn; to date I have met no one who is her equal at turning theoretical arguments into testable statistical models. She read various versions of the manuscript, and I continue to benefit from her learning and generosity. Ann Swidler's theoretical guidance and telling criticisms helped me clarify many obscure points and strengthen my argument. Michael Hannan was patient when I cavalierly rejected advice; in the end my obvious intellectual debt is probably the best apology.

Several friends and colleagues have provided invaluable assistance during the later stages of the project. David Brody, Alan Derickson, Ileen DeVault, Nancy Hewitt, Jeff Manza, and Charles Tilly read and made suggestions for improving the entire manuscript. Others read and commented on specific chapters; these include Richard Bensel, Glenn Carroll, Tony Fels, Gerald Friedman, Lawrence B. Glickman, Michael Hanagan, Ira Katznelson, Steve Leikin, Ronald Rothbart, Robert N. Stern, and members of the Berkeley Junior Faculty Americanists Group. Although I have been unable to incorporate all their advice and suggestions, the manuscript has been greatly improved by their kindness and critical acumen.

I am also indebted to many individuals for additional help. Leon Fink graciously shared his data on local third-party elections in 1886–1888. Daniel Jones at the New Jersey State Archives helped me hunt down sources. Mark Stern sent me his research on pottery workers and told me about archival materials I had not yet discovered. Daniel Dohan, Robert Freeland, Kurt Thompson, and Patricia Tweet provided research assistance. Elizabeth Rudd, my research assistant for the last two years, deserves special mention; she made important intellectual contributions to the final stages of this project and coordinated the details of manuscript preparation. Peter Agree, my editor at Cornell University Press, encouraged me from an early stage in the book's development.

Financial support was contributed by the Institute of Industrial Relations and the Committee on Research at the University of California, Berkeley, as well as by a National Science Foundation Dissertation Grant, a Mary Laura Bean Endowed Fellowship from the American Association of University Women, and a Grant-in-Aid of Research from the New Jersey Historical Society. The Center for Studies of Social Change at the New School for Social Research, where I spent six months of concentrated research and writing time, provided an office, a computer, and a lively intellectual community.

Permission has kindly been granted to quote from William Carlos Williams, *Paterson*. Copyright 1948 by William Carlos Williams. Reprinted by permission of New Directions Pub. Corp. An earlier version of Chapter 5 appeared as "Labor Organization and Class Alliance: Industries, Communities, and the Knights of Labor" in *Theory and Society* 17 (1988): 329–64. An earlier version of Chapter 7 appeared as "Disposition Is Not Action: The Rise and Demise of the Knights of Labor" in *Studies in American Political Development* 6 (Fall 1992): 272–321.

Finally, I would like to acknowledge two debts of a more personal nature. My mother has provided love and empathy throughout this project. She has also continued to teach me about social commitment and living life with a sense of adventure. Rick Jaffe has made it all worthwhile. This book is dedicated to him.

KIM VOSS

Oakland, California

THE MAKING
OF AMERICAN
EXCEPTIONALISM

Working-Class Formation
and the Knights of Labor

The late nineteenth century saw the emergence of many features that we today associate with "American exceptionalism."[1] In the mid-1870s the American labor movement did not differ significantly from labor movements in England and France, two countries at roughly the same stage of capitalist development. All were primarily movements of skilled craft workers, all shared broad similarities in rhetoric and behavior. By the early twentieth century, however, the American labor movement had begun to stand apart. Whereas workers in France and England had incorporated less-skilled wage earners into

---

1. The debate over American exceptionalism dates from the publication of Werner Sombart's 1906 book, *Why Is There No Socialism in the United States?* trans. Patricia M. Hocking and C. T. Husbands (rpt. White Plains, N.Y.: International Arts and Sciences Press, 1976). An insightful treatment of both Sombart and the issue of American socialism can be found in Jerome Karabel, "The Failure of American Socialism Reconsidered," *The Socialist Register* 18 (1979): 204–27. Other recent efforts to grapple with American exceptionalism include John M. Laslett and Seymour Martin Lipset, eds., *Failure of a Dream: Essays in the History of American Socialism* (Garden City, N.Y.: Anchor, 1974); Mike Davis, "Why the U.S. Working Class Is Different," *New Left Review* 123 (1980): 5-44; Michael Shalev and Walter Korpi, "Working Class Mobilization and American Exceptionalism," *Economic and Industrial Democracy* 1 (1980): 31–61; Sean Wilentz, "Against Exceptionalism: Class Consciousness and the American Labor Movement, 1790–1920," *International Labor and Working Class History* 26 (1984): 1–24; Eric Foner, "Why Is There No Socialism in America?" *History Workshop* 17 (1984): 57–80; Richard Oestreicher, "Urban Working-Class Political Behavior and Theories of American Electoral Politics, 1870–1940," *Journal of American History* 74 (1988): 1257–86; Byron E. Shafer, ed., *Is America Different? A New Look at American Exceptionalism* (Oxford: Clarendon Press, 1991); and Ian Tyrrell, "American Exceptionalism in an Age of International History," *American Historical Review* 96 (1991): 1031–55.

the labor movement and launched socialist or labor parties, workers in the United States were unable to build either a lasting broad-based labor movement or a powerful socialist party. Instead, dominated by the American Federation of Labor (AFL), the American labor movement eschewed the organization of less-skilled workers and the pursuit of political power. It was not until the New Deal, nearly sixty years after large-scale factories became prevalent in the United States, that less-skilled workers were successfully incorporated into the labor movement or that national unions actively tried to build political institutions.[2]

The organization of the Knights of Labor is a significant part of the story of why the American labor movement looked as it did on the eve of the twentieth century. Organized as a secret society by Philadelphia garment workers in 1869, the Noble and Holy Order of the Knights of Labor attempted to organize all workers, regardless of skill, race, or gender. In the early 1880s, it began a period of explosive growth, touched off by the Order's participation in a series of highly publicized strikes against the hated financier Jay Gould, a national symbol of corporate power. By 1886, the year of American labor's "great upheaval," the Knights had local assemblies in every state and organized between 8 and 12 percent of the industrial labor force. That same year, Knights members ran candidates for local office on independent labor slates in dozens of communities. These dramatic successes were followed by an equally spectacular decline; within five years the Order had collapsed as a viable national organization. This collapse effectively discredited working-class-based political mobilization in the United States for several generations.[3]

2. In 1912 the AFL did move into a formal coalition with the Democratic party, but I would not categorize this coalition as an instance of unions actively building working-class political institutions. As Gwendolyn Mink notes, this coalition was one in which unions were dependent on a middle-class party, rather than one in which a middle-class party was dependent on a significant labor wing. Moreover, as she points out, "from labor's standpoint, the tie was a slack one. Indeed, when union labor became politically tainted with class mobilization after World War I, the Democratic party surrendered to the contradictions of union dependence on a middle-class party, and the Democratic state, in pursuit of middle-class normality, broke its promises to union allies." *Old Labor and New Immigrants in American Political Development* (Ithaca: Cornell University Press, 1986), pp. 264–65.

3. In 1886, the Order's reported membership was 729,677. Bryan D. Palmer calculates, "cautiously," that this figure represents at least 8 percent of the work force. I believe that this figure is probably overly cautious; if we divide the total membership by the labor force employed in the industrial sector, which is where the Knights concentrated its organizational efforts, the figure is 11.76 percent. The latter figure is based on the total work force employed in manufacturing, construction, mining, and railway transport in 1886; I estimated it by interpolating the figures given in U.S. Bureau of the Census, *Historical Statistics of the United States* (Washington, D.C.: U.S. Government

In this book I explore the dynamics of solidarity in the Knights of Labor and the implications of the Knights' experience for our understanding of American class politics. It is a story of working-class formation, but in a specific sense: the coming together of loosely organized occupational groups as a collective political actor.[4] I ask how solidarity was actually forged between workers in skilled and less-skilled occupations and what determined the fate of these alliances. In answering these questions, I seek to illuminate the circumstances that promoted unity and fragmentation in the American working class.

The organization of the Knights of Labor provides a unique lens into the process of class formation. On paper the Order was a highly centralized union, but, in reality, it was a varied, decentralized association in which local assemblies exercised much autonomy. Members of each local assembly defined their own collective identity and chose their own organizing strategy. Locals had great latitude in setting goals and deciding tactics and thus were very responsive to local conditions. This makes the local assemblies of the Knights an ideal source for tracing the effects of both local conditions and workers' actions on working-class development.

In this book I pursue the topic of solidarity and disunity in the Knights by investigating the emergence and decline of these local assemblies. I focus on the locals of one important industrial state, New

---

Printing Office, 1975), pt. 1, p. 139. Palmer's figure is reported in "Social Formation and Class Formation in North America," in *Proletarianization and Family History,* ed. David Levine (Orlando, Fla.: Academic Press, 1984), p. 273. Because it is based on the Knights' peak membership, even this figure probably understates the Order's influence. The Order attained its greatest strength at different times in different communities and many more members "passed through" the Knights of Labor than were members at any one time. Jonathan Garlock estimates that over the course of the Order's history, more than three million workers were enrolled. See "A Structural Analysis of the Knights of Labor: A Prolegomenon to the History of the Producing Classes," Ph.D. diss., University of Rochester, 1974, pp. 222–32.

4. For an excellent survey of recent literature on working-class formation, see Ira Katznelson, "Working-Class Formation: Constructing Cases and Comparisons," in *Working-Class Formation,* ed. Ira Katznelson and Aristide R. Zolberg (Princeton: Princeton University Press, 1986), pp. 3–41. Katznelson urges that we move away from the essentialist assumption inherent in the traditional Marxist understanding of class formation that "classes 'in themselves' will, indeed, must act 'for themselves' at some moment." He suggests that an improved formulation would distinguish four separate dimensions of class formation: (1) the structure of capitalist development, (2) ways of life within capitalism, (3) group formation, and (4) collective action. Katznelson thus includes in his definition of working-class formation both the creation of a set of production relations (levels 1 and 2) and the creation of a working-class–based consciousness and politics (levels 3 and 4). I use the term only to encompass the latter process, but, like Katznelson, I too shed the assumption that production relations will mechanically determine class consciousness or class organization.

See also Katznelson's *City Trenches: Urban Politics and the Patterning of Class in the United States* (Chicago: University of Chicago Press, 1982), chaps. 2, 3, and 8.

Jersey, and systematically investigate the specific effects of community setting, industry characteristics, workers' actions, and employers' resistance on their rise and demise. In analyzing the creation of the locals, my primary concern is to understand how and when American workers were able to forge alliances across the skill divide. In analyzing the demise of the locals, my major goal is to discover whether (and, if so, to what extent) the Knights collapsed because it proved impossible for American workers to sustain such a class-based alliance.

Such systematic analysis can distinguish and weigh the various forces that shaped the labor movement in the United States. I had two objectives in undertaking it. I wanted to contribute, first, to our knowledge of the process of working-class formation and, second, to our understanding of the ways in which this process produced diverse political legacies.

In broad terms, I argue that until 1886, the American working class developed in ways that were generally similar to the ways the working classes in England and France developed. As elsewhere, craft workers played a key role, both in forging the early labor movement and, later, in mobilizing less-skilled workers. Craft workers did not always play this "craft radical" role in the United States, but, as I attempt to demonstrate, neither did they always play it elsewhere. Instead, building solidarity was everywhere a protracted project, and one that was easier in the community arena than on the shop floor. Community alliances between skilled and less-skilled workers were common in the Knights of Labor and were a large part of the reason why the Order mobilized so rapidly. Later this rapid mobilization would place severe strains on the Knights, but neither it nor the more commonly mentioned lack of solidarity on the part of skilled workers was the primary reason for the collapse of the Order's local assemblies. Instead, the mobilization of employer opposition, especially against skilled craft workers who maintained their allegiance to the Knights in the hostile years following the Haymarket bombing, was the most important reason for the decline of the Knights. Workers' response to this opposition, and the lessons they drew from their failure to triumph over it, in turn, helped to discredit broad-based political unionism as a model for labor movement development in the United States.

Alliances, Craft Organization, and Working-Class Formation

In examining the process of working-class formation in the Knights of Labor, this work focuses on alliances between skilled and less-skilled workers and especially on the role of craft organization in encouraging or hindering such alliances. It does so because in the late nineteenth century, creating a true class-based social movement entailed an alliance between the skilled, unionized heirs to the artisan traditions of the 1830s and the growing number of less-skilled factory workers. To see why, let us briefly consider the timing of labor movement development in the three countries that are most frequently discussed in recent social history—England, France, and the United States.

In each of these countries, a labor movement was initially built long before the factory proletariat came to dominate the population of wage earners. According to E. P. Thompson, English workers spoke and thought of themselves in working-class terms for the first time in 1832, and, as subsequent work by William Sewell and Sean Wilentz has demonstrated, French and American workers developed a similar language of class shortly thereafter.[5] In each of these countries, crafts people began to think and act as "workers," rather than just as members of this or that trade. Although the extent and content of this new collective awareness varied, in all three countries, the primary actors were skilled artisans who constructed similar criticisms of the developing capitalist economy. Thus, as Sewell notes, "The nineteenth-century labor movement was born in the craft workshop, not in the dark, satanic mill."[6]

Despite the title of E. P. Thompson's book, *The Making of the English Working Class*, it is more accurate to think of this early development of the labor movement as the first "moment" of class formation rather than as any final "making" of the working class.[7] Half a century later, when both the composition of the working class and the nature of capitalist development were dramatically different, the labor movement had to be remade if it was to remain a true working-class movement and not become simply a minority movement of skilled craftsmen. By the 1880s, large factories, not small shops, dominated the industrial landscape, and less-skilled workers outnumbered artisans in the labor force. On the shopfloor, traditional craft skills were in decreasing demand as mechanization and work reorganization created

5. E. P. Thompson, *The Making of the English Working Class* (New York: Vintage, 1966); William H. Sewell, Jr., *Work and Revolution in France: The Language of Labor from the Old Regime to 1848* (Cambridge: Cambridge University Press, 1980); Sean Wilentz, *Chants Democratic: New York City and the Rise of the American Working Class, 1788–1850* (New York: Oxford University Press, 1984).

6. Sewell, *Work and Revolution*, p. 1.

7. Eric Hobsbawm makes a similar point in his essay "The Making of the Working Class, 1870–1914," in his *Workers: Worlds of Labor* (New York: Pantheon, 1984), pp. 194–213.

more and more semiskilled jobs. In the larger economy, both skilled and less-skilled workers became enmeshed in national markets, a development that made it increasingly difficult for skilled workers to ignore the presence of less-skilled workers, even when they did not work next to them in the factory. Thus, before the decade ended, contemporary commentators recognized that a new, permanent class of proletarianized workers was emerging and argued that ameliorating the problems created by the new factories and work regimes required organizing around the common identity of wage labor.[8]

Such broad-based organization, however, was difficult to achieve. The rigors of the new industrial discipline and the high rates of geographical mobility depleted all wage-earners' organizational resources and were especially ruinous for the less skilled. At work, modern forms of discipline and sharp distinctions between different types of work isolated wage earners from one another; after work there were few hours remaining in the day to socialize. Ethnic and gender differences, too, often divided less-skilled workers from one another.

Work reorganization also undercut skilled workers' positions, but, unlike the less skilled, they frequently retained enough resources to act collectively. Craftsmen were more likely to be unionized; they generally had a better developed repertoire of collective action; and they were in a more strategic position at work. Thus, their participation and resources were crucial; without them, an inclusive labor movement was unlikely to be built.

The pivotal role of skilled workers is attested to in the burgeoning literature on nineteenth-century craft workers. Indeed, the importance of skilled workers to labor protest and rebellion in the nineteenth century has become something of an orthodoxy among scholars of the labor movement. Two opposing images recur in these studies. In one image, skilled workers play the role of craft radicals who spearhead revolutionary working-class movements; in the other, they act as conservative labor aristocrats who hinder the organization of other workers.[9] Underlying both images is the specter of technological

8. For France, see John Merriman, *The Red City: Limoges and the French Nineteenth Century* (New York: Oxford University Press, 1985), chap. 6; for England, see Henry Pelling, *A History of British Trade Unionism*, 3d ed. (London: Macmillan, 1976); for the United States, see Irwin Yellowitz, *Industrialization and the American Labor Movement, 1850–1900* (Port Washington, N.Y.: Kennikat Press, 1977), and Chapters 2 and 5 of this book. The ideas in this and the next two paragraphs were first elaborated in Carol Conell and Kim Voss, "Formal Organization and the Fate of Social Movements," *American Sociological Review* 55 (1990): 255–69.

9. The "radical artisan" image is the dominant one in most recent social history; see Thompson, *Making;* Joan Wallach Scott, *The Glassworkers of Carmaux* (Cambridge: Harvard University Press, 1974); Sewell, *Work and Revolution;* Victoria E. Bonnell, *Roots*

change, in the face of which craft workers are attempting to preserve their autonomy. The major difference is that radical artisans are led to support inclusive union strategies and class-based politics, whereas labor aristocrats respond with increasing exclusivity.

Most authors emphasize either one or the other of these images, but a close reading of the evidence suggests that neither image is entirely correct. Instead, skilled workers and craft organization played a contingent and contradictory role in the process of working-class formation.[10] Craft workers were at once radical and conservative; craft organization was simultaneously a nucleus for further working-class organization and an obstacle to it.

It is worth spending a moment demonstrating this point because it underlies much of the argument to follow. A majority of studies of radical artisans concern the French. Here, researchers are more inclined to search for worker solidarity, and their research strategies, as well as the nature of the records available, increase the likelihood that they will find it. Many studies investigate an important political struggle—a revolution, an uprising, a strike—in one particular town or region. A common procedure is to use arrest records to analyze

<hr />

of Rebellion: Workers, Politics, and Organizations in St. Petersburg and Moscow, 1900–1914 (Berkeley: University of California Press, 1983); Bernard H. Moss, The Origins of the French Labor Movement: The Socialism of Skilled Workers, 1830–1914 (Berkeley: University of California Press, 1976); Michael P. Hanagan, The Logic of Solidarity (Urbana: University of Illinois Press, 1980) and Ronald A. Aminzade, Class, Politics, and Early Industrial Capitalism: A Study of Mid-Nineteenth-Century Toulouse, France (Albany: State University of New York Press, 1981).

The "labor aristocracy" image is found primarily in the British and American literature. For Britain, see Eric Hobsbawm, Labouring Men (London: Weidenfeld and Nicolson, 1964), pp. 272–315, and Workers: Worlds of Labor, pp. 214–72; John Foster, Class Struggle and the Industrial Revolution (London: Weidenfeld and Nicolson, 1974); Gareth Stedman Jones, "Class Struggle and the Industrial Revolution," New Left Review 90 (1975): 35–69. A survey of the British literature can be found in John Field, "British Historians and the Concept of the Labor Aristocracy," Radical History Review 19 (1978): 61–85, and critiques are presented in H. F. Moorhouse, "The Marxist Theory of the Labor Aristocracy," Social History 3 (1978): 61–82, and "The Significance of the Labor Aristocracy," Social History 6 (1981): 229–35. For the United States, see Karl Marx and Frederick Engels, Letters to Americans, 1848–1895 (New York: International Publishers, 1953), p. 242; Philip S. Foner, History of the Labor Movement in the United States, 2d ed. (New York: International Publishers, 1975), 2: 437–39 and History of the Labor Movement in the United States, 1st ed. (New York: International Publishers, 1964), 3: 174–94; and Jean Monds, "Workers' Control and the Historians: A New Economism," New Left Review 97 (1976): 81–100. A more subtle and insightful treatment of the labor aristocracy in the United States is presented in Andrew Dawson, "The Paradox of Dynamic Technological Change and the Labor Aristocracy in the United States, 1880–1914," Labor History 20 (1979): 325–51.

10. A few studies have recognized this and begun to ask about alliances. See Michael P. Hanagan and Charles Stephenson, "The Skilled Worker and Working-Class Protest," Social Science History 4 (1980): 5–13; Hanagan, Logic of Solidarity; and Jeffrey Haydu, Between Craft and Class (Berkeley: University of California Press, 1988).

the participation rates of workers in different trades and then to link differential rates of participation with features of particular trades.[11] But focusing on moments of widespread collective action tends to emphasize common action by multiple trades within a community rather than to reveal exclusivist tendencies within trades. Obscured is the fact that artisans who stand at the forefront of radical political movements (those, in other words, whose occupational titles appear over and over again on arrest records) often are the very same artisans who close their trade unions to the newer, less-skilled operatives once these operatives are employed in large numbers. Such membership restrictions were practiced by the Parisian tailors, who, as Christopher Johnson discovered, were so active in the class struggles of the 1830s and 1840s.[12] Similar exclusivity was practiced by the artisanal glassworkers of Rive-de-Grier; yet, as Michael Hanagan shows, these same glassworkers provided the critical leadership and financial backing when the semiskilled metalworkers of Rive-de-Grier undertook a militant general strike in 1893.[13]

Studies of the British and American working class often emphasize the opposite features of class formation, highlighting exclusionary tendencies through studies of a single industry or trade, rather than moments of united action by a community of workers. Few studies inquire about interoccupational solidarity between skilled and less-skilled workers. In part this scarcity reflects a difference in sources. Particularly in the United States, no strong centralized state collected spy reports and arrest records. This scarcity also reflects different historical events. In France, the revolutionary uprisings that punctuated the nineteenth century provide a natural research focus. In the United States and Britain, in contrast, most researchers try to explain the retarded development of revolutionary movements. Hence the literature tends to draw examples from instances where workers rejected industrial unionism.

In the United States, as in France, asking different questions reveals

11. E.g., Charles Tilly and Lynn H. Lees, "The People of June, 1848," in *Revolution and Reaction,* ed. Roger Price (London: Croom Helm, 1975), pp. 170–209; Ronald Aminzade, "Revolution and Collective Political Violence: The Case of the Working Class of Marseille, France, 1830–1871," Working Paper 86, Center for Research on Social Organization, University of Michigan, 1973; William H. Sewell, Jr., "Social Change and the Rise of Working-Class Politics in Nineteenth-Century Marseille," *Past and Present* 65 (1974): 75–109.

12. Christopher Johnson, "Patterns of Proletarianization: Parisian Tailors and Lodeve Woolens Workers," in *Class Consciousness and Class Experience in Nineteenth-Century Europe,* ed. John M. Merriman (New York: Holmes and Meier, 1979), pp. 57–114.

13. Hanagan, *Logic of Solidarity,* chap. 4.

other tendencies. For example, David Montgomery has shown that, even in the United States (and even within single industries), craft workers' resistance to de-skilling occasionally formed the basis for common action between skilled and less-skilled workers.[14] Community studies of nineteenth-century American workers have also found instances of solidarity between skilled and less-skilled workers.[15]

In sum, if we are to understand the process and contours of working-class formation, particularly in the critical second moment when labor movements in France, England, and the United States were remade, we need to focus our attention on alliances and craft organization. We should not expect workers in any particular country always to play the role of either craft radicals or labor aristocrats. Instead, we should investigate the conditions that encouraged alliances between craft and craftless workers, the frequency with which these conditions occurred, and the fate of any alliances that were forged.

In this book I do so by examining local variation in the creation of alliances between skilled and less-skilled workers in the Knights of Labor. I ask three questions about the building of solidarity. First, I ask whether skilled workers tended to ally with less-skilled workers in the Knights. Second, I ask about the basis of alliances: were alliances more likely to occur at the community level (as they apparently did in France) or at the industry level? And third, I ask about the conditions that encouraged alliances.

Social Movements, Solidarity, and the Collapse of the Knights

The first half of this book demonstrates the important role alliances played in the emergence of the Knights. Coalitions, primarily between skilled and less-skilled workers in the same community, were common. In New Jersey, the Knights grew rapidly among less-skilled workers in large part because skilled craftsmen provided from their ranks many of the activists and organizational resources needed to initiate locals of less-skilled workers.

Sustaining a social movement, however, involves different chal-

14. David Montgomery, *Workers' Control in America* (Cambridge: Cambridge University Press, 1979).

15. Alan Dawley, *Class and Community* (Cambridge: Harvard University Press, 1976); John T. Cumbler, *Working-Class Community in Industrial America* (Westport, Conn.: Greenwood, 1979); Daniel J. Walkowitz, *Worker City, Company Town: Iron and Cotton-Worker Protest in Troy and Cohoes, New York* (Urbana: University of Illinois Press, 1978).

lenges from those faced in building one. Instead of mobilizing people, the challenge is to create enduring organization; in addition to expounding possible futures, leaders have to explain failures and defeats. It is possible that solidarity could decay under such changed circumstances. This, for example, is what Selig Perlman argues happened in the Knights. As less-skilled workers joined in increasing numbers, and as the Order became entangled in a series of difficult strikes, the skilled abandoned the Knights:

> [T]he struggle was one between groups within the working class, in which the small but more skilled group fought for independence of the larger but weaker group of the unskilled and semi-skilled. The skilled men stood for the right to use their advantage of skill and efficient organization in order to wrest the maximum amount of concessions for themselves. The Knights of Labor endeavored to annex their skilled men in order that the advantage from their exceptional fighting strength might lift up the unskilled and semi-skilled. From the viewpoint of a struggle between principles this was indeed a clash between the principle of solidarity of labour and that of trade separatism.[16]

To assess adequately the extent to which the Knights' failure reflects a breakdown of solidarity, one needs to recognize that other factors also affect the development and decline of social movements. Unfortunately, sociologists have paid much less attention to the development and decline of social movements than they have to their emergence. Nevertheless, it is possible to distinguish two broad theoretical perspectives on social movement decline: a classical model that focuses on processes such as oligarchization and conservatization which are internal to the movement, and a political process model that emphasizes the interplay between internal and external processes.[17] Gener-

16. Selig Perlman, "Upheaval and Reorganization (since 1876)," in *History of Labour in the United States*, ed. John R. Commons (New York: Macmillan, 1918), 2: 396–97.

17. Typically, everything written about social movements before the formulation of resource mobilization theory is now referred to as the "classical" model. This is less problematic for movement decline than it is for movement emergence, because there was only one model for understanding movement decline before that time—the one proposed by Weber and Michels that focuses on institutionalization and oligarchization. See H. J. Gerth and C. W. Mills, eds., *From Max Weber: Essays in Sociology* (New York: Oxford University Press, 1946), pp. 297–301; and Roberto Michels, *Political Parties* (Glencoe, Ill.: The Free Press, 1949). For a contemporary application of Michels's argument, see Frances Fox Piven and Richard A. Cloward, *Poor People's Movements: Why They Succeed, How They Fail* (New York: Vintage, 1979). A useful critique and extension of this model can be found in Mayer N. Zald and Roberta Ash, "Social Movement Organizations: Growth, Decay, and Change," in *Studies in Social Movements: A Social Psychological Perspective*, ed. Barry McLaughlin (New York: The Free Press, 1969). For the most com-

ally, labor historians implicitly adopt the lens of the classical theorists. Their tendency is to emphasize workers' actions and organizational dilemmas when explaining the failure of working-class movements. In the case of the Knights, scholars have pointed to the problem of leadership, to the Knights' unwieldy organizational structure, to factionalism, to tactical errors, and, most frequently, to the antagonistic competition of the national trade unions in their accounts of the Knights' collapse.[18] Factors external to the labor movement, such as the actions of employers and the changed political climate in the wake of Haymarket, are sometimes mentioned but rarely singled out as primary causes.[19]

The problem with such internal explanations is that they neglect the extent to which political opportunities and the response of other social groups affect internal organizational processes. Recently, social movement scholars have proposed a "political process model" for understanding this interaction. It suggests that a change either in the structure of political opportunities, in the response of other social groups, or in the organizational strength of the movement can diminish the ability of movement members to sustain collective protest. Most important, this model emphasizes the dynamic nature of the interaction:

---

prehensive elaboration of the political process model, see Charles Tilly, *From Mobilization to Revolution* (Reading, Mass.: Addison-Wesley, 1978), pp. 52–142, and for the best elaboration of the model with respect to movement decline, see Doug McAdam, "The Decline of the Civil Rights Movement," in *Social Movements of the Sixties and Seventies*, ed. Jo Freeman (White Plains, N.Y.: Longman, 1983), pp. 298–319, and *Political Process and the Development of Black Insurgency* (Chicago: University of Chicago Press, 1982).

18. Chapter 7 discusses past scholarship on the Knights' failure in greater detail. To summarize briefly: Philip Foner makes all these arguments, whereas Gerald Grob, Selig Perlman, and Lloyd Ulman stress the competition between the Knights and national trade unions. William Birdsall emphasizes the weakness of the Knights' organizational structure. Recent studies of the Knights by Leon Fink and Richard Oestreicher tend to downplay the competition between the Knights and the trade unions, and they are much more sensitive to the impact of employer opposition, but they, too, ultimately ascribe the primary causes of the Knights' collapse to internal factors. See Foner, *History of the Labor Movement in the United States*, Volume 2: *From the Founding of the American Federation of Labor to the Emergence of American Imperialism;* Gerald Grob, *Workers and Utopia* (Chicago: Quadrangle, 1969); Selig Perlman, "Upheaval and Reorganization"; Lloyd Ulman, *The Rise of the National Trade Union* (Cambridge: Harvard University Press, 1955); William C. Birdsall, "The Problem of Structure in the Knights of Labor," *Industrial and Labor Relations Review* 6 (1953): 532–46; Richard Jules Oestreicher, *Solidarity and Fragmentation: Working People and Class Consciousness in Detroit, 1875–1900* (Urbana: University of Illinois Press, 1986); Leon Fink, *Workingmen's Democracy: The Knights of Labor and American Politics* (Urbana: University of Illinois Press, 1983).

19. Leon Fink's more recent writings about the Knights constitute a partial exception to this statement; see "The New Labor History and the Powers of Historical Pessimism: Consensus, Hegemony, and the Case of the Knights of Labor," *Journal of American History* 75 (June 1988): 115–36.

tactics and goals, for example, affect the intensity of movement opposition, and movement organizations sometimes alter their tactics when faced with changed political opportunities.

My account of disunity and of the collapse of the Knights' local assemblies, which constitutes the second part of the book, builds on the political process model of social movements. Although my account is necessarily limited by the type of information available on locals, I attempt to give a dynamically attuned account and to put fragmentation between skilled and less-skilled workers into proper context. The story told is one in which employer countermobilization and state neutrality loom large. In the United States, economic concentration gave employers both the ability to enforce internal discipline within their ranks and the strategic leverage to hold out against their employees for a much longer period than their counterparts in England or France found possible. Thus, they were able to crush broad-based unionism before class-patterned ways of acting and thinking had established deep roots and become routine for the working class. Moreover, employers' disproportionate resources put the Knights in a nearly hopeless situation, against which the Order struggled by appealing to the small employers. This strategy, which drew on the rhetoric and understanding of a working-class republican world view, did not work, and it lost the Knights the support of both skilled and less-skilled workers.

To understand fully the collapse of the Knights, however, one must go beyond political process models of social movements. A political process account of the Knights' demise would end with the mobilization of employers' associations and the decline of workers' strike and political activities. But workers themselves drew lessons from these defeats, lessons that had an independent effect on both the longevity of local assemblies and future efforts to build broad-based unionism in the United States. Thus, I am also seeking to understand here why workers drew the lessons they did and to trace the consequences of those lessons for the development of the American labor movement.

Sources and Methods

This book uses both quantitative and qualitative methods in its attempt to reconstruct the forces at work one hundred years ago. The centerpiece of the analysis is a statistical investigation of the 323 Knights local assemblies in New Jersey. It is designed to evaluate the specific effects of community setting, industry characteristics, craft organization, and employer resistance on the rise and demise of the

Knights. Two parallel analyses are presented. The first examines the incorporation of less-skilled workers into the Knights; the second investigates the collapse of locals for both skilled and less-skilled workers.

I analyze local assemblies for historical, theoretical, and practical reasons. Historically, the locals were the basic unit of the Order. Theoretically, one of the key dimensions of working-class formation in this period was the spread of organization. As noted, by 1880, craft organization had long established roots among skilled workers—the key question was whether or not less-skilled workers would also organize. Only if they did would the working class be able to act collectively over the long run.

Practically, local assemblies provide the best systematic records we have of relations among skilled and less-skilled workers in the United States in the late nineteenth century.[20] Unlike the craft unions of the American Federation of Labor, the Knights allowed each local assembly to define its own organizational basis, placing neither institutional nor ideological constraints on the skill level of its members nor requiring individual locals to organize all occupations or skill levels. The composition of the Knights varied from the so-called mixed assemblies—open to all producers with the famous exceptions of lawyers, bankers, stockbrokers, gamblers, liquor dealers, scabs, and union spies—to trade assemblies, which organized workers around occupational and industrial identities. Workers used craft, industrial, ethnic, and sexual identifiers to describe their local trade assemblies within the Knights of Labor. Practitioners of the same trade could and did use different organizing strategies in different communities. For instance, molders sometimes organized around their craft identity in assemblies of "iron molders"; sometimes they organized around their identities as skilled workers in assemblies of "pattern makers and molders"; and sometimes they organized around their industrial identity, joining less-skilled workers in assemblies of "iron foundry employees."

Because each local enjoyed great freedom in the way it chose to designate itself, these designations reveal the degree to which workers

20. American archives generally lack the type of documents, such as arrest records and marriage registers, used in European labor history. Thus it is impossible to trace endogamy between skilled and less-skilled workers or to trace the involvement of skilled and less-skilled workers in labor conflicts by using arrest records. One approach might be to canvass local labor newspapers, attempting to distinguish communities where workers formed alliances from those where they remained divided. Such an approach, however, has two important drawbacks: Only scattered issues of many nineteenth-century newspapers remain in existence; and equally problematic, communities where no labor newspapers were published would be indistinguishable from communities where the working class was inactive.

organized across the skill gap. By coding the skill levels of the occupations designated by each local assembly, one can reconstruct the sequence in which the various skill levels were organized locally. For any particular community or local industry, this organizational history provides information on such matters as whether craft organization was ever established, whether less-skilled workers ever initiated a labor organization, and whether a formal alliance ever developed between skilled and less-skilled workers. This organizational history provides a systematic record of the relations among workers.

This quantitative approach offers several advantages. First, it extends recent community studies of the American working class in the nineteenth century.[21] We now have several studies that impressionistically evaluate the relative importance of the various forces that shaped the labor movement in the United States, but we have no studies that systematically distinguish and weigh the particular effects of different social and economic influences. Second, it provides a way of looking systematically at the role craft organization played in the creation and collapse of the Knights local assemblies. Third, by delineating a set of conditions that encourage and hinder worker alliance, a quantitative approach provides a baseline that could be used in future community studies to decide which kinds of cases might be most fruitfully compared.

For such complex historical processes, however, a quantitative study can provide only partial answers. Thus, two case studies are presented that illuminate and extend the quantitative findings. In Chapter 5, a brief case study of the Knights in Trenton clarifies the relationship between craft organization and the mobilization of less-skilled wage earners, first uncovered in the statistical analysis. In Chapter 7, the statistical relationship between employers' associations and the collapse of local assemblies is investigated in further detail through a study of an important lockout that took place in Newark in 1887.

The statistical information for this study was collected from a variety of sources. Using national records, the historian Jonathan Garlock had already compiled a nearly complete list of all Knights locals, along with their occupational composition and founding dates.[22] Unfortunately,

---

21. In addition to the Dawley, Cumbler, and Walkowitz studies cited in note 15 and to the Fink and Oestreicher studies cited in note 18, examples include Susan E. Hirsch, *The Roots of the American Working Class* (Philadelphia: University of Pennsylvania Press, 1978), and Steven J. Ross, *Work, Leisure, and Politics in Industrializing Cincinnati, 1788–1890* (New York: Columbia University Press, 1985).

22. Jonathan Garlock, *Knights of Labor Assemblies*, distributed by Inter-University Consortium for Political and Social Research (ICPSR 0029), Ann Arbor, Mich., 1973.

however, his data are incomplete. First, there are important gaps in the occupational information collected by the Knights' national office. Second, not all labor organizations in the late nineteenth century were associated with the Knights; in particular, trade unions of skilled craft workers were often unaffiliated with the Order. Because I needed as complete a record as possible of all local organizing efforts by community, and because information on nineteenth-century labor organizations, especially by community, is quite rare, these two deficiencies presented formidable problems.

New Jersey is one of the few states for which such information exists. Although not as completely or accessibly as one might wish, the New Jersey Bureau of Statistics collected valuable information on both the Knights' locals and those of other labor unions. In particular, their 1887 report identifies the occupation of workers in all labor locals, including the "mixed" assemblies of the Knights of Labor.[23] As discussed in Chapter 5, the information on the Knights contained in the 1887 report listed statistics only by an assigned office number; the location of the local was not given. Thus, it was necessary to cull information on Knights locals from various archival sources, such as local labor newspapers and the Terence Powderly Papers,[24] in order to identify the location of the locals included in the 1887 report. These additional sources also helped me fill in many of the gaps in the occupational information collected by the Knights' national office.

The New Jersey Bureau of Statistics also collected information on trade unions in its 1900 report.[25] Because both the 1887 and 1900 reports published founding dates and occupational composition for local unions, these two reports provided a preliminary list of all non-Knights locals. These I supplemented with information on union sponsorship of strikes reported in the 1887 report and by the United States Bureau of Labor Statistics for the period between 1881 and 1894.[26] These sources, combined with scattered information in AFL records, city directories, and local newspapers, provided a reasonably complete list of trade locals unaffiliated with the Knights.

23. New Jersey Bureau of Statistics of Labor and Industries, *Tenth Annual Report* (Somerville: State of New Jersey, 1888).
24. Terence Powderly was the highest elected officer of the Knights of Labor from 1879 to 1893.
25. New Jersey Bureau of Statistics of Labor and Industries, *Twenty-third Annual Report* (Camden: State of New Jersey, 1901).
26. United States Bureau of Labor, *The Third Annual Report: Strikes and Lockouts* (Washington, D.C.: Government Printing Office, 1888); United States Bureau of Labor, *The Tenth Annual Report: Strikes and Lockouts* (Washington, D.C.: Government Printing Office, 1895).

Once I had found good information on labor organizations, the next problem was to find enough information on communities and manufacturers to evaluate the effects of varying community and industrial environments on worker alliances. On the one hand, New Jersey was a good state for such an endeavor. It was one of the largest industrial states in the late nineteenth century, it had a diversified industrial base, and factory production dominated the economic landscape. On the other hand, good information about community-level industry is not readily available. The most obvious source, the federal census, reports manufacturing statistics only at the county level. Researchers often use county as a proxy for community, but this is inappropriate here because my research design emphasizes the impact of worker alliances within communities, thus necessitating that my unit of analysis correspond to workers' social reality in the late nineteenth century. A good solution was to use the schedules originally completed by the census takers when they collected the statistics that eventually were aggregated in the published census of manufactures. These schedules report information, such as number of employees and amount of horsepower used, for each establishment. By aggregating information from individual establishments, I found it possible to use these schedules to build a community-level data file. Although it was laborious to code the census schedules, this source had the advantage of including information on the average wages paid to skilled and "ordinary" employees in each establishment—information not reported in the published reports. The remaining statistical information was coded from the New Jersey state census and other published sources.

For the qualitative case studies, daily newspapers proved the most valuable sources. I also made several research trips to local archives in New Jersey to find additional materials. These included documents from public sources (government agencies, the New Jersey State Labor Federation, city directories, and the Works Progress Administration[27]) and private ones (J. P. McDonnell's[28] diary and the Gutman collection

27. The history of the WPA Papers is as follows: During the great depression of the 1930s, the federal government hired historians to research various topics. The project was halted, however, when World War II began. In New Jersey, research was done on local, ethnic, industrial, and labor history. Because many of the projects had not been completed when the war began, the research notes and source materials were boxed up and put into storage. Eventually, these boxes were obtained by the New Jersey State Archives in Trenton. The researchers transcribed and translated many articles from the local, labor, and ethnic press. In some cases, the newspapers have since been destroyed or lost, and this transcript is the only record that survives.

28. J. P. McDonnell was a labor activist who lived in Paterson.

at the New York Public Library, which was particularly helpful for information on Paterson and Newark).

All historical studies are plagued by problems of data availability, and this one is no exception. Especially in a work that puts a premium on systematic information, the surviving historical record forces a series of compromises and trade-offs. Obtaining systematic information on labor organizations meant choosing a state that has few surviving records on industrial composition. Focusing on locals enabled me systematically to distinguish and weigh the particular effects of social and economic influences on solidarity, but it limited my ability to analyze the effects of tactics and internal organizational characteristics on the collapse of the Knights. In addition, the depth of my case studies is entirely dependent on the availability of extensive local sources. My design required that my cases illuminate a particular set of relationships; thus, unlike the historian, who can tell the story best documented in the archives, I sometimes had to make do with less information than I wished. However, I believe that the advantages of a systematic approach overshadow the data difficulties.

These investigations come together in the following way: Part One provides the historical and comparative context for the events explored in the book. It begins in Chapter 1 with a discussion of the first critical moment of working-class formation in the United States, which occurred with the journeymen's revolt in the 1830s. By placing American developments in their comparative context, this chapter challenges the notion that the American labor movement has always been exceptional. Chapter 2 surveys the evolving nature of skilled and less-skilled work over the course of the nineteenth century, emphasizing changes that generated common grievances and experiences on the part of workers in the closing decades of the century. Chapter 3 examines the second moment of American working-class formation, which occurred in the 1880s with the dramatic growth of the Knights of Labor. This chapter provides an overview of the Knights' history, and analyzes the Knights' ideological and organizational innovations. These innovations are then assessed in the light of similar ones made by broad inclusionary labor movements in England and France.

Part Two shifts the focus to a systematic investigation of the circumstances that fostered solidarity and fragmentation in the New Jersey Knights. Chapter 4 depicts the setting for the empirical study, describing the workers, major industries, and growth of the Knights in New Jersey. Chapter 5 examines the foundations of solidarity in the New Jersey Knights; it looks specifically at how and why less-skilled workers were incorporated into the Order. Chapter 6 investigates the conditions that led skilled and less-skilled workers to organize together in the same local assemblies. The reasons for the decline of the Knights local assemblies in New Jersey are examined in Chapter 7.

The Conclusion is devoted to exploring the legacy of the Knights of Labor, and to drawing out the implications of this study for our understanding of working-class formation in the United States.

THE AMERICAN
LABOR MOVEMENT AND
LESS-SKILLED WORKERS
IN COMPARATIVE FOCUS

1

The First Moment of Working-Class Formation: The Journeymen's Revolt

The late nineteenth century was a critical period for the labor movement in England, France, and the United States. The first stirrings of a working-class consciousness had occurred half a century earlier in the 1830s, but the organizational structures and conceptual categories that had developed in those years largely ignored less-skilled workers. This stance was becoming increasingly untenable in the closing decades of the nineteenth century as craftless workers grew to be a substantial proportion of the labor force. A few labor activists in each country recognized this fact and tried hard to convert their fellow craft workers to new, more inclusive organizations and identities. They also attempted to formulate arguments and union structures that would appeal to less-skilled workers. As they did so, activists were forced to confront the language and organizational forms of the 1830s: What was to be discarded? What borrowed? What transformed?

The labor movement that was remade in the closing decades of the nineteenth century, therefore, was profoundly shaped by what had come before. If we are to understand the Knights of Labor—what it achieved, what it wished for, and what it might have accomplished— we must know something of the historical context in which it was formed. This chapter and the next two survey the ideological and organizational contours of the American labor movement from its first appearance in the 1830s through the mid-1880s, when the Knights successfully incorporated large numbers of less-skilled workers. It also situates the development of the American labor movement compara-tively. Thanks to the work of historians such as William Sewell, Jr., E. P. Thompson, Michael Hanagan, and Eric Hobsbawm, we now know a great deal about the French and English labor movements in the nine-teenth century. By comparing the two moments of working-class for-mation in the United States, France, and England, we will be able to assess whether or not the American labor movement in the nineteenth century indeed merits its reputation for having been "exceptional."

The Birth of the American Labor Movement: Artisans, Republican Ideology, and Craft Unions

The first working-class movement in the United States arose in the 1830s, a time when artisans still outnumbered factory workers. Some large textile factories were in operation, but, as yet, these factories em-ployed a minority of the wage-earning population.[1] Instead, most manufacturing was done by native-born workers, using traditional methods, in small independent shops.[2] Thus, few of the standard fea-

---

1. In 1840, 14 percent of all wage earners were employed in the cotton textile indus-try; perhaps an additional 5 percent worked in the wool industry according to the U.S. Bureau of the Census, *Historical Statistics*, p. 139, and Victor S. Clark, *History of Manufac-tures in the United States* (1929; reprint, New York: Peter Smith, 1949), 1: 570. Early textile factories are described in Jonathan Prude, "The Social System of Early New England Textile Mills: A Case Study, 1812–1840," in *Working-Class America*, ed. Michael H. Frisch and Daniel J. Walkowitz (Urbana: University of Illinois Press, 1983), and Thomas Dub-lin, *Women at Work* (New York: Columbia University Press, 1979).

2. Amy Bridges, "Becoming American: The Working Classes in the United States before the Civil War," in *Working-Class Formation*, ed. Ira Katznelson and Aristide R. Zolberg (Princeton: Princeton University Press, 1986), p. 168, estimates that roughly one-half of all nonagricultural wage earners were engaged in traditionally organized trades. The remainder of the industrial working class was employed either as domes-tic servants, outworkers, or day laborers in transportation and construction. Immigrant workers accounted for only a small proportion of each group. In cities such as Phila-delphia, New York, and Boston, for example, approximately 10 percent of the work force was foreign-born. Many of these immigrants were British, which meant that they shared language, religion, craft, and cultural traditions with American workers. The first three decades of the nineteenth century did bring a substantial increase in the ranks of industrial wage earners, but this growth resulted from natural increase and rural-to-urban migration, not from immigration. For the number of immigrant workers, see Bruce Laurie, *Working People of Philadelphia, 1800–1850* (Philadelphia: Temple University Press, 1980), p. 29; Bruce Laurie, *Artisans into Workers* (New York: Noonday Press, 1989), pp. 25–26; Sean Wilentz, *Chants*, p. 48, n. 51; David M. Gordon, Richard Edwards, and Michael Reich, *Segmented Work, Divided Workers* (Cambridge: Cambridge University Press, 1982), p. 62, and John Modell, "The Peopling of a Working-Class Ward: Read-ing, Pennsylvania, 1850," *Journal of Social History* 5 (1971): 71–95. Modell's study of a working-class ward in Reading, Pennsylvania, is the most detailed study we have of the ethnic origins of the working classes in this period. He used data from the 1850 cen-

tures we typically associate with industrialization—factories, capital-intensive methods, rapid technological development, and, in the United States, immigrant labor—were a part of workers' experience when the labor movement was first made. These workers' confrontation with the industrial revolution entailed equally disruptive but different changes: market expansion, labor-intensive techniques, and the sweating system. These changes, rather than factories and machines, caused artisans to organize unions and to create a new rhetoric of class.

To understand the radicalizing effects of economic changes in the 1830s, it is necessary to know something of the social and mental world of these early artisans. In the first two decades of the nineteenth century, artisans' work life looked much as it had the century before. Crafts in the United States developed free of most of the legal restrictions and long traditions common to European guilds, but they shared many of the features and goals of the European craft associations. In some cases, American artisans even adopted the insignia and ceremonies used by European craftsmen to maintain members' loyalty to the trade.[3] And like their European counterparts, American artisans possessed the expertise to create a complete product, relied on custom (rather than the demands of the market or of the master) to determine the pace, price, and quality of production, and thought of themselves as part of a fluid hierarchy that included master craftsmen, journeymen, and apprentices. Advancement through the ranks could no longer be taken for granted in the 1820s, but work routines, shop customs, and tools remained much as they had been a hundred years earlier.[4]

Obtaining a "competence" was very important for workers in these traditional shops.[5] To achieve a competence a young man first apprenticed himself to a master artisan, who taught him the "art and mystery" of a craft, and then he carefully accumulated the skills and capital required to become a master himself. This process was marked by reciprocal obligation and cooperative collaboration: masters frequently provided room and board for their apprentices, worked alongside of their journeymen, lent tools and raw materials to other masters, and

sus, and his figures thus reflect the Irish and German immigration in the 1840s. Even so, only one in four artisans, one in three laborers, and one in seven construction and transportation workers were foreign-born.

3. Sean Wilentz, "Artisan Republican Festivals and the Rise of Class Conflict in New York City, 1788–1837," in Working-Class America, ed. Frisch and Walkowitz, pp. 45–58.

4. Good accounts of artisans' work life can be found in Hirsch, Roots, chap. 1; Wilentz, Chants, chap. 1; and Dawley, Class and Community, chap. 2. A useful overview is presented in Laurie, Artisans, pp. 35–37.

5. Laurie, Artisans, pp. 44–45, discusses competences.

sometimes even sold their shops on favorable terms to especially liked workers. This training inculcated values and standards that went beyond the practical knowledge of how to make a hat or print a pamphlet: the apprentice also learned customary methods for producing goods, an appreciation for craftsmanship, and an abhorrence of speculation and entrepreneurship. Thus, as journeymen worked toward their competence, they were initiated into a moral universe that united both masters and journeymen. Frequently, ties between the two were further solidified by their joint membership in mutual aid societies founded to promote "the trade."[6]

A competence carried larger social and political connotations as well. The early American republic was a society marked by hierarchy and deference, where the rich and highborn used adjectives such as "meer," "illeterate," and "rough" to modify the word "mechanick" (the term most often used for artisan in early nineteenth-century America).[7] In the artisan's view, however, a competence set the skilled craftsmen apart from those truly unworthy of respect: the dependent poor and unskilled. Furthermore, it allowed artisans to assert a moral superiority over the wealthy. Drawing on the republican distinction between "producers" and "idlers," artisans argued that the craftsman —especially the self-employed master who owned his own shop and tools—should be considered an ideal citizen.[8] His competence provided the independence to make uncoerced political choices, and the modesty of his material resources encouraged diligence and virtue. A typical speech at a Fourth of July celebration in New York in 1809 expressed this sentiment: "In your hands must the palladium of our liberty rest. You cannot be inflated by distinction; you do not float like the ephemeral bubbles of pride and fashion, on the surface of society; nor are you of that uninformed class too low to be agitated with the current events, and who, like dull weeds, sleep secure at the bottom of the stream."[9] This view—that the competent urban craftsman was

6. Howard Rock, *Artisans of the New Republic* (New York: New York University Press, 1984), pp. 128–32; Wilentz, "Artisan Republican Festivals."

7. Quoted in Stuart M. Blumin, *The Emergence of the Middle Class* (Cambridge: Cambridge University Press, 1989), pp. 31 and 33. See also Rock, *Artisans*, pp. 4–8.

8. In making this argument, they received support from no less a hero than Thomas Jefferson who called artisans "the yeomanry of the city." This was the highest expression of praise from a man who considered the independent yeoman farmers the backbone of the republic. Jefferson's remark is found in a May 5, 1793, letter to James Monroe, quoted in Staughton Lynd, *Class Conflict, Slavery, and the United States Constitution* (Indianapolis: Bobbs-Merrill, 1968), p. 265.

9. John T. Irving, "An Oration Delivered on the Fourth of July 1809, before the Tammany Society, or Columbian Order, Tailors', Coopers', Hatters', Hibernian Provident, Masons', Shipwrights', House Carpenters', and Columbian Societies," p. 3, quoted in Rock, *Artisans*, p. 139.

the ideal citizen—was part of a larger reinterpretation artisans made of the nation's republican heritage. In constructing their own variation on republican themes, artisans were not alone: historians of the nineteenth century have recently discovered that groups and individuals of quite different circumstances and convictions claimed the mantle of republican ideas to pursue their interests and goals.[10] Federalists and

10. Indeed, a paradigm shift has occurred among many eighteenth- and nineteenth-century historians. It began with the work of Bernard Bailyn, Gordon Wood, and J. G. A. Pocock, each of whom analyzed American political rhetoric in the late eighteenth century. Their research led them to challenge the interpretation of older, "consensus" historians who believed that Lockean liberalism pervaded the ideology of the United States from its inception as a nation. Bailyn, Wood, and Pocock noted the vital importance of classical republican ideas among the generation that fought the revolutionary war. See J. G. A. Pocock, "Virtue and Commerce in the Eighteenth Century," *Journal of Interdisciplinary History* 3 (1972): 119–34; Bernard Bailyn, *The Ideological Origins of the American Revolution* (Cambridge: Harvard University Press, 1967); Gordon Wood, *The Creation of the American Republic: 1776–1787* (New York: Norton, 1972); Eric Foner, *Tom Paine and Revolutionary America* (London: Oxford University Press, 1976). Good overviews of this work and its influence can be found in Robert E. Shalhope, "Toward a Republican Synthesis: The Emergence of an Understanding of Republicanism in American Historiography," *William and Mary Quarterly* 29 (1972): 49–80, and Sean Wilentz, "Society, Politics, and the Market Revolution, 1815–1848," in *The New American History*, ed. Eric Foner (Philadelphia: Temple University Press, 1990).

Since the late 1960s, the majority of historians of early America have accepted the importance of republicanism for the revolutionary generation. Many, however, have challenged the notion that republicanism was the monolithic entity it often appears to have been in the work of Bailyn, Wood, and Pocock. The result has been a number of works that use the clash over different versions of republicanism as a way to understand political and social struggles in early American society. See, for example, Robert Kelley, "Ideology and Political Culture from Jefferson to Nixon," *American Historical Review* 82, no. 3 (1977): 531–62; Gary Nash, *The Urban Crucible* (Cambridge: Harvard University Press, 1979), and the essays in Alfred F. Young, ed., *The American Revolution: Explorations in the History of American Radicalism* (DeKalb: Northern Illinois University Press, 1976). An excellent overview of this literature is provided in Robert E. Shalhope, "Republicanism and Early American Historiography," *William and Mary Quarterly* 39 (1982): 334–56.

Eventually, historians of the nineteenth century also began to look for—and find—the language of republicanism in later periods, most notably as a language of protest and opposition. Labor historians in particular have used the concept of republicanism as an interpretive framework for understanding the development of workers' movements. Almost every influential labor historian writing today about the nineteenth century discusses republicanism in some form. Disagreement centers primarily around the extent to which working-class republicanism was a viable oppositional ideology, rather than around the existence of a working-class variant of republicanism. (Those who extend the lens of republicanism to understand the nineteenth-century labor movement include Wilentz, *Chants;* Leon Fink, *Workingmen's Democracy;* Steven J. Ross, *Workers on the Edge* (New York: Columbia University Press, 1985); Richard J. Oestreicher, "Terence V. Powderly, the Knights of Labor, and Artisanal Republicanism," in *Labor Leaders in America,* ed. Melvyn Van Tine and Warren Dubofsky (Urbana: University of Illinois Press, 1987); Linda Schneider, "The Citizen Striker: Workers' Ideology in the Homestead Strike of 1892," *Labor History* 21 (1982): 47–66; Victoria Hattam, "Economic Visions and Political Strategies: American Labor and the State, 1865–1896," *Studies in American Political Development* 4 (1990): 82–129; Amy Bridges, "Becoming American," pp. 157–96; William E. Forbath, "The Ambiguities of Free Labor: Labor and the Law in the Gilded Age," *Wis-*

Jacksonian democrats, mercantilists and artisans all argued that they were the *true* defenders of the new nation and tried hard to legitimate their refashioning of the revolutionary heritage. That radically different interpretations could be invested with plausibility reflects both the flexibility of key republican terms and the conflict between republican ideals and the societal changes wrought by an expanding market economy.

The republican tradition taught that the polity, economy, and society were interdependent and that a republican form of government could exist only with an independent, virtuous, and roughly equal citizenry.[11] Artisans' refashioning of these ideas reflected their inculcation in the moral universe of the small shop and their belief that masters and journeymen shared the same interests. As Sean Wilentz's careful study of urban artisans in this period demonstrates, they made a metaphorical association between the Republic and the trade. To them "independence" implied both the freedom to ply their craft without state or elite interference and the personal freedom to think and act without being coerced or unduly influenced by others. Their understanding of "virtue," however, limited the extent to which independence could become an endorsement of the pursuit of individual self-interest. Just as the journeyman and master must honor custom and the larger interests of the trade over their own individual gain, so citi-

---

consin Law Review (1985): 767–817; William E. Forbath, "The Shaping of the American Labor Movement," *Harvard Law Review* 102 (1989): 1109–56.)

The debate over the extent to which working-class republicanism provided a viable definition of American workers as a distinct class in opposition to other classes can be found in Wilentz, "Against Exceptionalism," and the "Responses," especially those of Nick Salvatore, "Response," *International Labor and Working-Class History,* 24 (1984): 25–30, and Michael Hanagan, "Response," *International Labor and Working-Class History,* 24 (1984): 31–36. A few nonlabor historians have also entered the fray; see John Patrick Diggins, "Comrades and Citizens: New Mythologies in American Historiography," *American Historical Review* 90 (1985): 614–38, and Fink, "New Labor History," for a reply.

I believe that the radicalism of working-class republicanism can best be addressed dynamically and comparatively, that is, by understanding both how it changed over time and how it compared with workers' ideologies elsewhere. Gaining such an understanding is one of the goals of this chapter and chapter 3.

11. This paragraph relies heavily on Wilentz, *Chants,* esp. pp. 14–15 and 92–97. Indeed, it should be noted that this section on American workers in the 1830s recounts more of Wilentz's argument than most historians will find necessary. I have summarized his work at some length because most sociologists will be unfamiliar with it or with the fact that there was a working-class and labor movement in the United States in the 1830s. My argument in this chapter and the next two requires that I demonstrate the existence of this early labor movement and provide enough detail so that my claims about America's unexceptional labor movement can be assessed. In addition, I want to demonstrate that working-class republicanism changed over the course of the nineteenth century. To do so, I must give the reader a reasonable feel for organized labor's world view in the 1830s.

zens in a republic must put the commonwealth above the needs of the individual. If citizens were unable to practice such virtue, then America, like the republics of antiquity, would become "enervated by luxury [and] depressed by tyranny," a land where "the [poor] will be found in a state of vassalage and dependence on the [rich]."[12] Their understanding of "equality" did not, however, develop this theme of rich and poor into a call for equality of economic condition. Instead, they emphasized something akin to the modern-day concept of equality of economic opportunity: if the trades were free to operate without the restraint of "offensive government," those who were diligent and virtuous would be able to obtain their competence. Thus their understanding of equality stressed legal rights and civic duties rather than economic equality. As they made abundantly clear, artisans believed that the small craftsman's shop was the embodiment of republican values and that those outside it had not been well trained for participation in the republic.

By the 1830s the traditional system of production that underlay artisans' interpretation of republicanism began to collapse in many trades, especially in the cities of the Northeast. As I have suggested, mechanization and technological advance played a relatively small part in the deterioration; far more important were expanding markets and improvements in transportation.[13] Merchants and craft entrepreneurs began to take advantage of this new situation by buying large stocks of raw materials on credit and by reorganizing production so that goods might be produced more cheaply. Strategies differed from trade to trade, but the underlying logic was ruthlessly similar: greatly intensify the division of labor and farm the simplest tasks out to low-paid workers. Historians now consider these types of arrangements, once seen as transitional or proto-industrial, as a second—and perhaps most common—route to mass manufacture.[14] All involved large numbers of underpaid workers, frequently women or recent migrants from the countryside, working at home or in sweatshops on simplified tasks. The most skilled work (for example the cutting of garments, the lasting of shoes, typesetting) remained the province of journeymen,

12. George James Warner, *Means for the Preservation of Liberty: An Oration Delivered in the New Dutch Church on the Fourth of July, 1797*, quoted in Wilentz, "Artisan Republican Festivals," p. 49.

13. Hirsch, *Roots*, pp. 16–20, makes this point with respect to Newark; Bruce Laurie, *Working People of Philadelphia, 1850–1880* (Philadelphia: Temple University Press, 1980), pp. 8–10, makes it for Lynn, Massachusetts; and Wilentz, *Chants*, pp. 108–12, makes it for New York.

14. See Wilentz, *Chants*, p. 113, and Laurie, *Artisans*, p. 39, for an elaboration of this argument.

but they now completed only a portion of the labor they once had. In the words of Wilentz, it was a "bastardization" of the artisan system.

Not everyone, of course, suffered or faced the indignity of proletarianization. Some trades, such as shipbuilding and jewelry making, were barely touched by these developments.[15] Even in the bastardized trades, there were opportunities for masters and journeymen willing to violate traditional standards and able to obtain credit.[16] But for the majority—of both journeymen and small masters—capitalist development meant falling wages, a glutted labor market, and the loss of status and independence.[17]

These developments touched off the nation's first union movement during the business slump of the late 1820s. Many journeymen, as we have seen, belonged to trade organizations that united journeymen and masters. Gradually, some of these mutual aid societies came to operate as trade unions, especially those organized in the bastardized trades.[18] Their members began to speak less of the "trade" and more of strikes, to describe the masters not as "mechanics" but as "unmanly and ungenerous," as "tyrants" "whose only object is to accumulate money."[19] Such rhetoric, as Wilentz has noted, indicates a shared sense of workers' feeling distinct from the masters and reflects "glimmers of a language of class." However, this consciousness of class remained quite limited before the 1830s. At no point did journeymen's societies in either New York or Newark, two of the cities where the early labor movement has been extensively studied, come close to embracing different trades.[20] And it was the "unfair" masters,

15. Hirsch, *Roots,* chap. 2; Wilentz, *Chants,* chap. 3.

16. For example, James and John Harper, founders of Harper Brothers, were master printers who created the largest publishing enterprise in the United States in those years. James Harper later became mayor of New York. See Amy Bridges, *A City in the Republic* (Ithaca: Cornell University Press, 1987), pp. 52–53; Wilentz, *Chants,* pp. 317–18. For other examples, see Edward Pessen, *Riches, Class, and Power before the Civil War* (Lexington, Mass.: D.C. Heath, 1973), who notes that such backgrounds were a rarity among the urban elite.

17. Recent historical research suggests that the period between 1820 and the Civil War was probably the most unequal period in American history. In the large cities of the Northeast, Edward Pessen reports that the top 1 percent of wealth holders owned about one-fourth of all wealth in the mid-1820s and about one-half of all property by mid-century. Williamson and Lindert estimate that in the nation at large the relative wealth of the top 10 percent of the population nearly tripled between the Revolution and the Civil War, with most of this concentration occurring from the 1820s to the late 1840s. See Edward Pessen, *Jacksonian America,* rev. ed. (Urbana: University of Illinois Press, 1985), p. 81, and Jeffrey G. Williamson and Peter H. Lindert, *American Inequality: A Macroeconomic History* (New York: Academic Press, 1980), p. 62.

18. Hirsch, *Roots,* pp. 84–85; Wilentz, *Chants,* p. 223.

19. Quoted in Wilentz, *Chants,* pp. 57–58.

20. Artisans in Philadelphia did briefly experiment with a citywide association of artisans, but it soon floundered. Laurie, *Working People,* p. 85.

along with the merchant elite, who were addressed with opprobrium, not all masters.

Journeymen's problems reached a wider audience and were given greater political significance when local Workingmen's parties organized in several cities in the late 1820s.[21] These local third parties achieved only moderate electoral success, and most of their platforms called for only modest reforms. However, they were important in the development of a working-class discourse because they publicized journeymen's shared grievances and helped reinvigorate the radical language of the American revolution.[22]

A much clearer language—and organization—of class developed between 1833 and 1837 under the aegis of the General Trades' Unions (GTU) and its national counterpart, the National Trades' Unions (NTU). It was in the GTU that journeymen from different trades first declared their common interests as wage earners and articulated their differences with capitalist employers and entrepreneurs. Eventually, they also developed a critique of the expanding capitalist economy that, although framed in an American vernacular, was every bit as radical as that developed by workers across the Atlantic.

The movement began in New York City, where a bitter fight for higher wages led journeymen carpenters in 1833 to send out an appeal for help to "every honest journeyman mechanic" in the city.[23] Journeymen of several other trades heeded the call, and within a month the strike was won. Roused by the expression of solidarity across craft lines, the city's journeymen created the GTU, a more formal expression of their mutualism. Essentially, the GTU functioned as a citywide

21. Bridges, *City*, pp. 22–24 and 103–5, and Wilentz, *Chants*, chap. 5, discuss this party in New York City; for a general overview, see Laurie, *Artisans*, pp. 79–83, and Pessen, *Jacksonian America*, pp. 270–76.

22. Party leaders also helped turn the labor theory of value into an attack on economic inequality and prevailing property relations. By the Jackson years, the doctrine that all wealth is derived from labor had become an article of popular faith. Because the concept of "labor" was supple and imprecise, that belief could be embraced by merchants and manufacturers, as well as by workers and farmers. Broadly defined, merchants, professionals, and bankers qualified as productive citizens. Narrowly defined, only those who worked with their hands were included. The more radical party leaders, such as New York's Thomas Skidmore and Philadelphia's William Heighton, conceptualized and popularized the more restrictive definition. See Wilentz, *Chants*, pp. 178–90, for a discussion of Owen and Skidmore; see Laurie, *Working People*, pp. 74–80, and *Artisans*, pp. 66–71, for an overview of both Heighton's and Skidmore's ideas. Daniel T. Rodgers, *Contested Truths: Keywords in American Politics since Independence* (New York: Basic Books, 1987), pp. 72–75, provides a very informative discussion of the revitalization of republican language in this period.

23. John R. Commons et al., eds., *Documentary History of American Industrial Society* (New York: Russell and Russell, 1958), 5: 208. For accounts of New York's GTU, see Wilentz, *Chants*, chap. 6, and John R. Commons et al., *History of Labour in the United States* (New York: Macmillan, 1918), 1: 357–83 and 395–411.

labor council: monthly meetings were held, policy was hammered out, the actions of member unions were coordinated, and funds were collected for operating expenses and strikes. But more than this, the GTU also attempted to build something akin to a movement culture: libraries and lyceums were established, guest lectures were arranged, rallies and demonstrations were organized. Most telling, it sponsored one of the nation's first newspapers devoted solely to the views and interests of journeymen.[24]

Over the next two years, similar citywide labor councils were initiated in more than a dozen urban centers, ranging from Philadelphia and Boston to Cincinnati and Newark.[25] Journeymen from virtually every sector of the urban economy organized at some point, although unionism flourished most in trades such as consumer finishing, building, and printing, where specialized tasks, and the sweating system were most pronounced.[26] By 1836, the ranks of organized workers had grown to include an estimated 300,000 members, a number that represents between one-fifth and one-third of all urban workers.[27] These numbers suggest a significant broadening of the movement as the NTU reached its peak membership. "Half-trained," sweated, and immigrant journeymen were welcomed in some trades as journeymen became more radicalized in the course of the movement. In Philadelphia, even unskilled dockworkers were eventually admitted.[28] These dockworkers were an exceptional case, however, for although the NTU represented a significant broadening of solidarity, its inclusiveness did not generally extend too far beyond the ranks of the skilled.

Employers reacted with outrage almost as soon as the GTU was organized. Entrepreneurs had their own brand of republicanism— one that equated moral justice with free competition in all arenas of social life. Collective action, they charged, was "subversive of the

24. *The Union* was started by the GTU; the *National Trades Union*, a daily penny paper, was begun by the NTU. Commons et al., *Documentary*, 5: 292–93, reprints the initial committee report recommending the establishment of the *National Trades Union*. Alexander Saxton, *The Rise and Fall of the White Republic* (London: Verso, 1990), chap. 4, notes that the radicalization of workers in those years also spurred a larger broadening of newspaper readership.

25. John R. Commons et al., *Documentary History of American Industrial Society* (New York: Russell & Russell, 1958), 6: 73.

26. Wilentz, *Chants*, p. 223; Hirsch, *Roots*, p. 84; Laurie, *Working People*, p. 88. A list of all trades organized in the years 1833–37 is given in Commons et al., *History*, pp. 472–77.

27. Commons et al., *History*, p. 424, gives the 300,000 figure; Laurie, *Artisans*, p. 84, provides the proportion. In some cities, the percentage of workers organized was probably much larger. Wilentz, *Chants*, p. 221, quotes the New York *Evening Post*'s calculation that two-thirds of New York's workingmen belonged to the GTU.

28. Laurie, *Working People*, pp. 99–100.

rights of individuals" and a violation of the "obligations of society."[29] They wished "to see all men, mechanics as well as others, receive an adequate compensation for their labor," but as employers, they were powerless to bring this about because "the true regulator of prices, whether of labor, goods, real estate or any thing else, is demand."[30] At times, their arguments went so far as to endow the emerging labor market with supernatural sanction: In condemning the carpenters' strike, for example, the New York *Journal of Commerce* argued: "All combinations to compel others to give a higher price or take a lower one, are not only inexpedient, but at war with the order of things which the Creator has established for the general good, and therefore wicked."[31] Typically, employers' editorials and resolutions also denied that recent economic changes had altered artisans' life chances. They staunchly maintained that all men who worked hard enough could still achieve a competence and eventually become rich. Unionization was thus, in their eyes, the action of lazy and incompetent workers.[32]

At first, union spokesmen countered such arguments by emphasizing labor's moderation and focusing their attacks on "dishonorable" employers.[33] Continued labor conflict, however, along with the highly charged political atmosphere that surrounded Andrew Jackson's reelection campaign and second term, undermined the moderate position.[34] By 1836 John Commerford, president of the New York GTU, saw the journeymen's movement in clear class terms. The enemy, he asserted was "capital"—a class of men that included exploiting masters, who with "deep and matured design" so controlled society that they could reward themselves by "filching from labor."[35] This theme was taken up by others, and terms such as "class" and "capitalists" began to appear with increasing frequency in union and strike documents.

Union leaders also began to attack employers' power to dictate the terms of wage labor with new, more radical arguments. Drawing on

29. Commons et al., *Documentary*, 5: 209 and 315.

30. Ibid., 5: 308–9.

31. Ibid., 5: 209.

32. For example, see the comments about the "dissolute, improvident" union agitators reported in Commons et al., *Documentary*, 5: 210.

33. Commons et al., *Documentary*, 5: 308, provides an example of the type of statements made by the early, moderate president of the NTU. See also Wilentz, *Chants*, pp. 238–39.

34. Jackson's efforts to mobilize working-class voters against the rechartering of the Bank of the United States was particularly important because they led workers to analyze the *particular* difficulties they were experiencing in the rapidly changing economy. Wilentz, *Chants*, pp. 240–41, discusses these developments in more detail, and Pessen provides a good overview of the so-called "Bank War," *Jacksonian America*, pp. 137–48.

35. Quoted in Wilentz, *Chants*, p. 241.

the labor theory of value, they began to claim that labor was property, not a market commodity. "We hold that our labor is our property," announced New York sailmakers in 1836, "and we have the inherent right to dispose of it in such parcels as any other species of property."[36] "As the mechanic is not possessed of any other property than his labor," elaborated a union delegate to the 1835 NTU, "he has an undoubted right to dispose of it on such terms and in such quantities as may answer his convenience."[37]

Moreover, journeymen drew a connection between their struggle to protect their property rights and their obligation as citizens to uphold the Republic. To "acquiesce" in the "violation" of their "constitutional and natural rights" as "American citizens," to "affi[x] a value to their own labor" (i.e., property) would "make dark the republican atmosphere of this boasted land of liberty, for a long and wicked reign of anarchy and despotism."[38]

As labor leaders made these claims about capitalists, labor, property, and the Republic, they offered a new, radical, and anticapitalist critique of workshop exploitation and proletarianization. They denied that labor was a commodity, thereby challenging one of the most fundamental assumptions of the capitalist system. In their view, journeymen were not victims of abstract and neutral economic laws; they were, instead, men dispossessed. And this dispossession not only degraded and impoverished workers but it also stripped them of their independence, thus threatening the Republic. All their battles were thus linked: the battle to set the price of their labor, to maintain their independence from "dictatorial" capitalist employers, to associate with one another freely, and to defend the Republic.[39] All had become the same struggle.

By 1835, these ideas had swept the organized labor movement and set the unions on a collision course with employers. One hundred and forty strikes, an unprecedented number that was almost six times the total for the preceding two years, took place in 1835 and 1836.[40] Many were successful, including a general strike for the ten-hour day in Philadelphia. In response, employers adopted increasingly aggressive

36. Ibid., p. 242.
37. Commons et al., *Documentary*, 6: 232.
38. Quotes are from two resolutions expressing the outrage of the GTU over the "dictatorial conduct" of employers' associations. In Commons et al., *Documentary*, 5: 287, 301. See also the widely disseminated "Ten-Hour Circular," written by members of the Boston Trades' Union in 1835, reprinted in Commons et al., *Documentary*, 6: 94–99.
39. Wilentz, *Chants*, pp. 242–48.
40. Commons et al., *History*, pp. 381–82.

tactics and rhetoric. In New York, they successfully used the courts to challenge the unions: in late winter a city court allowed master stone masons to sue journeymen for damages resulting from a strike; several months later merchant tailors had twenty journeymen convicted of conspiracy.[41] Between these courtroom battles, both the police and militia were called out to break a strike on the waterfront. Elsewhere, employers relied on their own combinations and solidarity to ensure that the United States remained, in the words of the judge in the tailors' conspiracy case, the "favoured land of law and liberty," where "the road to advancement [was] open to all."[42]

In this charged atmosphere, union leaders and labor journalists began to worry that a continual round of strikes might distract workers from the larger goal of social reconstruction. They began to seek "a more permanent solution," and soon many were advocating cooperative production as a way to "give workers absolute control over the disposal of . . . [their] labor."[43] Cooperatives, several argued at the annual convention of the NTU in 1836, would end "the division of workingmen into employers and journeymen." As Bruce Laurie points out, the discovery of cooperation marked a major tactical departure for the labor movement. Before, radicals had advocated antimonopoly politics as a way to defeat the market economy, but as workers began to experience the power allied against labor, journeymen turned to a more direct means of restructuring productive relations.[44]

Small cooperatives were set up in 1836, but these—as well as the GTUs, the NTU, and most local unions—were destroyed in the nation's first industrial depression that began in 1837 and lasted seven painful years.[45] In New York alone, more than one-half of all craft

41. See Wilentz, *Chants*, pp. 286–94, and Commons et al., *History*, pp. 404–12, for an account of these court cases and the protests they generated. Conspiracy had only recently been made a statutory offense in New York; these court cases set a precedent in sanctioning the use of these laws to undermine trade unions.

42. The words are those of Judge Ogden Edwards in his decision against the tailors; quoted in Commons et al., *History*, p. 410.

43. From a report on the 1836 convention of the NTU; quoted in Laurie, *Artisans*, pp. 89–90.

44. As yet, however, important features of the cooperative vision remained vague. Where, for one thing, was the capital for the new cooperative shops to come from? Banks were condemned out of hand and were unlikely to lend money in any event. Similarly, providing capital was not seen as the proper sphere of the government. Advocates of cooperation suggested "small weekly contributions" to local unions instead; eventually, they also suggested that the constitutions of central labor unions be amended so that funds collected for strikes could be used instead for cooperation. For an informative overview of cooperation in this period, see Laurie, *Artisans*, pp. 90–91.

45. On the depression, see Peter Temin, *The Jacksonian Economy* (New York: Norton, 1969).

workers lost their jobs; unknown numbers suffered the same fate else-where.[46] Workers took whatever work they could; those who were not turned out watched helplessly as employers ignored wage agree-ments. By summer the journeymen's revolt was over and the NTU and its affiliated city federations were dead.

Much had changed since 1833. Although journeymen failed to win control over their labor or to set up an alternative system of coopera-tives, they had—at least briefly—demonstrated what solidarity across craft borders could accomplish. In the process, they had forged orga-nizations and institutions that would serve as models when skilled workers once again mobilized in the 1840s and 1850s.[47] And they had transformed the political language of republicanism into a new lan-guage of class—one that introduced new terms such as "capitalists" while putting old terms such as "property," "rights," and "citizenship" to new uses.[48] By 1837 the old artisan republicanism had been split into two. There were now two distinct visions that clashed head on: One defined virtue as craft mutualism and condemned the "demon of individual gain"; the other emphasized the virtue of individual achievement and denounced the "idlers and loungers" who joined trade unions.[49] One was a working-class view that demanded that the economic sphere be subordinated to republican principles; the other, was a middle-class, or "free-labor" view that insisted that a virtuous republic could be ensured only if the economy was regulated by the laws of the market.[50]

I do not mean to imply that the GTUs evidenced a finely honed proletarianism or that the new language of class supplanted the old. Producerism, for example, still exerted a very strong hold on the minds of workers and of their leaders. Bruce Laurie notes that in the 1837 panic even radicals lashed out against the nonproducers, against the "money-changers," the idlers, the speculators, rather than against the capitalists.[51] But even before the panic, the small master who worked with his hands remained someone who could evoke both sympathy and solidarity from journeymen. The inclusion of small masters was

46. Wilentz, *Chants*, pp. 294–95; Commons et al., *History*, pp. 456–58.
47. On the national labor movement in those years, see Commons et al., *History*, and Ware, *Labor Movement*.
48. Rodgers, *Contested Truths*, provides an excellent discussion of the way the con-cept of "natural rights" was contested and interpreted in those years. See esp. pp. 72–79.
49. Quoted in Wilentz, *Chants*, pp. 247 and 285.
50. Ibid., pp. 240–48, 271–86, and 294–96; Forbath, "Ambiguities," pp. 773–79; Eric Foner, *Politics and Ideology in the Age of the Civil War* (New York: Oxford University Press, 1980).
51. Laurie, *Artisans*, p. 91.

debated in many GTUs; in Boston, they were eventually offered membership.[52] These debates are ambiguous in their implications: they both demonstrate the influence of producerist categories and provide evidence that workers were questioning the efficacy of these conceptual categories. Unlike a decade or two before, masters were now seen as a distinct and separate group; the question was whether or not an alliance was in the best interest of the GTUs.

The enormous boundary between skilled and less-skilled workers also remained intact in 1837. Even in the class-conscious atmosphere of 1835 and 1836, the NTU and its affiliated craft unions did not offer membership to female factory workers, male day laborers (with one notable exception), or many "half-trained" craftsmen.[53] At least one union leader, John Commerford, president of the New York City GTU, did grapple with a more inclusive vision: when trying to raise money for dockworkers who had been jailed during a strike, he argued that "like the mechanic, the stevedore has as good and just a right to ask what he pleases for his labor as the merchant has for his commodities."[54] But his argument went unheeded by his fellow union members. Moreover, although much of journeymen's new language of labor was universal, when one looks more closely, it becomes clear that journeymen often ascribed narrower meanings to many terms than is at first apparent. When, for example, they claimed that their labor was their property, they generally had skilled, not unskilled, labor in mind. That John Commerford felt it necessary to explain that a stevedore, like a mechanic, had property rights based on his labor hints at this, as does his audience's indifference. So, too, does the journeymen's use of the concept "independence" when they spoke of dictatorial employers. Women workers, day laborers, even many of the "half-trained" could not have had their independence threatened for they had no hope of a competence—and hence of independence—to begin with.

It was, in sum, an understanding of class boundaries that sharply distinguished the skilled from the less skilled while only tentatively drawing the line between the skilled and the small masters. But these limitations should not blind us to the enormous changes in perception and organization that had occurred. Historians such as Wilentz and Laurie point to the 1830s as a formative moment in the history of

52. Commons et al., *History*, p. 379; Wilentz, *Chants*, pp. 251–53.
53. The Philadelphia GTU did admit unskilled day laborers in 1836. See Laurie, *Working People*, pp. 99–100.
54. Quoted in Wilentz, *Chants*, p. 251. Wilentz notes that craft workers and laborers met in the charged spring and summer of 1836 to plan protest demonstrations. Nevertheless, laborers were not admitted to the New York GTU.

the American working class because artisans, cooperating for the first time across trade lines, took received republican wisdom and turned it into a compelling critique of the developing capitalist economy. Their class-based republicanism would shape labor's response to the developing capitalist economy for the next fifty years.

The Journeymen's Revolt in Comparative Perspective

Two key features of U.S. history are emphasized in almost every discussion of American exceptionalism: the early introduction of universal male suffrage and the strong cultural stress on individualistic strategies for social advancement. Because American workers were not forced to wage a protracted battle for the vote and citizenship rights, so the story goes, they were never pressured to build the kind of national organizations or the collectivist ideologies that maximized class consciousness in England and in most of Europe.[55] Recent studies of early labor movements across the Atlantic, however, challenge the exceptionalist assumption that American workers have always differed markedly from workers elsewhere. If we compare accounts of early journeymen's movements by such authors as Edward Thompson, William Sewell, Jr., and Sean Wilentz—all of whom identify these movements as formative for the development of working-class consciousness—we see extensive overlap in workers' grievances, language, organization, and alternative visions. In 1836 and 1837, despite the fact that they had voting rights and lived in a society where individualism was often championed, American journeymen used a vocabulary of class, participated in building organizations, and developed an alternative vision of the economy and society that looked very much like that of artisans in England and France.

Instead of retracing old ground by providing a narrative of the first moment of working-class formation in England and France, I will simply point out the similarities among the journeymen's movements. One of them lies in the underlying economic causes of artisan politicization. The three decades preceding the 1830s brought intensified competition among manufacturers and the subordination of direct producers to monopolizing middlemen on both sides of the Atlantic; the result was a reorganization of production that proletarianized artisan producers in many sectors of the economy. As one of the delegates to

---

55. In addition to the sources cited in the Introduction, note 1, see Arthur L. Stinchcombe, *Information and Organizations* (Berkeley: University of California Press, 1990), p. 279.

the NTU commented when comparing English and American workers, "no one will dispute that the same causes produce like effects."[56]

Another similarity can be found in the significant broadening of journeymen's organizations and solidarities in this period. In England, the years 1829–34 witnessed an unprecedented burst of craft union organization and action. As in the United States, this heightened activity soon led to the formal expression of cross-trade solidarity on the part of journeymen. The most notable example is the Grand National Consolidated Trades Union, initiated by Robert Owen in 1833. This national federation soon fell apart, but efforts to coordinate trade union action within towns continued, albeit on a more modest scale.[57] In France, where the Le Chapelier law of 1791 made trade unions illegal, solidarity was less formally organized, but it was nonetheless evident. Since the turn of the century, French artisans had used government- and church-sanctioned mutual aid societies and *compagnonnages* to pursue limited trade union goals. In the 1830s journeymen began to recast these older forms of associations by jettisoning both church and state tutelage and by openly engaging in efforts to regulate the conditions of their employment. For the first time, workers began to build informal and sometimes secret intercity networks that could coordinate actions across trade and city boundaries. Soon, appeals were being issued to all journeymen's associations, proposing that they "join hands to sustain each other" in order to "bring into being the bonds of the confraternity of proletarians."[58] Additional signs of journeymen's growing sense of class identity can be seen in the French strike wave that peaked in 1833 and in the emergence of several working-class newspapers in both France and England.[59]

56. Commons et al., *Documentary*, 6: 222.

57. Edward H. Hunt, *British Labour History, 1815–1914* (Atlantic Highlands, N.J.: Humanities Press, 1981), pp. 199–206; G. D. H. Cole and Raymond Postgate, *The Common People, 1746–1946* (London: Methuen, 1961), pp. 258–72.

58. Quoted in Sewell, *Work and Revolution*, p. 213.

59. On the strike wave, see Edward Shorter and Charles Tilly, *Strikes in France, 1830–1968* (Cambridge: Cambridge University Press, 1974), pp. 107–8, and Roger Price, *A Social History of Nineteenth-Century France* (New York: Holmes and Meier, 1987), p. 231. In Paris, three working-class newspapers were founded in 1830: *L'Artisan, journal de la classe ouvrière* (The Artisan, Journal of the Working Class); *Le Journal des ouvriers* (The Workers' Journal); and *Le Peuple, journal général des ouvriers, rédigé par eux-mêmes* (The People, General Workers' Journal, Edited by Themselves). In Lyon, two were published, *L'Echo de la fabrique* (The Manufacturers' Gazette) and *L'Echo des travailleurs* (The Workers' Gazette). See Sewell, *Work and Revolution*, pp. 197 and 207.

In England, the working-class press dates back to the 1825 founding of the *Trades Newspaper*. In 1831, the more widely read *Poor Man's Guardian* began publication. See also Thompson, *Making*, pp. 718–33, for a discussion of the unstamped press. A useful review of English developments in this period is provided in John Rule, *The Labouring Classes in Early Industrial England, 1750–1850* (London: Longman, 1986), pp. 288-307.

It was in the course of building these organizations and justifying these strikes that French and English artisans elaborated a language of class. The immediate cause of labor agitation was a ruptured political alliance between artisans and middle-class radicals. In both countries, workers had joined with middle-class activists to defeat a regime dominated by landed aristocrats, only to be subsequently denied full citizenship rights by the new government.[60] In France, it was the social and political struggles following the July Revolution of 1830 that radicalized artisans. Parisian workers felt betrayed when sympathetic treatment was not forthcoming from bourgeois officials whom workers had fought to install in power. The new bourgeois government initiated various liberal reforms—including a slight extension of the franchise, a reduction in the arbitrary powers of the monarch, and a guarantee of freedom of the press, but both the new "Citizen King" and the new legislature balked when workers came forward to demand controls on their trades. Workers' demands for uniform tariffs, shorter workdays, and regulation of machinery were dismissed as assaults on the "liberty of industry."[61] For workers, this betrayal was glaringly similar to the one they had experienced in 1789, when, as in 1830, they had borne much of the burden of the insurrection only to have the bourgeoisie desert them. This time, however, workers took up the language of republicanism and reshaped it to formulate a critique of wage labor, political exclusion, and the bourgeoisie's interpretation of "liberty."[62]

In England, the Reform Bill of 1832 represented a similar breakdown of a political alliance between workers and the middle class.[63] In agitating for the reform amid "probably the most serious disturbances to occur in nineteenth-century Britain," many middle-class leaders claimed that if reforms were not granted, working-class discontent might erupt into insurrectionary activity. When the Reform Bill extended the franchise to the bulk of the middle class but left workers very little to show for their support, in Thompson's words, a "line was drawn" between the two groups "with the crudity of an indelible pen-

---

60. William H. Sewell, Jr., "How Classes Are Made: Critical Reflections on E. P. Thompson's Theory of Working-Class Formation," in *E. P. Thompson: Critical Perspectives*, ed. Harvey J. Kaye and Keith McClelland (Philadelphia: Temple University Press, 1990), p. 70.

61. Sewell, *Work and Revolution*, pp. 195–96.

62. Sewell speaks of the "liberal discourse of the French revolution," rather than of republicanism, but, labels aside, he makes essentially the same point. See his "Artisans, Factory Workers, and the Formation of the French Working Class, 1789–1848," in *Working-Class Formation*, ed. Katznelson and Zolberg, pp. 55–67, and in *Work and Revolution*, chap. 9.

63. Sewell, "How Classes Are Made," pp. 70–71.

cil."[64] In the disillusionment that followed, English workers, like their French counterparts, took up the traditional language of political radicalism to justify their call for political and economic reform.

In the United States, there was no equally clear-cut moment at which the bourgeoisie attained political power and betrayed the working class. But American journeymen nevertheless felt a very real sense of betrayal. It rings through the writings of the period and derives from a coincidence that has gone virtually unrecognized in the literature on American exceptionalism: the enhancement of worker's political status and the degradation of their economic lot occurred almost simultaneously.[65] Mechanics were outraged because, after years of arguing that a workers' competence entitled him to a respected political voice, this political voice was finally secured at the very moment when the journeyman's competence—and thus his political independence and social respect—were snatched away.[66] American journeymen, I am arguing, traveled a different path to a similar sense of betrayal, a similar sense that their full inclusion in society was being denied.

Although the immediate causes of artisan radicalism differed on the two sides of the Atlantic, once the movements were under way, the transformation of existing ideas into a class-conscious discourse was a remarkably similar process. Much as American labor leaders used the language of republicanism, artisans in England and France appropriated the very language the bourgeoisie had employed in gaining political power, turning inherited values to radical ends. This was not a straightforward process of borrowing, however, for in each case, the appropriated language was too individualistic and too firmly rooted in the political rights of property to sanction two of labor's most critical claims: that workers had full political rights despite their lack of land and capital and that they, collectively, had a right to control the terms of their labor.[67]

We have already seen how American workers reinterpreted republicanism to make these claims. French labor leaders used the republican discourse of the French revolution to pursue lines of reasoning that were strikingly parallel. This was a complicated process that cannot easily be summarized; however, the major lines of argument and language redefinition should demonstrate broad similarities between the

64. Thompson, *Making*, p. 821.
65. An exception is Rodgers, *Contested Truths*, p. 73.
66. One example of a worker expressing such sentiment would be William Heighton, a Philadelphia shoemaker and labor activist. He argued that nonproducers had silently achieved a counterrevolution in the United States by usurping control of the government and rigging elections to benefit the privileged. For a discussion of Heighton's ideas, see Laurie, *Artisans*, pp. 66–72.
67. Sewell, "How Classes Are Made," pp. 70–71.

cases. Appropriating the producerist categories of the French Revolution, French labor leaders argued that because workers produced all of society's wealth, they were in fact the sovereign people, and that the bourgeoisie was in effect a new aristocracy. "We believe that the people is nothing but the working class," declared *L'Artisan* in 1830.[68] Yet the people were exploited, their property (in their labor) "expropriated," their "dignity as men" denied.[69] Why? Because the new aristocracy had instituted abusive forms of privilege that exempted the idle rich from labor and gave them an unjust monopoly of political power (through property restrictions on the franchise). Only by building "associations" of workers across trade lines could workers overcome their own oppression, and society's wrongs. As they made these arguments, French artisans redefined terms such as "people," "property," "aristocrat," and "privilege"; in the process they created a working-class discourse that, in William Sewell Jr.'s words, "established a solidarity between workers of all trades, empowered workers to make collective claims about the character and products of productive activities, gave them a moral claim to political power, and stigmatized wealthy property owners as privileged and greedy monopolists."[70]

English workers made similar assertions by stretching and reformulating the lexicon of English radicalism.[71] In 1832, as Thompson and

68. Quoted in Sewell, *Work and Revolution*, p. 199.
69. Quoted from Sewell, *Work and Revolution*, p. 215.
70. Sewell, "How Classes Are Made," p. 71.
71. English radicalism shared many ideological tenets and intellectual ancestors with American and French republicanism. As with republicanism, its critique of society was rooted in the corrupting effects of the concentration of political power and in the belief that moral societies were composed of free men equal in rights. It, too, was fiercely antiaristocratic, drew on notions of the common good and inalienable rights ("rights of the free-born Englishman"), and justified its call for democratic political reform by drawing a contrast between the producing and nonproducing classes. Moreover, many of the same texts shaped radicalism in England and republicanism in France and in the United States. Above all, Tom Paine's writings, especially *The Rights of Man*, were important in the development of radicalism.

Indeed, the parallels between what is termed "republicanism" in the French and American literature and what is referred to as "radicalism" in the English are so extensive in this period that one might be tempted to simply refer to all three as "republicanism." However, English historians are divided over the extent to which even the most plebeian and democratic of English radicals endorsed the dissolution of the monarchy, a defining feature of republicanism after the French Revolution. Gareth Stedman Jones, for example, believes that working-class radicals were republicans in this sense, but Dorothy Thompson claims that they were not. Gareth Stedman Jones, *Languages of Class* (Cambridge: Cambridge University Press, 1983), pp. 169 and 185; Dorothy Thompson, *The Chartists* (New York: Pantheon, 1984), p. 6. Adjudicating this debate is beyond the scope of this study, and thus I reluctantly adopt the term radicalism. Nonetheless, the important point remains the similarities of language and ideological tenets that underlay the language of labor in all three countries.

For useful discussions of English radicalism, see Thompson, *Making*, pp. 17–26, 77–

others have demonstrated, the "People" (or "the real people") became synonymous with the working class.[72] Property rights, too, were re-defined, much as they were by artisans in France and in the United States, first to include, and eventually to privilege, labor itself. This development is nicely illustrated in the contrasting statements of a weaver in 1823 and a Chartist in 1839:

> The weaver's qualifications may be considered as his property and sup-port. It is as real property to him as buildings and lands are to others.[73]

> The working class were told they had no need of the suffrage as they had no property to protect. They had indeed none save that which was in the strength of their arms; and from that property, every description of property arose, and therefore, theirs was the only property of real value and ought to be the first in the world to have legislative protection.[74]

185, 466–71, 603–30, and 807–36; Trygve R. Tholfsen, *Working-Class Radicalism in Mid-Victorian England* (New York: Columbia University Press, 1977), chap. 1; and Stedman Jones, *Languages of Class*, esp. pp. 102–7. On Tom Paine's influence, see E. Foner, *Tom Paine*, esp., chap. 7.

72. Thompson, *Making*, pp. 807–32; Stedman Jones, *Languages of Class*, p. 104. See also Tholfsen, *Working-Class Radicalism*, pp. 49–72.

Although Stedman Jones notes that "in radical terms, in 1832, the 'people' became the 'working classes,'" he is reluctant to see in this transformation the birth of a lan-guage of class. He is bothered by both the continuities in the new and old radical vocabulary and by the fact that the new, more radical rhetoric continued to identify the state, rather than the economy, as the ultimate source of oppression. His argument is provocative but ultimately unconvincing, largely because he appears to believe that one can speak of class consciousness only when a class discards old categories and rhetorics and adopts new ones in a single, sudden, transformative moment. My reading of his-tory suggests that the process is rarely this dramatic; instead new understandings get layered over older ones and only gradually displace them.

Joan W. Scott, "On Language, Gender, and Working-Class History," *International Labor and Working-Class History* 21 (1987): 1–13, notes that Stedman Jones's own evidence suggests that a new class-based language is emerging. In the quotes given in his text it is virtually impossible not to notice that workers are struggling to reshape their vo-cabulary in order to articulate their sense of distinction from masters, shopkeepers, and aristocrats. They sometimes address the question of whether or not to cooperate with various outside groups, especially masters, but when they do so, Scott argues, they are clearly debating tactics rather than identity.

Others have taken issue with Thompson for overstating the unity of the working class in 1832. R. Currie and R. M. Hartwell, in "The Making of the English Working Class?" *Economic History Review* 18, 2d ser. (December 1965): 633–42, for example, be-lieve that Thompson's own evidence demonstrates that the period was "rich in conflict between artisans, factory workers, and the labouring poor." I believe that this conflict existed but that it is a misreading of Thompson to think that it fatally undermines his argument. His case rests upon his ability to demonstrate the birth of a language and organization of class, not upon his ability to show the creation of a fully formed and universally shared class consciousness on the part of all proletarians.

73. Quoted in John Rule, "The Property of Skill in the Period of Manufacture," in *The Historical Meanings of Work*, ed. Patrick Joyce (Cambridge: Cambridge University Press, 1987), p. 106.

74. Quoted in Stedman Jones, *Languages of Class*, p. 109.

The term "aristocracy" was similarly stretched: the columns of the labor press began to refer to a "sub-aristocracy" of "the middle classes," who, like the traditional landed aristocracy, was "parasitic," unjustly "privileged," and engaged in "idle Profligacy."[75] Increasingly, this new "sub-aristocracy" was viewed as a "middle-class," distinct from—and often contrasted with—the "industrious" or "working classes."[76]

The parallel development of the labor movement in England, France, and the United States extends as well to the type of alternative system artisans envisaged. On both sides of the Atlantic labor leaders advocated various schemes for cooperative production, all of which were intended eventually to replace the developing competitive economy with a system of producers' cooperatives.[77] Supporters in each country recommended similar means for establishing cooperatives: initially, they would be capitalized by regular weekly contributions from workers, and eventually they would come to include more and more of the industry. These cooperatives, activists in all three countries explained, would allow workers to control the terms of their labor and to enjoy its full returns. The vision was everywhere rather utopian in that it relied, in Richard Price's words, "upon the possibility of implanting islands of cooperation within the sea of competition," and somehow having the islands expand to encompass the sea.[78] To skilled artisans at the time, however, it probably seemed somewhat less utopian than it does now; after all, it was a vision in which they would *recover* the independence, pride, dignity, and well-being their skills had once af-

75. Thompson, *Making*, ch. 16; Patricia Hollis, *Class and Conflict in Nineteenth-Century England, 1815–1850* (London: Routledge and Kegan Paul, 1973), pp. xx–xvi, 47–48, 52, and 72–85. See also D. G. Wright, *Popular Radicalism: The Working-Class Experience, 1780–1880* (London: Longman, 1988), p. 98, and R. J. Morris, *Class and Class Consciousness in the Industrial Revolution, 1780–1850* (London: Macmillan, 1979), p. 49.

76. Asa Briggs, *The Collected Essays of Asa Briggs*, vol. 1 (Urbana: University of Illinois Press, 1985), esp. pp. 14–20; Raymond Williams, *Keywords* (New York: Oxford University Press, 1983), pp. 63–64.

77. On the cooperative vision in the United States, see the earlier discussion in this chapter. On English cooperation, see Rule, *Labouring Classes*, pp. 296–98; Richard Price, *Labour in British Society* (London: Croom Helm, 1986), pp. 54–55; and Hollis, *Class and Conflict*, pp. 154–65. Sewell, *Work and Revolution*, pp. 202–6, and Moss, *Origins*, pp. 32–35, discuss cooperation in the 1830s in France.

In England, the utopian vision may have reached its apogee: members of the Builders Union argued in 1833–34 that cooperation would provide a peaceful method to reform parliament and the economy. Once the product of workers' labor was no longer appropriated by nonproducers, they contended, the corrupt parliament of privilege and monopoly would fall and be replaced by a very different parliament: "Every trade has its internal government in every town; a certain number of towns comprise a district and delegates from the trades in each town form the Annual Parliament, and the King of England becomes President of the Trades Union." Quoted in Rule, *Labouring Classes*, p. 296.

78. Price, *Labour*, p. 55.

forded. The important point is that both the vision and its impractical aspects were shared by French, English, and American workers.

A final similarity in the journeymen's movements of the 1830s lies in the boundaries and limitations of their emergent class consciousness. As in the United States, artisans in France and England were more inclusive of other workers in their language than in their organizations, and the language itself often masked exclusivist assumptions. In terms of organizations, French compagnonnage and mutual aid associations and English unions were composed almost entirely of skilled urban workers. At periods of peak activism, such as occurred at the height of the Owenism trade union phase, small overtures were made to craftless workers, but these were short-lived exceptions to the general rule.[79] As for workers' discourse, when "the working class(es)" or "the industrious" were counterposed to "aristocrats" or "capitalists," the referent of the former terms was an inclusive group of manual wage earners. But when property was reinterpreted to entail the full political rights of labor, the property holders signified were those who had skills, as both Joan Scott and John Rule have recently demonstrated.[80]

Corresponding ambiguities beset artisans' perceptions of small masters in France and England. As in the United States, small masters were sometimes welcomed to join journeymen's organizations and were included in their visions of political and economic reform. Even in the revolutionary fervor of 1848, for example, French workers advocated socialist schemes in which the distinction between workers and masters would explicitly be abolished as the two came together as associated owners of the means of production.[81] When we consider that small masters were as likely as workers to suffer from competitive capitalism and that masters too possessed the skills prized so highly

79. For example, the Operative Builders' Union, an association of craft unions in the building industry, may have briefly included laborers. Hunt, *British Labour History*, p. 201, claims that it did, and Rule, *Labouring Classes*, p. 296, writes that such workers were to be granted membership in the future when "they can be prepared with better habits and more knowledge to enable them to act for themselves, assisted by other branches who will have an overwhelming interest to improve the mind, morals, and general condition of their families in the shortest time."

80. Joan W. Scott, *Gender and the Politics of History* (New York: Columbia University Press, 1988), esp. pp. 107–8; Rule, "Property of Skill," pp. 99–118; John Rule, "Artisan Attitudes: A Comparative Survey of Skilled Labour and Proletarianization before 1848," *Bulletin of the Society for the Study of Labour History* 50 (1985): 22–31. Sewell would probably disagree with this assessment, for the implication of his work is that the ideology of the French revolution made it difficult for workers to claim skilled labor as a special, exclusive property. Despite this, Rule notes that a sense of a restricted right to follow a craft did, in practice, remain a fundamental assumption of French artisans. A test of competence was the primary condition for admittance to a compagnonnage, and as Moss's *Origins* demonstrates, French socialism developed on the basis of federating crafts for common purposes while preserving their individual autonomy.

81. Sewell, *Work and Revolution*, p. 283; Scott, *Gender and Politics*, pp. 98–100.

by journeymen, this hope that small masters might ally with workers should not be too surprising.[82] In addition, producerism remained an important strain of working-class thought, further clouding the situation. Indeed, one of the most commonly used terms of hostility in England was "parasitic capitalist," a phrase that nicely combined the old categories with the newer, more radical rhetoric.[83]

It would be going too far to claim that there were no important differences in the language and organization of class that developed in England, France, and the United States during the 1830s. There were some, largely of tone and emphasis, that to a certain extent still mark the working class in each country. For example, one can already find some of the famed, fierce insularity of the British working class: in 1834, James Morrison, editor of a union newspaper, *Pioneer*, wrote: "Orphans we are, and bastards of society."[84] Edward Thompson notes that the tone is one not of resignation but of pride. It is difficult to imagine either an American or a French worker claiming anything of the sort; both would be more likely to assert, perhaps a bit defensively, workers' superiority. Similarly, one comes across more talk of "arms," and "blood," in the French documents; there is clearly a greater willingness to wage civil war if the same demands the British and American workers made were not met.[85] Finally, French and English workers were likely to identify both the state and capitalist employers as the source of their distress, but American workers generally attributed their oppression primarily to employers.[86] American workers did speak of government corruption and often identified this as the source of workers' problems, but they tended to tie this corrup-

82. One might think that the distinction between those who were franchised and those who were not would have overlapped with the distinction between masters and journeymen. But many small masters were disenfranchised, especially in France.

83. See Hollis, *Class and Conflict*. She identifies this second, more radical rhetoric with Henry Hetherington, William Carpenter, and, above all, Bronterre O'Brien. But even their assaults on capitalism were underpinned by persistent contrasts between "productive" and "unproductive" labor.

84. Quoted in Thompson, *Making*, p. 832.

85. To take an extreme example, a song written in 1833 by a French tapestry worker begins: "To arms, Proletarian / Take as your battle cry: / Morality for all, for all equality, / Victory to labor! Death to idleness!" Quoted in Sewell, *Work and Revolution*, p. 214 (his translation). Some of the same threatening tone occurs in the English documents (see, for example, Thompson, *Making*, pp. 714–15) but it is less widespread, and it is almost absent in the songs and circulars of American workers.

86. In *Languages of Class*, chap. 3, Stedman Jones argues that Chartism cannot be understood as a class-conscious movement because English workers attributed their misery to political and legal oppression rather than to economic oppression. By his logic, American workers would be the most class conscious of the three. See pp. 95 and 105–7.

87. Although many people believe that universal white male suffrage was instituted

tion to the aggrandizement of power on the part of capitalists rather than to any inherent problem in the structure of the state itself. Unlike their European colleagues who tended to view the state as an active and hostile player in society, American workers generally saw the state as playing a more neutral role: it guarded the common good by ensuring that no one group or interest dominated the rest of society.

For anyone steeped in the writing about American exceptionalism, however, it is the similarities that are most notable. Imagine for a moment a cross-national choir of activists from the journeymen's revolts. As they sang together, some discordant notes would surely be heard. But much would harmonize as they lifted their voices to condemn idlers and celebrate producers, proclaim skill to be property and capital to be an unfair source of privilege, lament their loss of dignity and laud trade solidarity, denounce the new competitive economy and acclaim cooperation as the path to their liberation. Thus, if the earliness of universal suffrage and individualism did mitigate against class consciousness in the United States, it did not do so in any immediate or direct manner.[87] The first moments of working-class formation resembled each other much more than they differed.

---

when the American colonies achieved independence, such is not the case. Significant property qualifications for voting and eligibility for office remained in effect through 1824 in many states. After 1824, Rhode Island, Louisiana, Mississippi, Ohio, Connecticut, North Carolina, and Virginia continued to limit the franchise in important ways, but most states had established universal white male suffrage. Hence, with respect to the timing of working-class formation, universal white male suffrage was instituted in the United States about a decade before what is identified here as the first moment of working-class formation.

French males, however, were not far behind. Universal male suffrage was established there in 1848, about a decade after the first moment of working-class formation.

England did not establish universal male suffrage until much later, in 1918. The process by which universal suffrage was attained was also much more halting. In 1832, as noted, electoral reform enfranchised the urban middle classes. In 1867–68, a second electoral reform act reduced the income and property qualifications for suffrage, thus enfranchising many skilled workers. The third electoral reform of 1884–85 extended the vote to most workers, although it left domestic servants, poor relief recipients, and those who for one reason or another did not appear on the complicated registration lists disenfranchised. Only in 1918 were all restrictions on the franchise of male citizens removed; that same year women householders (and those married to householders) were given the right to vote. Thus, most English male workers were enfranchised a few years before the second moment of working-class formation, but universal male suffrage did not occur until after this second moment.

On suffrage requirements in the United States, see Pessen, *Jacksonian America*, pp. 150–53 and Chilton Williamson, *American Suffrage: From Property to Democracy, 1760–1860* (Princeton: Princeton University Press, 1960); on France and England, see Peter Flora et al., *State, Economy, and Society in Western Europe, 1815–1975* (Frankfurt: Campus Verlag, 1983), pp. 112–13 and 148–49. Neal Blewett, "The Franchise in the United Kingdom, 1885–1918," *Past and Present* 32 (Dec. 1965): 27–56, provides a useful discussion of England's third electoral reform act and its consequences.

2

Skilled and Less-Skilled Work,
1830–1880

The artisans are almost to a man red-hot politicians. They are
sufficiently educated and thoughtful to have a sense of their
importance in the state. . . . The unskilled labourers are a
different class of people. As yet they are as unpolitical as
footmen . . . they appear to have no political opinions whatever;
or, if they do possess any, they rather lead towards the
maintenance of "things as they are," than towards the
ascendancy of the working people.
—Henry Mayhew, 1849

We have seen that craftless workers remained at the margins of the
labor movements of the 1830s. Who were these workers and what
kind of work did they do? What changed—either about the organization of work or the character of the industrial labor force—that made
it possible in the closing decades of the nineteenth century for these
workers finally to be actively recruited into the labor movement?

English, French, and American less-skilled workers in the 1830s all
did work that was distinguished in several ways from craft work. They
received poorer wages, toiled at tasks that could be learned in shorter
amounts of time, endured less healthy working conditions, and had
little hope of ever gaining a competence. A substantial proportion also
worked in locations that were far removed from the large cities where
the movements of the 1830s were formed. Even those who labored in
urban areas lived in distinct social worlds. This, and the fact that many
were women and children, meant that skilled artisans found few similarities between their situation and that of the new, less-skilled proletariat created by the early industrial revolution.

When examining the American industrial economy of the 1830s, it is possible to distinguish three types of less-skilled workers: out-workers, unskilled laborers, and factory operatives. Outworkers were the most directly involved in urban manufacturing; as we have seen, in trades such as clothing and shoemaking they had become a significant proportion of the labor force. Official statistics were not collected, but most accounts indicate that women made up the bulk of urban out-workers in the 1820s and 1830s.[1] Some were the wives and daughters of day laborers or artisans who had fallen on hard times; the majority, however, were abandoned or widowed women supporting themselves and their children. The contractors for whom outworkers toiled made profits by keeping labor costs and overhead low. Already meager in the 1820s and 1830s,[2] wages fell to even lower levels in the 1840s when immigrant families desperate for work arrived in the nation's leading manufacturing centers.

Unskilled day laborers were also a part of the urban economy, although in most cities they were involved in transportation and construction rather than in manufacturing work. They did the loading, hauling, digging, and general labor that supported the manufacturing economy. Such work paid better than outwork, but employment was generally irregular. In the 1830s, the majority of day laborers were native-born rural migrants, although a noticeable minority in many cities were Irish immigrants. Somewhere between one-quarter and one-third of the urban labor force was employed as day laborers; together with outworkers, they probably accounted for about 40 percent of the urban working class.[3]

Factory operatives were employed almost exclusively in the cotton textile industry. Most worked in mills that had been built in small New England villages, far away from the daily experience of urban craftsmen. To most Americans, the word "factory" conjured up nightmarish images of dehumanized, machine-driven, dependent labor, and as a result labor recruitment was a perennial problem for textile entrepreneurs. The earliest factories hired poor rural families, including children, to run the spinning machines, but with mechanization, larger establishments became technically feasible, and it became dif-

1. One estimate by Matthew Carey, an antebellum businessman and philanthropist, put the number of women outworkers in the nation's four largest cities at 12,000 or 13,000 in 1831. Bruce Levine et al., *Who Built America?* (New York: Pantheon, 1989), 1: 249.
2. Christine Stansell, *City of Women* (Urbana: University of Illinois Press, 1987), pp. 106–15; Oscar Handlin, *Boston's Immigrants, 1790–1880* (Cambridge: Belknap Press, 1979), chap. 3.
3. Gordon, Edwards, and Reich, *Segmented Work*, p. 61; David Montgomery, "The Working Classes of the Pre-Industrial City, 1780–1830," *Labor History* 9, no. 1 (1968): 15.

ficult to find enough families willing to work in the textile mills. The solution, initiated in 1827, was to recruit young, unmarried Yankee farm women and to build dormitories to shelter them.[4] Turnover was high, but, as H. M. Gitelman notes, high rates were advantageous as long as the flow of women into the mills was sufficient to staff the machines: they reassured a nervous public that no permanent class of dependent wage earners was developing.[5] Overall, cotton textile employment accounted for about 14 percent of the manufacturing labor force in the 1830s.[6]

In sum, working conditions, pay, past experiences, expectations for the future, gender, ethnicity, and physical distance all set these workers apart from skilled urban craftsmen. Craftsmen's republicanism provided an interpretation of these differences that further magnified these divisive effects. Because they equated lack of independence with absence of virtue, craftsmen found it difficult to view day laborers, outworkers, or factory operatives as members of the same class. Women workers were particularly suspect. Most craftsmen believed that women's upbringing and nature made it impossible for them to organize for their own defense; they also feared that women's "weaker character" made them unable fully to resist the tyranny of employers.[7] This attitude was given public expression when the NTU declared women's manufacturing work to be "highly injurious to the best interests of the working classes."[8] Such attitudes obviously tended to discourage alliances across skill and gender lines.

In England and France, the same varieties of less-skilled workers were found in the industrial economy. However, the industrial and demographic mix of each country differed; thus variations existed in the distribution of workers across types and in the gender and ethnic makeup of the less-skilled work force. For example, women workers probably formed a larger proportion of the manufacturing work force in both England and France than in the United States; certainly this was the case after the 1840s (see Table 1). French women, moreover, were more likely to be employed as homeworkers, even when they spun or wove, than were either English or American women, in part

4. Gordon, Edwards, and Reich, *Segmented Work*, pp. 70–71; Dublin, *Women at Work*, pp. 23–57.
5. Howard M. Gitelman, "The Waltham System and the Coming of the Irish," *Labor History* 8 (1967): 227–53.
6. U.S. Bureau of the Census, *Historical Statistics*, p. 139.
7. Stansell, *City of Women* pp. 137–41.
8. Quoted in Stansell, *City of Women*, p. 138.

because the French produced more wool, linen, and silk than cotton.[9] Variation existed, too, in the numbers and ethnicity of non-native employees doing less-skilled work. Fewer immigrants found their way to France than to England or to the United States,[10] and those who did were predominantly Italian rather than Irish, as they typically were in Anglo-American cities.[11] However, language and regional differences within France meant that rural migrants were often almost as distinct from natives as were foreign immigrants.[12]

But these variations are less notable than the profound separation between skilled and less-skilled workers in everyday life in all three countries. As is true of the literature on the United States, virtually all studies of workers in early-nineteenth-century France and England make note of the great difference between artisans and unskilled workers. For example, Henry Mayhew, the preeminent chronicler of nineteenth-century London, observed in 1849 that, "in passing from

9. Louise A. Tilly and Joan W. Scott, *Women, Work, and Family* (New York: Methuen, 1987), pp. 69–70. For figures on the various types of textile production in each country, albeit for a later period, see Hanagan, *Logic of Solidarity*, p. 8.

10. In some French cities, notably Marseille, the number of Italian workers concentrated in low-skilled occupations approximated that of the Irish in English and American cities. But in most French cities, rural migrants did the jobs that immigrants did in England and in the United States. See William H. Sewell, Jr., "The Working Class of Marseille under the Second Republic: Social Structure and Political Behavior," in *Workers and the Industrial Revolution*, ed. Peter N. Stearns and Daniel J. Walkowitz (New Brunswick, N.J.: Transaction Books, 1974), pp. 75–116, esp. p. 80; Michael P. Hanagan, *Nascent Proletarians* (Oxford: Basil Blackwell, 1989), pp. 75 and 90, n. 42.

11. Thompson, *Making*, p. 429, notes that anywhere between one-fifth and one-third of the working population of Liverpool and Manchester was Irish, a number that exceeds those found in any city in the United States in the mid-1830s.

12. Eugen Weber, *Peasants into Frenchmen* (Stanford: Stanford University Press, 1976), p. 67, reports that French was a foreign language as late as 1863 for large numbers of Frenchmen, including almost half the schoolchildren. Instead they spoke what the French described as *patois*, a collection of various languages, dialects, and jargons traditionally spoken in French provinces. Hanagan, *Nascent Proletarians*, p. 72, notes that in Stephanois cities, rural migrants frequently spoke their own patois and kept to themselves, thus provoking antagonism among native workers who resented migrants for accepting lower wages.
The picture Weber and Hanagan present of regional difference and conflict between migrants and natives contrasts with William Sewell's discovery that in Marseille, trades open to migrants were more likely to support and participate in radical politics and militant protests. McDougall suggests that Weber's, Hanagan's, and Sewell's findings could all be right. She demonstrates that in Lyon, the majority of migrants who became militants were short-distance migrants, primarily from departments surrounding Lyon. Short-distance migrants were likely to speak the same language as natives and to find fellow countrymen when they arrived in Lyon. Thus, they were less likely to be perceived as different by natives and also less likely to provoke antagonism. See Mary Lynn McDougall, "Consciousness and Community: The Workers of Lyon, 1830–1850," *Journal of Social History* 12, no. 1 (1978): 129–45.

Table 1. Comparative development of labor and industry in England, France, and the United States

	England		France		United States	
Manufacturing	1851	1891	1856	1896	1850	1890
Wage earners in manufacturing (thousands)[a]	3,612	5,408 (50% increase)	3,097	4,619 (49% increase)	1200	4,390 (266% increase)
Female workers as % of total manufacturing workers[b]	35	36	35	37	24	20
Steam horsepower[c]	1,290	9,200	370	4,520	1,680	14,400
Steam horsepower per manufacturing worker[d]	.36	1.7	.12	.98	1.4	3.28
Urbanization and Immigration	1851	1891	1851	1891	1850	1890
Foreign-born as % of total population[e]	4.7	2.3	1.1	2.8	9.7	14.7
Urban dwellers as % of total population[f]	40.8	53.7	14.5	21.7	11.3	27.7
Secondary Sector	1851	1911	1851	1910	1850	1910
Wage earners in the secondary sector as % of total labor force[g]	48.1	51.6	26.9	33.1	17.6	31.6
Agriculture	1851	1901	1851	1891	1850	1900
Wage earners in agriculture as % of total labor force[h]	22.0	9.0	51.4	44.6	64.0	38.0

[a] English and French figures from B. R. Mitchell, *European Historical Statistics, 1750–1970* (New York: Columbia University Press, 1975), pp. 155 and 163; U.S. figures from U.S. Department of Commerce, *Historical Statistics of the United States, Part I* (Washington, D.C.: Government Printing Office, 1975), p. 139.

[b] English and French figures are computed from Mitchell, pp. 155 and 163; U.S. figures are from Edith Abbott, *Women in Industry: A Study in American Economic History* (1910; reprint, New York: Arno Press, 1969), p. 360.

[c] David S. Landes, *The Unbound Prometheus* (Cambridge: Cambridge University Press, 1969), p. 221. 1890 figures given are actually for 1888.

[d] Row 3 divided by Row 1.

[e] French statistics are from Gary Cross, *Immigrant Workers in Industrial France* (Philadelphia: Temple University Press, 1983), p. 21; English figures for 1851 are from N. L. Tranter, "The Labor Supply, 1780–1860," in *The Economic History of Britain since 1700*, ed. Roderick Floud and Donald McCloskey, (Cambridge: Cambridge University Press, 1981), I: 211, and for 1891 are from *Statistical Abstract for the United Kingdom* (Eighteenth Number) (London: His Majesty's Stationery Office, 1937), pp. 22–24. (English figures include people born in Ireland.) U.S. figures are from John Higham, *Send These to Me: Immigrants in Urban America* (Baltimore: Johns Hopkins University Press, 1984), p. 15.

[f] Urban population is defined as the proportion of the population residing in places of 10,000 or more residents. French and English figures are from Jan de Vries, *European Urbanization, 1500–1800* (Cambridge: Harvard University Press, 1984), Table 3.8, pp. 45–46. (English figures include Wales.) U.S. figures are computed from Department of Commerce, *Historical Statistics*, pp. 11–12.

[g] Aristide Zolberg, "How Many Exceptionalisms?" in *Working-Class Formation: Nineteenth-Century Patterns in Western Europe and the United States*, ed. Ira Katznelson and Aristide R. Zolberg (Princeton: Princeton University Press, 1986), p. 438.

[h] French figures are from Yves Lequin, "Labour in the French Economy since the Revolution," in *The Cambridge Economic History of Europe*, ed. Peter Mathias and M. M. Postan (Cambridge: Cambridge University Press, 1978), 7: 305–6; British and U.S. figures are from Philip S. Bagwell and G. E. Mingay, *Britain and America: A Study of Economic Change* (New York: Praeger, 1970), p. 60.

the skilled operative of the West End to the unskilled workman of the eastern quarter of London, the moral and intellectual change is so great that it seems as if we were in a new land, and among another race." [13] Sewell records a similar distance in his summary of the distinct worlds of proletarians and artisans in Marseille at mid-century: "proletarians were impoverished, oppressed, frequently illiterate, often without family ties, unorganized, nomadic, and to judge from their high crime rates, often personally disoriented"; in contrast artisans, "were moderately well-paid, respectable, literate, organized, and rooted in the city, in their trade, and in a long-standing urban corporate tradition." [14] Both Mayhew and Sewell are writing about male workers, but those who study female workers have discovered an analogous division between skilled artisans and women workers. Ideologically, "skill was . . . a male 'property,' " something a woman could not possess, no matter what her technical aptitude. [15] Thus even in cases where men and women did the same kinds of tasks, as for instance occurred in the Parisian garment trade, these tasks were generally carried out in physically distinct spaces and thought of as differentially skilled. In the 1830s and 1840s Parisian seamstresses worked at home for low pay at jobs that were, by definition, unskilled, but tailors were employed in a shop where they received better wages for tasks that were, again by definition, skilled. [16] Thus, in England and France, as well as in the United States, prevailing gender attitudes further accentuated what was already an enormous gulf between skilled and less-skilled workers.

It was only in the last quarter of the nineteenth century that the worlds of skilled and less-skilled workers began to converge. Enormous structural changes in the economy underlay the homogenization of the lives of the skilled and less skilled. These changes were most dramatic and rapid in the United States. In 1840, 800,000 Americans, or one out of every seven workers, had been engaged in the pursuits that define an industrial economy: manufacturing, mining, and construction. By 1890, over 6.5 million Americans, or one out of four, earned wages for such endeavors. [17] But the sheer volume of goods increased even more rapidly than the size of the industrial work force:

13. *Morning Chronicle*, Dec. 21, 1849, quoted in Hunt, *British Labour*, p. 99. Commentators continued to remark on the great distance between skilled and less-skilled workers in the 1860s and 1870s, as Royden Harrison makes clear in *Before the Socialists* (London: Routledge and Kegan Paul, 1965), pp. 27–29.

14. Sewell, "Social Change," p. 82.

15. Rule, "Property of Skill," p. 108.

16. Scott, *Gender and Politics*, p. 102.

17. Figures computed from U.S. Bureau of Census, *Historical Statistics*, p. 138.

by 1894, when the United States became the world's leading industrial power, her inhabitants produced almost one-third of the world's manufactured goods. The annual rate of growth of total output over the period 1846–78 was 4.2 percent, the highest in the world, and greater than France and Britain combined.[18] Increasing factory size went hand in hand with industrial growth. Between 1850 and 1880, the average number of wage earners per establishment grew from 53 to 197 in iron and steel, 60 to 115 in glass, 5 to 20 in agricultural implements, and 53 to 104 in carpets and rugs.[19] In the industrial state of New Jersey, the typical worker in 1880 was employed in a factory that had more than 100 workers on its payroll.[20] Mechanized production, too, became a common feature of the industrial landscape. Between mid-century and 1900, the amount of horsepower used in the United States increased more than 757 percent.[21]

These figures demonstrate the rapidity of the changes in the American economy, but they mask their erratic, uneven quality, especially after 1870.[22] From the 1830s through the early 1870s, industrial growth was rapid and more or less continuous: the number of wage earners grew steadily along with per capita output, profits, and investment.[23] This long boom came to an end when Wall Street crashed in 1873, triggering a round of bankruptcies and failures that put as much as one-quarter of the labor force out of work.[24] After the economy began to recover, systemic problems persisted. Boom years were followed by recession years at consistently shorter intervals until 1893, when another major depression rocked the economy, again ushering in a financial panic and throwing large numbers of wage earners out of work. Behind this new unstable pattern of economic growth lay a vicious cycle. Falling prices in the depression and recession years led manufacturers to reorganize work so as to decrease their costs of production. The pro-

18. Gordon, Edwards, and Reich, *Segmented Work*, p. 43.

19. U.S. Bureau of Census, *Special Report on Employees and Wages. Twelfth Census of the United States, 1890–1900* (Washington, D.C.: Government Printing Office, 1903), table 17, p. lxxii. Figures are given for specific industries, not for the nation as a whole, because aggregate data for the late nineteenth century are biased downward due to the inclusion of "hand and neighborhood" industries.

20. New Jersey figure is from the study data.

21. Calculated from Table 1.

22. Gordon, Edwards, and Reich, *Segmented Work*, pp. 49–54 and 94–99. See also David Montgomery, *The Fall of the House of Labor* (Cambridge: Cambridge University Press, 1987), pp. 46–57.

23. Industrial output, GNP, and the number of wage earners grew even in the decade of the Civil War. See Gordon, Edwards, and Reich, *Segmented Work*, p. 52.

24. Stanley Lebergott, *Manpower in Economic Growth* (New York: McGraw-Hill, 1964), p. 187; Robert M. Jackson, *The Formation of Craft Labor Markets* (Orlando: Academic Press, 1984), p. 133.

ductivity gains they achieved led to increased competition and ever greater supplies of manufactured goods; these in turn caused prices to fall even lower. Heavy investments by the government and private groups in transportation and communication further fueled the deflationary cycle because they dissolved many of the cost advantages that protected local producers from even wider competition.[25] As manufacturers scrambled to stay in business, they turned to pricing pools, trusts, and other combinations, but these had little long-term effect.[26] They also turned with renewed vigor to efforts to cut the costs of production. Tasks were subdivided, skills displaced, and steam and machine power substituted for human labor. Wage cuts, too, were tried, along with new payment schemes and experiments with more intrusive and systematic management techniques.

This drive for lower production costs permanently altered customary patterns of work and social life for both skilled and less-skilled workers. It is important to remember that, as in the 1830s, these developments occurred unevenly across industries and products; thus, throughout the period, wage earners continued to work in a variety of settings, using a miscellany of techniques. Nevertheless, it is possible to summarize the important changes that occurred in the lives of skilled and less-skilled workers in these years.

Consider first the skilled. Between 1840 and the onset of the depression in 1873, there had been a gradual increase in the number of skilled workers who found employment in mechanized factories. Outside of textiles and iron, however, those who did remained a minority. The depression and ensuing economic instability greatly expanded their numbers as manufacturers turned to new methods of production to lower their labor costs. As a result, by the 1880s a great many skilled workers spent their days in factories instead of small shops. Those who did, as Steven Ross has demonstrated, were essentially a new breed: neither as skilled as their counterparts of the 1830s nor as semiskilled as the emerging factory proletariat.[27] Unlike the handicraft artisan of the 1830s who produced a complete product, these "factory artisans" of the late nineteenth century were required to master only a few constituent operations. Rather than receiving a "price" for their product,

---

25. Alfred D. Chandler, *The Visible Hand* (Cambridge: Harvard University Press, 1977), pp. 79–205. For an informative discussion of the government's role in facilitating industrial growth in this period, see Carl Degler, *Out of Our Past*, 3d ed. (New York: Harper Colophon, 1984), pp. 261–64.

26. Montgomery, *Fall*, p. 47.

27. This paragraph and the next draw especially from Ross, *Workers on the Edge*, pp. 97–118. See also, Michael P. Hanagan, "Artisan and Skilled Worker: The Problem of Definition," *International Labor and Working Class History* 12 (Nov. 1977): 23–31.

they received a wage for their time. No longer were they responsible for organizing production in time-honored ways to ensure customary notions of quality; now they were employees of a capitalist who made goods with an eye to maximizing profits. Neither were they any longer the unchallenged managers of daily work life; now the hiring, firing, and assigning of tasks was increasingly done by foremen and factory superintendents. Moreover, realistic hopes for escaping wage-earner status had all but vanished.

It should be noted that not everything had changed. Some aspects of their work and lives remained much as they had for the artisans of the 1830s. Like the old handicraft artisans, the new factory artisans were highly skilled and relatively well-paid; they often controlled the pace of their own work and sometimes of a helper as well. In some trades, they even continued to own their own tools. But the surroundings in which they worked, the future they envisaged, and the autonomy they exercised had all been modified.

No systematic study has been undertaken that would allow us to estimate with any precision the number of skilled workers who were "factory artisans" in the 1880s. We know only that, beginning with the depression of the 1870s, their ranks expanded greatly. Laurie reports that across the nation a surge of post-depression capital investment eliminated pockets of manual work in many trades, and Ross in his detailed examination of industrial development in Cincinnati concludes that of the ten industries dependent on handicraft artisans there in 1840, nine had come to rely on factory artisans by 1880 (these were: boots and shoes, tobacco, printing and publishing, furniture, carriages and wagons, metalworking, machinery, hardware, and brewing).[28] Even with additional studies, exact figures will remain elusive because the transition was uneven, both within and between industries. Some manufacturers had the capital and insight to adopt new methods and machines quickly when others were unable or unwilling to do so. Many firms clung to older methods of production when others continued to rely on skilled workers to recruit and coordinate work teams even when more modern management techniques were known.[29] In addition, the state of technology imposed limits on reorganization and mechanization.[30] Thus some shops and even whole industries (for

28. Laurie, *Artisans*, pp. 116–17; Ross, *Workers on the Edge*, p. 95.

29. The iron and steel industry is the most studied example. See Katharine Stone, "The Origins of Job Structures in the Steel Industry," *Review of Radical Political Economy* 6 (1974): 115–70; Montgomery, *Fall*, p. 29; William Form, "On the Degradation of Skills," *Annual Review of Sociology* 13 (1987): 29–47, esp. 35.

30. David Brody, *Steelworkers in America: The Nonunion Era* (Cambridge: Harvard University Press, 1960), p. 16; Bruce Laurie and Mark Schmitz, "Manufacture and Produc-

example, hatmaking and baking) remained dependent on handicraft skills into the 1890s.[31] Nevertheless, skilled workers found fewer alternatives to factory employment as the years passed, and when they did uncover them, they usually discovered that the pay was poorer.[32] Thus, by the early 1880s, a substantial proportion of the skilled labor force worked in factories or knew fellow tradesmen who did.

Factory expansion and the reorganization of traditional crafts also profoundly altered the scope and nature of less-skilled work. Most dramatically, the number of semiskilled factory operatives rose sharply. Whereas in the 1830s only textiles were produced by such workers, by the 1880s a dizzying array of products were made at least partially by semiskilled operatives: these included steel, chairs, packaged meat, boxes, chewing tobacco, books, shoes, thimbles, carriages, hats, paints, soap, and railroad cars.[33]

There were three important means by which the population of factory operatives grew. One involved the direct substitution of operatives for craftsmen. This happened in most industries, but furniture provides a typical example. The cabinetmaker who fashioned furniture to order in the 1830s was largely replaced in the 1880s by a trio of factory artisan types—varnishers, carpenters, and finishers—and a virtual army of semiskilled operatives, including dowlers, scrapers, benders, machine hands, bench hands, singers, and rubbers.[34] The manufacture of train rails provides another example, one that illustrates the varying economic forces that led to the direct substitution of operatives for craftsmen. Before the Civil War, train rails were made out of wrought iron by highly skilled puddlers, other equally skilled craftsmen, a few helpers, and common laborers.[35] After the introduc-

---

tivity: The Making of an Industrial Base, Philadelphia, 1850–1880," in *Philadelphia: Work, Space, Family, and Group Experience in the 19th Century*, ed. Theodore Hershberg (Oxford: Oxford University Press, 1981), pp. 57 and 61.

31. Laurie and Schmitz, "Manufacture and Productivity," p. 64; David Bensman, *The Practice of Solidarity: American Hat Finishers in the Nineteenth Century* (Urbana: University of Illinois Press, 1985), pp. 38–39.

32. Ross, *Workers on the Edge*, p. 139; Laurie & Schmitz, "Manufacture and Productivity," pp. 99–101.

33. This paragraph and the next three draw especially from Montgomery, *Fall*, pp. 112–70, and Ross, *Workers on the Edge*, pp. 118–26.

34. Skill designation for furniture making found in U.S. Census Bureau, *Special Report*, pp. 1177–78; description of changes in furniture making in this period found in Ross, *Workers on the Edge*, pp. 100–104, and Montgomery, *Fall*, pp. 125–26. Unskilled workers, too, found increasing employment opportunities in the furniture factories of the 1880s: they did the sewing, packing, and cleaning.

35. Brody, *Steelworkers*, pp. 8–17; Bernard Elbaum and Frank Wilkinson, "Industrial Relations and Uneven Development: A Comparative Study of the American and British Steel Industries," *Cambridge Journal of Economics* 3 (1979): 276–77 and 283–84.

tion of the Bessemer converter, which made it possible to produce steel—the superior metal for rails—much more cheaply, the manufacture of rails no longer required the puddler or many of his ilk. Instead manufacturers hired "a swarm of specialists . . . , each of whom had to be highly competent at a particular task . . . but none of whom mastered an entire process in the flow of production."[36] Some of the new specialists are most accurately classified as factory artisans, but others, such as those who poured the molten steel into cast-iron molds, were semiskilled operatives, a designation that did not exist in the earlier iron factories.[37]

Another means by which the numbers of operatives grew was by the addition of supplementary departments to firms in which the primary product was still made by skilled craftsmen and their helpers. Skilled brass molders and drawers, for example, remained at the center of brass production into the twentieth century, but in the 1880s and 1890s brass mills began to add thimble, soldering, and packing departments that were staffed largely by women doing repetitious, specialized tasks.[38] Similarly, papermaking firms in New England continued to be dependent on the skills of paper-machine tenders, but the finished paper was, in the last decades of the century, trimmed, ruled, stamped, and backed by female operatives.[39]

The development of new industries was a third means by which the number of factory operatives increased.[40] Industries such as soapmaking, chemicals, and meatpacking were organized along factory lines from the beginning in the United States; they went through no artisan stage of production. Instead, from the start, production was characterized by a minute division of labor and low skills.[41] Often machinery was not installed in the earliest factories; instead profits were generated by the rationalization of tasks. The work rhythms of slaughterhouse workers, for example, assumed a "machine-like precision" even before the advent of a moving "disassembly" line.[42] When it occurred, technological change did not alter the basic organization

36. Montgomery, *Fall*, p. 29.
37. U.S. Census Bureau, *Special Report*, p. 185, describes pourers and ladlemen as semiskilled.
38. Montgomery, *Fall*, p. 125.
39. Judith A. McGaw, " 'A Good Place to Work.' Industrial Workers and Occupational Choice: The Case of Berkshire Women," *Journal of Interdisciplinary History* 10 (1979): 227–48; Montgomery, *Fall*, p. 125.
40. Ross calls many of these workers factory laborers rather than factory operatives. I chose the later term to emphasize the degree to which the regularity of work made the jobs these workers did increasingly similar to the work done by semiskilled operatives.
41. Ross, *Workers on the Edge*, pp. 118–20.
42. Ibid., p. 122.

of production. Instead, innovations such as refrigeration turned meat-packing into a year-round activity, thus providing more stable employment opportunities and making wage earners in the industry look less like the laborers they had initially resembled and more like other factory operatives.

This growth in the number of factory operatives, no matter which distinct path led to their employment, had enormous consequences for the development of the labor movement. Although certainly not ensuring that workers would organize across the skill divide, the expanding number of operatives altered and narrowed the chasm that separated craft and craftless workers. These new factory operatives had many more experiences in common with factory artisans than less-skilled workers in the 1830s did with handicraft artisans. First, both now worked in the same kind of settings. In the factory, skilled, semiskilled, and unskilled employees were all vulnerable to the fear of replacement, subject to arbitrary authority, and exposed to long hours and intensified production schedules. The existence of common grievances was certainly most obvious to skilled and less-skilled wage earners when they worked for the same employer. However, even when they did not, trends in the geography of factory location meant that factory operatives and artisans were now more likely to observe each other's working conditions and to hear of each other's complaints. Although in the 1830s factories had been built in rural areas to be near cheap water power, after the Civil War manufacturers' dependence on unharnessed rivers and streams was severed first by design improvements to the steam engine and later by the invention of electrical generators. Beginning in the 1870s, industrial growth was most rapid in metropolitan centers.[43] Thus, even when employed in different establishments, factory workers were more likely to be familiar with one another's situation.

Second, many factory operatives in the 1880s were male, but in the 1830s a majority had been women and children. Male factory operatives were paid on average about 80 percent more than women operatives; thus, they were more capable of supporting trade union organization.[44] Furthermore, an alliance between male factory artisans and

43. David M. Gordon, "Capitalist Development and the History of American Cities," in *Marxism and the Metropolis*, ed. William K. Tabb and Larry Sawers (New York: Oxford University Press, 1978), p. 39.

44. Computed from figures found in *Report on Manufacturing Industries at the Eleventh Census: 1890* (Washington, D.C.: Government Printing Office, 1895), p. 21. This figure is necessarily rough; the census did not distinguish skilled from less-skilled workers. Instead it reported average annual earnings per employee for all operatives, whether skilled or unskilled, and for pieceworkers. Because many less-skilled operatives were

male operatives required that artisans overcome only one prejudice—that against the less skilled, but an alliance between male factory artisans and female operatives necessitated a rethinking of two—against working women and against the less skilled. Thus, increases in the number of male semiskilled workers also heightened the probability of joint organization across the skill divide.

Of course, not all less-skilled workers in the 1880s could be characterized as factory operatives. Sweatshops and home production persisted, especially in the clothing industry (although, especially in the 1870s, factory organization was becoming common even there).[45] The demand for common laborers also remained high. The 1870 census classified 8 percent of the gainfully employed population as laborers, a proportion that had climbed to 12 percent by 1910. (Considering only the industrial labor force, this latter figure represents one-third of all workers in manufacturing and transportation.)[46] Here too, however, more and more of the actual laboring work was done in manufacturing establishments. The simple expansion of manufacturing, combined with incomplete mechanization and reorganization, resulted in an increased demand for laborers to fetch, carry, load, and clean up. Indeed, as David Montgomery has pointed out, the largest employers of laborers in the late nineteenth century were engaged in the most highly capitalized industries: railroads, steel, chemicals, mining, and metal manufacturing.[47]

But even when homeworkers and laborers worked in settings far removed from the factory, the social world in which they lived was less distinct from that of skilled workers than it was in the 1830s. The growing convergence in the experiences of skilled and less-skilled workers involved more than the mere facts of factory employment and expanding numbers of male operatives. It entailed a *sense* of decreasing social distance. A brassworker, testifying before a United States Senate committee in 1883, provides poignant evidence of this. He began his testimony by instructing the committee about the creation of a chandelier. He noted that fifteen years earlier chandeliers had been fashioned in their entirety by a single skilled craftsmen; now, he reported, twelve men and four machines had taken the place of that lone mechanic. When asked how this affected his work and social life,

---

paid by the piece, I took these figures for my calculations. A further source of possible error is the fact that the overall figure I give is based on only thirty industries: fifteen that employed a large proportion of females and fifteen that employed a small proportion of them.

45. Montgomery, *Fall*, pp. 117–22.
46. Ibid., pp. 59–60.
47. Ibid., p. 60.

the man responded first by discussing his relationship with his boss: "Well, I remember that fourteen years ago the workmen and the foremen and the boss were all as one family; it was just as easy and as free to speak to the boss as anyone else, but now the boss is superior, and the men all go to the superintendent or to the foreman; but we would not think of looking the foreman in the face now any more than we would the boss. . . . Off duty as well as on duty, we would not dream of speaking to him on the street. . . . The average hand growing up in the shop would not think of speaking to the boss, would not presume to recognize him, nor the boss would not recognize him either." He went on to describe his neighborhood: "The bronze workers as a rule live in tenement houses. They are surrounded by the poorest class, the cheapest class; the cheapest element of the laboring people, and they are no better than anybody else." And then he returned once again to remember an earlier day: "It was different then. A mechanic was considered somebody, and he felt he was somebody; he was a skilled mechanic, and he was considered above the poor laborer on the street."[48]

At the same time the blending of worlds was far from complete. Skilled workers, even in the most rationalized work setting still had more autonomy and higher wages than less-skilled workers. These provided a solid base on which to build trade unions and also established privileges that were worth protecting, sometimes at the expense of less-skilled workers. Moreover, like the brassworker, skilled craftsmen had collectively a memory of better times and greater social respect. Thus, when they sometimes claimed, as did a machinist to the same congressional committee, that they were "simply . . . ordinary laborer[s], no more and no less," it was often a bitter observation rather than a real assertion of solidarity.[49]

Furthermore, although the gender composition of the less-skilled work force had shifted so as to make alliances more likely, increased ethnic diversity introduced a new source of division. The first great waves of immigration to the United States had occurred in the 1840s and 1850s; by the eve of the Civil War, between one-third and one-half of the population of large cities had crossed the Atlantic from Britain, Ireland, or Germany. Immigration dropped off in the early 1860s and again in the late 1870s but expanded greatly in the 1880s.[50] The re-

48. U.S. Senate, *Testimony Taken by the Committee upon the Relations between Labor and Capital* (Washington, D.C.: Government Printing Office, 1885), pp. 741–43.
49. Ibid., pp. 755–59.
50. Richard A. Easterlin et al., *Immigration: Dimensions of Ethnicity* (Cambridge: Belnap Press of Harvard University Press, 1982), p. 4.

sult was an industrial working class that in the 1880s was composed of large numbers of immigrants and their children. Gutman and Berlin estimate that, along with blacks, these groups accounted for fully three-quarters of the industrial labor force.[51] The majority group, however, were not new arrivals, but the offspring of immigrants. Because these workers had been born and raised in the United States, the problem for those who sought to create an inclusive labor movement was not so much a lack of familiarity with America's republican heritage or unfamiliarity with wage labor.[52] Instead, the problem was one of differing—often competing—cultural heritages and allegiances.[53] Ethnicity was an additional source of division in a working class that, although growing more homogeneous, was still riddled with cleavages. Moreover, it was a division that tended to reinforce skill and industry differences. For instance, in Orange, New Jersey, a fairly typical mid-size industrial town, nearly one-half of all Irish immigrants were employed in unskilled jobs, but few German immigrants or native Americans were. Each ethnic group, too, tended to be found in a few skilled trades, rather than to be equally distributed throughout the crafts.[54] Thus, diversity was accentuated.

These impediments notwithstanding, rapid industrialization in the years following the Civil War narrowed many of the differences be-

51. Herbert Gutman and Ira Berlin, "Class Composition and the Development of the American Working Class, 1840–1890," in *Power and Culture*, ed. Ira Berlin (New York: Pantheon, 1987), pp. 380–95 and 385.

52. Historians have begun to argue that even first-generation immigrants rarely found republicanism a foreign ideology. Rowland Berthoff, "Peasants and Artisans, Puritans and Republicans: Personal Liberty and Communal Equality in American History," *Journal of American History* 69, no. 3 (1982): 579–98, for example, contends that republicanism's dual ideal of personal independence and communal equality grew out of a worldview that was essentially peasant and artisan in origin. Therefore, he suggests, it was "perennially renewed in its original form by successive waves of peasant and artisan immigrants." Berthoff emphasizes the conservative effects of immigrants' republicanism, but others stress its reformist and radical impact. For example, Foner in a study of the Irish Land League argues that the radical strains of republicanism expressed in the Land League helped both to "introduc[e] thousands of Irish-Americans to modern reform and labor ideologies" and "to transform specifically Irish grievances and traditions into a broader critique of American society in the Gilded Age." (See his "Class, Ethnicity, and Radicalism in the Gilded Age: The Land League and Irish America," in *Politics and Ideology in the Age of the Civil War* [New York: Oxford University Press, 1980], p. 151.) Suggestive essays along these lines can also be found in Dirk Hoerder, ed. *"Struggle a Hard Battle"* (DeKalb: Northern Illinois University Press, 1986), and Marianne Debouzy, *In the Shadow of the Statue of Liberty: Immigrants, Workers, and Citizens in the American Republic* (Saint-Denis, France: Presses Universitaires de Vincennes, 1988).

53. On competing cultural heritages, see Oestreicher, *Solidarity*, pp. 39–60.

54. Bensman, *Practice*, p. 143. Irish immigrants and their children were concentrated in the hatting industry, and German and native-born American skilled workers were more likely to be employed in the building trades and other crafts.

tween skilled and less-skilled workers in the United States, thus creating more realistic opportunities for those who might attempt to build an inclusive labor movement. Although the pace of industrial change was less rapid in England and France, a similar convergence of the worlds of the skilled and less skilled occurred in the closing decades of the nineteenth century in these countries as well. The deflationary crisis that spurred American manufacturers to reorganize production was a world wide phenomenon that also forced industrialists in France and England to come to terms with falling prices, profits, and interest rates. (Indeed, the whole period 1873–96 is known in the French and British literature as the "Great Depression.") They, too, experimented with technological innovation, new payment schemes, more systematic management techniques, and more extensive factory organization in a desperate struggle to lower the most controllable of their costs—labor. The upshot was everywhere the same: more common grievances and experiences among workers.

National economies differed, however, as did the set of restraints and opportunities managers faced as they attempted to create more profitable enterprises. In England the industrial system that manufacturers attempted to transform in the closing decades of the nineteenth century was one that, following a period of rapid mechanization and "factoryization," had evolved into an amalgam of old and new, manual and mechanized.[55] The story of the initial, textile phase of the industrial revolution is familiar and need not be recounted here. In the 1830s and 1840s a similar period of technological innovation and workshop reorganization had occurred in many capital-goods industries—steam engines, ships, iron rails, lathes. But by the 1850s this technological and organizational revolution, too, had exhausted itself. In its wake was left an economy only partially transformed, with few industries totally untouched by steam power and machinery and "fewer still where [the two] ruled unchallenged."[56] In this unevenly mechanized economy, early factory artisans organized and managed much of the actual production. These British craftsmen retained a great deal of responsibility for overseeing production and supervising less-skilled employees, much more, most studies sug-

55. Hobsbawm, *Labouring Men*, p. 317, calls the period "technically . . . conservative." The most influential article to develop this point is Raphael Samuel, "The Workshop of the World: Steam Power and Hand Technology in Mid-Victorian Britain," *History Workshop* 3 (1977): 6–72. For a good recent overview of the development of work practices in the period that stresses the irregularity of capitalist development, see Patrick Joyce, "Work," in *The Cambridge Social History of Britain, 1750–1950*, ed. F. M. L. Thompson (Cambridge: Cambridge University Press, 1990), 2: 131–94.

56. Samuel, "Workshop," p. 46.

gest, than the majority of their American counterparts in the 1870s and 1880s.[57] Their autonomy and supervisory duties rested on two features of mid-Victorian industrial organization. First, subcontracting arrangements—in which skilled employees agreed to manufacture a particular object or component at a designated cost—were widespread. These arrangements were popular because they allowed industry to meet sharp fluctuations in demand without having to incur a permanent burden of overhead costs and because they provided a cheap, easy way of supervising and coordinating the large numbers of helpers and unskilled workers drawn into the expanding industrial economy.[58] The second feature of British industrial organization in this period that enhanced the position of the factory artisan was the imperfect nature of early machinery. Technical kinks made many machines dependent on manual skill. The so-called "self-acting" mule, which was used to spin cotton yarn, provides a typical example. Although touted as "self-acting," early models of the machine actually demanded frequent manual interventions (particularly in the "nosing" and "strapping" operations) to prevent the yarn from snarling.[59]

57. William H. Lazonick, "Production Relations, Labor Productivity, and Choice of Technique: British and U.S. Cotton Spinning," *Journal of Economic History* 41 (1981): 491–516, esp. 506; Joyce, "Work," p. 151; Haydu, *Between Craft and Class*, pp. 60–89.

58. Samuel, "Workshop," provides numerous examples of the virtual army of unskilled workers who were drawn into the industrial economy in those years. They ranged from the grown men employed to bring seal skins to suppleness by jumping on them (one of Booth's investigators noted, "It is a curious sight, on entering a room, to see a row of . . . tubs each with its Jack-in-the-box bobbing up and down. Every man is naked except for a vest, and a rough cloth which is tied round his waist and attached to the rim of his barrel. With hands resting on either ledge up and down he treads. . . . Skins cured by this process are said to be softer and silkier."), to the teams of men in chains who dragged armor plates from the furnace to the factory floor, to the large number of job hands employed in the lace trade to do the preparation work and make good on the deficiencies of new labor-saving machinery. See pp. 20 and 46–47.

59. Price, *Labour*, p. 79, cites the example of the early self-acting "mules" that were installed in the 1830s and 1840s and that were used to spin cotton yarn. These machines were known as "self-acting," but the early models required some manual interventions to keep them running. "Certain motions—particularly nosing and strapping—demanded constant adjustment to prevent the yarn from snarling." (Nosing, according to William H. Lazonick, "Industrial Relations and Technical Change: The Case of the Self-Acting Mule," *Cambridge Journal of Economics* 3 (1979), 230–62, was done to compensate for the taper of the spindle so as to wind the yarn firmly and without snags into a bundle that was suitable for weaving. Strapping involved adjusting a screw that regulated the speed of the spindles in proportion to the diameter of the bundle. Failure to adjust it properly resulted in broken slivers of cotton yarn.) Price contrasts this state of affairs with a very different one in the United States, where, he claims, "mules were run by unskilled girls totally subservient to management." But the literature on the United States does not support such a sharp contrast. Mules in the United States were also run by men, indeed, often by craftsmen imported from England. But in the United States, mule spinning machines were introduced later (probably in the late 1840s and early

In order to avoid costly spoilage of the yarn, employers depended upon experienced mule spinners to oversee the self-acting mule. This need for manual intervention eventually was self-reinforcing because mule spinners tended to tune and adjust each machine "with little respect for the intentions of the maker or the principles of engineering. Before very long, no two mules were alike."[60]

These factory artisans, along with handicraft artisans in various older crafts such as cabinetmaking and tailoring, are often characterized as "labor aristocrats" in British labor history.[61] Because of their strong strategic position, they were able to build what were probably the most stable and resilient craft unions of the era.[62] These workers and unions were formidable opponents when manufacturers tried to implement managerial reforms or technological change.[63] Technologi-

---

1850s, according to Dublin, *Women at Work*, p. 138), by which time more of the kinks had been worked out. Thus the technical base for the power of mule spinners was absent in the United States.

60. Mule spinners' strategic position was further enhanced by the fact that cotton manufacturers were in a very competitive industry; thus, when employers introduced the self-acting mule, they were reluctant to disrupt production by challenging the supervisory responsibilities of cotton spinners. Lazonick believes this to be the biggest reason why mule spinners were able to retain their strategic position. Others, such as Harold Catling, *The Spinning Mule* (Newton Abbott, Eng.: David and Charles, 1970), put greater weight on the technical problems. If there were no technical basis for the strategic position of mule spinners, it seems as if some manufacturers would have gambled on dismissing spinners.

61. The classic statement is given by Hobsbawm, *Labouring Men*, pp. 272–315. For other references, see Introduction, note 9.

62. Reliable and comparable membership figures are not in existence, but some indication of the relative strength of craft unions in the United States and Britain can be seen by comparing rough membership figures given in David Montgomery, *Beyond Equality* (Urbana: University of Illinois Press, 1981), p. 140, and Hunt, *British Labour*, p. 251. Based on contemporary sources, Montgomery cites a figure of 300,000 for the number of union members in 1872, a year before the membership losses of the depression began. That figure represents 6.5 percent of the male industrial labor force (4,580,249 in 1870). Hunt cites the figure of half a million members in the late 1870s during the depression. This figure represents 10.5 percent of the male industrial labor force (4,746,000 in 1880). Thus, a higher proportion of male British industrial workers were unionized during the depression years than in the United States in the organizational upsurge of the early 1870s. (The total size of the male industrial labor force is computed from figures given in Montgomery, *Beyond Equality*, pp. 449–53, and Brian R. Mitchell, *European Historical Statistics, 1750–1900* [New York: Columbia University Press, 1975], p. 163.)

A further indication of the relative strength of British craft unions in this period is that in 1884, the Parliamentary Committee of the Trades Union Congress (the umbrella organization for British craft unions) reported that there was little point in English unions participating in international congresses until foreign workers were better organized. See Hunt, *British Labour*, p. 250.

63. As exasperation was rising, a frustrated spokesman for the boot and shoe manufacturers noted in 1892, "The men working the machines exercise all their ingenuity in making machine work as expensive as hand labour. There exists . . . a tacit understanding that only so much work shall be done within a certain time. . . . The unions

cal retooling, in particular, was also discouraged by another feature of the British economy: great sums of capital had already been invested in the first generation of factory machines, and manufacturers were reluctant to scrap them.[64] In addition, investment overseas now yielded higher returns than investment at home, and some economic historians argue that this created a shortage of capital for investment in the British industry.[65] Technological renovation did take place in this era but less so on the whole than in the United States.

It would be a mistake, however, to minimize the reorganization that did occur. Although the British economy was reformed in a more piecemeal manner than the American economy during the depression years, the effect of the changes was very similar: Factory artisans lost many of the responsibilities and privileges that set them apart from other workers; handicraft artisans began to find it more and more difficult to hold out against mechanization and downgrading, and new semiskilled jobs were created in a wide variety of old and new industries.[66] Thus, in the closing decades of the nineteenth century, British workers, like their American counterparts, came to share a wider variety of experiences, and as a result increasing attempts were made to overcome the divide between skilled and less-skilled workers.

---

are engaged in a gigantic conspiracy to hinder and retard the development of labour-saving appliances in this country. . . . It seems to be settled policy with the men not to try to earn as much money as possible per week, but as much as possible per job, in other words to keep the costs of production as high as possible." Quoted in Hunt, *British Labour*, pp. 290–91. This is almost the complete opposite of the workers' actions and goals in the machine shop that Michael Burawoy studied in Chicago in the 1970s; see his *Manufacturing Consent* (Chicago: University of Chicago Press, 1979).

64. P. L. Payne, "The Emergence of the Large-Scale Company in Great Britain, 1870–1914," *The Economic History Review* 20, no. 3, 2d ser. (1967): 519–42. Payne also notes that consumers of British products were less willing to accept mass-produced, standardized goods like those produced by American manufacturers. British firms tended to differentiate their product in order to insulate themselves from the pricing policies of their competitors. They were able to exploit the preferences of British consumers for articles exhibiting "craftsmanship." This, too, mitigated against wholesale technological innovation, as well as ensuring sufficient profits to avoid the desperation of American producers in this period.

65. D. N. McCloskey, "Did Victorian Britain Fail?" *Economic History Review* 23, 2d Ser. (1970): 446–59.

66. Jonathan Zeitlin, "Engineers and Compositors: A Comparison," in *Divisions of Labour*, ed. Royden Harrison and Jonathan Zeitlin (Brighton, Eng.: Harvester Press, 1985), pp. 185–250; Charles More, *Skill and the English Working Class* (New York: St. Martin's Press, 1980); Gregory Anderson, "Some Aspects of the Labour Market in Britain c. 1870–1914," in *A History of British Industrial Relations, 1875–1914*, ed. Chris Wrigley (Brighton, Eng.: Harvester Press, 1982); Price, *Labour*, pp. 93–104. Recently, some British labor historians have begun to emphasize the unevenness of these changes. This is an important corrective, but it should not be overdone. See, for example, Joyce, "Work," pp. 156–57.

Gender and ethnic differences, however, continued to cause difficulties for those who sought to extend unionism throughout the industrial labor force. The proportion of women workers remained steady, rather than decreasing as it did in the United States, and women began to find employment opportunities in industries that had traditionally been dominated by skilled male workers. In several industries, including machine making, tailoring, shoe manufacture, pottery, and printing, new production techniques allowed manufacturers to replace male workers with women.[67] Although some male workers adopted an attitude of tolerance toward their new female coworkers, many others reacted with hostility, an attitude that obviously impeded alliances across the skill divide.[68] Ethnic conflict between Irish and English workers also remained a source of division, although overt conflict may have abated somewhat as Irish immigration declined.[69] Jewish immigration beginning in the 1880s introduced a new division, one that also tended to reinforce skill and industry differences, but the number of Jewish immigrants to England in the closing decades of the nineteenth century was much smaller than the number of Irish immigrants to England earlier in the century.[70] Overall, however, in England, as in the United States, there were differences in the gender and ethnic composition of the skilled and less-skilled work force, and these remained an obstacle to working-class solidarity even as changes in the workplace created opportunities for expanded organization.

The French national economy on the eve of the depression con-

67. Hunt, *British Labour*, pp. 22–23.

68. For examples of craftsmen's hostility to female workers, see Zeitlin, "Engineers and Compositors," pp. 195–97, and Richard Whipp, "The Stamp of Futility: The Staffordshire Potters, 1880–1905," in *Divisions of Labour*, ed. Harrison and Zeitlin, pp. 87–113, esp. pp. 139–41 and 143–44. See also More, *Skill*, pp. 229–30.

69. Hunt, *British Labour*, p. 170, suggests that divisions between Irish and English workers declined beginning in the 1860s. He bases his reasoning on the fact that the Irish entering England were in less desperate straits than the 1840s immigrants and on the fact that the rate of immigration decreased. Thus he argues that there was a lessening of tensions because an increasing proportion of the Irish community was either British-born or had long been residing in Britain. However, Lynn H. Lees, *Exiles of Erin* (Manchester: Manchester University Press, 1979), and Michael Hechter, *Internal Colonialism* (Berkeley: University of California Press, 1975), both argue that the Irish in England maintained a distinct cultural identity, one that separated them from English workers, even when they had been born and raised in England. Irish workers' sense of difference was probably also reinforced by the fact that in London (and probably other English cities with large numbers of Irish workers), there was no shift of the Irish into skilled occupations, as often took place in American cities. See Lees, *Exiles*, esp. p. 259. Unfortunately, there have been very few studies of Irish immigrant workers in England, so for the present, we simply do not have the information to assess properly the extent of ethnic division in England.

70. Hunt, *British Labour*, pp. 176–87.

trasted sharply with the British.[71] The English economy was geared toward the production of capital goods for industry and medium-quality consumer items for an expanding middle class, and the French economy specialized in the production of finely crafted, luxury products for both domestic and international consumption. Most of these products, such as fancy silk ribbons, high-fashion clothes, and fine jewelry, were made by handicraft artisans who worked in small workshops or at home. A few products, such as cotton cloth, were produced in mechanized factories, but even these were often destined for the more expensive end of the market and hence relied on skilled workers. Thus, in the middle decades of the nineteenth century, the French industrial landscape was dominated more by small workshops —and its work force was more saturated with artisans—than either the American or the British economy.[72]

For many years, economic historians believed that this small-shop economy was "backward," especially in comparison with British industry.[73] Recent research, however, indicates that these handicraft artisans, toiling in their workshops, were highly productive.[74] Their continued survival, long past the time when traditional artisanal arrangements had been supplanted in many industries in England and the United States, rested on several interlocking features of French industry and society in this period. Most obviously the luxury market in which the French economy specialized put a premium on quality and craftsmanship, neither of which were easy to standardize or mechanize. The kind of inexpensive manufactured goods that were conducive to mechanized factory production were produced in France largely for the domestic market, but the expansion of this market was limited by the nation's very slow population growth, its gradual rate of

71. A good overview of the French economy through the "great depression" can be found in Sewell, *Work and Revolution*, pp. 143–61.

72. One estimate puts the percentage of workers employed at home or in small artisan shops in that period as high as 75. Cited in Ronald Aminzade, "Reinterpreting Capitalist Industrialization: A Study of Nineteenth-Century France," in *Work in France: Representations, Meaning, Organization, and Practice*, ed. Steven L. Kaplan and Cynthia J. Koepp (Ithaca: Cornell University Press, 1986), p. 395.

73. S. B. Clough, "Retardative Factors in French Economic Development in the Nineteenth and Twentieth Centuries," *Journal of Economic History* 6, Supp. (1946): 91–210; David Landes, "French Entrepreneurship and Industrial Growth in the Nineteenth Century," *Journal of Economic History* 9 (1949): 45–61; R. E. Cameron, "Economic Growth and Stagnation in Modern France, 1815–1914," *Journal of Modern History* 20 (1958): 1–13; C. P. Kindleberger, *The Economic Growth of France and Britain, 1851–1950* (Cambridge: Harvard University Press, 1964).

74. Patrick O'Brien and Caglar Keyder, *Economic Growth in Britain and France, 1780–1914* (London: Allen and Unwin, 1978). Until 1870, according to their estimates, labor productivity in France grew at rates comparable to those in Britain.

urbanization, and its large population of farmers (see Table 1). Small population increases and a large agricultural sector also combined to create a labor shortage and hence recruitment difficulties for many employers. Those who sought to induce workers into mechanized factories, heavy industry, or coal mines had an especially difficult time attracting and retaining employees.[75] Finally, French workers—especially urban artisans—engaged in a guerrilla war against factories and mechanization in these years that was more protracted and successful than any carried out in England or the United States. They organized, they struck, they protected their independence by refusing to sell their products to any single merchant, and then they played off against one another the many merchants who bought their wares. When no other tactic worked, they settled for lower wages and severely cut household consumption rather than accept jobs in mechanized factories.[76] One effect of this resistance was reduced wages. Phelps-Brown and Browne have calculated that real wages in France in the 1860s were between one-third and one-half lower than those in Britain and lower still than those in the United States.[77] This, of course, further slowed mechanization because it meant that employers would gain fewer savings by substituting machines for artisans.

The depression, however, marked a turning point in the war handicraft artisans waged against modern industry.[78] The worst effects of the depression did not hit France until the 1880s, but when they did, they were severe. The agricultural sector was especially hard hit, and as a result French farms were no longer able to support the large labor force that they had successfully absorbed before the depression. This ended the labor shortage, especially of less-skilled factory labor. At the same time, the economic crisis in the countryside also reduced peasant buying power, reducing the market for domestically produced consumer goods. Another, even more serious blow was dealt to the industrial sector when France's trading partners responded to the depression by erecting tariffs on foreign-made goods, thus shriveling the market for French luxury goods. (France did not immediately retaliate, and as a result cheap, foreign-made goods flooded the domestic market at the same time luxury goods sat unsold in warehouses.) Additional downward pressure on prices resulted when a new, centralized, and

75. Gérard Noiriel, *Workers in French Society in the 19th and 20th Centuries* (New York: Berg, 1990), pp. 33–71.
76. George J., Sheridan, Jr., "Household and Craft in an Industrializing Economy: The Case of the Silk Weavers of Lyon," in *Consciousness and Class Experience in Nineteenth-Century Europe*, ed. John M. Merriman (New York: Holmes and Meier, 1979), pp. 107–28.
77. Quoted in Hunt, *British Labour*, p. 108.
78. Noiriel, *Workers*, pp. 73–88.

coordinated railroad network was completed in the 1890s, creating for the first time a truly national market in France.

Together, these economic changes placed enormous pressures on French industry and eventually tipped the balance of power against the handicraft sector. Mechanization and technical innovation increased dramatically, especially in heavy industry and textiles. For example, in Lyon's silk industry, which had long been a bastion for handloom weavers, the total proportion of power-driven looms jumped from approximately 5 percent in 1873 to about 33 percent in 1900.[79] In the glass-bottle industry, technical change came in the form of a new furnace (the Siemens gas furnace), which allowed manufacturers to triple the number of bottles produced in an hour.[80] As in England and the United States, many such examples could be found. French manufacturers, too, tried speedups, and elaborate pay schemes and reorganized work processes. The upshot, as elsewhere, was an increased number of factory artisans and semiskilled operatives. By now, the story is a familiar one. The biggest difference in the French case is that these changes happened to a labor force in which there were more traditional handicraft artisans than in England or in the United States. This, and the continued survival of many extremely small shops, tended to slow the rate of change, but the overall effect was the same: more similarity in wage earners' work experiences.[81]

As in England and in the United States, there were at the same time persistent differences in the composition of the skilled and less-skilled work force that tended to offset some of the growing commonalities. Distinctive cultural allegiances imported to new areas of settlement by French migrants continued to limit the development of a common working-class identity in some communities, although the distinction between native and migrant workers tended to become a great deal less prominent in the closing decades of the nineteenth century.[82]

79. Ibid., p. 82.

80. Joan Wallach Scott, *The Glassworkers of Carmaux* (Cambridge: Harvard University Press, 1974), pp. 73–75.

81. For an overview of these developments, see Hanagan, *Logic of Solidarity*, pp. 3–32. Good descriptions of changes in the work experiences of skilled and semiskilled workers in these years can be found in Lenard R. Berlanstein, *The Working People of Paris, 1871–1914* (Baltimore: Johns Hopkins University Press, 1984), pp. 74–107; Donald Reid, *The Miners of Decazeville: A Genealogy of Deindustrialization* (Cambridge: Harvard University Press, 1985), chap. 6; and Michael P. Hanagan, *Nascent Proletarians: Class Formation in Post Revolutionary France* (Cambridge: Basil Blackwell, 1989).

82. Berlanstein reports that in Paris the Bretons resisted assimilation, forming a distinct community and constituting "one of the few bulwarks against working-class anticlericalism" in the years 1871–1914 (*The Working People of Paris*, p. 166). Peter N. Stearns, *Lives of Labor* (New York: Holmes and Meier, 1975), p. 58, notes that these same Bretons

Moreover, skill differences ceased to correspond so closely to the line between natives and migrants.[83] In contrast, cleavages between immigrant and French workers endured and generally tended to reinforce skill divisions.[84] Outside of a few areas, however, the number of immigrants was nowhere near the magnitude it was in the United States (see Table 1). Of more widespread importance was the continuing division along gender lines. As in England, women workers continued to make up one-third of the labor force, and gender differences tended to exacerbate skill and industry differences.[85]

This brief overview of the British and French economy in the nineteenth century suggests two main conclusions when compared with our discussion of developments in the American economy. First, it is clear that the depression years brought similarly dramatic structural changes to the industrial economies of France and England as it did to that of the United States. The result was everywhere a significant convergence of experiences and grievances across all sectors of the working class. Further evidence to this effect can be gleaned from studies of the period by historians and economists: repeatedly, words such as "homogenization" are used to describe this era of working-class history, no matter which of the three countries is being discussed.[86] Sec-

---

were sometimes recruited as strikebreakers, a practice that most certainly would have increased tensions between them and other workers.

On the other hand, Hanagan found in his study of cities of the Stephanois region that by the mid-1870s migrant groups had become more integrated into the urban working classes (*Nascent Proletarians*, pp. 79–80). In general, the literature on France suggests a lessening of hostility between migrants and natives in the last two decades of the nineteenth century.

83. Hanagan, *Nascent Proletarians*, p. 80. In Paris, this integration was aided by the process of social mobility. Berlanstein, *Working People*, p. 29, reports that unskilled day laborers were most likely to be children of propertyless rural laborers and that their children generally moved into machine-tending work.

84. Michelle Perrot, *Les Ouvriers en grève, 1871–1890* (The Hague: Mouton de Gruyter, 1974), pp. 170–71; Judy A. Reardon, "Belgian and French Workers in Nineteenth-Century Roubaix," in *Class Conflict and Collective Action*, ed. Louise A. Tilly and Charles Tilly (Beverly Hills: Sage, 1981); Donald Reid, *The Miners of Decazeville* (Cambridge: Harvard University Press, 1985), pp. 119–20. Hostility between native French workers and immigrants was heightened by employers' use of immigrants as strikebreakers. In Rive-de-Gier, for example, unemployed German glassworkers were used to defeat a ten-month strike in 1894. See Hanagan, *Logic of Solidarity*, pp. 112–13.

85. Louise Tilly, "Paths of Proletarianization: Organization of Production, Sexual Division of Labor, and Women's Collective Action," *Signs* 7, no. 2 (1981): 400–417; Marilyn J. Boxer, "Protective Legislation and Home Industry: The Marginalization of Women Workers in Late Nineteenth-Early Twentieth Century France," *Journal of Social History* 20, no. 1 (1986): 45–65.

86. For a French example, see Noiriel, *Workers*, chap. 3, esp. p. 74; for English examples, see Zygmunt Bauman, *Between Craft and Class* (Manchester: Manchester University Press, 1960), p. 144, and Joyce, "Work," pp. 6 and 131–94; for the United States, see Gordon, Edwards, and Reich, *Segmented Work*, p. 112 and passim. Even those who

ond, although there was a narrowing of the gap between skilled and less-skilled workers everywhere, there were fundamental differences in the industrial structure and in the composition of the labor force in each country. These differences shaped the opportunities and constraints labor activists in each country faced when they attempted to build a more inclusive labor movement.

In particular, American activists faced a set of circumstances that were in several respects more difficult than those faced by their colleagues in France and England. The figures in Table 1 indicate some. First, both the manufacturing labor force and the use of steam power expanded much more rapidly in the United States than in England or France. Thus, labor activists had to comprehend more quickly the nature of industrial change and act swiftly to counter its consequences. Second, workers in the United States had to cope with rapid urbanization at the same time as they contended with rapid industrialization. Between 1850 and 1890, America's urban population increased 2.5 times, while France's urban population grew 1.5 times and England's grew 1.3 times. Third, the industrial population of the United States was much more ethnically diverse. Table 1 presents figures for the percentage of foreign-born inhabitants, and these provide some indication of the magnitude of the differences: the proportion of foreign-born inhabitants in the United States was five times greater than in either France or England.[87] Only with respect to gender differences did American activists encounter a more homogeneous work force than their counterparts in England and France. In all other respects, American supporters of broad-based unionism faced a more formidable task: organizing an extremely diverse work force that was experiencing rapid change in several dimensions simultaneously.

Of course, the creation of inclusive unions was a difficult challenge in all three countries. Changes on the shopfloor and in the larger economy created new opportunities for expanded organization, but they did not automatically lead workers to adopt broader identities or reveal a set of strategies guaranteed to generate successful unions. In each country workers themselves had to discover the kinds of arguments, organizational forms, and tactics that would best overcome the skill divide.

---

reject the word "homogenization" often agree that the status and experience gap between skilled and less-skilled workers narrowed. Their rejection stems most frequently from discomfort with the assumption that this narrowing necessarily led in any straightforward way to any particular kind of class consciousness or collective action. See for example, Price, *Labour*, p. 11; Anderson, "Some Aspects," p. 2.

87. It would be useful to have data on immigrants working in manufacturing, but the data are just not available.

3

The Second Moment of Working-Class
Formation: The Knights of Labor

In the closing decades of the nineteenth century, the American, English, and French labor movements were remade. In each country, labor activists began to challenge restrictionist union practices and to question craftsmen's exclusionary beliefs. In the process they invented new organizing strategies and conceived of new inclusive ideologies.

In this chapter I examine the new strategies and ideologies promoted by the Knights of Labor as they rebuilt the American labor movement. These innovations and their effects are then assessed comparatively.

History and Ideology of the Knights of Labor

Between the journeymen's revolts of the 1830s and the Civil War, few efforts were made in the United States to extend labor organization beyond the ranks of skilled craft workers. As we have seen, the experiential distance between craft and craftless workers was simply too great. Even craft workers had difficulty maintaining their unions in those years, and thus for the American labor movement the period between the late 1830s and the late 1860s was one of retrenchment, not experimentation. Only in the years following the Civil War did things begin to change. Craft workers took advantage of the postwar boom to revive their local unions, and in a few trades they successfully built enduring national organizations for the first time. Many of these same workers also began to campaign for distinctly working-class legislation—factory regulation, mine laws, and especially the eight-hour day. They argued that such laws were necessary if the abstract right of free labor, won at Appomattox, was to have any real meaning. This line of argumentation soon drew them headlong into a national debate over what egalitarian ideals and republican traditions meant in post–Civil War America. It was in this milieu of renewed labor activism and charged political debate that the Noble and Holy Order of the Knights of Labor was organized.

The Knights grew to be the largest and most prominent of all Gilded Age labor organizations. But the beginnings of the Order were inauspicious. It was founded as a secret society by six Philadelphia garment cutters on Thanksgiving Day, 1869.[1] The men met to disband their local craft union, which had fought unsuccessfully for years to maintain wage rates in the trade. After dissolving the local, one veteran member, Uriah S. Stephens, suggested that the cutters use the occasion to create a new type of labor organization, one that would bring together all wage earners in a "great brotherhood." Craft unions, Stephens argued, were powerless to address the true cause of labor's degradation, which lay in "the present arrangement of labor and capital," whereby "capital dictated" and "labor submitted."[2] Only by organizing more broadly, he contended, would workers be able to achieve "emancipation" from "the thraldom and loss of wage slavery."[3] To realize these goals, Stephens advocated education, mutual aid, and cooperation.

In drawing a parallel between wage work and slavery, and in offering an alternative vision in which wage workers would be freed from such "slavery," Stephens was invoking themes that were common in the postbellum labor movement. Labor leaders in the decades following the Civil War frequently compared the plight of wage earners to that of chattel slaves and often spoke of the need to "free" workers from the "tyranny" of the "wages system."[4] Stephens's attempt to

1. Carroll D. Wright, "An Historical Sketch of the Knights of Labor," *The Quarterly Journal of Economics* 1 (1987): 139–43; John L. Butler, "History of Knights of Labor Organization in Pennsylvania," in *Fifteenth Annual Report of the Secretary of Internal Affairs of the Commonwealth of Pennsylvania. Part III: Industrial Statistics* (Harrisburg, Penn.: E.K. Meyers, 1888), pp. G31–G33.

2. Quoted in George E. McNeill, *The Labor Movement: The Problem of Today* (Boston: A. M. Bridgman and Co., 1887), p. 402.

3. Quoted in McNeill, *Labor Movement*, p. 408; Ware, *Labor Movement*, p. 74.

4. See, for example, David Montgomery's profiles of two very influential labor leaders of the post–Civil War period, Ira Steward and William Sylvis. Steward was the leader of the Machinists' and Blacksmiths' International Union (which Terence Powderly, a machinist, joined in 1871) and a leading theoretician of the labor movement in

define a broader solidarity was not totally unique either: the Knights of St. Crispin, a shoeworkers' union, had begun to incorporate semi-skilled factory workers in the late 1860s and the short-lived National Labor Union encouraged solidarity between organized trades unions in the early 1870s.[5] What was novel about Stephens's plan was the way in which it combined both trade and skill solidarity with an advocacy of secrecy. Stephens emphasized solidarity because his own trade union experience made him doubt the efficacy of craft unionism and because early religious training left him strongly committed to a nondenominational Christian brotherhood.[6] He embraced secrecy— and the ritualism that so often goes with secret societies—because his membership in the Masons and other fraternal organizations convinced him that secrecy was a powerful source of organizational stability and member loyalty. Secrecy, of course, also provided a shield from employers' blacklists, which often undermined unions in this period.

Secrecy was immediately embraced by the new union, but members hesitated before fully endorsing brotherhood. For the first year, a majority in the new union rejected proposals that they admit members from other trades. Eventually, however, the founding local began to allow "sojourners"—nonvoting members of other crafts who, it was hoped, would create locals in their own trades.[7] These sojourners, and the organizational abilities of the early activists, allowed the Knights to expand slowly in spite of the depression that destroyed most other labor organizations in the mid-1870s. The Order's earliest recruits were all skilled urban workers in Philadelphia and southern New Jersey. The skill barrier was broken only later, after the Knights spread to the coal fields of central Pennsylvania. Whole communities of mine workers—including some mine laborers—began to join, attracted, at least partially, by the Order's shield of secrecy.[8] The railroad

---

the 1860s and 1870s. Sylvis was president of the Iron Moulders' International Union and the dominant figure in the NLU. See Montgomery, *Fall*, and *Beyond Equality*, pp. 249–60. A very useful discussion of labor ideology in the post–Civil War era is presented in Forbath, "Ambiguities."

5. On the membership of the Knights of St. Crispin, see Dawley, *Class and Community*, pp. 143–48. For information about the National Labor Union, see Montgomery, *Beyond Equality*, chap. 4.

6. Ware, *Labor Movement*, pp. 26–28; Oestreicher, *Solidarity*, p. 89.

7. Ware, *Labor Movement*, p. 25. "Sojourner" is a masonic word; it refers to a member of another lodge. (Personal communication, Tony Fels, 1 August 1991.)

8. According to the list presented in Jonathan Garlock, comp., *Guide to the Local Assemblies of the Knights of Labor* (Westport, Conn.: Greenwood, 1982), the first assemblies to include mine laborers were Local Assemblies 96, 109, 136, 143, 148, and 150, all organized in Pennsylvania in 1875.

strikes of 1877 also resulted in the organization of some less-skilled railroad workers.[9] Thus, by 1879 when Stephens resigned and Terence Powderly took over the reins of leadership, the Order's 9,300 members included skilled workers from many trades and a smattering of less-skilled mine and railroad workers.[10]

Over the next three years the Knights spread beyond Pennsylvania and neighboring states to most major metropolitan areas in the United States. As the depression ended and the unemployment rate declined, economic circumstances were once again conducive to organization. A large number of the local assemblies established in this period were founded by craft workers who took advantage of the improved economic climate to reorganize local unions that had been destroyed in the depression years.[11] This time they organized under the auspices of the Knights, sometimes affiliating with national craft unions as well. (Dual affiliation was common even after the Federation of Organized Trades and Labor Unions, the precursor of the AFL, was created in 1881.) The absorption of these reactivated craft locals added a substantial number of energetic trade union leaders to the Order's ranks. They, along with the gradual abandonment of secrecy, boosted membership and publicity. By July 1883, the Knights' membership had grown to almost 50,000.[12]

Then, in 1884 and 1885, membership began to expand rapidly in the wake of highly publicized strikes by railroad shopmen against financier and railroad magnate Jay Gould. Gould, known as the "wizard of Wall Street," was perhaps the most hated of the robber barons, and the Knights' victory over his management electrified workers across the country. Something akin to what Doug McAdam terms "cognitive liberation" occurred as a result: workers who were ordinarily fatalistic began to demand change and to develop a new sense of power and efficacy.[13] National leaders of the Order tried to moderate this sense of efficacy, cautioning workers that strikes were difficult to win and should only be used as a last resort. However, local members and their elected officials were much less hesitant, and the railroad victories set off an unprecedented strike wave.[14] In its wake, thousands of

9. Ware, *Labor Movement*, pp. 36–37.

10. Stephens resigned after an unsuccessful bid for Congress. Membership figures given in Ware, *Labor Movement*, p. 66.

11. Garlock, "Structural Analysis," pp. 41–43; Fink, *Workingmen's Democracy*, p. 221 and *passim*.

12. Ware, *Labor Movement*, p. 66.

13. McAdam, *Political Process*, pp. 48–51.

14. Jeremy Brecher, "The Knights of Labor and Strikes, 1885–86," Paper presented at the Knights of Labor Centennial symposium, Chicago, May 17–19, 1979.

workers—particularly semiskilled and unskilled workers—joined the Order. By the summer of 1885, membership had doubled, and a local assembly had been established in nearly every city and mid-size town in the country.[15]

These new members had wide latitude in how they constituted their local assemblies. No constitutional constraints were placed on the skill level of local assembly members, nor were individual locals required to organize all occupations or skills. Instead, members of each local were allowed to define the assemblies' collective identity. This facilitated what Anthony Oberschall has labeled "bloc recruitment."[16] Work and community groups with established interpersonal ties and collective identities could easily be recruited as local assemblies. Officially, the only requirement was that locals identify themselves as either "mixed assemblies" (open to all producers with the exceptions of gamblers, stockbrokers, lawyers, bankers, liquor dealers, scabs, and spies)[17] or "trade assemblies" (open to workers of a specified occupation or industry). Coordination was provided by district assemblies, which also elected representatives to the national convention. Constitutionally, this national body (known as the General Assembly) was the supreme authority for the organization, and it elected the top executive officers, the General Executive Board. In practice, centralized control proved difficult, and the Order's organizational structure fostered local autonomy.[18] Thus, the Knights offered workers a chance to organize on their own terms within a context of broader solidarity.

The Order's rapid growth soon attracted public attention. Eventually, the "social question" (as the conflict between capital and labor was popularly known) became the most widely debated issue of the day. In 1883 the U.S. Senate was worried enough about strikes and class polarization to set up a committee of inquiry into the relations of labor and capital. By 1886 the question had grown so pressing that it became virtually impossible to open a popular journal or urban news-

15. Garlock, "Structural Analysis," part 4. Of the more than 400 cities with populations over 8,000, all but a dozen had local assemblies at some point during the Order's existence, and most had multiple locals.

16. Anthony Oberschall, *Social Conflict and Social Movements* (Englewood Cliffs, N.J.: Prentice-Hall, 1973), p. 125.

17. Initially, physicians were also excluded "because professional confidence might force the societies' secrets into unfriendly ears." So too were politicians whose moral character was considered too low and who were suspected of being unable to keep secrets. With the lifting of secrecy and the candidacy of Stephens for congress, both groups were eligible for membership. See Wright, "Historical Sketch," pp. 143–44; William C. Birdsall, "The Problem of Structure in the Knights of Labor," *Industrial and Labor Relations Review*, no. 6 (1953): 553–54.

18. Birdsall, "Problem"; Ware, *Labor Movement*, pp. 61–64; Garlock, "Structural Analysis," pp. 16–22.

paper without coming across an article or editorial justifying or more often condemning strikes, boycotts, and unions.[19] "Shall Capital or Labor Rule?" asked the title of an article in the *North American Review* in 1886; and *The New York Times* hysterically denounced the "strikers and boycotters" as "entirely un-American . . . [with] no real conception of what American citizenship is or implies."[20] Even the scholarly world of law journals was rocked by the quickening spiral of strike activity. One law review editorial, written on May 1, 1886, declared: "Strikes as now managed are notoriously lawless, reckless and dangerous conspiracies against the public peace and safety. They mean terror, incendiarism, violence, and bloodshed, and with these characteristics the law should deal, if patiently, yet decisively. . . . A mob of strikers is entitled to no more leniency than a mob of lynchers or common ruffians."[21] Nor was it only on the antilabor side that public discourse had grown so politicized. As Leon Fink notes, by the mid-1880s each specific industrial confrontation tended to take on wider significance. During an 1885 strike the Lansing, Michigan, *Sentinel* provided an answer of sorts to the law review editor: "This is not a strike," it proclaimed "but a grand labor revolution."[22]

Strikes, membership, and public scrutiny reached a crescendo in 1886, the year known in American labor history as "the great upheaval." Two events set the stage for that upheaval. First, in 1884 a dying organization, the Federation of Organized Trades and Labor Unions (FOTLU), passed a resolution calling for a general strike on May 1, 1886, to inaugurate an eight-hour workday. Powderly opposed the strike call, but the idea captured the imagination of Knights members. It was not simply the prospect of shorter hours that generated such widespread enthusiasm; equally important was the idea that workers would establish the length of the working day by their own actions. Rather than agitating for legislation, or incrementally negotiating individual contracts, as had been tried in the past, workers would demonstrate—in a single bold act—their ability to impose their own rules on work.[23] In spite of Powderly's opposition, assembly after assembly voted to strike on May 1, and many Knights organizers

19. A good survey of the kind of rhetoric used to discuss Knights and labor activism in 1886 can be found in Henry David, *The History of the Haymarket Affair* (New York: Farrar and Rinehart, 1936), pp. 36–42.

20. Henry Clews, "Shall Capital or Labor Rule," *North American Review* 142 (1886): 598–602; *New York Times* article quoted in David, *Haymarket*, p. 38.

21. Quoted in David, *Haymarket*, pp. 41–42.

22. Quoted in Leon Fink, "Class Conflict in the Gilded Age," *Radical History Review* 3, nos. 1–2 (1975): p. 63.

23. Oestreicher, *Solidarity*, pp. 145–146; Jeremy Brecher, *Strike!* (Boston: South End Press, 1972), chap. 2.

established new locals around the eight-hour issue. Again, workers flocked into the Order.

Second, in March 1886, Knights members struck at a Gould railroad for a third time. The demand was a daily wage of $1.50 for unskilled workers and reinstatement of a Knights member who had been fired for attending a union meeting. As had happened with the earlier Gould strikes, the conflict became a crusade, touching off a wave of highly publicized strikes and boycotts. By summer, Knights membership had climbed to more than three-quarters of a million workers. Workers of virtually every nationality and race and in nearly every industry were now Knights members. For the first time in American history, a national labor movement had been built from the bottom up.[24]

Many of these members participated in the demonstrations that prepared the way for the general strike that was set to begin on May 1. Eventually, some 340,000 workers joined the protest, and support grew each day. By May 4, it looked as if the movement would be a success. Then, at a public demonstration that night in Chicago, where more workers struck than anywhere else in the country, a bomb exploded as the police moved in to break the rally up. More than seventy policemen were injured, one fatally, and the police opened fire and killed or injured an undetermined number of demonstrators. Anarchist leaders who were addressing the crowd when the bomb exploded were immediately blamed for the bombing. Despite a lack of evidence that the anarchists or the Knights had anything to do with the bombing, antilabor sentiment intensified, and a backlash swept the nation faster than the protest message had. On the night of the bombing the General Executive Board of the Knights, meeting in St. Louis, called off their strike against Gould without winning a single demand.[25] Combined with the general failure of the eight-hour strikes, these developments suddenly reversed the Knights' explosive growth. In the aftermath of these defeats, workers began to leave the Order. Further membership losses occurred as the Order became embroiled in highly destructive factional battles. At issue were fundamental matters of strategy and tactics: Should the Order move to quell strike activity in light of the fierce antilabor climate? Should the growing numbers of independent labor candidates be openly supported? Should craft autonomy be curbed or encouraged within the Order? Should Terence Powderly retain his post as leader, particularly after his disavowal of

24. Oestreicher, "Terence V. Powderly," p. 47, makes the same point.
25. The account of the General Executive Board's actions following Haymarket comes from Nick Salvatore, *Eugene V. Debs: Citizen and Socialist* (Urbana: University of Illinois Press, 1982), pp. 68–69.

the Haymarket anarchists? Given the Knights' heterogeneous membership, these issues would have been difficult to resolve under the best of circumstances; against the backdrop of the country's first major red scare, they provoked confrontation, disillusionment, and decline.[26]

Adding fuel to the factional fires, the Order also became involved in a vituperative conflict over craft autonomy with the AFL, which was founded in December 1886. The dispute was an outgrowth of an internal fight within the Cigar Makers' International Union (CMUI, a non-Knights craft union) over the organization of unskilled workers who rolled cigars in New York City tenements. A dissident faction within the CMIU favored organization of the tenement workers, but the national leadership rejected their inclusion in the union on the grounds that they undercut the wages and working conditions of more skilled men already in the union.[27] One of the Knights' most radical districts, District Assembly 49 of New York City, sided with the dissidents, and the internal battle blossomed into a war that grew to engulf both national organizations. Although the war is often presented as having been swiftly won by the AFL, in reality, it was a messy business that lingered on for several years. Not until 1892 was the AFL, which supported the CMIU, indisputably the larger organization.[28] And only after 1899 did the AFL attain a membership that equalled the Knights' membership of 1886.

The Knights continued to play an important role in many areas through the 1890s, but the Order never again attained anywhere near the membership or power it had achieved in the mid-1880s. By 1890, membership had plummeted to 120,000 workers, and by 1893, when the national organization served briefly as a vehicle for an agrarian-socialist alliance, it was under 80,000.[29]

Assessing the reasons for the Knights' initial success and ultimate decline is the task of later chapters. The purpose here is to place the

26. On Haymarket, see David, *Haymarket*; on the southwest strike, consult Ruth A. Allen, *The Great Southwest Strike* (Austin: University of Texas Press, 1942); and for a very helpful discussion of the issues that divided the Order in 1886, see Oestreicher, "Terrence V. Powderly," pp. 50–56.

27. The factional fight was also about ideology and tactics. Briefly, the leaders of the CMIU wanted to reorganize the union to put more power into the hands of the international office, to increase dues and benefits, and to tighten discipline. The dissidents wanted more local autonomy, separate language locals, and to forge an independent labor party. For accounts of the conflict, see Patricia A. Cooper, *Once a Cigar Maker* (Urbana: University of Illinois Press, 1987), pp. 21–25; Ware, *Labor Movement*, chap. 11.

28. Shelton Stromquist, "United States of America," in *The Formation of Labour Movements, 1870–1914: An International Perspective*, ed. Marcel Van Der Linden and Jürgen Rojahn (Leiden, The Netherlands: E. J. Brill, 1990), 2: 552.

29. Richard Oestreicher, "A Note on Knights of Labor Membership Statistics," *Labor History* 25, no. 1 (Winter 1984), p. 107.

Knights' organizing strategy and ideology in a historical and comparative context. To that end, the Order's ideology must now be addressed.
Around what vision did the Order attempt to organize both skilled
and less-skilled workers?

The Knights offered workers a vaguely defined but powerful vision
of labor solidarity and cooperative social relations. Their ideology was
one that encouraged workers from different backgrounds to think
that their problems were related and to trust that collectively workers
would be able to create just and moral economic arrangements. It
was an evolving, often ambivalent, set of ideas, one that merits closer
scrutiny, both because of the role it played in uniting workers across
the skill divide and because it has often been unfairly caricatured
(most notably by those writing in the tradition of John Commons) as
hopelessly "backward-looking" and "middle-class."[30]

The Knights' ideology drew heavily on republican political ideals, as
had the GTU. Thus, workers' economic and shopfloor difficulties were
tied to a larger political critique. As one Knights member testified before Congress in 1883, "The political structure of this country is resting
on a sand heap, owing to the degradation of labor."[31] A New Jersey
activist developed a similar theme in an 1887 speech, calling on the
words of Abraham Lincoln to dramatize his point: "Lincoln said
labor should be above capital, and that capital could not have existed
without labor," but now "the aristocracy of America backed up by the
aristocracy of the old world is putting capital above labor in the structure of the American Republic."[32] George McNeill, an influential labor
activist and Knights official, articulated the same point more succinctly
when he declared "an inevitable and irresistible conflict between the
wage-system of labor and the republican system of government."[33]

The Knights did not, however, simply appropriate antebellum labor
rhetoric. The experience of industrial capitalism had transformed
workers' lives, and the Order's ideology reflected this transformation.
The working-class republicanism of the 1880s was more inclusive,
more democratic, more mutualistic, and more oppositional than the
working-class republicanism of the 1830s. Labor leaders in the 1880s

30. Perlman, "Upheaval"; Grob, *Workers and Utopia*. Influential syntheses by historians such as Samuel P. Hays, *The Response to Industrialism, 1885–1914* (Chicago: University
of Chicago Press, 1957); Robert H. Weibe, *The Search for Order, 1877–1920* (New York: Hill
and Wang, 1967); and Thomas Bender, *Community and Social Change in America* (Baltimore: Johns Hopkins University Press, 1978), incorporate this view of the Knights.
31. U.S. Senate, *Testimony*, 1: 218, Testimony of John S. McClelland, secretary of the
General Executive Board.
32. *Elizabeth Daily Journal*, May 7, 1887.
33. McNeill, *Labor Movement*, p. 459. McNeill first made the statement in 1877.

also advocated a larger role for the state and offered a more fully elaborated vision of the alternative society they sought than had the labor leaders of the 1830s.

First, the Knights spoke a language of inclusion that would have astonished the members of the GTU. In their declaration of principles they repeatedly described themselves as the "masses"—the "toiling," "industrial," "working," "laboring" *masses*. The term "masses" was one that the proud artisans of the GTU would never have uttered—to them it would have reeked of baseness, of commonness, of the mob. The Knights, in contrast, embraced the absence of distinction implied in the term "masses." They used it to emphasize the fact that the Order was open to all workers—whether unskilled, female, black, foreign-born, or independent craftsmen. And having opened the organization to a much more inclusive group of workers than any other American labor union, Knights leaders attempted to bridge the differences between these workers by continually stressing the importance of solidarity. "An injury to one is the concern of all," declared the Order's slogan.

Of course, differences in experience and expectations were not bridged overnight simply by the use of a new universalistic word. At first, as we have seen, the founding assembly did not admit members of other trades, much less of inferior skills. Something of this attitude lingered throughout the history of the Order, for it is clear that many skilled workers remained firmly attached to craft identities even as they sought the protection and power of a broader class organization. Moreover, the Knights' record on gender and racial equality was not always consistent with its high-minded principles. Chinese workers were excluded from membership, black workers were discriminated against in some local assemblies, and women were only grudgingly appointed to leadership positions.[34] Thus, it must be noted that the Order was not always successful in its attempts to overcome the skill, gender, and ethnic differences that divided the American working class. However, by the standards of the late nineteenth and early twentieth century, its success was extraordinary: thousands of local assemblies explicitly recruited less-skilled workers, and by 1887, nearly one-tenth of the Order's membership was female, and a similar proportion was black.

34. Foner, *History*, II: 56–74; New Jersey Bureau of Statistics, *Tenth Annual Report*, pp. 14–15. One of the first boycotts organized by the Knights in New Jersey was against Chinese laundry workers; Knights' leaders saw this as an action to support working women. See New Jersey Bureau of Statistics, *Ninth Annual Report*, pp. 202–3, and the *Bayonne Herald* (WPA newspaper collection), Dec. 11, 1886.

Second, whereas the journeymen of the GTU claimed property rights in their skills to justify their demands, the Knights claimed a more universalistic set of citizenship rights to legitimate their program. Knights leaders repeated the now-familiar argument that wage labor was a threat to the republic because it was creating a permanent, dependent class of citizens. But rather than simply calling for a return to the old days of independent proprietorship, the Knights argued that citizenship must now guarantee a basic set of economic rights for all wage earners. They especially emphasized the right to organize labor unions, to set wages according to union scale, and to toil only reasonable hours. Without these rights, the Order insisted, wage earners would be unfit for civic participation. Unless democracy was extended to the workplace, ensuring all citizens equality at work as well as equality before the law, it would be impossible to maintain a republican form of government. "We complain that our rulers, statesmen and orators have not attempted to engraft republican principles into our industrial system, and have forgotten or denied its underlying principles," George McNeill stated in 1877.[35] The Knights' preamble made a similar point, insisting that the "alarming" concentration of "great capitalists and corporations" must be "checked" because the dependence it engendered was corrupting workers' economic independence and their ability to function as competent citizens.

An additional argument was also made to support the Knights' claim to an expanded set of citizenship rights. Building on their belief that labor created all wealth, they added the argument that workers' inventiveness was the source of social and economic progress. This being the case, they demanded a fair share of the benefits of social progress and economic growth. Unless democracy was extended to industry, labor leaders contended, workers would never get their "fair share" of profits. Robert Layton, an axemaker and Knights official, made this point when he testified before a Senate committee in 1883. Comparing his life with that of his father, Layton noted that his father had made only about half as many axes in a day as Layton did, yet had lived much more comfortably. It was his own and other workers' productivity, Layton implied, that accounted for the advances in "material civilization," yet he and the others were forced to live more poorly than their parents.[36] Layton's complaint echoes throughout the Senate testimony and much of the labor oratory of the day: under the present

35. McNeill, *Labor Movement*, p. 456.
36. U.S. Senate, *Testimony*, 1: 37.

"system of wage labor," workers' productivity resulted, ironically, in more dependence, ignorance, and grinding poverty each generation.[37] Only by extending democracy to industry would this skewed state of affairs be ameliorated.

Third, in contrast to the GTU, the Knights argued that state action would be required to "secure for workers the full enjoyment of the wealth they create." At the national level, the Order demanded public ownership of the communication, transportation, and banking systems. At the state level, the Order sought health and safety laws, bureaus of labor statistics, and the "abrogation of all laws that do not bear equally upon capital and labor." In a country where state action was looked upon with great suspicion, granting the state even this limited role was a radical step. But as George McNeill argued, exceptional circumstances called for drastic action: concentrated capital had become "a greater power than that of the State, . . . a power that [was] quietly yet quickly sapping the foundations of majority rule."[38]

However, although the Knights were more willing than most of their fellow citizens to use the state as an instrument of social progress, they looked above all to mutualism to bring about their aims. Their call for self-organization and self-help extended beyond anything that the working class had previously attempted. "We have formed the Order of the Knights of Labor," went the organization's declaration of principles, "with a view of securing the organization and direction, by cooperative effort of the power of the industrial classes."[39] Members built a dense network of alternative institutions and practices, including local assemblies, boycotts, reading rooms, bands, parades, lecture circuits, cooperatives, and labor parties. The Order even established its own court system. These courts, organized at the local and district levels, heard cases involving violations against both the Order (such as scabbing and accepting substandard wages) and the civil law (such as wife beating and failure to pay boarding bills).[40] Such institutions

37. See Forbath, "Ambiguities," p. 806, for further discussion of this oft-mentioned theme.

38. McNeill, *Labor Movement*, p. 462. It was a limited vision of state action but, as Forbath notes, one that nevertheless unleashed severe criticism even in the pages of the liberal magazines where, only a few years before, abolitionists had themselves penned arguments in favor of an active democratic state to support their radical reconstruction position. See "Ambiguities," p. 489.

39. Butler, "History," p. G33.

40. On the Knights court system, consult Jonathan Garlock, "The Knights of Labor: A 19th-Century American Experiment with Popular Justice," paper presented to the Social Science History Association, Columbus, Ohio, Nov. 1978.

heightened workers' class awareness, gave them practical experience of mutualism, and helped make the Knights' vision of a producers' self-governing Republic tangible to members.[41]

Strikes and political action were other tactics of self-help used by the Knights, but these were not universally endorsed. As noted, Terence Powderly was skeptical about the value of strikes. He generally shunned labor actions that would make employers less receptive to persuasion and arbitration.[42] However, the rank and file, along with many local and district officials, pursued strikes avidly. The strike waves of 1886 and 1887 exceeded, in number of strikes, number of strikers, level of organization, and bitterness, anything undertaken in the 1830s.[43] Partisan political action was also pursued in the same years, often as a direct effect of heightened strike agitation. It, too, as we have seen, created internal dissension. Many within the Knights, including Powderly, feared that partisan politics would destroy the Order. Their caution notwithstanding, local labor parties with ties to the Knights campaigned in over 200 communities between 1885 and 1887.[44] In the 1830s, no similar political action had been attempted.

A final difference between the Knights and the GTU lay in the alternative vision each elaborated. Both championed cooperation as the best means to abolish the dependence of "wage slavery," but they had fundamentally different visions of the overall role and functioning of cooperative enterprise. In the 1830s cooperatives were seen as a way to uphold customary production practices and to provide artisans with competences. By the 1880s, cooperatives were seen as a way to "republicanize" industry; that is, as a way to reorganize work so that all workers—skilled and unskilled alike—would have an equal voice in deciding what to produce and how to produce it. In addition, the Knights' experience with cooperation was much more extensive: they successfully established many more cooperatives and sustained them much longer than had the journeymen of the 1830s.[45] These cooperatives were seen as both a practical means of self-help and a way to

41. Stromquist, "United States," pp. 553–54, borrows Lawrence Goodwyn's notion of a "movement culture" to describe these developments in the Knights.

42. Oestreicher, "Terence V. Powderly," pp. 51–53.

43. Brecher, *Strike!*, chap. 2.

44. Fink, *Workingmen's Democracy*, pp. 26–29.

45. Two hundred and ninety producer cooperatives were established between 1884 and 1888, and there were probably a few hundred cooperative stores established in the mid-1880s. See Steve Leikin, "The Practical Utopians: Cooperation and the American Labor Movement, 1860–1890," Ph.D. diss., University of California, Berkeley, 1992, chaps. 4 and 5, for an illuminating discussion of cooperation in the Knights of Labor.

demonstrate the moral superiority of a cooperative over a competitive economy.

All these differences indicate the extent to which Knights leaders and activists had to alter and extend the meaning of working-class republicanism in order to organize workers across the skill divide. In the 1830s, journeymen had developed a language that expressed for the first time an identity of class, but when they actually applied it, they applied it narrowly. With the Knights, the same words were pushed toward their universalistic and oppositional limits. Moreover, workers developed a clearer vision of the alternative future they wanted to create. In the near term, it was a future in which workers and employers would be on more equal terms and market forces would be regulated in the interests of industrial and political democracy. In the longer term, it was a future in which a decentralized cooperative system would replace competition.

Noting this transformation in the interpretation of working-class republicanism does not, however, adequately answer one of the key questions scholars have asked about the Knights' ideology. What were the political implications of the Knights' ideology: just how radical and oppositional was it?

Scholars have differed sharply in their assessment.[46] Because the Knights' ideology drew on republican ideas, and because it offered a vision of a future society in which workers would no longer be dependent wage earners, some historians have argued that the Knights' ideology was "backward-looking," and by implication, doomed. This was the interpretation given by the founders of American labor history and their followers. Gerald Grob, for example, argues that the Knights' emphasis on producer cooperatives and on the abolition of the wage system was hopelessly at variance with the direction of industrial society.[47] As such it was the final hurrah for an old utopian reform tradition that had long hobbled the labor movement. This line of argument, I believe, is misdirected. It assumes that discourses

46. In part, the disagreement derives from the complex and ambivalent set of ideas championed by the Order. Its ideology was not a fully elaborated or always internally consistent set of beliefs. Instead, as perhaps befits a decentralized organization in a rapidly changing age, the temper of the movement was experimental. "Any ism which conscientiously tries to improve the condition of the people should be considered on its own merits," wrote one labor journalist in 1885 (quoted in Oestreicher, *Solidarity*, p. 132). Workers struggled to grasp the great changes they were experiencing, and the conceptual categories and remedies they advocated evolved and shifted throughout the history of the organization.

47. Grob, *Workers and Utopia*, esp. pp. 187–88.

of modern labor movements break radically with the conceptual categories of past struggles. But we know from the study of other social movements that what E. P. Thompson calls the "legitimating notion of right" is a necessary element of most popular protest. Republicanism provided a language that inspired workers and legitimated their strikes, boycotts, and demonstrations.

Others interpret the Knights' ideology largely in terms of its producerist, class-blunting elements. Victoria Hattam, for example, argues that the Knights "considered themselves citizens and producers *rather than* workers or laborers" (my emphasis).[48] As a result, she believes, they attempted to represent both a middle-class and a working-class constituency, an effort that prevented them from functioning as a working-class movement. My reading of the Knights suggests that this argument is also flawed. It fails to note the ways in which older understandings of social divisions were layered on top of newer ones. Furthermore, it ignores the way that this layering shifted over time: the Knights' interpretation of social divisions was not the same in 1886 as it had been in 1869, or even 1883.

Hattam is certainly correct when she argues that producerist categories shaped the Knights' understanding of the world. In speeches and writings, Knights members sometimes still referred to themselves as producers and heaped scorn upon "idleness." Moreover, their greatest opprobrium was reserved for large, concentrated, monopolistic capital, a category that obviously had producerist overtones: references to "the alarming concentration of wealth," to "great corporations," and to "capital combinations" pepper their speeches and writings. Finally, and most damning according to scholars such as Hattam, the Knights identified their constituency as all producers, including employers.

However, Hattam is mistaken in her conclusion that the Knights' producerism prevented members from identifying themselves as workers. Words such as "wage earners," "employees," "labor," and "workers" appear much more often than the word "producers," both in the Order's declaration of principles and in official speeches.[49] And even the oft-repeated fact that the Knights allowed employers to be-

48. Hattam, "Economic Visions," p. 91.
49. In fact, the word "producers" does not appear in most versions of the Knights declaration of principles. In a few versions, the term "producing masses" does occur; however, it is used only once, while terms such as "workers," "employees," "industrial classes," and "laborers" are used repeatedly. See Butler, "History," pp. G33–G35; Ezra Cook, *Knights of Labor Illustrated* (Chicago: Ezra A. Cook, 1886), pp. 7–9; U.S. Senate, *Testimony*, 1: 2.

come members is less telling than it first appears. The Knights distinguished employers who had once been wage earners from those who had not; and they distinguished employers who paid union wages, abided by union rules, and respected their employees from those who did not. Only former wage earners who paid union wages and so forth were eligible for membership. In addition, it is clear that the boundaries drawn between producers, workers, and the wage class on the one hand and monopolists and capitalists on the other shifted and sharpened over time. In the Knights' initiation ceremony, which was written in 1869 by Stephens, the Order declared that it had "no conflict with legitimate enterprise, no antagonism with necessary capital."[50] By 1883, when Robert Layton, the national secretary of the Order testified before Congress, he stated that *capitalists* were ineligible for membership, although employers who respected labor (and met all the other criteria cited above) could join.[51] And by 1886, Knights members in Newark, New Jersey, were preventing *all* employers from marching in Labor Day parades.[52] Does this mean that producerist categories had completely lost currency among Knights members by 1886? No, but it does indicate that the balance between older and newer understandings of social divisions had shifted in favor of the latter.

Both the producerist and backward-looking indictments, I am arguing, are overdrawn. So, too, would be any effort to paint the Knights as socialists. Some members were socialists, and many have noted that the Knights' project differed little from the socialist project. Karl Marx's daughter, Eleanor, and her husband, Edward Aveling, for example, called the Order's principles and in particular its effort to establish an industrial co-operative system "pure and unadulterated Socialism."[53] But the means endorsed by the Knights to achieve this system were clearly different from the means pursued by most socialists. Frank Giddings, a labor journalist (and later an academic sociologist), tried to articulate this difference in 1886:

> Co-operation differs from socialism. . . . It does not ask the State to take possession of all capital, and manage all industry, and order all men in their industrial life as it orders regiments of soldiers. . . . There are those

50. Cook, *Knights*, p. 30.

51. U.S. Senate, *Testimony*, 1: 5. Along similar lines, Oestreicher reports that by 1885 any labor leader who tried to deny the existence of class conflict was going against the current of the labor movement, at least in Detroit. See *Solidarity*, p. 133.

52. See Chapter 7.

53. Edward Aveling and Eleanor Marx Aveling, *The Working-Class Movement in America* (1891; reprint, London: Arno Press, 1969), p. 137.

who favor socialism, because they despair of the possibility of improving social arrangements by any other means. William Morris, the English poet-socialist, who has long been a profit-sharing employer, holds that, short of socialism, co-operation stands no chance against a crushing competition. This is to over-look the vitally important truth, that there are monstrous evils associated with competition at present, which have grown up through the shameful neglect of the government to fulfill its primary functions of protecting equal rights and enforcing justice. The privileged corporations and monopolies, which exact tribute of all industry, are the creatures of government, and should be brought by government within proper limits of privilege and action. If this were done, and certain other wrongs, as those connected with unjust land-laws, were remedied, there would be no need of revolution and State socialism for the realization of co-operative ideals.[54]

How did the Knights intend to induce the government to protect equal rights and enforce justice? Here W. P. Cherrington, another labor journalist of the period, is illuminating. He compares the Knights' mission to that of the abolitionists: "African slavery on our soil, recognized by human law, was a false basis upon which to rest the structure of our free government, yet force was used to uphold it, and force, sanctioned by justice abolished it. It took a century or more to bring people to view slavery in its true light and recognize the slave as a man; so it may take some years to realize the fact that the present industrial system of our country is but chattel slavery, in fact, if not in name, and that the laws that sanction and uphold this system must be changed by the power of organized labor, mutual co-operation and mutual instruction."[55] Although they were willing to remind their fellow citizens that force might eventually be necessary, most Knights members in 1886 still believed that direct action, example, and agitation would be enough to bring about the social change they sought. They believed they had numbers, moral right, and, once they had organized broadly, greater power on their side. They were strengthened in their belief by the lessons they drew from the Civil War. In that conflict abolitionists had eventually changed public opinion, convincing their fellow citizens that slavery was incompatible with a republican form of government.

In sum, the Knights of Labor was a radical organization that chal-

54. Frank Giddings, "Cooperation," in *The Labor Movement: The Problem of Today*, ed. George E. McNeill (Boston: A. M. Bridgeman, 1887), p. 531.
55. W. P. Cherrington, *Exposition and Defense of the Principles, Demands, and Purposes of the Noble Order of the Knights of Labor* (Boston: Co-operative Printing and Publishing Co., 1886), p. 21.

lenged the status quo, but it was not a revolutionary association. Its vision was of a "workingmen's democracy" in which a broadly organized labor movement would champion and defend the public good within a regulated marketplace economy.[56] Often analysts try to assess this vision by applying a limited set of categories: revolutionary/quiescent, capitalist/anticapitalist, or even producerist/class conscious. But this set of categories, or any other borrowed from some external standard of "true" class consciousness, will never be adequate for any final assessment of the Knights or any other real-life workers' movement. To accomplish that, the Knights must be compared to real alternatives, those chosen by other workers facing similar circumstances and similar choices.

The Knights of Labor in Comparative Perspective

In both England and France broad inclusive unions emerged in roughly the same period that the Knights of Labor developed in the United States. In England such unions date from 1889 when the first "new unions" were organized, and in France they date from the closing years of the nineteenth century.

In England, the new unionism arose in the wake of two dramatic labor victories. These had the same kind of catalytic effect on English workers as the Knights' victories over Jay Gould had on American wage earners. The first involved a new union of unskilled gasworkers, which was initiated in London in March 1889. In August, the union demanded a shortening of the industry's grueling workday from twelve to eight hours without a reduction of pay. To universal surprise, the utility companies agreed within a few days. Shortly after this, another group of unskilled workers, the dockers, organized a union and went on strike. They demanded an end to the contract system and higher wages. In a tactically brilliant move, every day the strikers led a public parade around the city, carrying "stinking onions, old fish-heads, and indescribable pieces of meat," to show Londoners what the dockers had to live on. These demonstrations generated public sympathy, and eventually a group of prominent citizens intervened to help settle the strike. The workers won, and their victory touched off a wave of unionization, particularly among semiskilled workers in larger towns. By 1890, the seven largest of the new unions claimed 320,000 mem-

---

56. This is a paraphrase of Leon Fink's characterization in *Workingmen's Democracy*, p. 228. I have altered it to emphasize the Knights' inclusive organizing strategy.

bers, and the East End weaving shop where most trade union banners were made had turned out more banners than in any other year, before or since.[57]

These new unions immediately distinguished their brand of unionism from that of the "old" craft unions. The new organizations were inclusive, militant, political, and charged low dues, but established unions were exclusive, businesslike, hostile to social legislation, and demanded high dues. Most new unions were general rather than industrial unions; that is, they straddled a number of industries rather than organizing all workers in a given trade. They took this form in large part because strong and exclusive craft unions already existed in England's basic industries, and, as a rule, these established unions were hostile to the new unions. Thus, the new unions organized under and around existing union structures. Unlike the Knights of Labor, these new unions had no explicit mechanism by which craft workers could affiliate. Instead, new union leaders tried to nudge craft unions to broaden their membership requirements, but these efforts failed.[58]

Ideologically, these new unions were influenced by Britain's emerging socialist movement. Several explicitly socialist organizations had been founded in London in the mid-1880s, the largest and most important of which were the Social Democratic Federation (SDF) and the Fabian Society.[59] The membership of both organizations was small and predominantly middle class.[60] But its members were active in both the dockers' and the gasworkers' union. Karl Marx's daughter Eleanor, for example, provided organizational skills and general staff help in several disputes, and she also taught the leader of the gasworkers (Will Thorne) to read.[61] H. H. Champion, another middle-class socialist, edited a newspaper that served as the official organ for both the dockers and the gasworkers. The working-class socialists were even

---

57. Cole and Postgate, *Common People*, p. 428; Hunt, *British Labour*, pp. 162 and 305. For background on the new unionism, see Hunt, *British Labour*, and H. A. Clegg, Alan Fox, and A. F. Thompson, *A History of British Trade Unions since 1899*, vol. 1 (Oxford: Clarendon Press, 1964).

58. Hobsbawm, *Labouring Men*, pp. 179–203; *Workers*, pp. 152–75.

59. The SDF had actually been founded in 1881 as the Democratic Federation. It did not become an explicitly socialist organization, however, until 1884, when it changed its name. A good overview of these early socialist organizations is given in Henry Pelling, *The Origins of the Labour Party, 1880–1900*, 2d ed. (Oxford: Oxford University Press, 1965).

60. Pelling estimates that their combined membership numbered less than 2,000. See *America and the British Left* (London: Adam and Charles Black, 1956), p. 57.

61. Pelling, *Origins*, pp. 80–81, reports that Eleanor Marx Aveling also taught him about the Knights of Labor and that he originally opened the Gasworkers Union to all workers, irrespective of occupation because he was influenced by the Knights.

more active in the creation of the new unionism; serving as founders and leaders of both the gasworkers' and dockers' unions, as well as of several other new ones.[62]

British socialism was, however, a socialism of a decidedly reformist and pragmatic sort. In the late nineteenth and early twentieth century, Fabian ideas were much more influential in the labor movement than those endorsed by the more doctrinaire and revolutionary SDF, in part because the SDF was dismissive of trade unions. The Fabians advocated a policy of incrementalism. Socialism was seen as a system that would evolve logically out of progressive reforms, not as a system whose creation would require revolutionary action. These progressive reforms, they believed, could best be achieved by "permeation," that is, by getting nonsocialists to take up reform proposals and then impressing them with the rationality of socialism. As Cole and Postgate note, the Fabians proclaimed a socialist system as their objective but set out in practice to get not socialism but social changes pointing in a socialist direction: "[They] envisaged Socialism as a heap of reforms to be built by the droppings of a host of successive swallows who would in the end make a Socialist summer; and in this spirit [they] managed to express an essentially Socialist philosophy in terms of immediate proposals which made a strong appeal to many reformers who were by no means Socialists."[63] The temper of the socialists who were active in creating the new unions was more oppositional than the Fabians', but for the most part they, too, stressed reformist measures. For example, Keir Hardie, the most prominent spokesman for the socialist wing of the new unionism in the 1890s, concentrated his practical propaganda upon the statutory eight-hour day and the necessity for independent labor representation in parliament. The biggest dispute was over tactics: was direct action or parliamentary politics the best path to reform? At first, direct action probably had the largest number of supporters, but this changed when the new unions began to suffer serious setbacks in 1892. Much as had happened to the Knights in 1886, membership began to drop off dramatically in 1892 when a reaction against all unions set in. As a result, many socialists grew disillusioned with the efficacy of direct action as the single best means to better the lives of less-skilled workers. Thus, they began to concentrate more on political activities. In 1893, they established the Independent Labour Party (ILP), whose primary purpose was to run

62. Hunt, *British Labour*, p. 305.
63. Cole and Postgate, *Common People*, p. 423.

independent labor candidates for parliament. (At this time, approximately two-thirds of the male working class had the vote.)[64] The new party announced that its object was to achieve "the collective ownership of the means of production, distribution, and exchange," but, significantly, the founding convention rejected the motion that the new party be called the Socialist Labour Party.[65] Most members saw their role as coaxing the trade unionists of both "old" and new complexion away from the Liberal Party and into supporting the new party. They feared that calling themselves "socialists" would hinder their cause.[66]

Even this mild form of socialism met with resistance within the very groups the ILP most wanted to attract, the old unionists and the great mass of unorganized workers. The former remained suspicious of what they saw as the new unionists' and socialists' overemphasis on legislation and the government: they feared that such policies "would lead workers into craven dependence on the state." [67] The great mass of workers, too, were suspicious of state intervention. Based on an analysis of the popular and union press, Patrick Joyce argues that a distrust of the state and a celebration of collective self-help were deep-seated in the English working class.[68] Moreover, producerist values lingered among English workers, just as they did among American workers. Joyce reports that the usefulness and virtue of the honest, hardworking master was frequently emphasized and that such masters were included on the producers' side as workers continued to condemn idleness.[69]

---

64. The Reform Act of 1867 had enfranchised most urban workers, and another reform act in 1884 extended the vote to the majority of rural workers. However, about one-third of the male working class still was without the vote in the closing decades of the century for one reason or another: most commonly, they had had no stable place of residence when the register of voters had been prepared, they had once accepted poverty assistance, or they were neither householders nor tenants. See Blewett, "Franchise," pp. 27–56.

65. Quoted in Pelling, *Origins*, p. 118. The ILP's founding convention and the rejection of the "Socialist" label are also discussed in G. D. H. Cole, *A Short History of the British Working-Class Movement, 1789–1947* (London: George Allen and Unwin, 1948), pp. 249–51.

66. This caution received a vindication of sorts in the elections of 1895. The ILP ran twenty-eight candidates in the election, and they all lost, including Keir Hardie. That Hardie lost in spite of his popularity is usually attributed to the fact that he alone announced that he refused to work with the Liberal Party.

67. James Hinton, "The Rise of a Mass Labour Movement: Growth and Limits," in *A History of British Industrial Relations, 1875-1914*, ed. Chris Wrigley (Brighton, Eng.: Harvester Press, 1982), p. 32.

68. Joyce, "Work," pp. 68 and 121. See also James D. Young, *Socialism and the English Working Class: A History of English Labour, 1883–1939* (New York: Harvester Wheat Sheaf, 1989), Chap. 4.

69. Patrick Joyce, *Visions of the People: Industrial England and the Question of Class, 1848– 1914* (Cambridge: Cambridge University Press), pp. 120–21.

Working-class socialists recognized these popular attitudes and altered their rhetoric and goals accordingly. The economic analyses and prescriptions offered by the ILP rejected Marxism in favor of liberty, equality, and fraternity. The critique of capitalism they offered was more moral than economic, and no notion of a systemic crisis being inherent in capitalism can be found in their documents. Moreover, although they continued to advocate reforms such as the statutory eight-hour day, factory legislation, and a graduated income tax, leaders like Hardie argued that socialism also required self-help, "albeit self-help made possible by the state's adjustment of the profound inequalities of present, capitalist society."[70] Finally, the speeches and writings of ILP members made it clear that, although they believed that the working class had a historical role to play in the emancipation of society, they did not see class struggle as the motive force of history. What mattered most was the moral energy of the whole people or of the "commonwealth"; and the working class as both the majority of the population and the segment of society most in touch with this moral energy could create a society without class distinctions.[71]

At an ideological level, then, the socialism that infused the new unionism shared much with the working-class republicanism expressed by the Knights of Labor. Indeed, there are only two significant differences. First, although British working-class socialists placed limits on the role of state intervention, they nonetheless allotted it a larger role than did the Knights. Both the ILP and the Knights, for example, called for the eight-hour day. But the ILP demanded legislation to achieve it, and the Knights called on workers simply to refuse to work more than eight hours. Eventually, the socialist leaders of the new unionism decided to put their energy into organizing a labor party so that they would have a better chance of pushing the state to intervene in the economy. Second, although both organizations were vague on the future society they envisaged, the ILP was more so. The Knights advocated a cooperative industrial system, but the ILP called for collective ownership of the means of production, although it never specified what this meant in practice.

It is at the level of organization and longevity that we find the biggest differences between the new unionism and the Knights. As we have seen, the new unionism organized beneath and around the existing craft unions, rather than attempting to incorporate them or to ally directly with them. In addition, much of the leadership of the new unionism was explicitly socialist, which was not the case in

70. Ibid., p. 79.
71. Ibid., pp. 76–80.

the Knights. Many members of the Knights were avowed socialists, and much of the Order's ideology was protosocialist, but its national leaders did not have a socialist identity.

Most consequentially, the new unionism survived the rapid membership loss that followed its period of explosive growth, but the Knights did not. Eric Hobsbawm has noted that trade unions and other social movements often exhibit a general pattern of growth through discontinuous "leaps" or explosions. Often such explosions are followed by contractions that are almost as dramatic. Such was the case for both the new unionism and the Knights. The absence of adequate statistics on British trade unions before 1892 make it impossible to estimate the size of the contraction with precision, but, based on membership figures for the seven largest new unions, membership fell from 320,000 members during the movement's 1890 peak to 130,000 in 1892 and 80,000 in 1896. Thus, almost 60 percent of the membership had been lost by 1892, and almost three-quarters had fallen off by 1896. The comparable Knights figures are a 68 percent membership loss between 1886 and 1888, and a fall of 89 percent by mid-1892. Thus, the initial contraction looks as if it is comparable scale (the difference is only eight percentage points), but the subsequent fall is steeper for the Knights (the difference is 14 percentage points). Indeed, as we have seen, the downward spiral was never reversed in the Knights. The new unionism, in contrast, survived in spite of its reduced scale and lived to fight another day. Between 1911 and 1913, when there was another upsurge of militancy in England, the new unions that had been established in the 1889–92 period were there to provide institutional support and leadership for a second wave of militancy and organization. Thus, 1911–13 should be seen as a continuation or a second installment of the process started in 1889.[72] A similar wave of strike activity and conflict occurred in the United States after 1909, but by then the Knights were only a memory.[73]

The growth of broad, inclusive unions in France is not associated, as it is in the United States and Britain, with a period of sudden, explosive membership gains. Instead, broad-based unionization was a more gradual development. It took hold in the wake of two key precipitating events: the creation of the first French socialist workers' party in 1879 and the legalization of trade unions in 1884.

Before 1884 trade unions and mutual aid societies (which sometimes

72. Hobsbawm, *Workers*, p. 152. For his discussion of the often explosive growth of social movements, see *Labouring Men*, pp. 126–57.
73. Montgomery, *Workers' Control*, pp. 91–101, discusses the eruption of industrial conflict in the United States after 1909.

functioned as trade unions) endured a precarious existence. They were periodically tolerated but always subject to official persecution. In the 1870s the precariousness of their existence was felt even more acutely as the defeat of the Paris Commune brought renewed repression. Anxious to escape official disfavor, trade unions in this period were relatively conservative. Moreover, all were local unions, organized along craft lines.[74]

The creation of the Third Republic in 1877 led to a liberalization of the state's approach to labor unions. Working-class voters played a crucial role in the election of the middle-class leadership of the Third Republic, and once in power these leaders acted to retain this support.[75] In 1884, they enacted a law that copied almost exactly the wording of the 1824 law that had legalized English trade unions. Their hope was not only to ensure workers' votes but also to create a stable, conservative labor movement along mid-century English lines.[76]

This hope soon proved ill-founded. Taking advantage of the new mood of liberalization, militant workers had begun to build a working-class political movement even before trade unions were legalized. In 1879 the first French worker socialist party was founded, the *Parti Ouvrier Français*. This party subsequently underwent years of factional squabbles and bitter splits, but it and its descendants provided a large number of trade union leaders and activists who consistently pushed the trade union movement in broader, more inclusive directions.[77] They also shaped much of its ideological tenor, propelling it away from the practical, nonideological orientation of England's "old" unions.

In the decade following legalization, rhetoric stressing solidarity between skilled and less-skilled workers was common, although craft loyalties remained strong. Most of the locals founded in this period represented the more highly skilled trades.[78] Labor leaders did, however, look for ways to coordinate their activities. At the local level, the *Bourse du Travail* was created; it functioned as a combination labor

74. Val R. Lorwin, "France," in *Comparative Labor Movements*, ed. Walter Galenson (New York: Prentice-Hall, 1952), pp. 313–409; Price, *Social History*, pp. 240–49; Peter N. Stearns, *Revolutionary Syndicalism and French Labor: A Cause without Rebels* (New Brunswick: Rutgers University Press, 1971), p. 12; Gerald Friedman, "Politics and Unions: Government, Ideology, and the Labor Movement in the United States and France, 1880–1914," Ph.D. diss., Harvard University, 1985.

75. Universal male suffrage had been enacted in 1848.

76. Hanagan, *Logic of Solidarity*, p. 21. The French legislators, of course, had the 1870 English labor movement in mind when they legalized unions, not the labor movement of later years.

77. Gerald Friedman, "The State and the Making of the Working Class: France and the United States, 1880–1914," *Theory and Society* 17 (1988): 403–30.

78. Perrot, *Workers on Strike*, p. 40; Shorter and Tilly, *Strikes in France*, p. 150.

exchange, workers' club, and central labor union.[79] It gathered information about jobs, provided social, cultural, and educational facilities, and coordinated the activities of various unions. Often, the bourses were given financial support by local municipalities. At the national level, coordination was provided by craft unions. The first workers to establish these national craft unions were those in trades with a history of extralocal links, such as the hatters and printers. In 1895 delegates of the local bourses and the national unions came together and agreed to establish the *Confédération Générale du Travail* (CGT), which became the major labor federation of France.

The creation of the bourse and of the CGT eventually encouraged a broader organization of the working class. This happened in two ways. First, at the local level, militant craft workers began to support the strikes of less-skilled industrial workers, frequently providing leadership for new industrial unions in the process.[80] The bourses provided an important institutional avenue for this work. Second, at the national level and especially in the CGT, socialists pushed hard to get unions to adopt industrial organizing strategies. Advocates of industrial unions did not immediately carry the day, but as they slowly established more industrywide unions in the 1880s and 1890s they gradually convinced a majority of their fellow unionists to support broader organizing strategies. In 1900 the annual convention of the CGT voted to endorse industrial unionism as the preferred organizational form. In 1906, a majority of delegates voted to allow no new craft affiliates and to urge existing craft unions to amalgamate into industrial unions.[81] Thus, gradually in the 1890s and early 1900s, less-skilled workers began to join the union movement in larger numbers.

Structurally, the CGT shared much with the Knights of Labor. Both were low-dues organizations in which a variety of organizing strategies were tolerated. Unlike English "new unions," both allowed craft locals to affiliate. It is true that the CGT eventually outlawed the practice, but it was accepted in its formative years. Thus, both the CGT and

79. On the Bourse du Travail, see Lorwin, "France," pp. 321–24; Shorter and Tilly, *Strikes in France*, pp. 165–66; Jeremy Jennings, *Syndicalism in France: A Study of Ideas* (Houndsmills, Eng.: St. Anthony's/Macmillan series, 1990), chap. 2; Steven Lewis, "Reassessing Syndicalism: The Bourses du Travail and the Origins of French Labor Politics," paper presented at the Shifting Boundaries of Labor Politics conference, Cambridge, Massachusetts, March 12–14, 1993. Merriman, *Red City*, provides a very informative picture of the functions and fortunes of a bourse in one city, Limoges. See esp. pp. 181–83 and chaps. 7–8.
80. Hanagan, *Logic of Solidarity*.
81. For a discussion of these developments, see Friedman, "Politics and Unions," chap. 2, and Shorter and Tilly, *Strikes in France*, pp. 165–71.

the Knights of Labor provided workers with the opportunity to organize on their own terms within a context of broader solidarity. Both
also emphasized regional or geographical organization (the district assemblies served this function in the Knights, as the bourses did in the
CGT) and allowed national federations (the Knights allowed national
trade assemblies beginning in the 1880s).[82]

Ideologically, however, the CGT officially endorsed a policy of revolutionary syndicalism that was much more radical than the working-
class republicanism espoused by the Knights of Labor. As Peter
Stearns, a historian of French syndicalism, summarizes it, this philosophy emphasized three points: "complete hostility to the existing
system; a belief that the only way to attack this system was by economic rather than political means, notably a great general strike; and
a vague indication that the future society would be organized without a central political structure, on the basis of local economic units
directed by producers themselves."[83] This ideology was much more
extreme than anything sanctioned by the Knights of Labor, especially
in its total rejection of the economic and political system. It is difficult
to gauge the amount of actual support for revolutionary syndicalism
among rank-and-file French unionists. It is possible that a majority
were no more attracted to *revolutionary* syndicalism (as opposed to
reformist direct action) than were most Knights. The voting system
used by the CGT gave rights of representation to unions regardless of
size, and, therefore, overrepresented the views of smaller, more militant unions. Thus, the actual support for revolutionary syndicalism
among French workers has been the subject of intense historiographi-
cal debate.[84] Nevertheless, it is clear that at the level of formal organi-

82. The major structural differences have to do with centralization and the center
of gravity of the two organizations. The CGT was even more decentralized than the
Knights. Shorter and Tilly, *Strikes in France,* p. 169, offer this analogy to demonstrate
the extreme decentralization: "The CGT was much more like someone standing on a
table shouting exhortations during a bar-room brawl than a general directing his armies
across the field of battle." Moreover, the CGT had two, rather than one, centers of
gravity. Because locals could become member organizations of both the bourses and
the national federations, geographical and industrial axes were strong. In the Knights,
locals could become member organizations of either a district assembly or national trade
assembly; thus only one axis could provide a strong center of gravity. In the Knights,
geographical organizations were stronger than industrial federations.

83. Stearns, *Revolutionary Syndicalism,* p. 9.

84. Stearns is the leading proponent of the view that French syndicalism was "a
cause without rebels." Other historians of French history see Stearns's work as a useful
corrective but believe that he overstates the case. See Friedman, "Politics and Unions";
and Michelle Perrot, "On the Formation of the French Working Class," in *Working-Class
Formation,* ed. Katznelson and Zolberg, esp. p. 107. (She estimates that as much as one-
half of the membership of the CGT was more reformist than the official organization.)

zation, the CGT embraced a more radical ideology than the Knights of Labor. There were, however, even here some parallels in outlook, notably with respect to direct, economic action and the alternative future society each envisaged. These warrant further exploration.

The leaders of the CGT rejected political action for reasons different from those of the leaders of the Knights, but the rejection frequently had similar effects. Two developments turned the CGT away from the legislative arena. First, in the 1880s and 1890s union leaders came to bridle at the rein of political parties. Some of this resentment was natural; when socialist parties helped to organize the trade union movement in other countries, union leaders also discovered that the policies they adopted for day-to-day survival often conflicted with the dictates of socialist political theory.[85] And some of the resentment can be tied to the factionalism of the socialist movement; union leaders did not want sectarian battles and partisan loyalties to jeopardize union solidarity. Second, the CGT rejected political action because many activists had grown disillusioned with middle-class legislators. The brutal repression that followed in the wake of the Paris Commune had caused many workers to abandon their hope of creating a better world through cooperation with the middle class. Their experience with the Third Republic, under both "opportunist" and "radical" leadership, only confirmed their pessimism about the corruption and inefficacy of electoral politics.[86] Knights leaders also worried about the divisive effects of partisan politics and believed that party politics were profoundly corrupt. However, the majority of Knights members would not have supported a revolutionary general strike as an alternative. But in the short run, the kinds of activities endorsed were often similar. This was especially true of bourse activists. Fernand Pelloutier, the most influential trade union theorist-activist in the pre–World War I years and the guiding light of the bourses, believed that the ground for the Great Strike had to be prepared carefully first; thus he emphasized broad organization, educational work, and collective self-improvement in the short run. Like Powderly, he and many other syndicalists distrusted "partial" strikes for wages.[87] In their view, such strikes were doomed to failure. That there was an overlap in ideology is further demonstrated by the

85. See Hobsbawm, *Workers*, p. 153, for some examples.
86. Often French workers condemned politics in much the same language as did Knights members. Perrot in *Workers on Strike* reports that the word "politics" was almost always used by French strikers "in a pejorative sense, closer to 'political scheming'": "we refuse to become involved in your political intrigues"; "the present movement is outside of politics. . . ." For other examples, see p. 232.
87. This point is made by Hanagan, "Solidarity Logics: Introduction," *Theory and Society* 17 (1988): 318.

fact that Pelloutier and other syndicalists joined the French branch of the Knights of Labor, the *Chevalerie du Travail Française* in the 1890s.[88]

The alternative society French syndicalists wanted to create also bore a striking resemblance to the Knights' notion of a cooperative commonwealth. Syndicalists called for the "total emancipation" of workers through "the disappearance of the wage system and employers," an objective that could have come straight out of the Knights' declaration of principles.[89] The primary difference between the two organizations lies in the tactics endorsed to achieve this future. French workers, like their American counterparts, had once believed that the end of "the wage system" could be accomplished primarily by the creation of cooperative enterprises. Until about 1880, the only difference in the two cooperative visions had been that French workers also looked to the state for support in providing public credit and contracts. After the establishment of the Third Republic, however, they lost their faith that such state assistance could be achieved through the electoral system and began to endorse a great general strike, which would overwhelm the government and bring it to its knees. However, once the general strike had brought down the state, they planned to establish a social and political system that looked a lot like the cooperative commonwealth. It would be a society without classes or hierarchy where workers' associations would manage the factories and regulate the pace of industry.[90]

In addition to these parallels between French syndicalism and American working-class republicanism, there is one further similarity in the union movements: the persistence of producerist language. French unionists still used the term "producers" in their speeches and declarations, as did Knights' leaders.[91] This reflects the more widespread use of the term by French workers themselves, as Perrot has demonstrated in her examination of the language of French strikes. In France, as in the United States, workers continued to refer to themselves as "producers" and to use oppositionalist language that relied on producerist categories: capitalists were commonly condemned, for example, as "idle" "parasites," and "opulent" "monopolists" who did "little else than eat, drink and sleep while we labor."[92]

88. Ibid.
89. Quoted in Perrot, "On the Formation of the French Working Class," p. 187.
90. Moss, *Origins*, esp. chap. 5.
91. Perrot, *Workers on Strike*, esp. p. 223; Jennings, pp. 12, 31. Significantly, when Stearns expounds on syndicalist ideas, he frequently uses the word "producers." See *Revolutionary Syndicalism*, esp. p. 9.
92. Perrot, *Workers on Strike*, pp. 214, 222–24. Socialist thinking, too, often showed the influence of producerist categories. Haupt notes that French socialists often de-

In spite of these similarities, there are important differences that set the two movements apart. Two of these have already been noted: the CGT supported revolutionary means to achieve its ends while the Knights did not, and socialist parties were instrumental in creating broad-based unions in France but not in the United States. One final critical difference must also be emphasized: the CGT survived, but the Knights did not. It, and the larger French labor movement, have never achieved the same levels of organization as has the British labor movement, but, nevertheless, both the CGT and broad-based union-ism have had a continuous existence in France since the last quarter of the nineteenth century.[93]

In the closing decades of the nineteenth century the American, French, and English labor movements were more diverse than they had been in the 1830s. Ideologically, the dominant labor organiza-tion in each country embraced a different philosophy: The Knights of Labor espoused a set of beliefs I have called working-class republican-ism; the "new" unions endorsed socialism, and the CGT supported revolutionary syndicalism. Structurally, there were also dissimilari-ties: less-skilled English workers were organized in general unions, but less-skilled French and American workers were unionized along geographical and industrial lines. Politically, there were additional dif-ferences: the CGT supported revolutionary, nonparliamentary means to bring about social change, but both the "new" unions and the Knights supported constitutional methods. Finally, there were varying relationships between union organizations and working-class parties: In England, the ILP was founded by union activists, while in France, political activists founded unions. In the United States, Knights mem-bers organized local labor parties, but these were not officially en-dorsed.

However, there were also important similarities. Most important, activists in each country began to build inclusive unions in these years. In each case, ideological innovation was a necessary feature of the move to organize less-skilled workers. In England and France, social-

picted the petite bourgeoisie as in a "precarious and poverty stricken condition," and as the victims of large-scale capitalist exploitation. See Heinz-Gerhard Haupt, "The Petite Bourgeoisie in France, 1850–1914: In Search of the Juste Milieu?" in *Shopkeepers and Master Artisans in Nineteenth-Century Europe*, ed. Geoffrey Crossick and Heinz-Gerhard Haupt (London: Methuen, 1984), esp. pp. 111–12.

93. In 1913, on the eve of World War I, about 10 percent of French industrial workers were unionized, compared with 26 percent of their British counterparts. See Price, *Social History*, p. 247, for figures.

ism was the doctrine that encouraged greater egalitarianism and solidarity; in the United States working-class republicanism provided the ideological underpinnings for inclusive unionism.

In all three countries, producerist categories continued to shape workers' understanding of their situation. Everywhere workers used terms such as "producers" and "idlers," as well as "workers" and "employers." Contrary to what much of the literature seems to imply, American workers were not unique in their attachment to this older view of social divisions.

Finally, it is clear that alliances between skilled and less-skilled workers were everywhere a lengthy project. Disputes between craft workers and industrial workers and competition between sectional and inclusive organizations were common in all three countries. In the United States, competition occurred both inside and outside the Knights. In England, the old unions sometimes fought the new unions. And in France craft locals voted against endorsing industrial organization.

In other words, success was not a linear, straightforward march. Instead, it took time to build a unified labor movement. Critical issues of policy and structure had to be worked out, setbacks had to be reversed, crises had to be met.

All this needs to be considered as we assess the exceptionalism of the American labor movement in the 1880s. Certainly, the three labor movements were more different in the second moment of class formation than they had been in the first. But one would be hard-pressed to characterize the American labor movement as being backward or clearly headed down a different path from the one taken by French or English workers. Indeed, if we had undertaken our comparison in 1886, we, like Friedrich Engels and other British socialists, might have concluded that the American labor movement pointed the way for workers across the Atlantic.[94] Why it did not turn out that way is the subject for later chapters.

94. For Engels's view, see his preface to the American edition of the *Condition of the Working Class in England in 1844*. For the views of British socialists, see Pelling, *America*, pp. 62–64. Michael Mann, *The Sources of Power* (forthcoming), II, chap. 18, makes the same point.

AN EXPLORATION
OF SOLIDARITY IN
THE NEW JERSEY
KNIGHTS OF LABOR

4

Industry and Labor in
Nineteenth-Century New Jersey

From the broad sweep of comparative history, we now turn to the specific milieu in which the subjects of this book lived and labored. Workers experienced the enormous growth and change that took place in the American economy in the late nineteenth century, not in some average, typical set of circumstances but in particular workplaces, communities, and states. The specific setting for the organizational successes and failures, the alliances and divisions to be analyzed in the chapters that follow is New Jersey. In this chapter we take a glimpse at New Jersey's industrial development and at the legal and political environment that provided the backdrop against which workers organized. We also examine the Knights' activities and membership in the Garden State.

Industrial Development in Gilded Age New Jersey

New Jersey in the late nineteenth century was among the most industrial, urban, and ethnically diverse states in the Union. Located between two of the nation's oldest and largest ports (New York and Philadelphia) and endowed with winding rivers that could be harnessed for power and transportation, New Jersey began to develop as a manufacturing center early in the nineteenth century. In the post–Civil War years, however, the pace of economic development quickened, drawing new regions and new groups of workers into the erratic rhythms of the industrial economy. In the process, the social and economic map of the state was redrawn.

In 1834, when the NTU was formed, the typical economic unit in New Jersey was the self-sustaining farm household composed of individuals who had been born in New Jersey or in a nearby state. Residents who manufactured goods to sell to others were a small but growing minority. Most of them lived in Newark, Camden, Paterson, or in small commercial towns scattered throughout the state. A few also resided in rural hamlets where they used local materials to produce glass and iron.[1]

Only the workers of Newark and New Brunswick were active in the journeymen's revolt of the 1830s; most other communities had too few artisans plying the sorts of crafts that were disrupted by early industrialization to be drawn into the agitation. Paterson was an exception in that a large number of its residents struck, first in 1828 and again in 1835, but those who did were less-skilled factory operatives employed in the cotton textile industry. As was typical of such employees in this period, most were women and children, and they lived far from the union activists of Newark and New Brunswick. During the 1835 strike, a delegation of skilled workers from Paterson (most likely the machinists who built and repaired the textile machinery) attended a meeting of Newark's GTU, asked if they could join the Newark Union, and requested that Newark's mechanics take the cause of the "operatives of Paterson" into consideration. But although Newark's artisans may have felt some sympathy for Paterson's "factory girls," they were unwilling to make common cause with them and thus took no action on the request.[2]

Industrial development over the next several decades was to increase greatly the number and geographical concentration of New Jersey residents engaged in manufacturing. The ranks of both skilled and less-skilled wage earners multiplied rapidly, as did the urban neighborhoods in which most of them came to live. Workers of all trades and skill levels were brought into closer geographical proximity because industrial expansion tended to take place in New Jersey's rapidly growing cities, bypassing the homespun factories in the countryside.

Regionally, this development occurred in two stages. In the 1840s

1. Jeannette Paddock Nichols, "The Industrial History of New Jersey in the Middle Period," in *New Jersey: A History*, ed. Irving S. Kull (New York: The American Historical Society, 1930), pp. 583–615.
2. Frank T. de Vyver, "The Organization of Labor in New Jersey before 1860," Ph.D. diss., Princeton University, 1934, pp. 233–34.

and 1850s, Newark and several smaller cities located along a thirty-mile–wide corridor between Philadelphia and New York grew rapidly. Industrial entrepreneurs and railroad interests began to invest large amounts of capital, attracted by the region's proximity to the trade facilities of New York and by the iron ore and other raw materials of northwest New Jersey. The population of Newark, Jersey City, Elizabeth, Trenton, Camden, and Paterson expanded dramatically. In the two decades preceding the Civil War, these cities grew by an average annual rate of 10 percent, more than three times the annual rate of increase for the state as a whole. Especially in the cities located closest to New York, these high growth rates were fueled by immigration, largely from the British Isles and Germany. Immigrants from England and Germany often had skills that were in demand in the rapidly growing manufacturing concerns, whereas Irish immigrants more often found employment doing the backbreaking work of building the canals and railroads that made the accelerated rates of urban-industrial development possible.[3]

Most of these cities developed two or three primary industries in this period, a typical pattern of development throughout the nineteenth century. Paterson, as we have seen, began as a cotton textile town; but in the 1850s and 1860s, investment shifted to the construction of locomotives and to the capitalization of silk mills. Eventually, it became renowned as America's "silk city." Trenton, the state capital, developed as the center of the American pottery industry; it also had thriving iron and machinery works. Camden became known for its iron and glass factories and for its shipbuilding industry. Jersey City was the eastern rail terminus for New York City; besides its dock and railroad workers, it was best known for its sugar-refining and tobacco-processing factories. Entrepreneurs in Elizabeth tried their hand—often unsuccessfully—at carriages, hardware, and cordage in this period. Eventually, the city became home to the Singer Sewing Machine Company.[4]

Newark, dubbed a "monster workshop" by one of its mayors, was an exception to this pattern; its main industries were diverse throughout the nineteenth century. Its skilled work force, the city's low taxes, cheap rents, excellent shipping facilities, and close proximity to New York proved to be strong attractions for many different manufacturing concerns. Shoes, jewelry, felt hats, trunks, leather goods, thread,

3. Philip Curtis Davis, "The Persistence of Partisan Alignment: Issues, Leaders, and Votes in New Jersey, 1840–1860," Ph.D. diss., Washington University, 1978, chap. 1; Rudolph J. Vecoli, *The People of New Jersey* (Princeton: Van Nostrand, 1965), chap. 3.

4. Nichols, "New Jersey in the Middle Period," and "The Industrial History of New Jersey since 1861," in *New Jersey*, ed. Kull, pp. 892–940.

shirts, scissors, beer, and an array of other goods were produced there.[5]

After the Civil War, a second wave of rapid industrial development began, shifting the site of the most dramatic growth rates to smaller industrial towns such as Passaic and Bayonne, Garfield and New Brunswick. The older metropolitan centers continued to expand but not as quickly as these smaller cities. Many of the new industrial hubs were also located along the New York City–Philadelphia corridor, sometimes only short distances from the older metropolitan centers, but they generally had an entirely different character. Because they were home to newer industries such as petroleum refining, rubber making, and textiles, their work forces tended to include more factory operatives and laborers than cities such as Newark and Camden. These industries relied heavily on immigrant workers, and it was in the small industrial cities that the shock of industrialization, immigration, and urbanization was probably most disorienting in the Gilded Age.[6]

Outside the metropolitan corridor, several smaller industrial towns also developed in this period. In the south, small glassworks had been built in the eighteenth century in isolated communities near the pine forests, their location determined by the abundant supply of potash and sand found there. In the closing decades of the nineteenth century, a few of these glass-producing towns expanded and became small manufacturing and commercial centers. They were peopled primarily by native-born citizens, many of whom were the children and grandchildren of the early immigrant glassworkers. In the northwest region, small iron-producing towns such as Phillipsburg and Boonton also experienced a similar industrial expansion and diversification in this period.[7]

In sum, by 1880, New Jersey was a very different place from what it had been forty years before. According to the census, two-fifths of the working population was employed in the manufacturing sector of the economy, a figure that was twice the national average.[8] The industrial

5. *Board of Trade Report*, 1880, p. 14, cited in Samuel H. Popper, "Newark, N.J., 1870–1910: Chapters in the Evolution of an American Metropolis," Ph.D. diss., New York University, 1951, p. 17; U.S. Bureau of the Census, *Tenth Census: Social Statistics of Cities* (Washington, D.C.: Government Printing Office, 1886), p. 708.

6. Michael Howard Ebner, "Passaic, New Jersey, 1855–1912: City-Building in Post–Civil War America," Ph.D. diss., University of Virginia, 1974, pp. 9–12, chaps. 3–6; John F. Reynolds, *Testing Democracy* (Chapel Hill: University of North Carolina Press, 1988), pp. 10–11.

7. Reynolds, *Testing Democracy*, pp. 9–10; Robert D. Bole and Edward H. Walton, *The Glassboro Story* (York, Penn.: Maple Press Company, 1964), p. 165.

8. Census figures are summarized in New Jersey Bureau of Statistics of Labor and Industries (hereafter, NJBSLI), *4th Annual Report, 1881* (Somerville: State of New Jersey, 1882), p. 402.

concerns that engaged these wage earners were also more diverse than they had been in the past, with the textile, machinery, iron and steel, hardware, hat, leather goods, clothing, pottery, and glass industries among the largest employers (see Table 2). A majority of New Jerseyans now lived in urban areas, making the Garden State the second most densely populated state in the country and radically altering the population balance between urban and rural areas.[9] Finally, a much larger proportion of the state's residents, especially those employed in manufacturing, were now immigrants. About one in every three manufacturing workers in 1880 had been born outside the United States, most commonly in England, Ireland, or Germany (85.4 percent were from these countries).[10] Another third were the native-born children of foreign-born parents.

Living Standards and Work Settings

New Jerseyans, then, experienced all the massive changes recounted in Chapter 2, generally in a heightened and accelerated form. As in the nation at large, these changes had multiple and contradictory effects on New Jersey's working population. No longer were a majority of the state's factory workers women who lived in Paterson while the bulk of handicraft artisans were men who lived in Newark; now both skilled and less-skilled workers were typically male wage earners who worked in a factory setting. In addition, they often now lived in the same or adjoining neighborhoods. At the same time, industrial development in New Jersey introduced new sources of differences, while it only partially reduced the gradations of status and the varied industrial experiences that divided the working class. As we have seen, ethnic distinctions were now much more pronounced than in the past. Moreover, differences in pay, work methods, and future prospects all continued to divide workers along skill, trade, and industry lines. Some sense of these persisting divisions is documented in the annual reports published by the New Jersey Bureau of Statistics of Labor and Industries.

When the Bureau of Labor canvassed workers about their incomes in 1884, they discovered significant differences in living standards (see Table 3).[11] About 37 percent of New Jersey workers surveyed earned

9. Nichols, "New Jersey since 1861," pp. 917 and 919–20.
10. NJBSLI, *5th Annual Report, 1882*, p. 402; Reynolds, *Testing Democracy*, p. 7.
11. The Bureau of Labor provides little information about how it actually selected respondents for its questionnaires. Random sampling was not used, and these figures should only be taken as suggestive. However, the bureau did a good job at drawing from a representative selection of occupations.

Table 2. Principal manufacturing industries of New Jersey, 1880

Industry	Number of establishments	Number of employees	Average size of establishment	Percentage increase in average establishment size, 1870–1890	Percentage increase in number of employees, 1870–1890
Boots and shoes	89	3,318	37	174	67
Brick and tile	107	2,749	26	103	150
Chemicals	41	1,272	31	225	1470
Clothing, men's	186	3,239	17	79	−12
Foundry and machine shop	188	8,205	44	161	8
Glass	27	3,578	133	16	107
Hats and caps	79	5,567	70	79	140
Iron and steel[a]	40	4,792	120	114	115
Jewelry	68	2,234	33	−38	17
Leather[b]	62	2,688	43	158	116
Liquors, malt	49	1,121	23	218	122
Petroleum refining[c]	3	2,400	800	NA[d]	NA
Pottery and clay products	49	3,180	65	85	267
Printing and publishing	93	1,061	11	2	691
Rubber and elastic goods	15	1,091	73	NA	NA
Sewing machines	8	3,311	414	NA	NA
Shipbuilding	93	930	10	130	90

	1	2	3	4	5
Textiles					
Total^e	188	24,279	129	63	351
Cotton goods	24	4,836	203	98	150
Dyeing and finishing	18	2,198	122	NA	NA
Silk and silk goods	106	12,549	118	39	514
Woolen goods	27	3,363	125	395	282
Tobacco^f					
Chewing, smoking, snuff	6	3,165	538	5986	6358
Cigars and cigarettes	283	902	3	-50	25
Trunks and valises	15	1,723	115	-3	-30

Source: The 1880 figures reported in columns 1–3 are compiled from U.S. Department of the Interior, *Abstract of the Eleventh Census* (Washington, D.C.: GPO, 1894), Table 3, pp. 154–55. Columns 4–5 are calculated from figures reported in the U.S. Department of the Interior, Ninth Census, Vol. 3, *The Statistics of Wealth and Industry* (Washington, D.C.: GPO, 1872), Tables 8–10, pp. 454, 474, 547–49, and 614, and the U.S. Department of the Interior, Twelfth Census, *Manufactures* (Washington, D.C.: GPO, 1902), Pt. 2, Table 3, pp. 541–42.

[a] The 1870 figures include the following categories: "Iron pigs," "Iron forged and rolled," "steel, cast and not specified."

[b] In 1880 an establishment engaged in both tanning and currying made a separate report for each branch of the industry and was counted twice. Thus the figure given in the census is an overcount and is not reported here. I estimated the number of establishments by taking the midpoint between the 1870 and 1890 figures.

[c] In 1880, "petroleum refining" was the subject of a special report, and figures were not reported in the general statistics of manufactures. Figures reported here are from Bureau of Statistics of Labor and Industries, *Fifth Annual Report, 1882* (Trenton: State of New Jersey, 1882), pp. 50–52; and Bureau of Statistics of Labor and Industries of New Jersey, *Sixth Annual Report, 1883* (Somerville: State of New Jersey, 1883), pp. 133–34.

[d] Figures for 1870 not available. Some of these are new industries.

[e] Total includes "carpets and rugs," "shoddy," "hosiery and knit goods," and "worsted" in addition to those reported separately.

[f] The 1880 figures for tobacco are from the U.S. Department of the Interior, Tenth Census, *Statistics of Manufactures*, Table IV, pp. 151–54. The 1890 figures include a tobacco establishment omitted from the federal census returns. See the New Jersey Bureau of Statistics of Labor and Industries, *Sixteenth Annual Report, 1893* (Somerville: State of New Jersey, 1894), p. 10.

Table 3. Annual incomes of New Jersey workers, sampled in 1884

Income	Number of workers surveyed	Percent total workers surveyed
$500 or less	427	37
$501–$799	505	44
Over $800	212	19

Source: New Jersey Bureau of Statistics of Labor and Industry, *Seventh Annual Report, 1884* (Somerville: State of New Jersey, 1885), pp. 4–65; income categories are from David Montgomery, "Labor in the Industrial Era," in *A History of the American Worker,* ed. Richard B. Morris (Princeton: Princeton University Press, 1983), pp. 96–98.

annual incomes of less than $500, which meant that they made wages that were insufficient to provide a family of five with an adequate diet (the average working-class family had 4.8 members).[12] A majority of workers in industries that relied heavily on less-skilled operatives —textiles, rubber, paper, clothing, and hatmaking—reported to the Bureau of Labor that their yearly wages put them in this poverty category. So, too, did most laborers and miners. Workers with such low incomes generally lived in the most crowded and rundown sections of town, and those among them who were married men sent their wives and children to work.

A slightly larger portion of the workers surveyed by the Bureau— 44 percent—earned between $500 and $799 a year. Most shoeworkers, potters, carriage makers, carpenters, iron workers, machinists, cigarmakers, leatherworkers, and harnessmakers who reported their incomes to the Bureau of Labor fell in this category. Thus, this income group included skilled factory artisans, a few better-paid factory operatives, and deskilled handicraft artisans such as cigarmakers. As long as these workers remained employed and had wives who were able to budget carefully, they could expect to avoid poverty and to enjoy a limited number of life's amenities. Typically, they lived in less-cramped quarters than did their poorer colleagues and sometimes in better neighborhoods as well. Their income would have allowed them to eat cheaper cuts of meat most nights and to enjoy an occasional outing. In years of steady employment, they should also have been able to afford union dues.

Nineteen percent of the workers polled by the Bureau of Labor were paid wages that allowed them to live relatively prosperous lives, often

12. Montgomery's income groups are based on the cost of living in the late 1880s. Given that it was a deflationary era (which means that goods would have cost more in 1884 than at the end of the 1880s), these estimates should not be too far off, even for the earlier period). Average family-size figure is based on statistics given by the NJBSLI, *Eighth Annual Report, 1885,* p. 149.

in neighborhoods that were similar to those inhabited by the lower middle class. A majority of New Jersey's glassworkers and locomotive engineers made such incomes, as did substantial numbers of printers and carpenters. These were the workers who had the greatest financial resources to contribute to the labor movement, but they were also the ones whose living standards set them furthest apart from the growing numbers of less-skilled industrial workers.

Ethnic background and living standards were not the only sources of difference within the New Jersey working class. A great deal of diversity also characterized working conditions. Average factory size in the state's principal industries varied from 3 in cigarmaking to 800 in petroleum refining (see Table 2). Shopfloor practices also varied extensively, even within the same industry. Shoeworkers in one Camden factory, for example, were unionized and received uniform wages, but employers in other Camden factories informed the Bureau of Labor Statistics that there was "no regularity in production or uniformity in price [wages]."[13] Finally, levels of mechanization also differed greatly. In the silk industry, the number of power looms used in weaving tripled between 1875 and 1880 and quadrupled again by 1890, and the machinery for throwing silk was so improved that by 1890 unskilled women and children had replaced men.[14] In hatting, on the other hand, falling profits and an intensely competitive environment made investment in machinery prohibitively expensive for most employers. Instead, manufacturers relied on cutting piece rates and subdividing the labor process to generate profits.

These diverse work situations and living standards were reflected in the remarks made to the Bureau of Labor when in the early 1880s workers were asked about conditions in their trades.[15] Hatters and cigarmakers tended to complain about convict labor, pauper immigration, tenement house work, child labor, and low wages, whereas skilled ironworkers often earned enough to have savings but despaired about long hours, irregular work, rum, and selfishness. Several silk-workers complained about the suffering caused by machinery, one declaring that "improvements should be regulated in such a manner that we will not suffer by their introduction" and another expressing outrage that "although machinery produces more now, we get ten to fifteen percent less in wages than ten years ago."[16] Leather workers, on the other hand, did not mention machinery but did lament

13. NJBSLI, *Seventh Annual Report, 1884*, p. 103.
14. Clark, *History*, 2: 453–54.
15. Remarks culled from NJBSLI, *Sixth Annual Report, 1883*, pp. 113–24; *Seventh Annual Report, 1884*, pp. 237–56; *Eighth Annual Report, 1885*, pp. 214–28.
16. NJBSLI, *Eighth Annual Report, 1885*, p. 226.

subcontracting, long hours, and poor ventilation. Filemakers, tailors, cigarmakers, and laborers all complained about immigrant labor but differed as to what they thought ought to be done about it, a few suggesting that the true conditions of workers in America be publicized so that immigrants would have more realistic expectations, others advocating that immigrant labor be banned altogether, and one ambitious soul urging international unionization. Machinists and blacksmiths, for their part, commonly complained about piecework, long hours, and bad working conditions.

Yet despite different complaints and varying emphases, there were common themes in workers' remarks that cut across skill, industry, and ethnicity. Thus, in their own remarks, workers gave hints of the common grievances and experiences that I suggested in chapter 2 might be used by labor activists to build a unified labor movement. Almost every group of workers objected to the long hours they worked (the average working day was ten hours) and to the irregularity of employment. As one silkworker told the Bureau of Labor,

> We are employed any number of hours daily, from one to thirteen, as there is no limit to a day's work, nor does any one know when his day's work is done. For example, last January and February I worked only about thirty hours per week, and had to provide for our little home; while in May and June I had to work from seventy-four to seventy-eight hours weekly, in hot, stifling rooms, where the thermometer ranged from 90 to 110 degrees. As to our earnings, we are left entirely at the mercy of the boss. When times are dull, our wages are cut down; and if we grumble, we are told that there are plenty waiting to take our place. In busy times we are worse off yet, for then we are told that we are making too much time and money. We should not be allowed to work longer than a regular day, say of eight hours.[17]

Most also complained about wages, although they sometimes differed in the reasons they gave for their disgruntlement: a hand at a rolling mill told the investigator that "poverty is degrading," whereas a hatter complained that he was unable to clothe his family as it should be done, and a filemaker asserted that his wages were not a "fair" share of profits.[18] Moreover, complaints were frequently heard about employers' efforts to redefine work and pay practices. The specific problem in each industry varied, but there was a common frustration at workers' subordination to the will of employers. Child labor and

17. NJBSLI, *Seventh Annual Report, 1884*, p. 243.
18. NJBSLI, *Sixth Annual Report, 1883*, pp. 114 and 123; *Seventh Annual Report, 1884*, p. 224.

immigrant labor were also frequently condemned. Almost everyone wanted compulsory education, as a way both to ensure the education of their own children and to keep low-wage child labor out of the workplace. Immigration, too, was a big concern, although there was also variation in how much hostility was directed at immigrants themselves, as opposed to at those who misled them about the true conditions of labor in America or at those who used them to cut wages.

These common themes were the ones that Knights' activists tried to build on when they set about organizing New Jersey's diverse labor force. Using the program and ideology discussed in the preceding chapter, they attempted to address workers' practical concerns, as well as their more diffuse unease about the direction of society. Labor organizers counseled workers to ignore the differences in skill, work experience, and background that four decades of rapid industrialization had wrought, urging them to concentrate instead on the common difficulties and inequities that the new industrial system imposed on them all.

The Legal and Political Setting

As Knights activists attempted to build a labor movement that united New Jersey's diverse group of workers, they found that their room for maneuver, strategic choices, and, ultimately, fate were all shaped by the political and legal environment in which they operated. That this was the case was not always obvious as elected leaders regularly espoused a laissez-faire ideology when it came to economic and social issues. But, ideology aside, there is no getting around the fact that the state dictated many of the rules by which workers' battles with employers were fought, both on and off the shopfloor. Its role was clearly visible when government officials authorized the use of local policemen, state militias, or federal troops to protect strikebreakers, as occurred episodically in Gilded Age New Jersey.[19] Its role was more

19. The national guard or local police were used to protect strikebreakers several times in Gilded Age New Jersey. During the railroad strikes in 1877, the governor of New Jersey, Joseph D. Bedle, used several armed regiments of the national guard to ensure that strikers did not stop the trains in New Jersey. Local police were used to protect strikebreakers in the course of strikes by Paterson silkworkers in August 1880, January 1884, and March 1894; by Standard Oil workers in Bayonne in May 1882 and August 1886; by employees at the Singer Sewing Machine Company in Elizabeth in March 1886; by coal handlers in several communities in January 1887; by Newark steelworkers in April 1888; by Newark coach drivers in October 1889; by Newark sewing machine workers in August 1893; and by Passaic woolworkers in January 1895. See Vecoli, *People of New Jersey*, p. 85; *New York Times*, Aug. 29, 1880; *New York Tribune*, Jan. 19, 1884; *New*

subtle when the state legislature decided against using its authority over corporate charters as a way to regulate business activities. But in both cases state actions had important consequences for the labor movement. Thus, to understand the Knights' tactics and achievements in New Jersey, it is important to understand something of the American state in this period.

Over the past decade, much has been written about the peculiar structure of the American state in the nineteenth century. No matter whether it is viewed from the perspective of England or France—or, for that matter, of any other European nation—state power was remarkably diffuse. There was no central authority; instead power was divided among autonomous local, provincial, and national governments, and within each of these governments, in turn, authority was shared by legislative, executive, and judicial officials.[20] No other nation had anywhere near such a fragmented structure; it was, as Ira Katznelson notes, "the world's first political system of participatory federalism."[21]

York Times, Mar. 9, 1894 (all excerpted in the Gutman Papers, New York Public Library); *Bayonne Herald,* May 13, 1882, and Aug. 28, 1886 (both excerpted in the WPA Papers, New Jersey State Archives,); *Elizabeth Daily Journal,* Mar. 17, 1886; *New York Tribune,* Jan. 16, 1887; *Newark Evening News,* Apr. 4, 1888, and Oct. 10, 1889; *New York Tribune,* Aug. 29, 1893, and Mar. 9, 1894 (excerpted in the Gutman Papers).

Sheriffs and mayors were sometimes reluctant to call out the police to protect strike-breakers. They discovered that doing so increased their vulnerability at the polls and that it was also periodically ineffective because the police were sometimes the kin and neighbors of the strikers. Thus, they occasionally refused to call out the police, even when factory owners requested protection. For this reason, employers began to rely more on Pinkerton guards. This, too, could have political consequences for local politicians because they were usually asked to deputize the Pinkertons. Sometimes, as a way of giving something to each side, they also deputized strikers. This happened, for example, in the strike against Clark Thread Works in Newark in February 1891. (See Box 15, Gutman Papers, which includes excerpts from many newspapers about the Clark strike.)

More often, however, the arrival of the Pinkertons spelled disaster for strikers. (It certainly did during the strike by ironworkers in Millville in September 1886, and it contributed to the failure of the coal handlers' strike in January 1887.) Thus, beginning in 1886, the State Labor Congress began to push for legislation that would outlaw the deputization or use of Pinkertons during strikes. However, workers could not get the legislature to pass such a law. (See *New York Times,* Sept. 14, 1886; *Newark Evening News,* Aug. 14, 1886; *New York Tribune,* Jan. 16, 1887; and the "Report of the Eighth Annual Session of the Federation of Trades and Labor Unions of the State of New Jersey Held in New Brunswick, August 30, 1886," Rutgers University Archives.)

20. Martin Shefter, "Trade Unions and Political Machines: The Organization and Disorganization of the American Working Class in the Late 19th Century," in *Working-Class Formation,* ed. Katznelson and Zolberg, p. 209.

21. Ira Katznelson, "Working-Class Formation and the State: Nineteenth-Century England in American Perspective," in *Bringing the State Back In,* ed. Peter Evans, Dietrich Rueschemeyer, and Theda Skocpol (Cambridge: Cambridge University Press, 1985), p. 273.

An unusual set of institutional arrangements evolved for managing this fragmentation. Social scientists have offered a number of formulations that attempt to capture the nature of these arrangements, but none has proved as useful or influential as the one coined by Stephen Skowronek: a state of "courts and parties."[22] The courts interpreted and administered the law of the land, while political parties staffed and coordinated the nation's political institutions.[23] The legal system and the party system most profoundly affected the strategic choices of the labor movement.

The legal system in nineteenth-century New Jersey offered few protections from the insecurities of wage labor or from the hazards of factory employment. There were no minimum wage laws, no health and safety regulations, no laws specifying the conditions that constituted "just causes" for termination. In New Jersey, a law was passed in 1851 that prohibited the employment of children and declared ten hours as the standard working day, but both prohibitions were widely disregarded, as the law included no enforcement mechanism.[24] Thus, if workers wanted to enforce this law or to impose any new restrictions on employers' prerogatives, they were obliged to rely on their own collective actions. However, workers who decided to go this route by organizing unions and striking often ran afoul of state conspiracy laws.[25] Throughout the nineteenth century, conspiracy laws were the principal means by which labor was regulated, not only in New Jersey but across the nation. State courts differed, however, both among themselves and over time in how broadly they interpreted conspiracy statutes. After the Civil War, as workers came to rely on more formal mechanisms to pursue their union and strike goals, they increasingly came into sharper conflict with the courts.[26] New Jersey courts were especially sweeping in their application of conspiracy laws to meet heightened worker militancy in the immediate postwar years. In one often-cited 1867 case, they ruled against several employees who

22. Stephen Skowronek, *Building a New American State* (Cambridge: Cambridge University Press, 1982), chap. 2.

23. Shefter, "Trade Unions," p. 209; Skowronek, *Building*, pp. 25–29.

24. NJBSLI, *Eighth Annual Report, 1885*, pp. 263–64.

25. Recall the experience of the journeymen tailors during the agitation of the 1830s. See Chapter 1 in this book.

26. Traditional accounts of the development of labor law often claim that the *Commonwealth v. Hunt* decision put an end to conspiracy convictions in 1842. However, considerable documentation now exists that demonstrates that, although conspiracy indictments declined (along with union activity) in the 1840s and 1850s, they resumed again when industrial conflict increased after the Civil War. See Christopher L. Tomlins, *The State and the Unions* (Cambridge: Cambridge University Press, 1985), pp. 44–49; Montgomery, *Beyond Equality*, pp. 146–47; Hattam, "Economic Visions," pp. 106–10.

had threatened to quit as a body if their employer did not discharge nonunion members. Such behavior was intolerable, argued the Chief Justice of the New Jersey Supreme Court: it constituted "an unwarrantable interference" in their employer's affairs, one that "would disarrange his business."[27] Similar rulings were made in other conspiracy cases that same year, greatly increasing the risks involved with union activities.

The legal doctrine that regulated business activity in New Jersey was very different, and in the closing decades of the nineteenth century it came to be applied in such a way as to extend employers' power over both labor and the legislative branch of the government. Corporate charters were the primary means by which government regulated business in the nineteenth century. The authority to issue these charters was vested in state legislatures, as was the ability to repeal them or modify their terms. Formally, then, states had the authority to sanction or condemn a wide range of business activities, including mergers, trusts, and alterations in capitalization. This was a potentially very effective tool for proscribing corporate activity. Many states had used it earlier in the nineteenth century, imposing various restrictions on corporations in the name of public interest. After the Civil War, public officials in many states again turned to corporate charters as a way of restricting trusts and other forms of large-scale enterprise.[28]

By the late nineteenth century, however, efforts to use incorporation powers as a way to regulate business activity ran counter to the direction in which courts were moving in their interpretations of property rights and in which many states were moving in their efforts to attract investment. Beginning in the late 1860s, prominent jurists, most notably U.S. Supreme Court Justice Stephen J. Field, began to reinterpret the "sacred right" to private property in such a way as to make it unconstitutional for state legislatures to limit the rights of employers to do what they pleased with their property.[29] The definition of property was expanded so that it went beyond tangible proprietary things, such as factories and mines, and came to include intangible things, such as "value" in the marketplace. Potential earning power or profitability slowly came to be considered property by the courts, and hence any

27. NJBSLI, *Eighth Annual Report, 1885*, p. 275.

28. Tomlins, *State and Unions*, pp. 21–30. For a more extended discussion of these matters, see also Morton J. Horwitz, *The Transformation of American Law, 1780–1860* (Cambridge: Harvard University Press, 1977); and Lawrence M. Friedman, *A History of American Law*, 2d ed. (New York: Simon and Schuster/ Touchstone Books, 1985), chaps. 3 and 8.

29. Forbath, "Ambiguities"; Tomlins, *State and Unions*, esp. pp. 27–28.

state regulation of industry that diminished profits became a potential "taking" or "deprivation of property" subject to judicial invalidation. This was a profound change, and it had enormous consequences for both workers and the larger society. One way of understanding its importance is to compare it with workers' efforts to define their skill as property in the 1830s. Such a definition would have entailed a fundamental reinterpretation of property rights on a similar scale to that which occurred in the late nineteenth century. The difference is, of course, that workers were completely unsuccessful in their efforts, whereas the new corporate attorneys that cited Justice Field and his ilk slowly convinced the courts to accept their redefinition.[30]

Competition among states for investment after the Civil War also clashed with attempts to use incorporation laws to restrict business practices. New Jersey had an additional incentive in this competition: the state was financed almost entirely by corporate fees and railroad taxes. After the Civil War, when the cost of running the state government exceeded tax revenues, the governor and legislators began to search for new ways to raise funds, and they arrived at the solution of making New Jersey's incorporation laws so attractive that large numbers of companies would come to the state for charters.[31] Thus, New Jersey came to play a major part in aiding the creation of trusts in the 1880s. Further, when a nationwide revolt against trusts swept the country in the late 1880s, and state after state passed antitrust legislation, the New Jersey legislature remained stubbornly committed to its course. It not only refused a bid by New Jerseyans to outlaw trusts; it modified the state's general incorporation law to permit formation of holding companies.[32] Especially after the U.S. Congress passed the Sherman Antitrust Act in 1890, the New Jersey holding company replaced the trust as the legal arrangement used to merge a number of single-unit enterprises operating facilities in several states into a single, large, consolidated enterprise.[33] For these actions, the state earned various unflattering nicknames: "The State of Camden and Amboy" (a railroad company), "The Home of the Trusts," and, most famous, "A Traitor State."

30. Indeed, this redefinition was the basis by which the courts eventually came to recognize corporations as legal "persons," protected by the due process clause of the Fourteenth Amendment.

31. John W. Cadman, Jr., *The Corporation in New Jersey* (Cambridge: Harvard University Press, 1949), p. 449.

32. Thomas Flemming, *New Jersey: A Bicentennial History* (New York: Norton, 1977), pp. 147–48.

33. Chandler, *Visible Hand*, pp. 319–20.

Thus, while making legal decisions that significantly limited workers' collective ability to pursue their interests, New Jersey courts, along
with the state legislature and federal courts, were also making decisions that significantly increased employers' room to maneuver in their
conflicts with workers. New Jersey's labor press frequently noted and
condemned this disparity. In 1886, for example, the *Trenton Sunday
Advertiser*, a pro-Knights newspaper, commented ruefully on a court
case in which a union boycot was declared illegal "because it tended
to injure a man's income." The judge, declared the *Advertiser*, "forgot
to consider that a workingman's wages is his income as much as the
profit made by a business, and yet capitalists are not amenable to law
when they combine to clip wages by reductions, store orders, scrip or
screens." [34]

Knights activists in New Jersey wanted to change this state of affairs; early on, they began to push for laws that would alter the hostile legal environment in which they found themselves. Since male
workers had voting rights, there were two obvious political strategies that activists might choose to pursue this goal: they could create
a new political party to push class-specific legislation, or they could
work within the established multiclass parties to accomplish legal reform. For a number of reasons, the second strategy was less risky
and difficult than the first. To understand why, consider the nature of
partisan loyalty and electoral politics in late-nineteenth-century New
Jersey. New Jersey was among the last of the states to adopt white
manhood suffrage, but, even so, most male workers had the franchise
by the 1830s. Thus, for the first several decades during which they
had voting rights, New Jersey workers made up only a small minority
of the state's population, and one disproportionately located in a few
urban areas. To achieve any of their most important political goals—
changing the state's conspiracy laws or passing shorter-hours legislation—would have necessitated winning a majority of votes across the
state, something workers had little hope of accomplishing outside of
the major political parties. Thus, even workers who had a high level
of class consciousness joined one of the two major parties, sometimes
with the hope of pushing labor reform by allying with reformist elements in the middle class and sometimes merely to deal with nonlabor
concerns. As a result, most workers adopted partisan identities that
had little to do with their status as workers. These partisan identities became increasingly salient over time, enhanced by the fact that
party organizations were much more stable than labor organizations.

34. *Trenton Sunday Advertiser*, Jul. 25, 1886.

Other features of the political system further solidified partisan identities: parties tended to recruit members and to build loyalty by stressing ethnic solidarities and cultural interests (for example, temperance, Sabbath observance), they instituted patronage and informal welfare programs when in office, and they were highly effective at grafting the rituals and symbols of mass democracy onto partisan politics.[35] By the Gilded Age, partisanship was deeply embedded in New Jersey, and the working class was divided by competing party loyalties.[36]

These partisan loyalties were expressed in an electoral context that was very different from the one we are familiar with today. First of all, almost everyone eligible to vote did so. Average turnout in New Jersey in the 1880s was 82 percent of the electorate.[37] Second, most political offices were closely contested. For example, the governor's race in New Jersey was never won with more than 54 percent of the vote in any election between 1869 and 1892.[38] In the legislature, the party balance was also very close, with control over each house shifting frequently. Third, elections were an important form of public entertainment. They routinely involved huge rallies, torchlight processions, long, patriotic orations (through which everyone apparently sat), and a great deal of hoopla. Election Day itself was a holiday, and many people treated voting as an all-day social affair, going to the polls early, then gossiping with their friends as they followed the returns (sometimes gambling on them as well).[39]

Political parties were responsible for administering elections as well as for running political campaigns. As today, they were responsible for organizing conventions, unifying the party behind a single slate, and raising money, but they also actually conducted the elections, right down to printing and distributing the ballots. As reformers often lamented, this arrangement sometimes facilitated fraud and corruption.[40] More significant, however, for anyone interested in third-party

35. Bridges, "Becoming American," pp. 157–96; David Brody, "Labor Movement," in *Encyclopedia of American Political History*, ed. Jack P. Greene (New York: Scribner's, 1984), pp. 709–27, esp. pp. 711–13.

36. On the partisanship of New Jersey workers, see Reynolds, *Testing Democracy*, chap. 2; on workers' partisanship more generally, see Michael E. McGerr, *The Decline of Popular Politics* (New York: Oxford University Press, 1986), chaps. 1–2.

37. Calculated from Reynolds's estimates, in *Testing Democracy*, p. 177, table A.1.

38. Richard P. McCormick, "An Historical Overview," in *Politics in New Jersey*, ed. Alan Rosenthal and John Blydenburgh (Rutgers, N.J.: The Eagleton Institute of Politics, 1975), pp. 1–30, esp. p. 8.

39. An excellent description of election day can be found in Reynolds, *Testing Democracy*, chap. 1.

40. On vote buying, ballot fraud, and other types of corruption in Gilded Age New Jersey, see McCormick, "Historical Overview," p. 9, and Reynolds, *Testing Democracy*, chap. 1.

politics, it also made it very expensive and difficult to mount a political campaign.

Thus, in the Gilded Age, at a time when four decades of rapid economic development had added significant numbers of industrial wage earners to the voting rolls, thereby strengthening the potential political position of the working class, the party system made it risky for labor unions to wade too deeply into the political fray. Because partisan loyalties went deep, any discussion of independent political action ran the danger of dividing union members into hostile camps. (This is why so many nineteenth-century unions outlawed partisan politics at union meetings.) Moreover, mounting a third-party challenge, especially for higher offices, was a daunting proposition, beyond the resources of most labor organizations.[41]

In sum, the party system in the late nineteenth century tended to shape the strategies of the labor movement in two ways. First, it put enormous obstacles in the path of labor leaders who considered forays into third-party politics. As David Brody has remarked, workers in the United States were denied not the right but the room to participate.[42] Second, elections were closely contested, regularly won by only a small proportion of the vote, and this encouraged labor activists to try to play the two parties against each other to garner support for labor reform.

Taken together, then, courts and parties had a powerful institutional effect on the labor movement. Both conspiracy laws and the courts' gradual extension of property rights increased the difficulties and risks entailed in unionization and strike activity.[43] However, efforts to advance working-class interests in the political sphere rather than in the industrial sphere soon led workers into even more dangerous waters. There were gains to be made by lobbying because of the highly competitive electoral situation, but these gains were limited to the extent that neither party wanted to become so identified with the working class as to lose its multiclass character. But if workers turned to third-party politics instead, they faced the very real hazard of dividing and ultimately disorganizing the labor movement. Thus, the distinc-

41. Moreover, balloting was rarely secret. Thus, anyone casting a vote for a labor candidate ran the risk not only of being ostracized by more traditional friends but of intimidation by an employer.

42. Brody, *Labor Movement*, p. 713.

43. Collective action was doubly difficult when both conspiracy laws and extended property rights for employers coexisted, but each alone also exerted a powerful influence. Indeed, once New Jersey workers had successfully launched a battle to repeal the conspiracy laws, it was the extension of property rights that was to play the most significant role.

tive American state presented workers with very difficult strategic choices—and some rather unyielding political realities.

The New Jersey Knights

We have seen that industrial development in New Jersey created opportunities for expanded organization of the working class while leaving intact crucial divisions that could easily undermine efforts to build the sense of common plight required for broader unionization. In addition, we have also seen that the nineteenth-century state of "courts and parties" put significant obstacles in the path of expanded working-class organization, on both the industrial and political front. What strategies did Knights activists in New Jersey pursue in light of the opportunities and constraints they faced? And how well did they succeed at organizing New Jersey's diverse labor force?

The history of Knights organization in New Jersey began quite early. Skilled stonecutters initiated one of the first non-Philadelphia locals in Trenton in late 1873.[44] Four locals were organized in Camden soon after, as was a district assembly in 1874. But before long the deepening depression weakened or destroyed these assemblies, and although workers in a few communities made efforts to start new locals in the mid-1870s, few survived very long. Only later when the economy began to recover were sturdier locals initiated. By 1879, local assemblies were active in twelve of New Jersey's forty-nine cities and towns. The majority of these were located in the glass towns of southern New Jersey, many of which, as noted, had begun to expand rapidly in this period. Glassworkers were highly skilled and well-paid workers, and they saw in the Knights a chance to pursue traditional craft goals in the context of a growing national organization.[45] In central and northern New Jersey, mixed assemblies were more often the first Knights locals to be initiated. Available evidence suggests that these early mixed assemblies, although formally open to all, were composed largely of skilled craft workers drawn from a variety of trades. The workers in

44. There are discrepancies in the historical record over the month in which this assembly was founded. The NJBSLI, *Tenth Annual Report, 1887*, p. 16, claims that the local was organized in 1873, which would have made it the first local initiated outside of Pennsylvania. In *The Labor Movement in the United States, 1860–1895: A Study in Democracy* p. 30, Ware states that it was probably formed in January 1874, which means that it was founded the same month as the local assembly of gold beaters (LA 28) in New York City.

45. Dennis Zembala, "Glassworkers in the Knights of Labor: Technology, Labor, and the Roots of Modernism," paper presented to the Knights of Labor Centennial Symposium, Chicago, May 17–19, 1979.

Table 4. Knights of Labor assemblies in New Jersey: Year founded by organizing strategy

| | Organizing strategy | | | | | | | |
	Craft[a]	%[b]	Sectional assembly of less-skilled workers	%	Quasi-industrial	%	"Mixed"	%
Year founded	Number	%[b]	Number	%	Number	%	Number	%
1873–78	7	70	0	0	2	20	1	10
1879–82	10	29	8	23	5	14	12	34
1883–85	20	35	26	46	7	12	4	7
1886	36	19	60	31	72	38	24	13
1887–95	10	34	12	41	7	24	0	0
Total	83		106		93		41	

Note: Includes local assemblies that organized in towns with populations exceeding 2,500. See text (below and p. 148) for definition of organizing strategies.

[a] Includes six "preceptories" of LA 300.

[b] Percentages do not always add to 100 due to rounding error.

these early assemblies often went on to form new locals better tailored to their situations. Local Assembly 1288 of Paterson, for example, "attracted" workers of "similar trades," who in turn left to form a variety of trade locals.[46] A few of these mixed locals appear to have also functioned something like district assemblies, coordinating activities with the non-Knights craft locals that began to reorganize in the late 1870s and agitating for the creation of city trades councils.[47]

Over the next few years, the Knights grew slowly but steadily. The character of this growth can be discerned from the figures in Table 4, which presents a breakdown of local assemblies organized by year. Trade assemblies are classified according to their organizing strategy: If the local enrolled only skilled workers, it is classified as a craft assembly; if it organized unskilled and semiskilled workers but no craftsmen, it is characterized as a sectional assembly of less-skilled workers; if it organized across the skill divide or was open explicitly to all workers in a factory or industry, it is classified as a quasi-industrial assembly. This table suggests that the earliest membership gains in New Jersey, as elsewhere, tended to be among skilled craft workers.[48] If we

46. NJBSLI, *Tenth Annual Report, 1887*, p. 174.

47. Both LA 1364 of Newark and LA 1362 of Trenton performed many of the functions of district assemblies.

48. On the early organization of craft workers outside of New Jersey, see Garlock, "Structural Analysis"; and Fink, *Workingmen's Democracy*.

had more information on the occupational composition of the mixed assemblies in their early years, the prominence of craft workers would probably be even more conspicuous because, as we saw above, many of the early mixed assemblies were actually aggregations of skilled craftsmen.

In the glass-producing towns, Knights members undertook important strikes over scrip payment in 1880, but, for the most part, the Order concentrated on legal reform rather than industrial strife in the early 1880s.[49] Representatives of fourteen local assemblies and ten reorganized craft locals met in October 1879 to found what would prove to be the nation's first state labor federation, the New Jersey State Labor Congress.[50] The purpose of the Congress was to give organized labor a political voice, primarily by educating the public, canvassing legislative candidates, and endorsing only those politicians who would agree to support labor legislation. The Congress concentrated its efforts on four reforms: an end to the use of convict labor, the elimination of wages paid in scrip, the abolition of child labor, and the repeal of conspiracy laws. As we have seen, the party balance was very close in these years, and the Labor Congress achieved at least modest success in all four areas. Prison labor was restricted in 1881; it was the easiest victory because it had the support of many manufacturers who resented cheap competition almost as much as workers did. Scrip wages and child labor proved more difficult. Scrip payment was formally abolished in both 1880 and 1881; but each time glass manu-

49. Hattam contends that the Knights of Labor and the trade unions had sharply contrasting views of the necessity of legal protections for collective action and hence that the courts played a differential role in the development of the two organizations. In particular, she maintains that the Knights did not put much effort into repealing conspiracy legislation or obtaining legislation that would allow for the incorporation of labor unions but that the trade unions did. Knights leaders, she suggests, believed that once the country was returned to the republican path, protections like those involved in the repeal of conspiracy laws or the incorporation of trade unions would be unnecessary; thus there was no reason to push such legislation. The actions of the Knights in New Jersey call her argument into question. They were instrumental in creating the State Labor Congress, which pushed for both of these measures. See Hattam, "Economic Visions," p. 99 and passim.

On the strikes over scrip payment, see NJBSLI, *Tenth Annual Report, 1887*, pp. 163 and 165.

50. Ira Kerrison Papers, Box 1, Organization—2nd Draft Folder. In 1883, when the delegates to the Labor Congress decided to make the organization a permanent body, its name was changed to the Federation of Organized Trades and Labor Unions of the State of New Jersey. Because its name is identical to that of the national FOTLU, the precursor to the AFL, some readers might assume that the trade unions were the dominant force in the creation of the Labor Congress. As Leo Troy, *Organized Labor in New Jersey* (Princeton: Van Nostrand, 1965), pp. 52–57, makes clear, such was not the case. The New Jersey group was not affiliated with the national federation.

facturers successfully blocked the inclusion of enforceable sanctions in the legislation.[51] In 1883 a new child labor law was passed, and it provided for the appointment of a factory inspector to help enforce the law. However, in an era without automobiles, it proved impossible for one inspector to cover the whole state. Moreover, employers and parents were openly evasive and uncooperative.[52] The inefficacy of these two reforms led workers to complain about dishonest and double-dealing politicians.[53] Certainly, many of these complaints were justified; but of equal importance was the state's limited capacity to administer many of the laws passed in these years. Here, in other words, the labor movement ran up against not only the limitations of its ability to push working-class legislation through the existing party system but also the state's administrative weakness.

The Congress's most important legislative victory was the repeal of the conspiracy law in 1883.[54] In the words of one legal historian, this was the "Magna Carta" for trade unionism in New Jersey. Although it was still legal for employers to dismiss workers for joining a union, or to require "iron-clad" or "yellow-dog" contracts (in which employees had to agree not to join unions as a condition of employment), this law significantly decreased the risks of collective action.[55] Combined with labor's frustration over its limited success on the reform front, it helped to spur organizational gains and eventually helped to encourage workers to rely more heavily on strikes to achieve their goals.[56]

51. Indeed, the practice persisted at least until the turn of the century. See Philip Charles Newman, *The Labor Legislation of New Jersey* (Washington, D.C.: American Council on Public Affairs, 1943), pp. 65–68.

52. Ibid., p. 113.

53. NJBSLI, *Seventh Annual Report, 1884*, pp. 237–56; *Eighth Annual Report, 1885*, pp. 214–28.

54. It permitted workers "by peaceful means, [to] persuad[e], advis[e], or encourag[e] other persons to enter into any combination for organizing, leaving, or entering into the employment of other persons." Quoted in Newman, *Labor Legislation*, p. 25.

55. Over time, the state courts would gradually curtail labor's right to organize by limiting the definition of "peaceful means" and "lawful ends." And, as in other states, New Jersey courts would eventually rely on labor injunctions to limit workers' rights to organize and strike. See Newman, *Labor Legislation*, pp. 25–37, and Hattam, "Economic Visions."

56. The Labor Congress did not cease pushing legal reform. At each convention, delegates submitted labor measures that the Congress then endorsed or voted down. Resolutions submitted by Knights delegates included a weekly wage bill, ballot reform, a bill to incorporate trade unions, and an anti-Pinkerton bill. See "Report of the Sixth Annual Session of the Federation of Organized Trades and Labor Unions," October 6, 1884, pp. 6–7; "Report of the Eighth Annual Session of the Federation of Organized Trades and Labor Unions," August 1886, and newspaper accounts of the New Jersey State Labor Federation found in Boxes 1 and 2, Irvine Kerrison Papers, Rutgers University Library. (The State Labor Congress adopted a formal constitution and established itself as a permanent organization at its third annual meeting in 1883; upon doing so,

After the repeal of the conspiracy law, the pace of Knights' organizing accelerated. Skilled workers continued to organize new craft assemblies, but, most significantly, increasing numbers of locals were organized whose membership included less-skilled workers. As Table 4 demonstrates, nearly three dozen such locals were instituted between 1883 and 1885. In 1886, an average of two per week were founded.

Strike activity also increased dramatically. Buoyed by membership gains, encouraged by the national Knights' victories over Jay Gould, and freed from the threat of conspiracy prosecution, Knights members and their local officials grew less cautious about industrial strife. In the charged and highly politicized atmosphere of 1886, workers began to strike over a much wider range of grievances than they had in the past. They now struck to assert collective control over the employment relation (for equalization of pay, against the use of boycotted material, for reinstating employees, etc.) and in sympathy with other workers. They also used strikes to prevent employers from backsliding on agreements made with their employees. And, of course, they struck for the eight-hour day. Overall, the dominant tactics of the movement were shifting dramatically, away from education and lobbying to direct action. And direct action worked—strikers won their demands in 75 percent of the establishments in which they struck in 1886.[57]

Workers began to engage in boycotts, too, often in conjunction with strikes over union recognition. In East Orange, for example, the Seabury and Johnson pharmaceutical company (the predecessor to Johnson & Johnson) fired twenty female employees in April 1886 for joining the Knights, and the Essex County Trades Assembly organized a boycott against the company's products in response. Similar boycotts were called in support of rubber and brickworkers in Trenton and women hat trimmers in Orange.[58]

This conflict soon spilled over into the political arena. This time, however, many Knights members were impatient with lobbying and turned insistently to putting their candidates in office. This was a con-

---

it also changed its name to the New Jersey State Federation of Organized Trades and Labor Unions. It was not affiliated with the national FOTLU, and it did not identify until later with the craft unionist point of view.)

57. U.S. Bureau of Labor, *The Third Annual Report*, pp. 930–31.

58. NJBSLI, *Ninth Annual Report, 1886*, pp. 212–14; *Trenton Sunday Advertiser*, Dec. 12, 1886; David Bensman, *Practice*, pp. 131–50. One might quarrel with my categorization of the Orange Hatters' Boycott as a Knights effort. Bensman's account of the conflict centers on the role of the hat finishers, who had affiliated with the Knights in 1885 but who remained staunchly craft conscious. He does not point out that the trimmers' union over which the conflict originally broke out was in fact a local assembly of the Knights of Labor. See Garlock, *Guide*, p. 284.

troversial move in many communities where labor activists still feared that partisan politics would fracture labor unity. Proponents of the electoral strategy frequently concentrated their efforts on contesting one or two seats, rather than attempting to organize a whole slate of candidates. In some cases, they also took advantage of the greater financial and organizational resources of the major parties by preparing "pasters," small slips of paper printed with the name of the labor candidate that could be glued over the name of either a Democratic or Republican candidate on the preprinted ticket.[59] Important labor party campaigns were waged in Newark and Paterson in 1886, and in 1887 the use of Pinkerton guards and a bitter strike defeat led directly to an independent labor slate in Bayonne and Jersey City.[60] In 1886 the hatters of Orange organized a workingmen's party after the failure of the boycott in support of the hat trimmers. Similarly, a strike defeat led Passaic Knights to ally with the Democratic Party in 1886 and then to field an independent ticket in 1887.[61]

59. This happened in Newark when Knights activist Henry Beckmeyer ran for Congress in 1886. In fact, Reynolds reports that Democratic party workers carried the pasters as well. Labor candidates also printed up ballots that were exactly like the Republican and Democratic ticket except that they inserted the name of Beckmeyer rather than of the regular party candidate. Reynolds, pp. 45–46; *Newark Evening News*, Oct. 21, 1886; Nov. 3, 1886.

60. In Paterson, two state assemblymen and a city alderman were elected (*Trenton Sunday Advertiser*, Nov. 28, 1886; Herbert Gutman, *Work, Culture, and Society in Industrializing America* [New York: Vintage, 1977], p. 278). The election in Newark ended in a costly defeat for labor (NJBSLI, *Eighth Annual Report, 1886*, pp. 203–5; *Trenton Sunday Advertiser*, Nov. 7, 1886).

In Jersey City, the United Labor Party was successful in electing some municipal officials (five—out of twenty—freeholders and a fire commissioner) and in defeating "the Pinkerton thug nominee" for police commissioner who had sworn in the Pinkertons in the course of the coal handlers' strike, electing instead a Labor-Democratic candidate (*John Swinton's Paper*, Apr. 3, 1887; Apr. 10, 1887; Apr. 17, 1887). *John Swinton's Paper* declared, "The Labor men have shown that, while they may not in all cases be able to elect their candidates, they can defeat either party" (*John Swinton's Paper*, Apr. 24, 1887). In the case of at least one office, there were accusations of fraud (*John Swinton's Paper*, May 8, 1887).

61. In Orange, the Workingmen's party won numerous local offices, including council seats in two wards and positions among the assessors and on the school board. Their candidate for state assembly lost by only four votes. See Bensman, *Practice*, p. 147.

In Passaic, a temporary alliance between the Democratic party and a coalition of labor organizations in Passaic County, including the Knights, won victories in the legislative contest of November 1886. Then, following deterioration of this relationship, the labor coalition fielded an independent ticket in the general election of 1887, contributing to the resurgence of Republican candidates at the polls. See Ebner, "Passaic," pp. 135–36.

Fink, *Workingmen's Democracy*, pp. 28–29, presents a table of Knights of Labor political tickets, 1885–88. His table does not include Passaic or Orange. In the case of Orange, it might be argued that the political impetus came from the hatters' unions rather than from the Knights. After all, two members of the hat finishers' union (along with a foreman at a hat factory) were the organizers of the Workingmen's Party (Bensman, *Practice*,

Who were the members who joined the Order's ranks in 1886 and 1887, swelling the tide of strikes and independent political action? Based on a canvass of the state's labor organizations, the New Jersey Bureau of Statistics of Labor and Industries, reported that the Order had 40,275 members in New Jersey in early 1887.[62] Most (71.2 percent) were employed in manufacturing. A wide range of industries were represented, with the greatest numbers of Knights members engaged in making machines and metal products, textiles, leather, pottery, and apparel (see Table 5). In terms of ethnicity, there were almost equal numbers of native- and foreign-born workers (see Table 6). The Order was therefore somewhat unrepresentative of the working-class population in the Garden State, which was 68 percent native-born. In part this probably reflects the Knights' success at recruiting less-skilled workers, who were more likely to be foreign-born. Irish immigrants, who were generally less skilled than either British or German workers, joined the Knights in especially large numbers; they were twice as numerous in the Knights as in the larger working class, and British and German workers were about one and one-half times more numerous in the Knights than in the labor force. Finally, the Knights were less successful at organizing women than immigrant workers; although women accounted for almost 20 percent of the wage-earning population, they only made up 11 percent of the Knights' membership. And the Order actively excluded the small number of Chinese workers who settled in the Garden State.[63]

As for overall influence, in 1887 roughly 8 percent of all New Jer-

---

p. 142). However, the hat finishers were affiliated with the Knights at this time; in addition, several local hatting assemblies were active in Orange. Fink's table also reports that a successful Knights-sponsored campaign was waged in Washington, New Jersey. I do not mention this instance because there is evidence that this campaign may have been more of a temperance campaign than a labor contest (*Journal of United Labor*, Apr. 30, 1887).

62. NJBSLI, *Tenth Annual Report, 1887*, pp. 15–16, reports that the combined membership of the Knights and trade unions in 1887 was 57,962. But it goes on to cover several caveats. First, the Bureau points out that this figure includes workers who held membership in both organizations, a group the NJBSLI estimates at 5,000. Then it notes that, given the troubles of the Knights, the figures are probably more accurate for late 1886 or early 1887 than they are for mid-1887. It states that 53,000 is a good estimate of the total size of the labor movement in New Jersey in late 1886 or early 1887. I use the 40,172 figure the bureau reports for late 1886-early 1887. The figure includes dual members.

63. NJBSLI, *Ninth Annual Report, 1886*, pp. 202–03. In 1885, District Assembly 51 in Newark negotiated with a laundry owner in Belleville to have him discharge thirty-five Chinese men and hire white women in their stead. The labor activist who reported this event to the Labor Bureau seemed to have had somewhat conflicting feelings about it because he noted that "no charge was made against the Chinese of working under wages; on the contrary, they were said to stick up for good wages in true American fashion." Clearly, there were limits to solidarity, especially when it came to the Chinese.

Table 5. Knights of Labor membership in New Jersey by industry, 1887

	Number of Assemblies	Percent of Total	Membership	Percent of Total
Trade Assemblies				
Manufacturing	*140*	*59.1*	*24,658*	*61.2*
Machinery and metal products	38	16.0	6,750	16.8
Textiles	27	11.4	6,598	16.4
Leather and leather products	15	6.3	2,907	7.2
Clay and stone products	13	5.5	2,665	6.6
Food, drink, tobacco	11	4.6	867	2.2
Apparel, including hats	10	4.2	1,914	4.7
Glass	9	3.8	418	1.0
Chemical and rubber	5	2.1	757	1.9
Transportation equipment	4	1.7	721	1.8
Paper and paper products	2	.8	69	.2
Lumber and wood products	1	.5	50	.1
Printing and engraving	1	.5	37	.1
Misc. manufacturing	4	1.7	905	2.2
Nonmanufacturing	*39*	*16.4*	*4,162*	*10.4*
Transportation	18	7.6	2,005	5.0
Building	14	5.9	1,536	3.8
Services	4	1.7	464	1.2
Retail and wholesale trade	3	1.2	157	.4
Mixed assemblies[a]	*58*	*24.5*	*11,455*	*28.4*
Manufacturing			4,439	11.0
Nonmanufacturing			1,680	4.2
Laborers[b]			2,147	5.3
Occupations not reported			3,189	7.9
Totals	*237*[c]	*100.0*	*40,275*[d]	*100.0*

Source: Adapted from the *Tenth Annual Report of the New Jersey Bureau of Statistics of Labor and Industries, 1887* (Somerville: State of New Jersey, 1888), pp. 28 and 30; and Leo Troy, *Organized Labor in New Jersey* (Princeton: Van Nostrand, 1965), p. 48.

[a] Number of members in mixed assemblies with manufacturing occupations. The NJBSLI used the Knights' official criteria to define mixed assemblies; hence some of the assemblies defined here as mixed are analyzed as trade assemblies in Tables 7 through 13. See p. 76 for the Knights' definition of mixed assemblies and p. 148 for the definition used in the statistical analysis reported in Chapters 5 through 7.

[b] Number of members in mixed assemblies who are classified as "laborers." Laborers worked in both manufacturing and nonmanufacturing industries.

[c] Total number of assemblies excludes four assemblies not reporting membership.

[d] There is a discrepancy in the figures reported by the NJBSLI. When the bureau presents aggregate statistics, total membership is reported as 40,172. However, when the tables giving detailed occupation figures are summed, the total is 40,275. This latter figure is the one reported above and by Troy.

Table 6. Gender and nativity of Knights of Labor members in New Jersey, 1887

	Knights of Labor members		Total wage earners[a]	
	Number	%[b]	Number	%
Total	40,172[c]	100	570,738	100
Male	35,772	89	459,467	80.5
Female	4,400	11	111,271	19.5
Total reporting place of nativity	35,623	100	570,738	100
American born	16,999	47.7	387,247	67.9
Irish	7,280	20.4	57,169	10.0
German	5,082	14.3	58,019	10.2
British	3,140	8.8	31,040	5.4
Other	3,122	8.9	37,263	6.5

Source: NJBSLI, *Tenth Annual Report*, p. 15, and Table 116 of U.S. Department of the Interior, *Report on the Population of the United States at the Eleventh Census: 1890*, Part 2 (Washington, D.C.: Government Printing Office, 1892).

[a] The statistics are for 1890, the closest census year to 1887 for which nativity breakdowns are available. The figures for American-born workers include native white and black workers.

[b] Percentages add to more than 100 due to rounding error.

[c] As noted in Table 5, there is a discrepancy in the total membership figures reported by the NJBSLI. When the bureau presents detailed statistics of occupations, total membership sums to 40,275. However, when aggregate membership is given and when the gender figures are tallied, total membership is presented as 40,172. The latter figure is reported above.

sey wage earners were members of the Order.[64] (To put this figure in perspective, it should be noted that it approximates the percentage unionized in the national labor force at the end of World War I and in late 1936, the year the CIO began its famous sit-down strikes against General Motors in Flint, Michigan.)[65] If we restrict our attention to manufacturing workers, the Knights' influence is more conspicuous. Between 13 and 15 percent of all workers engaged in manufacturing in New Jersey in 1887 were members.[66]

64. Margo A. Conk, *The United States Census and New Jersey Urban Occupational Structure, 1870–1940* (Ann Arbor: UMI Research Press, 1978), reports that the working population of New Jersey in 1880 was 396,878 and 570,738 in 1890. These figures are the ones given in the censuses and include agricultural workers, professional workers, trade and transportation workers, and manufacturing workers. It should be noted that they also include some employers but that it is impossible to estimate how many. To arrive at the figure (7.75%) reported here, I calculated the average number of new employees per year, added them to the 1880 figure, and used this sum (518,180) as the divisor.

65. For national membership figures, see Irving Bernstein, "The Growth of American Unions," *American Economic Review* 44 (1954): 301–18.

66. The percentage is reported as a range because the actual figure varies depend-

In 1887 the New Jersey Knights began to experience many of the setbacks that characterized the national organization. Many of the candidates who ran received a large minority of votes but ultimately lost. Those who won discovered that, without experience and party organization, they had little real power. Moreover, in the wake of Haymarket, the percentage of failed strikes increased dramatically: 63 percent ended in a defeat for workers in 1887.[67] Perhaps most devastating in terms of timing and publicity was the failure of a general strike among coal handlers and longshoremen along the New York–New Jersey shore in early 1887. The strike was against six railroad corporations that supplied coal to most of the Northeast, and the rhetoric surrounding it was very similar to that of the anti-Gould strikes: it was seen as a contest of labor against united monopolists.[68] The strike began after the wages of the unskilled coal shovelers at Elizabethport, New Jersey, were reduced, but soon freight handlers, railroad hands, boatmen, and longshoremen all struck in sympathy. Because both the boatmen and longshoremen were members of trade unions, whereas the other workers belonged to the Knights, the strike represented united action by the two labor groups at a time when tensions between the Knights and the trade unions nationally were running high. Its failure reflected the strength of railroad companies, court intervention, and mismanagement on the part of the strike leaders.

As with many of the titanic conflicts in the mid-1880s, deciding which of these factors played the largest role would require carefully weighing the evidence. Certainly the struggle is an important chapter in the history of the development of the labor injunction, which eventually replaced conspiracy laws as the primary mechanism for state regulation of labor.[69] But strike leaders also misplayed their hand, over-

---

ing upon the categorization used. For instance, the census does not distinguish laborers employed in manufacturing from those employed at building sites and other nonmanufacturing concerns.

67. These percentages are based on figures reported in NJBSLI, *Tenth Annual Report*, *1887*, p. 244.

68. One important difference was that the shortage of coal, given that it was winter, undermined some public support. The coal shortage hurt the small dealers and small consumers most because coal carriers and owners hired enough strikebreakers to supply wholesale consumers. With the shortage, these wholesale dealers were able to charge inflated prices. The poor, who bought their coal by day, were affected by the strike "instantaneously; not only in the rise of price, which rapidly advanced, but also in the stoppage of charitable doles and gifts, both public and private" (New York Bureau of Statistics of Labor, *Fifth Annual Report for the Year 1887* [Troy Press Company, 1888], pp. 332 and 356; see also *New York World*, Jan. 14, 1887).

69. Traditionally, labor injunctions could be used only when a public utility or public carrier was in receivership. During the great upheaval, as Tomlins, *State and the Unions*, p. 50, notes, courts made them available to railroads, even when they were not in re-

estimating their own strength and underestimating that of their opponents. The strike was conducted by New York City's District Assembly 49, a stronghold of anti-Powderly and especially anti-trade union sentiment.[70] The composition of the strike's leadership, coupled with its defeat, exacerbated internal dissension within the Knights in New Jersey. In the wake of the strike's failure, organizing activity slowed considerably.

Employers, strengthened by the national antilabor sentiment, began to adopt increasingly aggressive tactics against organized labor. Some employers, especially in towns such as Burlington or Phillipsburg, had been intransigent all along. They simply fired any worker who refused to leave the Knights.[71] But after Haymarket, more employers began to form associations with the express purpose of defeating the Order. Newark was a center of such activity. In 1886 its clothing, leather, hat, and shoe manufacturers all founded employers' associations.[72] Besides turning to tactics such as lockouts, blacklists, and iron-clad oaths, they petitioned the legislature for the reinstatement of the conspiracy laws in order to halt the wave of boycotts and strikes.[73]

Conflict with the trade unions also began to exact a toll. The 1880s had witnessed the birth and reorganization of dozens of craft locals in New Jersey. Some of these had affiliated with the Knights, and others had remained aloof; however, generally cooperative relations reigned

---

ceivership on the grounds that "the courts had a general duty to protect any carrier against such interference as would prevent it from fulfilling its obligation to serve the public at all times." On the courts' involvement in the coal handlers' strike, see *New York World*, Jan. 14, 1887.

70. On the strike, see New York Bureau of Statistics of Labor, *Fifth Annual Report 1888*, pp. 327–85; NJBSLI, *Tenth Annual Report, 1887*, pp. 232–42; Selig Perlman, "Upheaval and Reorganization," pp. 420–22. John Swinton, a respected labor journalist, believed that the strike's failure was due in large measure to the mismanagement of District Assembly 49. Perlman notes that Swinton generally refrained from taking sides in the internal fights of the labor movement; thus his judgment is a sober one. See *John Swinton's Paper*, Feb. 13, 1887; Feb. 20, 1887; Feb. 27, 1887.

On the importance of cooperation between the Knights and the trade unions, see *John Swinton's Paper*, Jan. 30, 1887; Feb. 6, 1887.

Although the leadership of District Assembly 49 (the so-called Home Club) and Powderly were definitely hostile to each other until mid-1886, there was at least a temporary alliance between the two in June-July 1886. Grob, *Workers and Utopia*, p. 116, suggests that Powderly may have joined forces with District Assembly 49 in order to maintain his position. Whatever the reality, the Knights in New Jersey saw District Assembly 49 as anti-Powderly. See Andrew Clarke to Powderly, Apr. 26, 1887, microfilm reel 22, Powderly Papers, and the *Trenton Sunday Advertiser*, Aug. 8, 1886.

71. U.S. Senate. *Testimony*, pp. 205–6; NJBSLI, *Ninth Annual Report, 1886*, p. 220.

72. NJBSLI, *Ninth Annual Report, 1886*; Clarence Bonnett, *Employers' Associations in the United States* (New York: Vantage, 1956), esp. chap. 3.

73. Bonnett, *Employers' Associations*, p. 258.

through 1886 at both the state and local level. The Order was the larger organization (over 40,000 members compared with 18,000 trade union members in 1887), and it controlled most leadership positions in the Labor Congress.[74] Then, in 1886, a dramatic battle on the floor of the State Labor Congress openly pitted members of the two organizations against one another. This fight also generated antagonisms within each organization, between elements responsive to the positions of the other side. The Knights' candidate won the office both that year and the following one, indicating continued dominance. But by 1890 the Knights' strength had dwindled, and compromise with the trade unions was no longer in the cards. The Labor Congress that year rejected the credentials of two of the few Knights assemblies in attendance, and the Order was too weak to mount an effective challenge.

Many local assemblies were active in the late 1880s and early 1890s, a few surviving in New Jersey until the turn of the century. Indeed, new locals continued to be organized until 1895. But as Table 4 shows, the organizing momentum was never recovered. Instead, the organizational impetus rested increasingly with the trade unions. As Table 7 indicates, this signified a shift in the locus of organization. Fewer locals included less-skilled members, and correspondingly more were founded by skilled craft workers: out of a total of 289 locals, 29 percent organized the less skilled and 71 percent organized the skilled.[75] Most striking of all, little effort was made to incorporate both skilled and less-skilled workers in the same union. Only 6 percent of all trade unions adopted a quasi-industrial organizing strategy.

The shift to trade unions also implied a shift away from the organization of manufacturing workers. Trade union membership was concentrated in nonmanufacturing industries, particularly building and railway transportation. By the turn of the century, the problems of less-skilled workers in manufacturing were remote from the concerns of most union members. Moreover, these union members constituted a much smaller proportion of the labor force. In 1899 and 1901, surveys by the Bureau of Labor put total union membership at about 15,000, that is, 3,000 fewer workers than had belonged to non-Knights locals alone in 1877.[76]

In sum, the Knights of Labor did succeed for a time in organiz-

74. Trade union membership figures are from NJBSLI, *Tenth Annual Report, 1887*, pp. 24 and 26. Accounts of Labor Congress in these years can be found in the Kerrison Papers.
75. It is important to note that the trades union category is made up of all non-Knights labor unions, not just locals affiliated with the AFL.
76. Troy, *Organized Labor*, p. 73.

Table 7. Trade union locals in New Jersey: Year founded by organizing strategy

	Organizing strategy					
	Craft		Sectional assembly of less-skilled workers		Quasi-industrial	
Year founded	Number	%	Number	%	Number	%
1834–71	16	76	5	24	0	0
1877–82	21	68	10	32	0	0
1883–85	27	79	7	21	0	0
1886	13	62	7	33	1	5
1887–91	63	73	14	16	9	10[a]
1892–95	66	69	22	23	8	8
Total	206		65		18	

Note: Includes local unions that organized in towns with populations exceeding 2,500.
[a] Percentage adds to less than 100 due to rounding error.

ing New Jersey's diverse labor force. As a result the Order was able to permanently dismantle conspiracy legislation and to temporarily impose greater democracy on the shopfloor. In the end, however, workers were unable to sustain the Knights organizations they had built, and the Order declined. As a consequence, less-skilled manufacturing workers remained largely unorganized until the 1930s.

The description offered here of New Jersey's industry, politics, and labor movement should help to fill in the background for the types of events analyzed statistically in the next three chapters. It cannot, however, take the place of those statistics. Although we now know that the Knights in New Jersey organized workers on both sides of the skill divide, we do not yet know to what extent actual solidarity was achieved. We do not know, for example, how actively craft workers aided the organizational efforts of less-skilled workers. Nor do we know to what extent craft loyalties were ultimately responsible for the Knights' decline. Perhaps, as Perlman suggests, skilled workers were simply unwilling to remain Knights members once less-skilled workers joined in large numbers. How we finally judge the meaning of the Knights' success and collapse will depend on the answers to these questions.

5

The Foundations
of Solidarity

At the end of the nineteenth century when rapid industrialization was narrowing many of the differences between skilled and less-skilled workers, the Knights of Labor provided an obvious organizational vehicle for uniting workers around their new, common interests. At the same time, craft identities remained strong, even among the skilled workers who joined the Knights. The question pursued in this chapter is: What was the relationship between existing craft organization and the recruitment of less-skilled workers into the Knights of Labor?

This is an important question for two reasons. First, it is critical for our understanding of the rise and demise of the Knights. As demonstrated in the Introduction, creating a true class-based social movement in this period entailed an alliance between the skilled, unionized heirs to the journeymen's revolts of the 1830s and the growing number of less-skilled factory workers. It may be that the Knights failed because the kinds of links that were forged in working-class movements elsewhere were not forged in the Order. For example, it may be that craft workers in the United States were particularly attached to sectional interests ("job conscious," Selig Perlman called it) and thus that they were more likely than craftsmen elsewhere to ignore or actively suppress the unionization of their less-skilled colleagues. If so, it would suggest that the Order of the Knights of Labor, from the beginning, was built on a shaky foundation.

Second, an examination of how craft organization affected the incorporation of less-skilled workers into the labor movement is important for our understanding of the larger process of working-class formation. As noted, we currently have conflicting images of the role craft organization played in fostering working-class movements. In one image, skilled workers play the role of craft radicals who spearhead revolutionary working-class movements; in the other they act as conservative labor aristocrats who hinder the organization of less-privileged workers. Earlier, it was suggested that when one closely examines the evidence, it quickly becomes apparent that neither image fully captures the role craft workers actually played in working-class movements. Instead of always acting as craft radicals or labor aristocrats, skilled workers frequently played both roles, alternately behaving in ways that furthered and hindered broad-based organization. The challenge for researchers is to specify better the conditions that encouraged each outcome. A systematic study of the conditions under which craft organization pushed in one direction or the other in the Knights should help us to advance our knowledge of the role of craft workers in working-class formation. More specifically, it should help us to discover whether craft workers were more likely to facilitate alliances at the community level (as research on France indicates) or within industries (where American and British historians have generally looked for such alliances).

In this chapter I report a statistical study of craft organization in the Knights and follow it up with a case study that illustrates and extends the quantitative analysis. The statistical study uses information on the sequence in which various skill levels were organized in each New Jersey community to assess the extent to which craft organization promoted or hindered the incorporation of less-skilled workers into the labor movement. In addition, because a wide variety of factors other than the presence of craft organization is likely to affect the organization of less-skilled workers, the statistical analysis also investigates other aspects of the industrial and community context and weighs their influence. It is to a discussion of the types of community and industrial forces that were likely to encourage or discourage unionism among less-skilled workers that we now turn.

The Local Context of Worker Organization

Few studies of modern-day unionism address the local conditions that encourage or discourage unionization. Instead, they focus on broad economic trends, national-level political environments, and general characteristics of industrial sectors.[1] Even the growing body of quantitative studies of strike activity commonly ignores the community as a locus of industrial conflict.[2] Given the amount of centralization that characterizes both labor unions and business enterprise today, this may be a reasonable strategy, but it is clearly inappropriate for a historical period in which there was a great deal less concentration and coordination and a great deal more local autonomy and variation.

Guidance on which local factors might affect organization of the less skilled in the Knights, therefore, cannot be found in the sociological literature on late-twentieth-century unions. Instead, the most relevant literature is that which concerns working-class consciousness and collective action. This literature is voluminous and offers a variety of theoretical approaches. The most helpful of these, and the ones examined here, are culled from historical studies that emphasize the role of the workplace, the composition of the labor force, and the industrial structure of the community.

Workplace and Industrial Factors

Marx was perhaps the earliest scholar to stress the role of the workplace in shaping labor organization and activism. In large factories, he suggested, physical proximity and the elaborate division of labor would enhance worker solidarity.[3] In large factories, workers were estranged from both the act of production and their employers, but in

1. Orley Ashenfelter and John H. Pencavel, "American Trade Union Growth: 1900–1960," *Quarterly Journal of Economics* 83 (1969): 434–48; David Britt and Omer Galle, "Industrial Conflict and Unionization," *American Sociological Review* 37 (1972): 46–57.

2. See, for example, James R. Lincoln, "Community Structure and Industrial Conflict: An Analysis of Strike Activity in SMSA's," *American Sociological Review* 43 (1978): 199–220, and P. K. Edwards, *Strikes in the United States* (New York: St. Martin's Press, 1981).

3. For Marx's views on workers' estrangement, see Karl Marx and Frederick Engels, *The German Ideology: Part One with Selections from Parts Two and Three and Supplementary Texts*, ed. C. J. Arthur (New York: International Publishers, 1970); and Karl Marx, *Economic and Philosophic Manuscripts of 1844* (Moscow: International Publishers, 1961). Marx discusses the importance of labor concentration in facilitating class solidarity and collective action, in *Karl Marx: Selected Writings*, ed. David McLellen (Oxford: Oxford University Press, 1977), pp. 214 and 929. Jon Elster, *Making Sense of Marx* (Cambridge: Cambridge University Press, 1985), p. 355, points out that Marx never says explicitly that it is the concentration of workers in the workplace, rather than in housing and residence, that is the decisive factor. However, almost everyone who has read Marx agrees with Elster that, given what Marx says elsewhere about the importance of trade unions, the decisiveness of the workplace can be inferred. For the discussion of small craft shops, see Karl Marx, "Germany: Revolution and Counter-Revolution," in *Selected Writings of Karl Marx*, ed. V. Adoratsky (New York: International Publishers, 1936), p. 470.

small craft shops workers made the whole product and worked side by side with their employers. In the latter, Marx noted, workers were markedly less class conscious and less involved in workers' organizations. With somewhat less enthusiasm, Durkheim offered a similar line of argument in *The Division of Labor in Society:* "Small-scale industry, where work is less divided displays a relative harmony between worker and employer. It is only in large-scale industry that these relations are in a sickly state."[4]

Many others have argued for a similar "size effect" on workers' behavior,[5] although some evidence points in the opposite direction. For example, Ingham suggests that large factories can encourage individualistic behavior and discourage group solidarity, an argument that is given a theoretical foundation by Mancur Olson.[6] Further, a growing number of historical studies contend that smaller workshops were at least as conducive to unionization and militant action as large factories.[7] Most of these studies, however, concern skilled workers threatened by technological change, not less-skilled workers. This suggests that mechanization and deskilling provided the commonality of circumstances usually found only in large factories. In the case of less-skilled workers, technological change rarely posed the same kind of threat as it did to skilled workers; and it is unlikely that small shops were as likely to lead to the unionization of less-skilled workers.

Although technological change rarely affected less-skilled workers in the same way it affected skilled workers, a large body of literature indicates that it nevertheless had both direct and indirect effects on the unionization of less-skilled workers. Technological change, as we saw in Chapter 2, tended to increase and stabilize employment opportunities for factory workers while also equalizing working conditions. Consequently, it was likely to encourage unionization directly. At the same time, the "radical artisan" literature suggests that technological change also indirectly promoted less-skilled organization because it spurred skilled craftsmen to aid the organizational efforts of

4. Emile Durkheim, *The Division of Labor in Society* (New York: Macmillan, 1933), p. 356.

5. E.g., Elster, *Making Sense of Marx*, p. 355; Gordon, Edwards, and Reich, *Segmented Work*, pp. 116–26; Seymour Martin Lipset, Martin A. Trow, and James S. Coleman, *Union Democracy* (Garden City, N.Y.: Anchor Books, 1962).

6. Geoffrey K. Ingham, "Organizational Size, Orientation to Work and Industrial Behaviour," *Sociology* 1 (1967): 239–58; Mancur Olson, *The Logic of Collective Action* (Cambridge: Cambridge University Press, 1965).

7. Cecelia Bucki, "Dilution and Craft Tradition: Bridgeport, Connecticut, Munitions Workers, 1915–1919," *Social Science History* 4 (1980): 105–24; Craig Calhoun, "Transition in Social Foundations for Collective Action," *Social Science History* 4 (1980): 419–51; Hanagan, *Logic of Solidarity*; Scott, *Glassworkers*.

less-skilled industrial workers. There is disagreement, however, over whether it was slow or rapid technological change that was most likely to spur alliances. Based on his analysis of English and American machinists, Haydu claims that sudden change was more likely to promote solidarity across the skill divide; however, Hanagan's study of French workers led him to conclude that gradual, not rapid, technological change was more likely to prompt skilled workers to support the unionization of less-skilled workers.[8]

Just as similar conditions and common grievances tend to encourage solidarity, so, studies indicate, internal stratification within an enterprise is likely to promote fragmentation. Skill remained one of the most important sources of stratification. Although technological changes and economic crises in the late nineteenth century provided a basis for joint action between skilled and less-skilled workers, significant differences in life chances and working conditions endured, and any aspect of the labor process that reinforced the division between skilled and less-skilled workers was likely to impede the organization of the latter. Subcontracting arrangements and piecework, for example, have both been linked to exclusive behavior on the part of skilled workers.[9] Similarly, the labor aristocracy theorists have argued that large wage differentials hampered the organizational efforts of less-skilled workers.

Composition of the Labor Force

Workers often built unions that encompassed more than one enterprise, and equally important, they interacted with one another off as well as on the shopfloor. Hence a number of researchers link working-class composition to labor solidarity. Although not always explicitly spelled out, their arguments apply equally well to a variety of spheres: the workshop, the local industry, and the community.

It is often argued that the diversity of ethnic identities among workers in the United States tended to undermine the development of class solidarity.[10] Continual waves of immigration created serious

---

8. Hanagan, *Logic of Solidarity*; Haydu, *Between Craft and Class*.

9. Hobsbawm, *Labouring Men*, pp. 272–315; Foster, *Class Struggle*; Dan Clawson, *Bureaucracy and the Labor Process* (New York: Monthly Review Press, 1980); Montgomery, *Workers' Control*.

10. Oscar Handlin, *The Uprooted* (Boston: Little Brown, 1951); Eric Hofstader, *Age of Reform* (New York: Knopf, 1955), pp. 180–84; Stanley Aronowitz, *False Promises: The Shaping of American Working-Class Consciousness* (New York: McGraw-Hill, 1973), p. 164; Gabriel Kolko, *Main Currents in American History* (New York: Harper and Row, 1976), pp. 68–69; Gerald Rosenblum, *Immigrant Workers: Their Impact on American Labor Radicalism* (New York: Basic Books, 1973), pp. 151–54.

and lasting divisions—between native and newcomer, between recent and established immigrants, between those of different national and religious groups. As Oberschall notes, such cross-cutting loyalties significantly impede joint action.[11] Adding to the difficulty, employers were able to take advantage of ethnic cleavages to deflect "aggression on capital" onto "defense against immigrants."[12]

Often ethnic or gender differences overlapped skill and wage hierarchies; in these cases, as the labor economists have demonstrated, the divisive effects of each was enhanced.[13] Such overlap almost invariably occurred in the case of women workers. Because women generally took jobs only in the towns where their husbands and fathers worked, their mobility in the late nineteenth century was severely restricted. For this and a variety of other cultural reasons, the majority of jobs open to women were poorly paid and were characterized by exploitative working conditions.[14] Such jobs left women with few resources to invest in building unions or participating in collective action.[15] Equally damaging, women's segregation into low-paying, less-skilled positions made it easy for male workers to view female workers as competitors rather than as colleagues. Thus, when women composed a large percentage of the work force, most research indicates that less-skilled workers were generally less likely to be organized.

One should not, however, overestimate the extent to which homogeneity facilitated collective action. Although ethnic cleavages generally obstructed the development of working-class organization, the same line of reasoning would not apply in all instances. If, as the Trenton pottery manufacturers complained about the English potters, a particular ethnic group was more likely for cultural or historical reasons to support labor unions, then their presence could actually aid the development of unionization even as it contributed to the

11. Anthony Oberschall, *Social Conflict*, p. 129.

12. John R. Commons, "Is Class Conflict in America Growing and Is It Inevitable?" *American Journal of Sociology* 13 (1908): 761–62.

13. Gordon, Edwards, and Reich, *Segmented Work*; Jill Rubery, "Structured Labour Markets, Worker Organization, and Low Pay," *Cambridge Journal of Economics* 2 (1978): 17–36.

14. Alice Kessler-Harris, "Where Are the Organized Women Workers?" in *A Heritage of Her Own: Toward a New Social History of American Women*, ed. Nancy Cott and Elizabeth Pleck (New York: Simon and Schuster, 1979), pp. 343–66.

15. For a description of the difficulties Lenora M. Barry, an organizer appointed expressly to further the organization of women in the Knights of Labor, encountered in New Jersey, see NJBSLI, *Tenth Annual Report, 1887* (Somerville: State of New Jersey, 1888), pp. 202–6. Susan Levine discusses Barry's national activities in "Labor's True Women: Domesticity and Equal Rights in the Knights of Labor," *Journal of American History* 70 (1983): 323–33.

ethnic diversity of a community. Similarly, familial ties sometimes provided a basis for common action between skilled men and less-skilled women, especially in multiple-industry towns.[16] Equally important, in at least some instances, skill stratification aided the organization of less-skilled workers. When Hanagan compared three French towns— one predominately artisanal, one predominately industrial (i.e., composed of less-skilled workers), and one mixed artisanal/industrial—he found that trade unionism was weakest in the predominately industrial town. In the other two towns, skilled artisanal workers played a key role in involving industrial workers in unions and strike actions.

Nature of the Community

A worker's social consciousness, like that of any individual, is to a large extent influenced by the immediate social context, and many studies connect this context (as opposed to the characteristics of the workers themselves) to worker cohesion.[17] In their comparative studies of nineteenth-century communities, both Cumbler and Hanagan stress the importance of residential patterns in accounting for variations in labor solidarity.[18] When workers were concentrated in working-class neighborhoods, physical proximity encouraged informal contact and reinforced shopfloor solidarities; moreover, in Cumbler's study of Lynn, Massachusetts, such communal sociability encouraged the development of informal working-class institutions that mitigated the fragmenting effect of immigration.

A similar line of argument is often applied to one-industry towns. In such communities large numbers of workers who share similar life chances and grievances are concentrated. Moreover, the sense of cohesion that springs from shared work experiences is enhanced by the town's predominantly one-class nature and its geographical isolation. Kerr and Siegel were the first to draw attention to this phenomenon (the "isolated mass") in a systematic way, and their formulation re-

16. Carol Turbin, "Beyond Conventional Wisdom: Women's Wage Work, Household Economic Contribution, and Labor Activism in a Mid-Nineteenth-Century Working-Class Community," in *To Toil the Livelong Day*, ed. Carol Groneman and Mary Beth Norton (Ithaca: Cornell University Press, 1987), pp. 47–67; Johanna Brenner and Maria Ramas, "Rethinking Women's Oppression," *New Left Review* 144 (May–June 1984): 33–71.

17. For a highly engaging discussion about how community experiences affect workers' images of society, see D. Lockwood, "Sources of Variation in Working-Class Images of Society," *Sociological Review* 14 (1966): 249–67.

18. Hanagan, *Logic of Solidarity*; Cumbler, *Working-Class Community*.

mains highly influential.[19] However, the evidence for their argument is mixed. McDougall argues that Lyon's single-industry status served as an important precondition for the development of class consciousness in the first half of the nineteenth century, and Walkowitz applies a similar logic when explaining the labor agitation that rocked Cohoes, New York, in the 1880s.[20] Similarly, Griffen and Griffen suggest that Paterson's (New Jersey) reliance on the silk industry in large part explains the development of its cohesive and militant working-class consciousness.[21] But Hareven and Langenbach's description of Manchester, New Hampshire, paints a much more pessimistic picture: in one-industry towns, employer paternalism ties workers to employers, and the absence of alternative employment generally makes the employee highly vulnerable to employer power.[22] In their quantitative investigation of French strikes, Shorter and Tilly report that single-industry towns had lower strike rates and fewer grievances involving worker organization questions than did large metropolitan areas.[23]

This leads Shorter and Tilly to suggest that larger cities provided associational possibilities that more readily supported both unionization and strike activity.[24] Gutman, however, proposes the opposite relationship and directs our attention to important differences in the social structure of small and large American cities in the late nineteenth century. Examining the editorial stance of small-town and big-city newspapers, Gutman argues that the "social environment in the large American city after the Civil War was more often hostile toward workers than that in the smaller industrial towns." In large cities "the social structure . . . unavoidably widened the distance between social and economic classes," freeing the hand of the city manufacturer in his dealings with his employees, but in small towns "a good deal of prolabor and anti-industrial sentiment" was found among the middle and upper classes. Moreover, Gutman adds, a prolabor atmosphere was cultivated in small industrial towns because workers made up a larger percentage of the electorate and participated actively in local politics.[25]

19. Clark Kerr and Abraham Siegel, "The Interindustry Propensity to Strike—An International Comparison," in *Industrial Conflict*, ed. Arthur Kornhauser et al. (New York: McGraw-Hill, 1954).

20. McDougall, "Consciousness"; Walkowitz, *Worker City*.

21. Clyde Griffen and Sally Griffen, *Natives and Newcomers* (Cambridge: Harvard University Press, 1978).

22. Tamara Hareven and Randolph Langenbach, *Amoskeag* (New York: Pantheon, 1978).

23. Shorter and Tilly, *Strikes in France*, pp. 287–95.

24. Ibid., pp. 225–83.

25. Herbert Gutman, "The Worker's Search for Power: Labor in the Gilded Age,"

This brief review suggests several characteristics of workers' industrial and community context that might affect worker solidarity—and by extension—the ability of less-skilled workers to organize collectively. A statistical investigation of those factors for which it is possible to gather systematic evidence provides a fuller understanding of how the local context shaped working-class organization in the late nineteenth century. It also serves as the necessary background for our examination of the role of prior organization.

Data

To investigate the organization of less-skilled workers, we must first define a unit of analysis which clearly identifies a collection of workers who might potentially organize. Because all Knights locals, whether craft or industrial, generally organized within local industries, I chose the latter as the unit of analysis.

I consider each local industry as a separate unit of analysis; for example, the workers employed by the silk industry in Paterson constitute one unit of analysis, those employed in Paterson's cigarmaking shops represent another, and the potters of Trenton compose a third.

This unit of observation offers several advantages. First, it defines a group of workers who could pursue a variety of organizing strategies. As discussed in Chapter 3, some locals organized around craft identities, and others chose more broad-based association. Second, a local industry generally defines both a labor market and a natural social collectivity. The actions of any group of workers within a local industry might reasonably affect the actions of other workers in that industry. Thus it makes sense to look at whether the presence of craft locals affected the development of less-skilled organization within local industries. We can also distinguish the effects of pre-existing organization elsewhere in the community and investigate their differential impact in and outside of the local industry. Third, this unit of analysis allows the investigation of both community and industrial effects; thus it is possible to differentiate the effects of such factors as technological change and one-industry dominance.

I included all forty-nine New Jersey towns that had more than 2,500 inhabitants (see Appendix 1 for a list of communities), but only local manufacturing industries were analyzed. Industries were categorized according to the classification scheme presented in Appendix 2. In

in *The Gilded Age: A Reappraisal*, ed. H. Wayne Morgan (Syracuse: Syracuse University Press, 1963), pp. 31–53.

all, 543 local industries were coded. The average number of establishments in each local industry was 6.3.

Local industry characteristics were measured from information listed on the manuscript schedules of the 1880 Census of Manufactures.[26] For each establishment that produced more than 500 dollars worth of goods, these schedules reported the name of firm and type of product; number of men, women, and children employed; hours worked and wages paid; average daily wage for "skilled mechanics" and "ordinary laborers"; value of materials and value of product; capital invested; annual wage bill; and amount of horsepower used. Some important firms were omitted from the manuscript schedules, however, and in these cases, other sources, including the annual reports of the New Jersey Bureau of Statistics, were used to fill in the missing data.[27]

I measured craft organization and the emergence of locals of less-skilled workers by constructing organizational histories of every industry and town in New Jersey between the years 1880 and 1894. To create these histories, I compiled information on the location, founding and dissolution dates, and occupational composition of all local labor organizations, including those organized as Knights of Labor assemblies and those organized as trade unions (i.e., independently of the Knights). Using the sources discussed below, I eventually coded 652 local labor organizations.

I pieced together data on Knights local assemblies from several

26. Evidence about the local context of workers' actions in the late nineteenth century is limited. Thus, even my restricted theoretical discussion of the community and industrial context of worker organization brought to light several features I cannot measure. For example, I would very much like to have systematic evidence on working-class residential patterns or the number of skilled workers in a particular community or even the percentage of the electorate that earned wages. However, none of this information is available for even a significant minority of the communities considered here. We shall instead try to make the most of the data we do have and try to point out instances where more detailed study of one or two cases might clarify ambiguities.

27. The most important limitation of this source is that it provides measurement of the industrial context at only one point in time. Unfortunately, the 1890 manuscript schedules, which might have been used to assess the impact of industrial changes, were destroyed in a Commerce Department fire in the 1920s. Hence, with one exception, changes in the labor process are not measured. This is an important limitation because changes in the labor process often affected the way workers thought and acted. Moreover, in instances where dramatic changes occurred in the industrial context between 1880 and 1895, the variables include substantial measurement error. This measurement error is confined to cases in which local industries, already existing in 1880, changed markedly over the study period. When altogether new industries developed in a community, there was less of a problem because these local industries were simply not included in the analysis. See Kim Voss, "Working-Class Formation and the Knights of Labor," Ph.D. diss., Stanford University, 1986, app. 3, for more details on the coding of the manuscript census.

sources. I began with the information coded by the historian Jonathan Garlock, who compiled data on every local assembly mentioned in official Knights publications.[28] His data included an official assembly number for almost every Knights local organized in New Jersey, but, because of gaps in the national sources, he was unable to code occupational designations or founding and dissolution dates for many New Jersey assemblies. To fill in this missing information, I relied on the 1887 report of the New Jersey Bureau of Statistics of Labor and Industries, newspaper accounts of local Knights activities, city directories, and letters written by New Jersey Knights to the leaders of the Order, Terence Powderly and John W. Hayes.[29] The 1887 report of the New Jersey Bureau of Statistics of Labor and Industries was a particularly important source because it identified the occupations of workers in mixed assemblies. However, this report also presented special difficulties. In order to maintain the anonymity of the local assemblies the author of the report identified each assembly by an assigned office number rather than by locale or by an official assembly number. Before I was able to use any of the information in the bureau's report, I had to link it to an official assembly number or locale. By combining sources, I successfully linked 170 of the 230 assemblies in the different sources.[30]

The information collected by the Knights' national office offers one important advantage: it provides a reasonably accurate list of all local assemblies ever in existence during the study period. No comparable list of local trade unions exists. Hence, I had to consult several sources to piece together a comprehensive list of New Jersey trade unions. Some sources, such as the 1887 and 1900 reports of the New Jersey Bureau of Statistics of Labor and Industries, provide a census of all trade unions in existence in a particular year along with their founding dates.[31] Other sources, such as a few local newspapers, list all active labor organizations in a particular year.[32] The problem with using

28. Garlock, *Knights.*

29. The Powderly and Hayes correspondence encompasses 109 reels of microfilm and is organized by date. It is not indexed by state, and the only way to locate letters is to go through each reel. I went through all of the Hayes correspondence, which was much less voluminous than the Powderly letters, and I canvassed the Powderly letters for the years 1886 and 1887. These years were chosen because the additional information thereby gained could be used to help decode the 1887 report of the NJBSLI.

30. For further details, see Voss, "Working-Class Formation," app. 4.

31. NJBSLI, *Tenth Annual Report, 1887;* NJBSLI, *Twenty-third Annual Report, 1900.*

32. The following newspapers sporadically published trade union directories: *New Jersey Unionist, Paterson Labor Standard, Trenton Sunday Advertiser,* and *American Potter's Journal.* I also canvassed the following lists of trade locals published in the Proceedings of the American Federation of Labor (found in the American Federation of Labor records, microfilm edition, published in Frederick, MD, by University Publications of

these sources as an accurate sample of all New Jersey trade unions is that they are biased in favor of successful (i.e., surviving) unions and unions that were active in years in which records were published. In order to counter this bias, I combined these sources with the 1887 and 1894 strike reports compiled by the U.S. Bureau of Labor Statistics. These strike reports present information on all strikes between 1881 and 1894 by locality, giving the occupations of all strikers and noting union sponsorship. I used the information on union-sponsored strikes to check the biases of the trade union list I had pieced together from the New Jersey Bureau of Statistics and from local newspapers. I reasoned that, if the trade union list included a union for most of the occupational groups involved in union-sponsored strikes (in the relevant locality), then the trade union list could be considered reasonably complete. When I compared the trade union list with the information on union-sponsored strikes, I found that, for the 1881–86 period, 94 percent of the occupational groups involved in union-sponsored strikes were recorded as organized on the trade union list. For the 1887–94 period, 82 percent of the occupational groups were included on the trade union list. In cases in which the trade union list was incomplete, that is, in which no union was recorded as organizing the occupational group involved in a union-sponsored strike, I added a trade union for the relevant occupational group (and locality) to the list. Each of these new trade unions was assigned a life span of one year.[33]

After I had coded the occupational designations of the Knights local assemblies and the names of the trade unions, I assigned skill levels for all manufacturing occupations by using the Census Bureau's *Special Report*.[34] This report classified occupations based on how

America, 1985) between 1888 and 1897: delegates' lists, per capita tax lists, and the list of locals that contributed to the Homestead Defense Fund. Additional information on trade union locals was found in the 1899 report of the Essex County Trades Council in *Illustrated History of the Essex Trades Council and Affiliated Unions*, published by the Essex County Trades Council (Newark, N.J., 1899), in the reports of the annual sessions of the New Jersey Federation of Trades and Labor Unions, in Troy, *Organized Labor*, and in the WF-10 boxes of the WPA papers.

33. In a few cases I added an additional year to the life of a trade union based on the information provided by the strike data. My rule was to add a year to the life of a trade union if a union-sponsored strike involving an occupation organized by a trade union on my list occurred within one year of the dates I knew the union to be in existence. For example, if Newark blacksmiths were involved in a union-sponsored strike in 1893 and my trade union list indicated that a blacksmiths' union was active in Newark between 1888 and 1892, I would extend the life of the blacksmiths' union until 1893.

34. Census Bureau, *Special Report*. This report was the final product of a study commissioned by the Census Bureau in 1901. Researchers studied job titles in detail by going to factories, examining work processes, and consulting payroll lists. There is no evidence that this information was ever used to compile occupational statistics in the

much "judgement, ability, experience and supervisory duties" they required. For example, glassblowers and patternmakers were typical "skilled" craft workers; bolt makers and machine tenders typical "semi-skilled" workers; and laborers and bobbin boys typical "unskilled" workers. Nonmanufacturing occupations were classified in a similar manner, using the Census Bureau's 1915 occupational classification.[35]

After I had coded the skill level of the occupations represented in each local, I classified each union and local assembly as using one of four organizing strategies: a "craft" strategy of organizing only skilled workers; a "quasi-industrial" strategy of organizing both skilled and less-skilled workers, a "sectional" strategy of organizing less-skilled workers around narrow, occupational identities; and a "mixed" strategy of organizing everyone in a community. (Table 8 presents the details of the classification scheme.) The "mixed" designation was reserved only for those Knights assemblies that did not organize particular occupations or industries, regardless of whether they were officially denoted as "trade" or "mixed" assemblies.[36]

---

census, although the reasons why this was not done remain obscure. Conk, *U.S. Census*, provides an excellent discussion of the difficulties the issue of skill presented to census officials.

Most manufacturing occupations were located in the *Special Report*. The primary exceptions were occupations with the word "maker" in the title (such as "brushmaker" or "filemaker"). Unless there was evidence to the contrary in New Jersey sources, I classified makers as semiskilled workers because this practice was generally followed by the Census Bureau.

New Jersey's pottery industry used somewhat different terminology than that used in the *Special Report*. In cases of ambiguity, I relied on Marc Stern, "The Potters of Trenton, New Jersey, 1850–1902: A Study in the Industrialization of the Skilled Trades," Ph.D. diss., State University of New York at Stony Brook, 1986, chaps. 3 and 5, and table 15.

35. These sources, including the *Special Report*, probably underestimate the skill required for some occupations in the late nineteenth century. Because New Jersey industrialized earlier than many other states, this is less of a problem than it would be if, for example, I had chosen to study the Knights in Michigan. Nonetheless, the world of work did change between 1880 and 1900 in ways this study cannot measure. Inasmuch as no similar survey of occupations was undertaken in the earlier decade, one can only note the limitation and remain aware of the potential bias it might introduce.

36. The "mixed" designation was in reality a residual category. National officials of the Knights preferred it to the "trade" designation and sometimes required locals organizing on an industrial basis to form "mixed" locals. The "mixed" designation was also used in situations where there were too few workers in specific occupations to form trade assemblies. In classifying the organizing strategy of local assemblies, I attempted to disentangle these different uses of the "mixed" designation, and to treat all locals that organized particular occupations and industries in the same manner, regardless of whether they were officially recorded as trade or mixed locals. For an extended discussion of the variety of "mixed" locals, consult Garlock, "A Structural Analysis of the Knights of Labor," pp. 53–56, and for some New Jersey examples, see NJBSLI, *Tenth Annual Report, 1887*, pp. 46 and 59–64.

Table 8. Organizing strategies: All New Jersey labor organizations

Type of organizing strategy	Knights of Labor[a]		Trade union	
	Number	%	Number	%
Exclusive craft strategy	83	25.7	206	71.3
A single skilled occupation	66		158	
Multiple skilled occupations	17		48	
Strategy of incorporating less-skilled workers				
Quasi-industrial strategy	93	28.8	18	6.2
Skilled and semi-skilled occupations	11		5	
Skilled and unskilled occupations	2		1	
All workers, on an explicitly industrial basis	80		12	
Sectional strategy	106	32.8	65	22.5
Semi-skilled occupations	91		51	
Unskilled occupations	13		14	
Semi-skilled and unskilled	2		—	
"Mixed" Strategy[b]	41	12.7	—	—
Total	323	100.0	289	100.0

[a]I could not identify the occupational composition of forty officially designated trade locals. Of these, twelve "lapsed" before the start of the study period and one was founded after the study period.

As might be expected, it was more difficult to identify the occupational composition of assemblies that existed only briefly. Twenty-nine of the assemblies with missing occupational compositions were in existence for less than one year.

[b]If a local assembly was officially recorded as a "mixed" assembly but (1) my sources provided an occupational designation for the local and (2) it included workers in only a few industries, I treated the local like a "trade" assembly. Thus, for the purposes of this study, the "mixed" category includes only those assemblies that organized in a classic mixed pattern (i.e., a variety of occupations and industries) and those that designated themselves as mixed and for which I had no other information. See p. 148, n. 36.

Once I had characterized all locals according to organizing strategy, I constructed a record for each local industry of when various types of labor organization originated and disappeared. I used this record to measure both prior organization and the emergence of organization among less-skilled workers.

Variables

Three broad categories of variables are included in the statistical study of the conditions that promoted the organization of less-skilled workers in the Knights of Labor: variables that measure industrial circumstances, variables that indicate the community context, and variables that describe the types of labor organization located in each local industry at the beginning of each year.

Industrial Factors

Seven aspects of the industrial environment are included in the analysis. With the exception of technological change and horsepower per worker, all variables refer to the local industry, and all are measured for one year, 1880.

Average Size of Establishment. The average number of workers per establishment in the local industry. It is hypothesized that larger factories will encourage the organization of less-skilled workers.

Wage Differential. This variable is defined as the percentage difference between the wages paid to skilled workers and the wages paid to "ordinary laborers" in 1880.[37] Small wage differentials suggest that craft and less-skilled workers share common grievances and life situations, which should encourage craft workers to support other workers' organizational efforts. Consequently, it is expected that less-skilled workers will organize more rapidly when wage differentials are low.

Percentage of Female Employees. This measure is defined as the percentage of female employees in the local industry. Women workers were employed almost exclusively in less-skilled jobs, and their wages were generally lower than those of less-skilled men. Thus, they had fewer resources to invest in organization. It is expected that a high percentage of female employees will tend to decrease the probability that less-skilled workers organized.

Number of Establishments. This variable is defined as the number of factories in the local industry. (The logged value of this variable is used in the analysis.) Having multiple establishments in a local industry should encourage rapid labor organization because workers' dependency should make it difficult to organize when there are few employment options.

Horsepower per Worker. This variable is defined as the average amount of horsepower per worker, measured at the industry level (i.e., there

37. Skilled and ordinary wages have each been weighted by the number of employees in each firm. "Ordinary laborers" are not precisely defined in the census, but the closest correspondence to the categories used here is to semiskilled workers (cf. Stephan Thernstrom, *The Other Bostonians: Poverty and Progress in the American Metropolis, 1880–1970* [Cambridge: Harvard University Press, 1973], p. 337). The mean skilled wage in New Jersey in 1880 was $2.09 per day, and the mean "ordinary" wage was $1.13. The average wage differential was 0.91, indicating that skilled workers took home roughly 91 percent more money than less-skilled workers.

is one figure for silk manufacture in all of New Jersey; missing data made it impossible to calculate this variable for each local industry). Because mechanization tended to stabilize employment for many less-skilled workers, it is expected that more rapid organization of less-skilled workers will occur in industries characterized by high levels of mechanization.

Technological Change. Technological change is defined as the increase in horsepower per worker between 1880 and 1890, a figure intended to measure the pace of mechanization and innovation. I calculated this measure by combining information on horsepower included in the 1880 manuscripts with industry-level figures given in the 1880 and 1890 Census of Manufactures.[38] Because of missing data and because the 1890 figure is not broken down by community, this variable is also calculated at the industry level. A large body of literature suggests that technological change facilitates labor organization because it challenges the sharp cleavages between the status and interests of craftsmen and less-skilled workers. However, two very different arguments are made about the pace of technological innovation. For example, Hanagan argues that gradual technological change is more conducive to alliances across the skill divide, and Haydu suggests that sudden and far-reaching challenges are most likely to promote broad-based solidarities. No prediction is made in advance about this variable; it is included to provide systematic evidence that will allow us to begin to adjudicate between these two arguments.

Capital-to-Labor Ratio. This variable is defined as the number of dollars invested in the local industry divided by the annual wage bill for that industry. It is included to compensate for the high level of aggregation in my technological change indicators. Technological change in the late nineteenth century was highly capital intensive, and high capital-to-labor ratios should indicate higher levels of technological improvements;[39] they measure the level of mechanization in workers' immediate environment, whereas the horsepower variables measure technical innovation at an industrywide level. It is expected that high levels of capital investment will encourage the rapid organization of less-skilled workers.

38. A better way to have done this would have been to have used the 1890 manuscript schedules, but they were destroyed in a Commerce Department fire in the 1920s.

39. Laurie and Schmitz, "Manufacture," p. 71; Gordon, Edwards, and Reich, *Segmented Work*, pp. 141 and 252–53.

Community Variables

Information on the community context was gathered primarily from the New Jersey State Census; thus, variables are measured for 1875 and 1885.

Community Population. The log of the township population. As noted, Shorter and Tilly suggest that unionization develops more rapidly in large metropolitan areas, whereas Gutman argues that small industrial communities were more conducive to worker organization in the United States in the late nineteenth century. Shorter and Tilly's hypothesis accords better with what we know about the spread of other social movements, and thus, it is expected that less-skilled workers will organize more rapidly in more populated communities.[40]

One-Industry Town. A dichotomous variable (i.e., a "dummy" variable) coded "one" when a single manufacturing industry dominated the locality. I gathered information for this variable from the manuscripts of the manufacturing census, and it is thus measured only once, in 1880. Following Shorter and Tilly, a locality was considered a one-industry town if one manufacturing industry employed more than 50 percent of the total work force engaged in manufacturing and if there was no other manufacturing industry that accounted for more than 15 percent of the work force.[41] The community was also classified as a one-industry town if a single manufacturing industry had more than 60 percent of the workforce, and the next largest industry had less than 20 percent.[42] It is expected that less-skilled workers will organize less rapidly in one-industry towns.

Ethnic Diversity. Ethnic diversity is calculated for each community according to the following formula:

$$Hi = 100(1 - \sum p_i^2),$$

where p_i is the proportion of the population in that community born

40. Shorter and Tilly, *Strikes in France*, pp. 225–83; Gutman, "Workers' Search for Power." For a discussion of urbanization and other social movements, see Claude Fischer, *The Urban Experience* (San Diego: Harcourt, Brace, Jovanovich, 1984), pp. 123–26.
41. Shorter and Tilly, *Strikes in France*, p. 293.
42. Shorter and Tilly's classification scheme was modified in the following respects: since they had information on the total size of the work force, they only included *arrondissements* in which blue-collar industries composed more than 40 percent of the work force. I did not have figures on the size of the total work force, so my classification uses no such cutoff. Moreover, my classification refers only to manufacturing industries while they were able to include other "blue-collar" industries such as mining, construction, and transportation. On the basis of these modifications, twenty of the forty-nine communities studied were one-industry towns. See Voss, "Working-Class Formation," chap. 4, for further details.

in location i.[43] This variable was included because ethnic diversity presumably made it harder for workers to organize.

Organizational Factors

The organizational measures distinguish Knights of Labor organization from trade union organization and the organizational field of the local industry from that of the community. Four variables indicate the extent of craft organization.

Knights of Labor (KOL) *Craft Organization in the Local Industry.* A dummy variable coded "one" when there was at least one Knights of Labor assembly present in the local industry that organized skilled workers on a craft basis. This variable measures the impact of prior craft organization in the local industry and tests whether it helped or hindered the organization of less-skilled workers.

Trade Union (TU) Craft Organization in the Local Industry. A dummy variable indicating the presence of a trade union in the local industry that organized skilled workers on a craft basis. This variable also measures the impact of prior craft organization in the local industry. Trade union organization is differentiated from Knights of Labor organization because the two groups differed in both ideology and style. Historians writing in the tradition of John Commons portray the trade unionists affiliated with the AFL (and its precursor, the FOTLU) as tne quintessential labor aristocrats and thus would predict that trade union organization in the local industry would be likely to discourage the organization of less-skilled workers.[44]

Knights of Labor (KOL) *Craft Organization in the Community.* A variable coded "one" when there was at least one Knights of Labor assembly present in the community that organized skilled workers on a craft basis; it indicates the presence of a Knights assembly in any local industry other than the industry of observation. It is included to measure

43. The only countries of origin for which birth statistics were given in the 1885 New Jersey State Census were: (1) Germany; (2) Ireland; (3) other foreign-born; and (4) the United States. I was unable to calculate this measure for 1875 because the state census did not include ethnic breakdowns in its 1875 report. More troubling, systematic information was unavailable to measure ethnic diversity in local industries, so it is measured at the community level.

See Rein Taagepera and James Lee Ray, "A Generalized Index of Concentration," *Sociological Methods and Research* 5 (1977): 367–83, for a discussion of the advantages and disadvantages of this index, the Herfindahl-Hirschman index, as compared to alternative indices of concentration. In addition, see Stanley Lieberson, "Measuring Population Diversity," *American Sociological Review* 34 (1969): 850–62.

44. See, for example, Grob, *Workers and Utopia*, p. 60.

whether craft workers were more likely to facilitate the unionization of less-skilled workers in their community or in their local industry.

Trade Union (TU) Craft Organization in the Community. A dummy variable indicating the presence of a trade union in the community that organized skilled workers on a craft basis. As they would with the other measure of trade union craft organization, Commons and his students would suggest that this variable will be negatively related to the formation of less-skilled Knights assemblies.

The discussion of prior organization has concentrated thus far on the effects of craft organization. However, the presence of other forms of prior organization would also be likely to affect the development of Knights organization among less-skilled workers in any particular local industry. Consequently, comparing the impact of other forms of prior organization with craft organization should clarify the interpretations of any impact of craft organization on less-skilled workers' organizational development. I include four indicators of noncraft organization:

Trade Union (TU) of Less-Skilled Workers in the Local Industry. A dummy variable coded "one" when there was at least one trade union that included less-skilled workers in the local industry. Because a trade union that incorporated less-skilled members would almost certainly compete for the same workers as a Knights assembly in the same local industry, it is expected that this type of organization will impede the development of Knights of Labor organization.

Trade Union of Less-Skilled Workers in the Community. A dummy variable coded "one" when there was at least one trade union that included less-skilled workers in the community. This type of organization is likely to have contradictory effects on the development of new Knights organization among less-skilled workers in a local industry. On the one hand, when no direct competition over membership is involved, less-skilled organization of any variety should function as a positive model for new less-skilled organization. But, on the other hand, differences in philosophy between the Knights and the trade unions might be more salient than the commonality of less-skilled status.

Knights of Labor (KOL) Organization of Less-Skilled Workers in the Community. A variable coded "one" when there was at least one Knights assembly that included less-skilled members from any industry in the community. This variable is included because an assembly of less-skilled workers anywhere in a community is likely to serve as a positive model for the development of other such assemblies.

Knights of Labor (KOL) Mixed Assembly in the Community. A dummy variable indicating the presence of at least one mixed assembly in the community. It is included because the jurisdiction of mixed assemblies overlapped that of all other labor organizations. Therefore, it is likely that mixed assemblies would have competed with other forms of organization.

Analytical Methods

I used event-history analysis to identify the conditions that encouraged the organization of less-skilled workers. This statistical technique models variation among local industries and over time in the annual rates at which the Knights incorporated less-skilled workers. Specifically, I used a log-linear specification to estimate how vectors of independent variables altered the rate of emergence of Knights organization incorporating less-skilled workers, where the "rate of emergence" is defined as the instantaneous probability of forming one or more such local assemblies in a local industry where none currently exist. No distinction is made in this analysis between "quasi-industrial" and "sectional" organizing strategies; both are considered as organizations for less-skilled workers. There were seventy-eight cases of organizational emergence in New Jersey between 1880 and 1895.

The analysis proceeds in two stages. First, I estimated a model that examined the impact of community and industrial variables on the incorporation of less-skilled workers into the Knights (reported as Model 9a). Second, I created a more inclusive model that adds the set of dummy variables indicating the forms of labor organization already established in the community (Model 9b). I treated the improvement in fit by substituting the second model for the first as an indicator of whether existing organization affected the founding of new organization among less-skilled workers.

The second model (9b) incorporates period effects. Because the Knights of Labor grew at a much faster rate before 1886 than after (see Chapter 4), I allowed the parameters of the organizational variables to differ from the first time period (1880–86) to the second one (1887–95). This enabled me to examine whether different forms of organization had varying effects in the two time periods. Period effects were not included in the first model because, largely as a result of being measured so infrequently, the effects of the community and industrial variables do not vary significantly in the two time periods (based on

Table 9. Impact of industrial, community, and organizational factors on the rate of emergence of Knights of Labor organization among less-skilled manufacturing workers in New Jersey, 1880–1895

Independent variables	Model 9a[a]		Model 9b[b]			Model 9c[b]		
	Coefficient	Standard error	Coefficient	Standard error	Impact	Coefficient	Standard error	Impact
Industrial factors								
Establishment size	.006**	.001	.007**	.001	1.65	.007**	.001	1.65
Log establishments	.39**	.12	.45**	.13	1.61	.43**	.12	1.58
Wage differential	.15	.19	.22	.20	1.14	—	—	—
Technological change	.23**	.09	.21	.11	1.28	.23**	.08	1.31
Horsepower/worker, 1880	-.01	.13	-.046	.14	.94	—	—	—
Capital-to-labor ratio	-.08	.06	-.099	.06	.45	-.098	.056	.45
Percent female	.17	.56	-.43	.63	.92	—	—	—
Community factors								
Log population	.65**	.16	.35	.27	1.49	.49*	.22	1.75
One industry	-.02	.30	.16	.34	1.17	—	—	—
Ethnic diversity	-.006	2.5	.02	.03	1.001	—	—	—
1880–1886 time period								
Intercept	-11.3	1.6	-10.5	2.4		-9.8	1.9	
Organizational factors[c]								
Craft organization								
KOL craft in local industry	—	—	-.98	.67	.37	-.84	.61	.43
TU craft in local industry	—	—	-.23	.46	.79	—	—	—
KOL craft in community	—	—	1.07**	.41	2.92	1.01**	.37	2.74
TU craft in community	—	—	-.67	.48	.51	-.73	.45	.48
Less-skilled-workers' organization								
TU less skilled in local industry	—	—	-.016	.57	.98	—	—	—
TU less skilled in community	—	—	-.026	.41	.97	.018	.41	1.02
KOL less skilled in community	—	—	.50	.32	1.65	.51	.31	1.66
Mixed KOL in community	—	—	.31	.38	1.36	—	—	—

1887–1895 time period

	9a[a]			9b			9c[b]		
Intercept	-14.2	1.7		-15.2	2.8		-14.2	2.3	
Organizational factors[c]									
Craft organization									
KOL craft in local industry	—	—	—	3.69**	1.10	39.8	3.63**	1.04	37.7
TU craft in local industry	—	—	—	-.06	1.27	.9	—	—	—
KOL craft in community	—	—	—	1.92	1.45	6.81	1.90	1.42	6.7
TU craft in community	—	—	—	-2.39	2.09	.09	-2.67	2.02	.07
Less-skilled-workers' organization									
TU less skilled in local industry	—	—	—	-.50	1.26	.61	—	—	—
TU less skilled in community	—	—	—	3.59	2.16	36.2	3.30	2.01	27.0
KOL less skilled in community	—	—	—	-.91	1.51	.40	-1.08	1.52	.34
Mixed KOL in community	—	—	—	.04	1.38	1.04	—	—	—
X^2[d]	240			280.09			276.21		
(d.f.)	(11)			(27)			(16)		

* p < .05; ** p < .01 (two-tailed tests)

Note: 78 events; 3,087 total spells covering 513 local industries for the period 1880–95. 30 local industries were dropped because of missing data. Maximum likelihood estimates are from event-history analysis. All models fit significantly better than a constant-rate model (.001 level). See text (pp. 149–55) for definitions of emergence and independent variables. Including information on organizational factors significantly improved the fit (X^2 associated with substituting 9b for 9a is 40.09 with 16 d.f.), but the more complete model 9b is not significantly better than model 9c (X^2 of 3.88 with 11 d.f.).

[a] The intercept is allowed to vary in the two time periods so that, when Model 9a is compared to Model 9b, the resulting improvement in fit reflects only the addition of the organizational variables, not the inclusion of period effects.

[b] The parameters of the industrial and community variables are constrained to have the same effect in both time periods. The parameters of the organizational variables are allowed to vary from the first time period to the second.

[c] Organizational factors measure whether locals of each type were present in the community or industry at the beginning of the calendar year.

[d] X^2, −2 log likelihood, measures the improvement in fit produced by substituting a maximum-likelihood estimate of a model including listed covariates for the null model assuming a constant rate.

a *t*-test comparison of parameters).[45] Thus, in Model 9b, I constrained the parameters of the community and industrial variables to be the same in each time period.[46]

Table 9 also reports a reduced form of Model 9b. Model 9c eliminates clearly nonsignificant variables in order to stabilize coefficient estimates for the significant factors.

Interpreting the coefficients in Table 9 is much like interpreting unstandardized regression coefficients. Positive coefficients indicate that the independent variable increased the probability of union formation, and negative coefficients indicate that the variable decreased the likelihood that less-skilled workers would organize. More specifically, they indicate approximately the amount by which a unit change in each independent variable increases the (logged) rate at which less-skilled labor organizations are founded per year (controlling for other variables).[47]

Table 9 also presents an "impact" column that is included to provide the reader with a more intuitive interpretation of the coefficients. The impact column indicates the factor by which a standard change in the value of each independent variable multiplies the rate of organizational emergence when other variables are held constant at their mean values. The standard change used is the shift from 0 to 1 for dummy variables and the shift from one-half a standard deviation below the mean to one-half a standard deviation above the mean for continuous variables. For instance, the impact column for the dummy variable indicating the presence of a Knights of Labor craft assembly in the community reports a figure of 2.92 in Model 9b. This signifies that the founding rate was almost three times higher when this type of Knights assembly was present (again, controlling for other variables).

---

45. I estimated some models in which I allowed everything but the technological change variables to vary in the two time periods. However, I had too few cases in the second time period for the models to converge with this specification. When models do not converge, the parameter estimates are unstable. It should be noted that the (admittedly unstable) parameter estimates for the background variables did not differ significantly for the two time periods. This suggests that constraining the background variables was an appropriate way to specify the models used here.

46. A reduced model is one that eliminates nonsignificant variables in order to produce more stable parameter estimates. Model 9c eliminates the variables not significant at the .2 level in Model 9b.

47. The qualifier "approximately" is necessary because the model being estimated has a log-linear specification. For a linear specification, the change in the founding rate is a constant multiple of the change in each explanatory variable (other things being equal). But for a log-linear specification, the size of the change in the founding rate depends upon the magnitude of the rate. See Appendix 3 for a brief introduction to event-history analysis, and Nancy Tuma and Michael T. Hannan, *Social Dynamics: Models and Methods* (Orlando: Academic Press, 1984), pp. 157–65, for a discussion of event-history parameters.

Statistical Findings

Model 9a estimates the rate at which the Knights incorporated less-skilled workers as a function of community and industrial context. It indicates that less-skilled workers were more likely to establish a Knights of Labor local when they were employed in industries undergoing rapid mechanization, worked in local industries characterized by large factories, and lived in more urbanized towns. Interestingly, none of the factors that are often mentioned in accounts of American exceptionalism appear to explain local variation in the degree to which less-skilled workers organized in the Knights of Labor: neither the ethnic-diversity parameter nor the wage-differential parameter is significant. Similarly, none of the remaining community and industrial variables are significant in Model 9a.

Model 9b suggests that the effects of the organizational variables had a significant impact on the rate at which less-skilled workers founded Knights of Labor locals. When Model 9b is substituted for Model 9a, the resulting improvement in fit is statistically significant at the .001 level.[48] Although some of the organizational parameters are not significant individually, as a group they improve the predictive power of Model 9b.

Moreover, Model 9b indicates that some types of prior organization played a different role before and after 1887. Here, however, a word of caution is in order. The rate at which less-skilled workers founded new local assemblies declined dramatically after 1886. Before 1887, less-skilled workers in sixty-eight local industries initiated Knights locals, but after 1887 workers were able to establish Knights organization in only ten previously unorganized local industries. The large standard errors and extreme values of the coefficients shown in Table 9 reflect the small number of events being modeled in the second time period. Because the creation of less-skilled assemblies was so rare after 1887, the post-1886 findings must be interpreted cautiously.

First, consider the pre-1887 period: a time of rapid growth for the Knights in both New Jersey and the nation. With one exception, organization emerged more rapidly among the less skilled where other kinds of Knights locals were already established. The presence of craft organization in the community was particularly influential, making

---

48. For a discussion of significance tests and event history analysis, see Paul D. Allison, *Event History Analysis*, Sage University Paper series on Quantitative Applications in the Social Sciences (Beverly Hills: Sage Publications, 1984), pp. 20–21. For a more general discussion of significance tests, consult Ramon E. Henkel, *Tests of Significance*, Sage University Paper series on Quantitative Applications in the Social Sciences (Beverly Hills: Sage Publications, 1976).

less-skilled workers nearly three times as likely to initiate a local assembly (i.e., the impact coefficient for this dummy variable is 2.74 in reduced Model 9c). The presence of other kinds of Knights locals also appears to have encouraged the organization of less-skilled workers. The parameters for the two dummy variables indicating the presence of mixed assemblies and assemblies of less-skilled workers in other local industries both have positive signs.

However, in contrast to the dummy variable for the presence of a craft assembly in the community (significant at the .01 level), neither parameter for the two other dummies indicating the presence of Knights organization in the community is significant. One factor affecting the significance level of the latter dummy variables is the degree to which the three types of Knights organization clustered. In statistical terms, multicollinearity among the three variables tends to inflate the standard errors of the coefficients, decreasing the value of the F-ratios used to indicate statistical significance. Hence, in this case we should be cautious in interpreting the significance level as an indication of unimportance. Rather, the test of the variables as a group, as well as our understanding of multicollinearity, suggests that the presence of any Knights organization in the community probably increased the rate at which less-skilled workers initiated local assemblies.

Nevertheless, the magnitude and significance of the three parameters differ substantially. Although all three types of local assemblies served as models of organization for less-skilled workers, craft assemblies provided the most important model and may have played a more active role in encouraging less-skilled workers to organize.

One type of Knights organization may have discouraged the organization of less-skilled workers. The sign of the dummy variable indicating the presence of a skilled craft assembly in the local industry is negative, which suggests that in the local industry the presence of a skilled assembly may have decreased the rate at which less-skilled workers organized. Here, in other words, we may have some mild support for exclusionary tendencies on the part of skilled craft workers, even in the Knights of Labor. However, this parameter is not statistically discernible at the conventional .05 level, and, given its dramatic shift in the second time period, a more nuanced interpretation is called for. Such an interpretation is advanced when the second time period is discussed below.

Last, the parameters for all forms of trade unionism have negative signs, but none are significant. The most cautious interpretation is that, if trade unions had any impact, the general direction of their joint effect is toward reducing the founding rate of Knights of Labor assemblies of less-skilled workers.

Turning to the post-1887 period, some intriguing differences in organizational effects are apparent. The most dramatic is in the parameter of the dummy variable that indicates the presence of a Knights craft assembly in the local industry. Negative, although not significant, in the early time period, this parameter is positive, large and statistically significant in the post-1887 period. The shift in this parameter suggests that during the period when the Knights were battling repression, internal dissension, and general decline, craft workers in the Knights may have ceased fighting the organization of their less-skilled colleagues and may have begun assisting in the development of less-skilled workers' organization. It should be recalled that the evidence for the negative effect of craft organization in the local industry in the early period was inconclusive—it hinged on a sign of a parameter that was not statistically significant. One reason for the nonsignificance of the parameter might be that within the local industry skilled craft organization had an indeterminate effect—sometimes skilled craft workers aided less-skilled workers when they began to organize, but at other times craft workers either ignored the organizational efforts of their less-skilled fellows altogether or actually disrupted their organizational efforts. In that case, when this dummy variable is included in the model with all the other indicators of Knights organization, the other indicators reflect the general positive effect of organization, but only the negative effect of the presence of a craft assembly in the local industry is indicated in its parameter estimate. Then, in the second period there is a shift; but, given the low number of events, we cannot be confident that it is as dramatic as it seems in Table 9. A certain amount of indeterminacy in the role of prior craft organization in the local industry would be consistent with the findings in both time periods.

Discussion of Statistical Findings

These findings challenge several of our assumptions about American workers, as well as some recent hypotheses about the conditions that are most likely to encourage broad-based worker organization.

In terms of the industrial and community variables, the results are contrary to Herbert Gutman's proposition that small industrial communities were more conducive to worker organization in the late nineteenth century than were large, urban communities. Following Gutman, American labor historians have tended to look for working-class solidarity in small, one-industry towns; my findings suggest that they have missed the most likely arena for alliances between skilled and less-skilled workers.[49]

Empirical findings also cast doubt on Michael Hanagan's suggestion that slow technological change encouraged skilled workers to help less-skilled workers organize. Instead, they accord better with Haydu's argument that sudden innovations were likely to spur alliances across the skill divide. Although my analysis did not examine the effect of mechanization on alliances in any direct fashion, it did suggest that rapid, not slow, technological change increased the probability that less-skilled workers would organize in the Knights of Labor.

These results also call into question the extent to which ethnic diversity systematically hindered unionization. To be sure, ethnic diversity was measured only within the community, but it had no significant impact on the rate of organization among less-skilled workers. However, anecdotal evidence suggests that this may say more about the Knights' ability to manage ethnicity than about the ease with which New Jersey workers overcame ethnic tensions. The Knights' organizational flexibility allowed workers to choose between organizing multiethnic or single-ethnicity locals. Moreover, in districts where members were ethnically diverse, translators were secured for meetings, and tutors were sometimes hired to teach English. But beyond these measures, Knights leaders made astute use of ethnic bonds when building and maintaining their organization. For example, officers of a South Amboy local wrote to John Hayes, then leader of the Knights, asking him to send a Polish organizer so they might entice the new Polish dockworkers to join their assembly. In 1887, "Sister Ryan" of Newark wrote to Powderly with a similar request: she wanted him to use his influence to help get an Irish Catholic elected as a delegate to the General Assembly so that Irish members of the district would not

49. This finding calls into question the periodization adopted by Ira Katznelson and his collaborators. In two influential books, Katznelson argues that America's unique pattern of working-class formation stems in large part from the radical division between the politics of work and the politics of community in the United States. Katznelson believes that the institutional set that supported the divorce of workplace and community issues (that is, political parties organized around community concerns and trade unions organized around workplace interests) was largely in place by the 1860s. After that the die was cast, except perhaps in small communities where the two spheres were not yet so radically divided. This chapter provides strong evidence that community remained the important arena for labor organization even in large urban areas until 1886. See Katznelson, City Trenches, and Katznelson and Zolberg, eds., Working-Class Formation, especially Katznelson's introductory overview and Martin Shefter's essay, "Trade Unions and Political Machines."

feel unrepresented in the Order. Powderly himself seems to have been especially sensitive to the need to manage ethnicity, sometimes to the point of deceit. In 1887, he wrote to "Brother Wright" asking him to talk to Local Assembly 8732 in Smithville, Pennsylvania. Powderly had recently addressed a meeting in Smithville, and while there he was asked to recommend a "good Scotchman" who might speak at a later date. No one immediately came to mind so Powderly mentioned someone with a Scotch name and then wrote to the man, asking him to go and not "make them any the wiser as whether you are Scotch or not if they think you are and it will make any Scotch converts." In any case, it is clear from the event-history analysis that ethnic diversity did not slow the organization of less-skilled workers in New Jersey.[50]

Finally, these findings suggest that different dynamics underlie the relationship between craft organization and class alliance within the community and within the local industry. Within the community, skilled-workers' organization generally encouraged the mobilization of less-skilled workers, but within the local industry, it played an inconsistent role. Before 1887, its presence may have impeded the development of the organization of less-skilled workers, but after 1887 it facilitated it.

These results, then, provide little support for the notion that craft workers in the United States acted as outright labor aristocrats. Even outside of the Knights, the empirical findings provide little support for that hypothesis. However, the results do imply that labor may have had difficulty overcoming the sectional organization of craft workers in the local industry. Even in the Knights of Labor, an organization committed to labor solidarity, workers seem sometimes to have been unable to overcome the vestiges of craft exclusiveness when competition between skilled and less-skilled workers was most direct.

At the same time, it should be emphasized that the pattern observed for craft organization within the Knights of Labor—that is, the fact that craft organization may have encouraged exclusiveness within local industries while still encouraging the organization of less-skilled workers elsewhere in the community—is quite like that observed by Hanagan in late-nineteenth-century France. Thus, it does not appear that the Order of the Knights of Labor was built upon a flimsy or comparatively weak foundation.

However, before we emphasize too strongly the importance of the

---

50. *Sunday Chronicle*, Aug. 6, 1899; *Journal of United Labor*, May 7, 1887; Ed Gallagher to John Hayes, Feb. 28, 1893, microfilm reel 5, *Hayes Papers*; Sister Ryan to Powderly, Sept. 3, 1887, microfilm reel 23, *Powderly Papers*; Powderly to Brother Wright, Aug. 31, 1887, microfilm reel 48, *Powderly Papers*.

community as a locus of solidarity between skilled and less-skilled workers in late-nineteenth-century New Jersey, we need to know a great deal more about how actively craft workers supported the organization of less-skilled workers. Hanagan's work on artisans and industrial workers in late-nineteenth-century France presents detailed information on the activities of skilled workers—he was able to demonstrate that skilled craftsmen provided leadership, financial aid, and important moral support to the strike efforts of less-skilled industrial workers. In contrast, the analysis presented here demonstrates only that prior organization of craft workers in the Knights of Labor coincides with the more rapid organization of less-skilled workers. It provides little information about the actual links between craft organization and the emergence of organization among less-skilled workers. Moreover, it offers few particulars as to why skilled workers may have been concerned with less-skilled workers in their communities, much less why they may have been more concerned with less-skilled workers in other industries than their own. The evidence that I have used up to this point will not allow further exploration of these issues. To find answers to these questions, it is necessary to examine other types of historical evidence.

Uncovering Mechanisms: The Knights in Trenton

If we step back for a moment and consider the ways in which existing organizations might affect the creation of new ones, we can identify at least three ways in which craft organization might have functioned at the community level. First, craft organization may have provided a nucleus of people who actively mobilized less-skilled workers. This, as we have seen, is what Hanagan found in the French communities he studied. Second—a notion equally consistent with the quantitative findings—craft organization may have served merely as a model that less-skilled workers imitated. According to this scenario, once Knights organization was established among skilled craft workers, the universalism of the Knights' message and the self-activity of the less-skilled workers would have been enough to generate the findings we observed in the statistical analysis. The fact that skilled workers were generally looked up to and emulated might account for the relatively greater impact of craft as opposed to other kinds of Knights organization. Third, less-skilled workers may have actively sought skilled workers' aid. In this scenario, craft organization again functions as a model, but less-skilled workers are the initiators of contact. Less-skilled workers who observed the activities of skilled-workers' assemblies could have approached assembly members and requested assistance and resources.

To see whether craft organization functioned in any of these ways, let us look more closely at the role of skilled-workers' locals in the development of the Knights of Labor in one community, Trenton. The narrative focuses on the actions of skilled potters, the largest group of skilled craftsmen in Trenton, which was the center of the American pottery industry.

The first trades assembly of potters was established by the skilled hollow-ware pressers in Trenton in late 1882.[51] It was followed in early 1883 by another assembly of skilled potters, the kilnmen.[52] Each of these groups had a history of union activity dating back to 1862, but neither union had survived a bitter strike and lockout that occurred in 1877.[53] Prior to forming their own Knights locals, each group had joined Mixed Assembly 1362, which was reorganized in June 1882 by potters and other skilled workers.[54] Soon, however, both the pressers and kilnmen left to form their own assemblies. These locals took an active role in the city's tiny labor movement; together with representatives of Trenton's few craft unions, they established the city's first Trade and Labor Council. Soon, the organized potters also became prominent activists in the State Labor Congress.[55]

51. Hollow-ware pressers made items such as large cups, jugs, bowls, vases, tureens, basins, and teapots. They took processed clay, flattened a small amount of it into a pie-crust shape (called a "bat") with a hammer, smoothed its surface with a steel knife (this revealed latent defects in the clay and fixed them), and took a mold and pressed clay into it. The molds were usually in two parts (for complicated pieces, additional parts were necessary), and once the clay had been pressed into both parts, the two pieces were brought together tightly. Using a potters wheel, or "whirler," the presser then sponged out all superfluous clay, patting, smoothing, and trimming until the inside of the dish was perfectly smooth. The mold, with the dish inside of it, was then taken to dry. The mold was made of plaster, which rapidly absorbed water, and after the dish was dry, the presser finished the piece by trimming and sponging its surface. For descriptions of the labor process in pottery factories, see Stern, "Potters," chap. 3; *Trenton Sunday Advertiser*, May 22, 1887; and *Harper's*, 62, February 1881, pp. 357–69. For the occupational designation of the assembly, see NJBSLI, *Tenth Annual Report, 1887*, p. 158.

52. The kilns and the operations that went on in firing the pottery accounted for much of the risk in the industry. The kilnmen put the polished ware in clay boxes (called "saggers"), using supports or packing them with sand, as necessary, put red clay around them, and placed them in the oven. Each oven held 2,000 to 3,000 filled saggers. Each section of the kiln achieved a different temperature and various types of pottery required more or less heat; thus the skill and experience of the kilnmen was very important.

53. NJBSLI, *Tenth Annual Report, 1887*, pp. 157–58; Garlock, *Guide*.

54. This mixed assembly was founded in 1879, but it collapsed a year later and was resurrected again in 1882.

55. *Trenton Sunday Advertiser*, Apr. 8, 1883; Apr. 15, 1883; Dec. 20, 1885; Stern, "Potters," pp. 481–82.

One early member of the kilnmen's local, Philip Tallon, "at once became impressed with the exalted principles of the Order" and took "a deep interest in its success" from then on. He became "one of the most energetic agitators for a District Assembly," which could coordinate the organizing activities of the Knights in Trenton and render aid in the case of labor disputes.[56] District Assembly 90 was founded in the summer of 1883, and Tallon was sent as a delegate for his local assembly. Another kilnman, Thomas Corbett, served as the first master workman (the highest elected office) of District Assembly 90.[57]

The Knights grew slowly in 1883. With the exception of an assembly of cigarmakers, they made few organizational gains, and their growth in membership was confined primarily to skilled workers. The pottery assemblies held picnics to recruit new members and raise money and, along with other Knights locals, generally opted for nonconfrontational tactics. They did, however, speak out on issues of concern to the larger working class (condemning the kinds of working conditions that "factory girls" generally faced and agitating against the "ticket of leave," a practice whereby employers required new workers to present a voucher certifying that they had left their last employer in good standing), but in general they acted with a great deal of restraint.[58]

This cautious approach was abandoned in early 1885, when the pottery manufacturers attempted to reduce potters' wages. A strike was called, and for the first time in Trenton's history manufacturers were forced to sit down and negotiate a settlement with their workers. "Within a fortnight," six new pottery assemblies were organized.[59] Two of these new locals included less-skilled members, although skilled workers represented the greatest concentration of membership in potters' locals throughout the Knights' tenure in Trenton.[60] By July the pottery locals had almost 1,000 members between them.[61]

The potters' success in achieving legitimacy sparked a period of growth for the Knights in Trenton. Three new locals were initiated by workers outside the pottery industry in 1885, all three quasi-industrial

56. *Trenton Sunday Advertiser*, Sept. 5, 1886.
57. Ibid.
58. *Trenton Sunday Advertiser*, Apr. 29, 1883; Stern, *Potters*, 481–82.
59. *Trenton Sunday Advertiser*, Feb. 1, 1885.
60. NJBSLI, *Tenth Annual Report, 1887*, p. 43, reports the membership figure. The assessment that two of these locals included less-skilled workers is based on the study data. Local Assembly 3549, the decorators' local, was organized along quasi-industrial lines, including both skilled and less-skilled decorators (some of whom were women); LA 3548, the jiggermen's and dishmaker's local, eventually adopted the same organizing strategy, including clay carriers and wedgers in their local, although it is unclear whether they did so from the beginning or not. See Stern, "Potters," p. 525.
61. Stern, "Potters," p. 502.

locals that included less-skilled members. Significantly, two of these (the brickmakers' and rubber workers' locals) were created by workers whose factories were located in the same neighborhoods as the potteries.[62] Because many workers in Trenton lived close to where they worked, it is likely that potters, brickmakers, and rubber workers also resided near one another.[63] In any event, Philip Tallon appears to have played a crucial role in nurturing these new assemblies. The *Trenton Sunday Advertiser* reported that his "untiring efforts" were recognized in various ways, one of which was the presentation of a "handsome gold ring" by the local brickmakers' assembly.[64] His help, along with that of District Assembly 90, was probably crucial in the organization of both the rubber workers and the brickmakers. These two locals almost immediately became embroiled in long, expensive labor disputes, each of which quickly evolved into tests of strength for the Knights.[65]

At the beginning of 1886, Tallon was commissioned as an organizer at the recommendation of District Assembly 90. In the first seven months of his commission, he initiated eight new locals, seven of which were composed of less-skilled workers. Indeed, he was such a successful organizer that, "at the request of prominent members" of District Assembly 90, he withdrew from his pottery local rather than resign as organizer when his own local assembly left District Assembly 90 to create a new National District Assembly of Potters in July 1886.[66] Instead, he transferred his membership to Mixed Local 1362.[67]

In Trenton, then, craft organization seems to have functioned in all three of the ways outlined earlier. First, in the person of Philip Tallon (and possibly other members of District Assembly 90 such as Thomas

62. Jessie Rose Turk, "Trenton, New Jersey, in the Nineteenth Century: The Significance of Location in the Historical Geography of a City," Ph.D. diss., Columbia University, 1964, pp. 316–17 and 330–31. Stern estimates that approximately one-third of all potters lived outside of the city limits, but the others, according to Turk, tended to live near the pottery works.

63. There are two other possible linkages among these workers that may have contributed to the pattern of organization observed in Trenton. First, one of the large brickmakers in town also manufactured saggers, the clay boxes used by kilnmen to hold and protect ceramic ware while it was fired (see Turk, "Trenton," p. 317). Second, all the locals for less-skilled workers organized in 1885 included at least some Irish workers. Tallon himself was Irish. (Biographical details about Tallon are given in *Trenton Sunday Advertiser*, Sept. 5, 1886, and in Stern, "Potters," pp. 527 and 531; information about the ethnic composition of New Jersey locals is available in NJBSLI, *Tenth Annual Report, 1887*, pp. 42–44.)

64. Sept. 5, 1886.

65. *Trenton Sunday Advertiser*, Jan. 31, 1886; May 9, 1886; June 27, 1886; Aug. 8, 1886; Nov. 21, 1886; NJBSLI, *Tenth Annual Report, 1887*, pp. 161–62.

66. *Trenton Sunday Advertiser*, Sept. 5, 1886.

67. Ibid.

Corbett), the craft organization of skilled potters provided a committed core of activists. The pottery locals contributed to this effort financially through assessments and other donations to the District Assembly, which in turn directed organizing activities, paid Tallon's salary, and presided over not only the potters' strikes but also the explosive conflicts that followed in the wake of unionization by the rubber workers and brickmakers.

Second, even apart from the activities of Tallon and District Assembly 90, the success of the potters in negotiating a settlement with their employers encouraged other workers to emulate their example. It is interesting to note that the settlement included a wage cut; workers perceived this as positive because employers sat down with a committee of the Knights of Labor and together hammered out a settlement. Hence, it may have been the respect accorded to the potters' arbitration committee (a committee that included Terence Powderly) that inspired some of the workers to join the Knights. (Granted, the cut was less than the employers felt the slump demanded, and hence the potters did achieve some success, but it was the legitimacy that seems to have so impressed the workers.) But whether or not this is true, it is clear that such success could only have helped Tallon in his organizing activities.

Third, there is also some indication that less-skilled workers sought the aid of their skilled counterparts. There is no evidence that the three assemblies initiated in 1885 were organized by a Knights organizer or by another assembly. It is likely that, inspired by the success of the potters' locals, rubber workers, brickmakers, and ironworkers all established their own assemblies. However, it is clear that, at least in the case of the rubber workers and brickmakers, they then relied on Tallon (as signified by the "handsome gold ring") and on the resources of District Assembly 90 to maintain their fledgling locals.

The Importance of the Knights' Organizers

The example of the Trenton potters also provides a response to another of our questions: Why did skilled craft organization within the Knights have a stronger and more consistent effect at the community level than within the local industry?

One answer clearly lies with the Knights' organizers. The impressionistic evidence suggests that the pattern of organization in Trenton was fairly typical. Knights organization spread first to skilled workers as it reactivated old craft locals; when several locals had been established, they initiated a district assembly, which then appointed and paid for one or two organizers.[68] Each organizer received a daily wage, and often a small sum for every local he established.[69] This system could generate rapid growth, and some complaints were registered about untrustworthy organizers. However, given the potential for abuse, it is remarkable that the system worked as well as it did. Organizers were often officials of the district assembly and, because their commissions automatically expired each year, they were dependent on the good will of the district assembly to retain their jobs. Hence, an organizer who engaged in irresponsible organizing would soon be removed, unless, of course the district assembly encouraged such behavior.[70]

An organizer was commissioned to initiate locals in all trades in the district. This in and of itself would explain part of the reason why the presence of craft organization had such a strong effect. In addition, it may provide part of the explanation as to why the community effect was stronger than the industrial effect, at least in the pre-1887 period.[71] When an organizer looked around a community for likely groups to organize, less-skilled workers may have appeared more promising in local industries where craft organization had not been established. First, if skilled workers had already established a local assembly, attempts to organize the less skilled might lead the less skilled to seek admission into the skilled-workers' locals. If they were admitted, no

68. Fink also found that skilled workers were the earliest members of the Knights and that the first Knights assemblies were often revitalized craft locals. See Fink, *Workingmen's Democracy*, pp. 50–53, 75–78, 119–20, 154–56, and 184–88.

Technically, the district assembly recommended organizers and the grand master workman confirmed them. (See Perlman, "Upheaval and Reorganization.") This system gave control over the organizers to the district assemblies, and, although the General Assembly tried repeatedly to wrestle this control away from the district assemblies, it managed only to restrict some of the organizers' actions (i.e., not allowing organizers to initiate strikes).

69. Perlman, "Upheaval and Reorganization," p. 346. I have found no evidence of female organizers in New Jersey; hence I use the masculine pronoun to refer to organizers. But the Order's national office did appoint at least one female organizer, Leonora M. Barry, who was commissioned in 1886. See Susan Levine, "Labor's True Women."

70. For instance, when District Assembly 17 of St. Louis adopted a higher rate of pay ($6 for each new local organized and $5 for every local reorganized), "this provision was virtually an encouragement to an unscrupulous organizer to violate the provision of the General Assembly that said that an organizer must not offer special inducements to former members to rejoin the Order" (Perlman, "Upheaval and Reorganization," p. 380). It should also be noted that in March 1886, the Order's executive board became alarmed at the rapid rate of growth (in February, 515 new locals were organized nationally in one month) and suspended organization for forty days. See Ware, *Labor Movement*, p. 68.

71. In the Knights' later years, there was an erosion of the organizer system in almost every district. At a minimum, the district assemblies had less money to hire organizers as fewer members paid assessments.

new local would be created, and the organizer would receive no commission. Because most organizers were committed labor activists, such a possibility would have been unlikely to prevent the organizer from eventually targeting such less-skilled workers, but it could have led him to try organizing other less-skilled workers first. Second, if an organizer began by concentrating his energies on the less-skilled colleagues of already organized craft workers, he might potentially have encountered resistance from craft workers who did not wish to see them organized. Because the organizer was often a skilled worker himself, he would have been sensitive to any ambiguity surrounding the relations between craft workers and their underlings.[72] Hence, if he sensed ambivalence, his most likely course would have been to organize other workers first. Third, when looking around the community and attempting to decide where to concentrate his organizing efforts, an organizer might suppose that, if the potential existed in industries where the craft workers were already organized, then the craft workers would have already undertaken the organization of their less-skilled fellows. If an organizer acted in any one of these ways, the result would contribute to the community effect we observed in Model 9b.

The Community Arena

But if the Knights' practice of hiring district organizers accounts for a portion of the community effect, it raises a prior question: Why did the Knights choose the community as the basic unit of organization in the first place? And why did the community as a basic unit of organization appeal to the skilled workers who were some of the Knights' earliest members?

Here I think the social historians would rightfully point out that in the late nineteenth century, "the local community constituted the main arena of intellectual, social, and political life."[73] To this we might add workers' past experience with craft organization. As the *Trenton Sunday Advertiser* saw it in 1886, "capitalists would like to see a return to trades unions, where each trade acting alone would be whipped in detail, but the workers have had some experience on that line."[74] This theme was echoed again in 1890 when the Trenton Potters debated

72. This statement is based on Perlman's assessment ("Upheaval and Reorganization," p. 346) that organizers were generally officers of the district assembly, and on organizers' occupations reported in Fink, *Workingmen's Democracy*, and in scattered sources about the occupations of organizers in New Jersey.

73. Walkowitz, *Worker City*, p. 13.

74. Apr. 4, 1886.

severing their ties with the now-failing Knights. In the discussion, a generational split was evident in the attitudes of different groups of workers toward the Knights. Older workers remembered the weaknesses of separate trade organizations and fought the younger members who could not remember the 1870s and did not understand why they should have to pay assessments for nonpottery workers while the latter were on strike.[75]

For skilled workers such as these potters, the importance of community seems to have been in part a pragmatic issue. Much like the artisanal glass and file workers described by Hanagan, the potters increasingly depended on organization to maintain their wage rates and their position on the shopfloor.[76] For them, an attack on any union or against any group of workers anywhere in their town seemed nothing but a prelude to an attack on their own organization. Moreover, if workers, whether skilled or not, could successfully organize large portions of the working-class community, they could bring much greater pressure to bear on recalcitrant employers. This is reflected in the Knights' widespread use of boycotts. Workers in one factory or industry were often not strong enough to force concessions or union recognition, but with the help of a communitywide boycott, they could not only refuse to buy the products of the offending employer, they could also prevent the housing and feeding of strikebreakers by enlisting the aid of shopkeepers.[77] In addition, they could hope to win over local public opinion and to ostracize factory owners whose local authority, as Gutman points out, was not yet legitimated. This tactic, of course, not only highlighted the importance of community-based organization, it made it at least as important to organize workers outside the industry as inside it.[78]

This brings us, finally, to the issue of power. As a skilled glassworker told the New Jersey Bureau of Statistics in 1884: "The working people must rise in a body. The glass blowers are too isolated from the great body of wage-workers, and while they themselves, because of their better wages, may occupy a higher social position, yet if all workingmen would come together in one great organization, their power, both socially and politically, would be much greater."[79] There is little doubt

75. Stern, "Potters," pp. 557–62.
76. Ibid., pp. 536–54.
77. For New Jersey examples, see David Bensman, *Practice*, pp. 131–49, and reports about the actions of merchants in South Amboy during the coal handlers' strike in the *New York Sun*, Jan. 27, 1887.
78. Gutman, *Work*.
79. NJBSLI, *Seventh Annual Report, 1884*, p. 239.

that this search for political power was the foundation of the Knights' appeal for many workers, both skilled and unskilled. Through combination, these workers hoped to win not only the day-to-day battles but also to establish a cooperative commonwealth that would abolish the ruthless economy that unjustly reduced workers, whose labor produced all wealth, to mere wage slaves.[80]

The community was a natural arena for an organization that placed such great emphasis on combination and cooperation. As the *Boston Labor Leader* noted, the special strength of the Knights lay "in the fact that the whole life of the community is drawn into it, that people of all kinds are together . . . , and that they all get directly the sense of each others' needs."[81]

Summary

This examination of how Trenton workers joined the Knights helps to clarify the relationship between craft organization and the recruitment of less-skilled workers into the Knights. The statistical analysis suggested that, within the community, the presence of craft locals encouraged the organization of less-skilled workers but that, within the industry, craft locals may sometimes have impeded the rapid unionization of less-skilled workers. In Trenton, pottery workers were among the first to join the Knights and initiate local assemblies. Drawing on long traditions of craft pride and autonomy, they founded craft locals. These locals provided the organizer, resources, and moral support needed to build a labor movement. In erecting that movement, the organizer focused most of his efforts on the larger community rather than on his own industry. He did so, perhaps, because as a skilled man himself, he sensed among his coworkers a certain wariness about organizing their own helpers. He may also have had some of his own pecuniary interests at heart. Certainly, however, he and other craftsmen in the Knights also believed that communitywide organization was the best way to win better working conditions in the short run and to create a cooperative commonwealth in the future.

Within the Knights, then, community, rather than industry, was the most promising foundation on which to build an inclusive labor

80. For the Knights' views on combination and cooperation, see Jama Lazerow, "The Knights of Labor: Boston as a Case Study," and Richard Schindehutte, "Organized Labor and Class Struggle: The Knights and 'All of Labor,' 1870–1890," both presented at the Knights of Labor Centennial Symposium, Chicago, May 17–19, 1979.

81. Feb. 5, 1887, quoted in Fink, *Workingmen's Democracy*, p. 14.

movement. This was also true of France, where workers eventually constructed a lasting alliance among skilled and less-skilled workers. Thus, from a comparative perspective, the pattern of mobilization observed in the Knights was not exceptional; on the contrary, the edifice around which American workers attempted to erect a working-class movement was quite strong.

6

Organizing Together,
Organizing Apart

Industrial unionism is socialism with its working clothes on.
—William Haywood

Not all scholars or labor activists would go as far as "Big Bill" Haywood in their claims about industrial unions, but most would agree that unions that unite skilled and less-skilled workers in the same local usually strengthen members' sense of working-class solidarity and that locals restricted to a single occupation or skill level tend to reinforce sectional identities. For less-skilled workers, industrial forms of association also offer clear advantages because they provide greater negotiating strength and collective resources than sectional associations. And from the vantage point of this book, industrial forms of organization are one clear marker of alliances across the skill divide.[1]

In this chapter I examine the organizing strategies adopted by Knights assemblies that included less-skilled workers. I distinguish two such strategies: a quasi-industrial strategy of offering membership to both skilled and less-skilled workers, and a sectional strategy of organizing unskilled and semiskilled workers but not craft workers. I ask whether there are systematic differences in the conditions that encouraged one organizing strategy rather than the other.

One purpose of pursuing this question is to clarify the effects of existing craft organization on the unionization of less-skilled workers

---

1. Melding skilled and less-skilled workers together in a local assembly was by no means the only important kind of alliance that occurred among workers in the Knights. When Trenton potters raised money after employers locked out less-skilled rubber workers, and when skilled hat finishers in Orange struck in support of the organizational efforts of semiskilled, female hat trimmers, both were allying with less-skilled workers. But references to such events are fleeting and scattered, largely because few labor newspapers from these years survive.

within local industries. In the preceding chapter, we saw that such organization sometimes encouraged and sometimes impeded the emergence of assemblies of the less skilled. By distinguishing sectional and quasi-industrial forms of less-skilled-workers' locals, we will be able to examine whether skilled-workers' craft assemblies in the local industry tended to obstruct any kind of organization of less-skilled workers or only quasi-industrial organization. If the latter is true, we would be less likely to label skilled workers as labor aristocrats with respect to their own underlings and more likely to argue that once skilled workers were organized around a craft identity, it became difficult to recruit them to broader forms of organization. From my recent study of the Knights in the iron and steel industry, I concluded that craft locals in iron and steel counties encouraged the organization of less-skilled workers but steered the new locals into sectional forms that were less likely to survive and thrive, thus over the long run limiting the Knights' potential.[2] A systematic investigation of the broad range of local industries in New Jersey will allow us to assess whether this was a more general occurrence.

An examination of the organizational strategies of less-skilled workers also provides further insight into the role of Knights organization of skilled workers within the community. Now that we have discovered that this type of Knights organization was more important than any other organizational factor in encouraging less-skilled workers to unionize, it would be helpful to know whether it also encouraged joint organization across the skill divide or channeled less-skilled-workers' assemblies into sectional forms.

Variables and Analytical Methods

The statistical analysis reported here parallels that discussed in the preceding chapter. Event-history analysis is again used to identify the conditions that facilitated the founding of Knights of Labor locals that incorporated less-skilled manufacturing workers. This time, however, the event-history analysis models variations among local industries and over time in the annual rate at which quasi-industrial and sectional locals were established.[3] All 154 locals that recruited less-skilled

2. Conell and Voss, "Formal Organization and the Fate of Social Movements."
3. The models used in this chapter are somewhat more complicated to estimate than the ones used in the preceding one. They incorporate both repeated events (i.e, the founding of all less-skilled workers' locals are included) and multiple kinds of events (i.e., quasi-industrial locals distinguished from sectional locals). One simplifying as-

manufacturing workers are included. Numbered among these are the first assemblies that appeared in previously unorganized local industries and those that formed in local industries in which less-skilled workers had already established a local.[4] As Table 8 indicated, these assemblies were almost equally likely to pursue sectional and quasi-industrial strategies: seventy-two (46 percent) were quasi-industrial assemblies, and eighty-three (54 percent) were sectional assemblies.

All the industrial and community variables described in Chapter 5 are included in the models reported here. With three exceptions, the organizational measures are also identical. The first exception consists of the replacement of the two variables that indicate the presence of a trade union of less-skilled workers in the local industry and in the community by the following variable:

Trade Union (TU) of the Less Skilled. A dummy variable coded "one" when at least one trade union organizing less-skilled workers was present in *either* the local industry *or* the community.

This variable was collapsed to reduce the complexity of the model.[5] In addition, I included two new variables describing the types of organizing strategies found among less-skilled workers in the local industry:

---

sumption had to be made: that the founding of the two types of locals operated independently at each moment in time. In reality, of course, the existence of each type of organization is likely to affect the founding of the other type. I built this into my models by including (time-varying) dummy variables that indicate the presence of quasi-industrial and sectional organization in each local industry. The RATE program does simultaneous estimation for multiple types of outcomes, and I used it for the estimates I report here.

4. The data do not permit a partitioning of emergence by organizing strategies because the date of organization is recorded in years; in cases where both a quasi-industrial and sectional assembly were born in the same year, there is no way to know which one came first. Thus, I had two choices. I could either maintain the focus on emergence by modeling the birth of each type of less-skilled-workers' local, or I could ignore the distinction between first and subsequent organization. I chose the latter course for two reasons. First, I originally focused on the emergence of less-skilled-workers' organization because I reasoned that the initial creation of organization by any particular group is the hardest to accomplish. Therefore, isolating the first appearance would allow us better to observe the role of skilled workers in sharing or withholding their resources. Having discovered that organization of skilled workers promoted organization of less-skilled workers, I found no equally compelling reason to isolate the first appearance of a particular organizing strategy. More important, because I was unable to partition the dependent variable analyzed in Chapter 5, if I had modeled only the first appearance of quasi-industrial and sectional locals, I would have had a hybrid analysis that was difficult to interpret. Second, by ignoring the distinction between first and subsequent organization, I could make use of all the information I had on the formation of less-skilled-workers' locals.

5. Note that the parameters of these two measures were not significant in either Model 9b or 9c. In addition, neither variable is the focus of theoretical attention. For both these reasons, these were the best measures to collapse.

Knights of Labor (KOL)*Quasi-Industrial Organization in the Local Indus-try.* A dummy variable coded "one" when at least one assembly organizing workers on a quasi-industrial basis was present in the local industry.

Knights of Labor (KOL)*Sectional Organization of the Less Skilled in the Local Industry.* A dummy variable coded "one" when at least one assembly organizing less-skilled workers on a narrow, sectional basis was present in the local industry.

These variables were not included in the earlier analysis because it was limited to the emergence of organization among less-skilled workers who at the time lacked organizational vehicles. That meant, by definition, that when either sectional or quasi-industrial assemblies including less-skilled workers were initiated, the local industry was eliminated from the risk set for the analysis. Here, however, the first appearance of a local is not isolated, and local industries are not elimi-nated from the risk set when less-skilled workers unionize.

The inclusion of these two variables makes it possible to investigate whether the establishment of a particular form of Knights organiza-tion among less-skilled workers interfered with the development of alternative forms. Once a group of workers was organized on a nar-row basis, it might have been harder to recruit them to broadly-based organization and vice versa. (Organizing strategies are distinguished for the Knights but not for the trade unions because there was little variation in the organizing strategies pursued by trade union locals in New Jersey.)

As in the preceding chapter, the analysis proceeded in two stages. First, I estimated models in which the independent variables reflected the nature of the community and of the industrial context. Second, I estimated models that included these independent variables plus a set of variables indicating the form of labor organization already estab-lished in the local community. As in Chapter 5, the latter models in-corporated period effects.

This time, however, models that include only the community and industrial variables are not reported. The primary purpose of this chapter is to compare how the independent variables affected the de-velopment of quasi-industrial and sectional locals. This comparison requires the estimation of the more inclusive models. Thus, I merely report that adding the organizational variables significantly improved the fit of both models (at the .001 level). Given that prior organization played such an important role in the emergence of Knights organiza-tion of less-skilled workers, this finding is not surprising. However, it is important to keep it in mind as we discuss the different ways in which this pre-existing organization affected the development of each type of less-skilled-workers' local.

I also report here only the reduced form of the fully specified models. These models are the same as the fully inclusive models except for the fact that I eliminated clearly nonsignificant variables in order to stabilize coefficient estimates for the significant factors.

Statistical Findings

Table 10 reports the results of the event-history analysis. As in Table 9, I report coefficients, standard errors, and an "impact" column.[6]

When one compares first the overall models, it is readily apparent that, although there were differences in the contexts that shaped quasi-industrial and sectional organizing strategies, these differences were primarily ones of degree rather than kind. Rarely does a parameter have a different sign in the two models; instead most disparities are a matter of magnitude and significance. Thus, my discussion of the models highlights parameter differences that either are significant at the .05 level (based on a *t*-test) or where one parameter is significant at the .1 level *and* is at least twice as large as the other.

Turning first to the industrial variables, Table 10 reports that the parameter for establishment size is exactly the same in both models. Big factories promoted organization among less-skilled workers but did not shape the organizing strategy. In contrast, numerous factories, which also encouraged the development of both types of less-skilled assemblies, disproportionately increased the rate at which sectional locals developed. Since numerous factories in a local industry generally meant more workers employed in the same occupation, this finding suggests that when a large organizational base existed for a particular occupation, workers were likely to pursue labor organization that capitalized on sectional identities.

High wage differentials and rapid technological change encouraged sectional but not quasi-industrial organization. In the case of wage differentials, the parameters in the two models are significantly different, a finding that suggests that large wage differentials channeled workers into narrowly based organizations. The tendency of large wage differentials to channel organization into narrow forms supports a modified

6. See Chapter 5 for a description of the impact column and a discussion of how the event-history coefficients should be interpreted.

version of the labor aristocracy argument according to which large wage differentials will tend to promote sectional interests.

The parameter for technological change has a significant positive effect on the development of sectional locals and an insignificant effect on the development of quasi-industrial locals, but the difference between the two parameters is not statistically significant. Thus, rapid technological change probably encouraged the organization of less-skilled workers but did not significantly shape the organizing strategy adopted.

Large capital-to-labor ratios impeded the organization of sectional locals but had little impact on quasi-industrial locals. This suggests that high levels of mechanization discouraged the organization of workers along narrow, sectional lines.

Last, the proportion of females in the local industry was the only industrial variable that had a significant effect on the development of quasi-industrial assemblies, but not on the development of sectional assemblies. The presence of female workers apparently hampered the development of quasi-industrial locals. As noted in Chapter 5, women workers generally had few resources for investing in organization; in addition, they were often viewed by males as competitors. This finding suggests that workers were rarely able to bridge the distance between male and female workers.

Turning next to the community variables, Table 10 indicates that large, ethnically diverse towns increased the founding rate of quasi-industrial local assemblies, but neither population size nor ethnic diversity had a significant impact on the development of sectional assemblies. The positive parameter for ethnic diversity is contrary to conventional wisdom; it implies that separate ethnic communities might encourage unity as well as fragmentation. Since the Knights allowed workers in the same industry to organize separate locals for each ethnicity, ethnic ties may have provided an associational base for quasi-industrial locals. That is, ethnic ties may have been one way for workers to bridge the distance between skilled and less-skilled employees.[7] Given that my measure of ethnic diversity is highly correlated with the percentage of foreign-born workers, this finding also suggests that the diverse traditions of the immigrants made some of the foreign-born workers more friendly to the class appeal of the

---

7. Here is one place where we are hindered by lack of information about the ethnic composition of local industries; before advancing this claim more strenuously, we would want such information.

Table 10. Impact of industrial, community, and organizational factors on the rate of development of different types of organization among less-skilled manufacturing workers in New Jersey, 1880–1895 (reduced models)

Independent variables	Sectional organizing strategy, model 10a[a]			Quasi-industrial organizing strategy, model 10b[a]		
	Coefficient	Standard error	Impact	Coefficient	Standard error	Impact
Industrial factors						
Establishment size	.008**	.001	1.78	.008**	.001	1.78
Log establishments	1.15**	.14	3.38	.62**	.13	1.93
Wage differential	.65**	.22	1.48	.14	.24	1.09
Technological change	.23**	.09	1.31	.13	.09	1.17
Horsepower/worker, 1880	—	—	—	—	—	—
Capital-to-labor ratio	-.26**	.11	.12	-.01	.04	.92
Percent female	-.40	.62	.92	-1.90**	.77	.68
Community factors						
Log population	.02	.23	1.02	.55*	.28	1.87
One industry	—	—	—	—	—	—
Ethnic diversity	.03	.04	1.002	.09**	.03	1.006
1880–1886 time period						
Intercept	-9.7	2.6		-17.2	3.0	
Organizational factors[b]						
Craft organization						
KOL craft in local industry	-.66	.37	.52	-1.18*	.53	.31
TU craft in local industry	—	—	—	—	—	—
KOL craft in community	.76*	.36	2.13	1.57**	.47	4.80
TU craft in community	.02	.51	1.02	-1.83**	.55	.16
Mixed KOL in community	—	—	—	—	—	—

Less-skilled-workers' organization						
TU less skilled	.25	.43	1.28	-.58	.48	.56
KOL sectional in local industry	.56	.31	1.76	-.23	.41	.80
KOL quasi-industrial in local industry	—	—	—	—	—	—
KOL less skilled in community	.17	.32	1.19	1.07**	.39	2.93
1887–1895 time period						
Intercept	-12.3	2.8		-88.1	—c	
Organizational factors[b]						
Craft organization						
KOL craft in local industry	2.60*	1.17	13.50	2.03*	.93	7.67
TU craft in local industry	—	—	—	—	—	—
KOL craft in community	.57	1.30	1.77	26.6	—c	—d
TU craft in community	-1.89	1.80	.15	2.32	—c	—d
Mixed KOL in community	—	—	—	—	—	—
Less-skilled-workers' organization						
TU less skilled	2.08	1.77	8.01	15.3	—c	—d
KOL sectional in local industry	-.98	1.41	.37	-.49	1.14	.61
KOL quasi-industrial in local industry	—	—	—	—	—	—
KOL less skilled in community	-.83	1.37	.44	24.6	—c	—d
Model X²[e]			437.06		307.74	
(d.f.)			(21)		(21)	

* p < .10; ** p < .05 (two tailed tests)

Note: 155 events; 3,754 spells covering 513 local industries for the period 1880–95. 30 local industries were dropped because of missing data. Maximum-likelihood estimates are from event-history analysis. See text (pp. 149–55 and 175–78) for definitions of development and independent variables. Both models fit significantly better than a constant-rate model (.001 level).

[a] The parameters of the industrial and community variables are constrained to have the same effect in every time period. The parameters of the organizational variables are allowed to vary from the first time period to the second.

[b] The organizational factors measure whether assemblies using particular organizing strategies were operating in the county at the beginning of the calendar year.

[c] Standard errors for variables included in the model are not reported when their values are greater than ten times the parameter value.

[d] The impact estimates are not reported when the value of the standard error is greater than ten times the value of the parameter estimate.

[e] X², −2 log likelihood, measures improvement in fit produced by substituting a maximum-likelihood estimate of a model including listed covariates for the null model assuming a constant rate.

Knights of Labor and more likely to put it into practice by organizing quasi-industrial locals than were native-born workers.

Turning finally to the organizational field, the figures in Table 10 indicate several differences in the way in which existing labor organization shaped the development of sectional and quasi-industrial local assemblies in the pre-1887 period. Only the presence of a skilled-workers' Knights assembly in the community affected the founding rate of sectional locals, whereas several organizational variables significantly affected the founding rate of quasi-industrial locals. The presence of any Knights organization in the community generally facilitated the development of quasi-industrial organization. A Knights craft assembly in the community had the greatest impact: quasi-industrial locals were almost five times more likely to be initiated when craft workers were already organized in a Knights assembly elsewhere in the community. But other Knights assemblies incorporating less-skilled workers in the community also had a substantial effect, increasing the rate of quasi-industrial organization almost 300 percent. In contrast, the presence of a skilled-workers' Knights assembly in the local industry is negatively related to the development of quasi-industrial locals. Last, the presence of a skilled trade union in the community also discouraged the development of quasi-industrial locals. Interestingly, this apparent competition between the Knights and the trade unions seems not to have affected the development of sectional locals.

Two of these findings are of particular interest for the light they shed on questions raised in Chapter 5 about the role of skilled-workers' Knights organization. First, although the presence of such an assembly in the community encouraged the development of both sectional and quasi-industrial organization, it disproportionately promoted the development of quasi-industrial locals. New assemblies offering membership to less-skilled workers were about twice as likely to be organized along quasi-industrial lines as along sectional lines when craft workers had already established a local in the community. Second, the presence of a skilled-workers' Knights assembly in the local industry tended to impede the organization of less-skilled workers, no matter which organizing strategy we examine. When considered together, these two findings imply that before 1887 Knights organization for skilled workers in the community was more likely to encourage the organization of the less skilled when skilled workers were not already organized in the local industry. This provides support for the arguments I developed in Chapter 5 as to why craft organization within the Knights had a stronger and more consistent effect at the community level than within the local industry. I contended that the Knights' system of organizers was part of the explanation and then went on to spell out some of the reasons why an organizer might have been more likely to organize less-skilled workers in industries where the skilled were not currently organized. The findings presented in Table 10 provide supporting evidence for a key line in that argument: the presence of a skilled-workers' Knights assembly in the community did indeed tend to encourage disproportionately the development of organization of less-skilled workers in industries where the skilled were not already organized into the Knights of Labor. Moreover, this facilitation effect more often resulted in the creation of quasi-industrial locals than of sectional locals. When industries without craft assemblies were organized by the Knights, quasi-industrial organizing strategies were favored.

After 1887, craft organization within the industry no longer impeded the unionization of less-skilled workers. Instead, it facilitated both quasi-industrial and sectional locals, and it was the only organizational variable to affect significantly the founding of either form of local assemblies of the less skilled. This is very similar to the results presented in Table 9, but, unfortunately, the same cautions must also be applied when interpreting the results for the later period in Table 10. Because all local assemblies of less-skilled workers are considered in this chapter, a few additional foundings are observed after 1887 (six in the case of quasi-industrial locals and eight in the case of sectional locals), but, in Models 10a and 10b, these additional events are being partitioned into two categories. Especially in the case of quasi-industrial locals, the small number of events being modeled produces unreliable parameter estimates. Hence, once again we can only treat the estimates for the second time period as suggestive.

Discussion of Statistical Findings

These findings help to clarify the conditions that were most likely to encourage broad-based union locals in the Knights of Labor, and it also elucidates the effects of craft organization on the recruitment of less-skilled workers into the labor movement.

In terms of industrial and community contexts, the results suggest that large wage differentials, labor-intensive production techniques and multiple establishments tended to encourage workers to organize narrowly rather than broadly. Urban residence, immigrant communities, and male-dominated work settings tended to promote organization across the skill divide.

As for craft organization, these findings again highlight the different relationship between craft organization and class alliance within the community and the local industry. Within the local industry, craft organization in the Knights' early years generally slowed the recruitment of less-skilled workers, no matter whether we consider sectional or quasi-industrial locals. Only after the crisis of 1886 do craft workers appear to have overcome their wariness about aiding the organization of their underlings. After 1886 the presence of craft assemblies facilitated the organization of both sectional and quasi-industrial locals of less-skilled workers.

Within the industry, then, craft organization had an inhibiting rather than a channeling effect on the unionization of less-skilled workers before 1887 and an encouraging rather than a channeling effect after 1887. Thus, it does not appear that Knights craft organization in New Jersey industries had the same kind of invariant channeling effect it did in the iron and steel industries; instead, its effect was mediated by historical circumstances.

At the community level, however, craft organization in the Knights generally encouraged the unionization of less-skilled workers throughout the Order's history. Moreover, it channeled less-skilled workers' assemblies into quasi-industrial forms. This finding is consistent with arguments made in Chapter 5 about how organizers reasoned and about the importance of the Knights' community focus.

Once again, then, we find that community ties were crucial in bridging the differences between skilled and less-skilled workers.

7

The Decline
of Solidarity

The weight given to the failure of the Knights of Labor in histories of the American labor movement is one thing that sets the "old" labor history apart from the "new." When earlier generations of historians and labor economists wrote of the Knights, they emphasized the failure of the Order, citing it as prima facie evidence that American workers lacked class consciousness.[1] Practitioners of the "new" labor history, in contrast, tend to focus less attention on the Knights' failure, highlighting instead the Order's ideology, strike actions, and initial success at organizing broad sectors of the working class. For them, these provide clear proof that American workers were capable of acting collectively in ways that rival their supposedly more class-conscious European colleagues.[2]

Both generations of labor historians make assumptions about the relationship between consciousness and organizations that, from a sociologist's viewpoint, are problematic. The "old" labor historians assume that it is possible to read backward from the lack of a successful working-class movement to a lack of interest in such movements. The "new" labor historians make the inverse mistake, implying that uncovering oppositional consciousness is as good as finding radical institutions.

1. Perlman, "Upheaval and Reorganization"; Grob, *Workers and Utopia.*
2. Wilentz, "Against Exceptionalism."

Both generations, in other words, tend to mistake collective dispositions for collective actions. They tend to assume that groups of people
who share motivational constructs or are disposed to behave in certain ways will automatically find ways to transform these dispositions
into behavior. Conceptualizing class formation as a social movement
alerts one to this fallacy. Those who investigate social movements
pay careful attention to the several steps that intervene between disposition and action, and adopting their analytical insights provides
a way of developing an improved, historically sensitive explanation
for the shape of the American working class. In minimalist outline,
we need to recognize that it is through organization and mobilization
that people constitute themselves as a class. This means that the conditions that lead people to see the world in class terms may not be
the same as those that sustain organizations created to act on such a
vision; and we need first to investigate the circumstance that encourage both the worldview and organizational longevity in critical moments of labor movement development. Second, we need to attend
to the interaction between ideology and organizational development.
One thing that a social movement organization does, as Scott McNall
points out, is to explain past failures, current defeats, and possible
futures; the explanations offered affect members' tactics as well as the
growth of the organization.[3] Moreover, the rapidity of organizational
growth feeds back on this process, affecting both solidarity and commitment. Finally, just as protesters' actions alone do not determine
the outcome of a social movement, workers are not the only participants in the process of working-class formation: employers and the
state play an equally important role in shaping a labor movement.

Taking seriously the distinction between disposition and action, in
this chapter I provide an explanation of the Knights' collapse that
recognizes both the class consciousness of its appeal and the inability
of Knights members to sustain local organizations initiated as an expression of that class consciousness. After reviewing in more detail the
explanations others have offered of the Knights' decline, I report on
two statistical studies of the Knights' collapse in New Jersey, one that
focuses on the demise of skilled-workers' locals and the other that con-
centrates on the failure of less-skilled-workers' locals. Both highlight
the destructive impact of employers' associations, a finding that I pursue further through a comparative examination of American, French,
and English employers' associations. Concluding that American em-

---

3. Scott McNall, *The Road to Rebellion* (Chicago: University of Chicago Press, 1988),
esp. chap. 1.

ployers' associations were stronger, but that this fact alone cannot completely explain the impact of the Knights' defeat on the American labor movement, I look more closely in a case study at the relationship between workers' organization, Knights ideology, and employers' actions in one New Jersey city, Newark.

Why Did the Knights Collapse? Old Views and New Agendas

The standard historical account of the Knights' decline, and the one that remains most influential among political sociologists, was offered at the end of World War I by Selig Perlman, a student of John R. Commons.[4] He treated the Order as a single, unified national entity and analyzed it in relation to the organization that would eventually supplant it, the AFL. In Perlman's view, skilled workers in the United States were unwilling to jeopardize their stronger bargaining position in order to improve the situation for less-skilled workers; thus, when less-skilled workers flooded into the Knights, skilled workers fled the Order and joined the AFL. Perlman assumes an inherent opposition between craft and class interests (and hence, between craft and craftless workers), but subsequent work by Ulman strengthens the plausibility of Perlman's account by providing a reason why American workers might have been particularly craft conscious.[5] He points out that economic development involves twin problems for any labor movement: it simultaneously deskills workers and extends labor and product markets. By stressing the first of these problems at the expense of the second, Ulman argues, the Knights essentially gambled that the leveling influence of technological change would be great enough to make allegiance to the Order a matter of self-interest for skilled workers. But, in Ulman's view, the impact of the market turned out to be greater than that of technological change in the United States, thus dooming the Knights.

Like Perlman and Ulman, Philip Foner also interprets the Knights as a single, national organization, but he rejects the argument that the Order failed because its structure could not be adapted to the needs of skilled workers. He points out that the Order was actually highly flexible in meeting the organizational needs of its varied membership, adding that the Knights were destroyed by the national leaders and

4. Perlman, "Upheaval and Reorganization," and *A Theory of the Labor Movement* (New York: Macmillan, 1928).
5. Ulman, esp. pp. 374–77.

the ease with which non-working-class members could obtain membership. These middle-class members, he argues, betrayed the rank and file.[6]

Recently, labor historians have rejected both explanations. They argue, as I have, that any explanation that treats the Knights as a single, national organization is both misleading and incomplete because it necessarily distorts our interpretation of what was actually a varied, decentralized association. To understand the Order, they insist, one must see it as composed of thousands of local assemblies, each pursuing, with relative autonomy, local goals and strategies. In their effort to rewrite a history of the Order that avoids the pitfalls of the older accounts, they have undertaken detailed studies of the Knights in industrial cities such as Detroit and Cincinnati (where the Order's dramatic growth in membership in the mid-1880s laid the groundwork for highly militant and massive May Day strikes in 1886), as well as in communities such as Rutland, Vermont, and Milwaukee, Wisconsin (where the Knights' upsurge resulted in important independent labor politics).[7] To one degree or another, each of these studies take the Commons-Perlman view as a point of departure, and together they present much evidence to refute the view that the Knights were unable to serve the needs of skilled workers or were somehow unfitted to the American environment. They also have added greatly to our understanding of the importance and meaning of the Knights. But they have been less helpful in providing a general explanation of the Knights' collapse because their local focus tends to generate highly specific interpretations.[8] To the extent that a general theme has emerged, it is one of internal dissension, although not along the simple, dichotomous lines suggested by Perlman, Ulman, or Foner. Instead of emphasizing the division between the Knights and the AFL, or between skilled and less-skilled workers, they see the roots of factionalism lying in industrial diversity and ethnic difference. The clearest implication of their work is that the interaction between dif-

6. Foner, *History*, pp. 157–60.
7. Fink, *Workingmen's Democracy*; Oestreicher, *Solidarity*; Ross, *Workers on the Edge*.
8. For example, Ross argues that the Knights' ability to forge a strong sense of solidarity resulted from the decision made by Cincinnati's mayor to call out the local militia in the course of the May Day strikes. This act so outraged Cincinnati's workers, who felt that they were law-abiding when those in power were not, that they temporarily transcended their separate and often opposed identities as citizens and workers. However, because this unity was based on actions taken by those outside the working class, it did not hold, and the Knights collapsed amid increasingly bitter battles over ideology and tactics. Because few mayors reacted to the May Day strikes by calling out the militia, it is difficult at this juncture to weave Ross's explanation for the Knights' failure into a more general explanation.

fering industrial circumstances and varying ethnic combinations will lead to distinct factions in different communities. Thus, they leave us with a research agenda rather than an explanation for the Knights' collapse: we need to gradually accrue case studies until we have enough to be able to distinguish the broad recurrent impulses that worked toward the same end in many communities across the country.

However, before scholars proceed to write a new history of the Knights (and by extension, of the American labor movement) by accruing individual case studies, all organized around the theme of internal factionalism, it makes sense to consider whether or not such factionalism is a cause or a symptom of collapse. As social movements fail, they often disintegrate into factionalism, but this does not mean that factionalism alone led to the failure. (For example, the civil rights movement was plagued by factionalism in its waning years. Does this mean that factionalism caused the collapse of the movement?) Thus, we need to know whether ethnic and industrial diversity always led to factionalism and collapse in the Knights, or whether other factors, especially those suggested by social-movements research (such as workers' resources, speed of growth, and oppositional strength), encouraged both factionalism and collapse. The best way of finding out, now that we have these case studies to build on, is to undertake a systematic study of the general conditions that lead to the collapse of Knights locals.

A Quantitative Exploration of the Knights' Collapse

The statistical analysis reported here is designed to identify the organizational and community features that contributed to the failure of local assemblies and, hence, to see how well the various explanations given for the Knights' demise account for the pattern of local assembly failures in New Jersey. Once again event-history analysis is used, but this time it is used to investigate the circumstances that led to the collapse instead of the emergence of local assemblies. Specifically, a log-linear specification is used to estimate how vectors of independent variables altered the rate of collapse of Knights of Labor local assemblies. All local assemblies that organized manufacturing workers and were active in New Jersey towns between 1879 and 1895 are included in the analysis.[9]

9. Since the statistical models in this chapter focus on local assemblies of skilled workers as well as those of less-skilled workers, the period of analysis is extended back one year to 1879 when several local assemblies of skilled workers were founded. Altogether, 207 local assemblies were active in this period and were originally included

I examine local assemblies of skilled and less-skilled workers separately. Since the defection of skilled workers looms so large in the Commons-Perlman-Ulman accounts of the Knights' demise, I begin by reporting on my analysis of the collapse of skilled-workers' local assemblies.

Two features of this analysis should be borne in mind. First, I examine formal dissolution, not incremental membership loss (for which data are simply unavailable). Some locals lost large numbers of members and fell on hard times and yet persisted as organizational entities; in this analysis such locals are indistinguishable from more successful assemblies.[10] Second, the term "longevity" is used in a relative sense—a few locals remained in existence a decade and a half, but the majority were in existence only a few years. (The average life of skilled-workers' locals was almost four years, whereas it was three years for less-skilled-workers' locals).

I chose independent variables that, given available evidence, would allow an assessment of the arguments given for the Knights' collapse and parallel the earlier analyses of the Knights' emergence. All the variables described in Chapter 5 are included in the models reported here.[11] Moreover, because sustaining a social movement involves distinct resources and actors, I added extra variables to the models of local assembly dissolution. Two of these measure further aspects of the local labor movement:

Knights of Labor (KOL) *Assembly for Less-Skilled Workers in the local industry.* A variable coded "one" when a local assembly of less-skilled workers was present in the local industry. If Perlman is correct, skilled locals will be more likely to collapse when less-skilled workers are organized.

Election Victory. A variable coded "one" when labor party candidates won. As Fink suggests, politics were often a spillover effect of Knights organization. Thus, the victory of a third-party ticket was likely to benefit the Knights, even when they had not officially endorsed the ticket.[12]

---

in the analysis; nine were later dropped because of missing data. In all, 97 percent of all New Jersey locals were founded between 1879 and 1895.

10. Dissolution dates were coded as follows: For locals that had their charters revoked by the national office, and for those that were formally declared "lapsed" because of failure to pay dues, the date of these events was recorded. For other locals, there is no known date of termination. In such cases, I assigned dissolution dates according to the last reference I found in either national or local sources.

11. These variables are described on pp. 149–55.

12. Election information was gathered from Fink, *Workingmen's Democracy*, pp. 28–29; Foner, *History; John Swinton's Paper;* and local newspapers. I am indebted to Leon Fink for providing additional information about the dates of elections reported in his book.

I included one measure of employers' organization. I found data on these organizations in Clarence Bonnett's *History of Employers' Associations in the United States,* as well as in scattered local sources:

Employers' Association. A variable coded "one" when a manufacturers' association was present in the local industry. This variable measures the actions of employers; it is expected that when employers mobilize, workers' organizations become more difficult to sustain.

Finally, the varying historical context of the Knights' rise and demise is measured by two variables:

National KOL Death Rate. The crude death rate for local assemblies in the national Knights of Labor. This variable, which is measured for all years of the Order's existence, is included as a control for the possibility that local variation in the failure rate of Knights assemblies merely reflects the Knights' national pattern of collapse.

Prior to 1887? A variable coded "one" for years prior to 1887. After the Haymarket bombing and the loss of the third railroad strike against Jay Gould, the Knights had a much more difficult time maintaining membership and sustaining organization.

I also originally included several measures of strike involvement in the model because of the expectation that strike success would strengthen local assemblies. In addition, I also analyzed the presence of a national craft union in the industry, but none of these variables had any impact on longevity, and they are not included in the models reported here.

Statistical Findings

The Collapse of Skilled-Workers' Locals

Table 11 presents the results of the event-history analysis. Rather than displaying the fully specified model, Table 11 includes only the coefficients and standard errors for the reduced model.[13] As in Table 9, I report coefficients, standard errors, and an "impact" column.[14] In Table 11, the impact column indicates the factor by which a "standard change" in the value of each independent variable multiplies the

13. Normally, failure-rate models include an estimate of the rate of declining age dependence over time, and both the model presented in Table 2 and the one presented in Table 3 were originally estimated using a Makeham law specification. However, the data on the local assemblies do not display the usual form of age dependence—or for that matter any apparent form of monotonic age dependence—and the more sophisticated models did not significantly improve on the constant-rate models used here. See Appendix 3 for further discussion.

14. See Chapter 5 for a description of the impact column and a discussion of how the event-history coefficients are interpreted.

Table 11. Impact of industrial, community, and organizational factors
on the rate of failure of skilled Knights of Labor local assemblies
in New Jersey, 1880–1895 (reduced model)

Independent variables	Coefficient	Standard error	Impact
Intercept	−6.74	2.66	
Industrial factors			
Wage differential	—	—	—
Number of establishments	−.11	.22	.86
Establishment size	−.0022	.0020	.73
Technological change	−.88*	.39	.78
Capital-to-labor ratio	.17*	.08	1.56
Percent females	—	—	—
Community factors			
Population	.40	.28	1.72
One-industry town	1.45*	.62	4.28
Ethnic diversity	—	—	—
Election victory	−.78	.65	.46
Organizational factors[a]			
Craft organization			
KOL craft assembly in local industry[b]	—	—	—
KOL craft assembly in community	.66	.45	1.93
Trade union craft in local industry	—	—	—
Trade union craft in community	—	—	—
Less-skilled-workers' organization			
KOL less skilled in local industry	—	—	—
KOL less skilled in community	—	—	—
Employers' association	.90*	.41	2.47
Time factors			
Prior to 1887?	−.60	.40	.55
National factors			
National KOL failure rate	.0012*	.0005	1.42
X^{2c}	37.77		
(d.f.)	(11)		

* p < .05 two-tailed test

Note: 49 events; 206 spells. 3 local assemblies were dropped because of missing data.
Maximum-likelihood estimates are from event-history analysis. Model fit is significantly
better than a constant-rate model (.001 level). See text (pp. 149–55 and 189–91) for definitions of failure and independent variables. Only coefficients for the reduced model
are reported. Variables that were clearly not significant were eliminated in order to obtain stable coefficient estimates for the significant factors.

[a] Organizational factors measure whether locals of each type were present in the community or industry at the beginning of the calendar year.

[b] Indicates the presence of at least one assembly of less-skilled workers in the local
industry in addition to the assembly being analyzed.

[c] X^2, −2 log likelihood, measures improvement in fit produced by substituting a
maximum-likelihood estimate of a model including listed covariates for the null model
assuming a constant rate.

rate of organizational *collapse* when other variables are held constant at their mean values. As in the earlier event-history models, a "standard change" is the shift from "0" to "1" for dummy variables and the shift from one-half a standard deviation below the mean to one-half a standard deviation above the mean for continuous variables.

Overall, the results suggest little support for the standard explanations of the Knights' collapse. This can be seen most readily by looking at the first column of Table 11. None of the organizational factors had a significant effect on assembly failures: neither the presence of Knights assemblies of less-skilled workers nor the presence of trade union locals had any impact on the failure of skilled Knights locals. Thus, the Commons-Perlman argument is not confirmed; there is no evidence that skilled workers left the Knights to join the trade unions when less-skilled workers joined the Order in large numbers. Some support is found for Ulman's reasoning that the Knights appealed to skilled workers whose crafts were undergoing technological change, but additional analysis of industry differences shows no support for the other half of his argument: to the extent that one can measure variations in product and labor markets by industry, there is no evidence that the skilled left the Knights in response to the development of the market.

In a very indirect sense, the significance of the national failure-rate measure provides some support for Foner's argument that national-level leadership policies and problems undercut the Knights. Local assemblies in New Jersey tended to fail when the national failure rate was high. However, this variable does not overshadow the effects of the other variables in Table 11, which indicates that national-level events occurred within the context of, and interacted with, local conditions. Foner's other argument, that the Knights were betrayed by increasing numbers of middle-class members, fares less well when confronted with available evidence. The New Jersey Bureau of Statistics of Labor and Industries provides a list of all the occupations represented in New Jersey's local assemblies in 1887. Out of a total of 40,000 workers, only 113 have middle-class occupations, which hardly seems a large enough number to speak of betrayal.[15]

15. This figure was obtained by adding up the number of clerks, storekeepers, physicians, and teachers in the mixed assemblies. It is possible that some of the trade assemblies included employers; NJBSLI, *Tenth Annual Report, 1887*, does not indicate whether the members of the trades assemblies are employers or employees. Based on my reading of New Jersey newspapers, I think that Foner exaggerates the number and influence of middle-class members, at least in the urban areas. Many of the employers that were in the Knights were those such as the editors of the *New Jersey Unionist* and *The Sunday Advertiser*. All labor movements generally had activists like them. As will be discussed, I don't think that the problem was actual middle-class membership; instead it lay in the Knights' strategies for combatting employers' associations.

Interestingly, Table 11 suggests that ethnic diversity (at least at the community level) had no effect on the survival of Knights locals. Similarly, electoral victory does not seem to have contributed in any direct sense to the longevity of the Knights.

Instead, these results indicate that the failure of the Knights among skilled workers had more to do with employers' strategies and with the industrial situation than it did with trade union policy or the Knights' appeal to less-skilled workers. Skilled-workers' locals lived longest when they were organized in labor-intensive settings and when technological change was rapid. Locals organized in one-industry towns, in contrast, tended to be short-lived, just as they did when employers initiated employers' associations. The negative effect of one-industry towns calls into question recent arguments about the fragmenting effects of industrial diversity, as does the fact that population had no effect on longevity. Indeed, skilled locals were over four times more likely to fail when they were organized in one-industry towns.[16] Employers' associations also had a devastating effect on skilled-workers' locals—they collapsed two and one-half times faster when the employers organized.

The Collapse of Less-Skilled-Workers' Locals

It is clear from Table 11 that, at least in New Jersey, skilled-workers' locals did not collapse because less-skilled workers joined the Knights. But what was the relationship between locals of skilled and less-skilled workers in the Knights? Was it characterized by competition or cooperation? And did the two types of locals draw on similar or different sources of support?

Table 12 provides some answers to these questions. It investigates the relationship between the collapse of locals of less-skilled workers and the organizational and contextual variables described above. The model presented in Table 12 parallels that shown in Table 11, except that it includes time periods. Thus the model in Table 12 measures the extent to which the effects of the independent variables differ in their relationship to longevity before and after 1886.[17]

Because there are time-period effects, the story told in Table 12 is

16. Employers in one-industry towns frequently organized boards of trade and boards of manufactures that functioned much like employers' associations. Thus it is likely that the one-industry town variable partially measures the impact of employers' organizations.

17. Although the inclusion of time periods adds to the complexity of Table 2, it also improves the model's fit greatly. Period effects were not estimated for the models reported in Table 1 because there were too few cases to support a more complex model.

more complicated than that told in Table 11. Factors such as wage differentials and number of establishments had a significant and identical effect on the longevity of locals of less-skilled workers in both time periods. The former tended to decrease the viability of locals of less-skilled workers (a finding that reinforces labor aristocracy arguments), and the latter tended to increase longevity throughout the study period. In contrast, other factors had different effects before and after 1886. Before 1887 average factory size was positively correlated with longevity, but in later years, it had the opposite effect. Similarly, employers' associations had a positive effect in the first period and a negative one in the second. Finally, several factors had a significant impact in only one time period. The proliferation of locals of less-skilled workers, for example, tended to overburden resources in the first period, thereby decreasing the probability of survival of all assemblies of the less skilled in a local industry. The remaining statistically significant variables, including the presence of a skilled-workers' assembly in the local industry, the percentage of female employees, one-industry towns, and the national failure rate had no significant impact on the longevity of assemblies of less-skilled workers in the early period, but it did so in the later time period (a period when, it is important to note, the majority of locals of less-skilled workers failed).[18]

Overall, these findings do not support arguments about hostility or competition between skilled and less-skilled workers, either within

18. In general, these findings are plausible and can be interpreted in a relatively straightforward manner. However, the coefficient for percentage of females requires additional comment. The percentage of females in the labor force in the local industry has a large and positive effect on survival in the post-1886 period. Two very different interpretations of this result are possible. First, it is possible that the membership of local assemblies reflects the composition of the labor force and thus that this finding indicates the viability of locals with female members in the difficult post-1886 period. This interpretation would support the work of Kessler-Harris and of Turbin, who argue that although women were more difficult to organize, once organized they could be much more militant than men (see Kessler-Harris, *Out to Work,* and Turbin, "Beyond Conventional Wisdom," p. 58.) But it is equally likely that the membership of the local does not reflect the composition of the local industry; in that case, this finding would suggest that male workers had an additional incentive to maintain organization when the threat of female substitution was great. To get a rough indication of which interpretation fits the evidence, I generated a list of all less-skilled locals that survived five years or longer and identified the eight of these that were located in local industries with higher-than-average percentages of females. I then matched these with the membership data on the locals given in the 1887 Report of the New Jersey Bureau of Labor Statistics. Of these eight locals, one was an exclusively female local, four had some female representation (varying from a low of 5 percent to a high of 29 percent), one had no female members, and two could not be matched. Thus, it appears that the coefficient for the percentage of females should be interpreted as indicating that locals with female members tended to survive longer.

Table 12. Impact of industrial, community, and organizational factors on the rate of failure of Knights of Labor local assemblies of less-skilled workers in New Jersey, 1880–1895 (reduced model)

Independent variables	1880–1886			1887–1895		
	Coefficient	Standard error	Impact	Coefficient	Standard error	Impact
Intercept	-2.06	.78		-1.16	.38	
Industrial factors						
Wage differential[a]	.42*	.17	1.25	.42*	.17	1.25
Number of establishments[a]	-.27**	.09	.67	-.27**	.09	.67
Establishment size	-.008**	.003	.36	.004**	.001	1.67
Technological change	—	—	—	—	—	—
Capital-to-labor ratio	—	—	—	—	—	—
Percent females	.91	1.12	1.20	-1.76**	.64	.71
Community factors						
Population	—	—	—	—	—	—
One-industry town	-.38	.57	.68	-.86**	.24	.42
Ethnic diversity	—	—	—	—	—	—
Election victory	.21	.45	1.23	.70	.63	2.0
Organizational factors[b]						
Craft organization						
KOL craft assembly in local industry	-.46	.48	.63	-.78**	.29	.46
KOL craft assembly in community	—	—	—	—	—	—
Trade union craft in community	—	—	—	—	—	—
Trade union craft in local industry	—	—	—	—	—	—

Less-skilled-workers' organization						
KOL less skilled in community	2.50**	.54	12.2	.36	.23	1.43
KOL less skilled in local industry[c]	−2.50*	1.06	.08	.52*	.26	1.68
Employers' association	—	—	—	—	—	—
National factors						
National KOL failure rate	−.0004	.001	.88	.001**	.00	1.36
X^2 [d]	102.70					
(d.f.)	(18)					

*p < .05 two-tailed test; **p < .01 two-tailed test

Note: 149 events; 575 spells. 6 local assemblies were dropped because of missing data. Maximum-likelihood estimates are from event-history analysis. Model fit is significantly better than for a constant-rate model (.001 level). See text (pp. 149–55, 189–91, and 194) for definitions of failure and independent variables. Only coefficients for the reduced model are reported. Variables that were clearly not significant were eliminated in order to obtain stable coefficient estimates for the significant factors.

[a] The coefficients for wage differential and number of establishments were constrained to be the same in the two time periods.

[b] Organizational factors measure whether locals of each type were present in the community or industry at the beginning of the calendar year.

[c] Indicates the presence of at least one assembly of less-skilled workers in the local industry in addition to the assembly being analyzed.

[d] X^2, −2 log likelihood, measures the improvement in fit produced by substituting a maximum-likelihood estimate of a model including listed covariates for the null model assuming a constant rate.

the Knights or between the Knights and the trade unions. The presence of a skilled-workers' craft local, whether affiliated with the Knights or the trade unions, did not contribute to the collapse of local assemblies of less-skilled workers. The presence of trade union locals had no effect at all, and the presence of a Knights skilled-workers' assembly in the local industry had a positive effect on the longevity of assemblies of less-skilled workers. Indeed, the biggest problem in terms of competition seems to have been among less-skilled workers themselves.

Instead, these findings provide a picture of locals doing relatively well in a variety of situations through the end of 1886, so long as wage differentials were not too high and resources were not spread too thin by organizational proliferation of less-skilled-workers' assemblies in a single industry. After 1886, however, workers found themselves in more hostile circumstances, and a narrowing of their social base of support seems to have occurred. Small shops, one-industry towns, and high percentages of female employment (these last two tended to go together) provided the best chance of survival for local assemblies of less-skilled workers in the later period.

The varying effect of employers' associations before and after 1886 is worthy of note. One interpretation is that the presence of an employers' association encouraged the survival of local assemblies of less-skilled workers through 1886 but discouraged it thereafter. However, it would be equally consistent with the finding to argue that the direction of the relationship actually goes in the opposite direction—to wit, that this coefficient reflects a tendency for the organization of less-skilled workers to spur employers' organization. This latter interpretation fits best with the anecdotal evidence, and it is the one I adopt here.[19]

Two comparisons will help to illuminate the larger significance of these findings. The first illustrates the difference between the conditions that encouraged less-skilled workers to organize in the Knights of Labor and those that sustained such organizations once established; the second demonstrates the different sources of support for locals of skilled and less-skilled workers.

First, consider the differences between the set of conditions that encouraged the organization of the less skilled and those that sustained it. Chapter 5 demonstrated that the Knights used community ties to

19. See the case study of Newark later in this chapter; Bonnett, *Employers' Associations;* and F. W. Hilbert, "Employers' Associations in the United States," in *Studies in American Trade Unionism,* ed. Jacob H. Hollander and George Barnett (New York: Henry Holt, 1906), pp. 183–217.

mobilize less-skilled workers. Skilled workers were more likely to aid the organization efforts of their less-skilled colleagues outside of their industry than inside of it. This stands in sharp contrast to the findings presented in Table 12 that shows that community ties between workers do not seem to have played a large role in sustaining organization. It is only in one-industry towns, where community and shopfloor ties overlap, that we see any evidence of community ties undergirding union survival.

Moreover, as can readily been seen in Table 13, which summarizes all the statistical findings, many of the other conditions that encouraged the organization of the less skilled had only a marginal effect on longevity. This is true of technological change and town size, both of which were correlated with formation but not survival. Taken together with the negligible impact of worker support at the community level, this comparison indicates that the factors that encourage workers to see the world in class terms (and hence create a Knights local assembly) differ from those that sustain such organization.

Next, compare Table 12 with Table 11. Only two factors, the presence of an employers' association and the national failure rate, affected the survival of assemblies of skilled and less-skilled workers in a similar manner. When employers organized, both types of assemblies tended to collapse, at least after 1886. In addition, both types of assemblies were adversely affected by the national demise of the Knights. But beyond these two factors, each type of assembly seems to have been susceptible to different pressures and to have drawn on different bases of support. Thus, although the decline of the Knights does not appear to have grown out of a general failure of solidarity, there do appear to have been, with the two exceptions noted above, different underlying dynamics of failure for the two types of assemblies. For example, it seems that the effect of industrial diversity, which has played a prominent role in recent discussions of the Knights' collapse, tended to undermine only assemblies of less-skilled workers.

Two overall conclusions about the failure of the Knights local assemblies follow from this statistical analysis. First, few of the explanations currently given for the failure of the Knights receive much support. The Knights' decline, at least as measured by the failure of the New Jersey assemblies, was not due to a failure of solidarity between skilled and less-skilled workers, nor due to competition between the Knights and the trade unions. Indeed, the type of solidarity most difficult to sustain—that between skilled and less-skilled workers in the same industry—did not fail at all. Instead, it played an important role in sustaining assemblies of less-skilled workers in the difficult years

Table 13. Summary of factors affecting the founding and survival of Knights of Labor local assemblies

	Less-skilled-workers' locals				Skilled-workers' locals
	Founding		Survival		Survival
	1880–1886	1887–1895	1880–1886	1887–1895	1880–1895
Industrial factors					
Wage differential	+++	+++	– –	– –	
Number of establishments	+++	+++	+++	+++	
Establishment size	+++	+++	+++	– – –	
Technological change					++
Horsepower/worker, 1880					
Capital-to-labor ratio					– –
Percent female				+++	
Community factors					
Population	++	++			
One-industry town				+++	
Ethnic diversity					– –
Election victory					

Organizational factors

KOL craft assembly in local industry		+ + +	
KOL craft assembly in community	+ + +	+ + +	
KOL less skilled in local industry			− − −
KOL less skilled assembly in community			
Craft trade union in local industry			
Craft trade union in community			
TU less skilled in local industry			
TU less skilled in community			
Employers' association		+ +	− −
Time-trend factors			
National KOL failure rate (Prior to 1887?)		− −	− −

Note: The entries in the table are the signs of coefficients in event-history models of the rate of founding and survival of Knights of Labor local assemblies. The "survival" columns reproduce the information in Tables 11 and 12; the only difference is that the signs are reversed here so that the entry shows the relationship of the factor in Column 1 to the survival of Knights of Labor local assemblies. The "founding" column reproduces information found in Table 9.

Key: + + or − − = sign of coefficient in reduced model, significant at the .05 level.
+ + + or − − − = sign of coefficient in reduced model, significant at the .01 level.

after 1886. Similarly, ethnic diversity, at least when measured at the community level, does not appear to have undermined Knights assemblies. Industrial diversity, on the other hand, did tend to affect negatively the viability of less-skilled (but not skilled) Knights assemblies. Second, both types of assemblies tended to be affected differently by most industrial and organizational settings. Only two factors, the national failure rate and the presence of an employers' association, had similar effects on both. Although it is no surprise that the national decline of the Knights tended to rebound on the New Jersey assemblies, the negative impact of the employers' association on both kinds of assemblies (at least after 1886) should be emphasized and analyzed further. It suggests that those of us who seek to understand the American labor movement too often focus on its internal dynamics. We need to look more carefully at the activities of employers.

The Knights, Employers' Associations, and the State

As we have seen, employers' associations played a key role in the collapse of the Knights in New Jersey. New Jersey is certainly not the nation, and we would want to know a great deal more about the importance of employers' associations elsewhere in the United States before placing undue emphasis on their role, but if we assume for the moment that this New Jersey finding can be generalized, it raises an intriguing possibility: perhaps the reason the Knights collapsed completely, while the new unionism in Britain and the CGT in France survived, has more to do with the consciousness and actions of employers than with those of workers. Perhaps employers in the United States organized more rapidly, brought more resources to the battle, and fought more bitterly than their European counterparts. Perhaps, in other words, it is time to turn the old arguments about American exceptionalism on their heads.

This is the conclusion of a small but growing body of literature.[20]

20. Earlier this century at least one comparative researcher made a similar evaluation. Arthur Shadwell, who in the 1900s surveyed British, American, and continental industrial relations, offered the following assessment: "Nothing has struck me more in the course of this investigation than the remarkable difference in attitude towards trade unions displayed, in private, by employers in [England] and in [the United States]. I have not heard a single word in favor of trade unions from any employer in . . . America. . . . [E]mployers [there] hate and dread unions. In England I have met no such feeling at all. I have heard the unions unfavorably criticized and sometimes condemned, but without bitterness; I have far more often heard from employers and managers fair

For example, James Holt, in a comparison of iron and steelworkers in the United States and Britain, concludes that American employers simply had greater financial resources and political power with which to fight unionism and that this is the primary reason why British steelworkers forged a successful union (and one that was eventually open to less-skilled workers) in the late nineteenth century while American workers did not.[21] Sanford Jacoby reaches a similar judgment after reviewing the evidence on management practices in England and in the United States.[22]

Aside from the explicitly comparative literature, additional support for this line of argument can be gleaned from the literature on the new unionism. Several British historians have noted that the employers' counteroffensive against the new unions was "feeble." Eric Hobsbawm, for example, explicitly argues that the new unions were still in existence in 1911–13 when a second period of explosive growth occurred, because employers made few attempts "to eliminate unions altogether or to deny their right to exist."[23] Similarly, Alan Fox notes that, although a few "unrepresentative" British employers founded associations specifically to destroy the new unions, most "had little stomach" for "American-style" union busting, "with its attendant unrestrained brutality and lawlessness."[24] British employers were "ever ready to grumble about the unions and represent them as responsible for most of their industry's ills," he notes, but few were willing to pursue a "knock-down, drag-out fight" to defeat them.

Further, Peter Stearns's and Gerald Friedman's articles on French employers provide grounds for believing that American employers were unusually successful at combining to defeat labor unions. French employers were notably hostile to the organizational efforts of their

---

and even friendly expressions of opinion" (Arthur Shadwell, *Industrial Efficiency* [London: Longmans, Green and Co., 1906], p. 11, quoted in Ross McKibbin, *The Ideologies of Class* [Oxford: Clarendon, 1990], p. 30).

21. James Holt, "Trade Unionism in the British and U.S. Steel Industries, 1880–1914: A Comparative Study," in *The Labor History Reader*, ed. Daniel Leab (Urbana: University of Illinois Press, 1977), pp. 166–96.

22. Sanford Jacoby, ed., *Masters to Managers: Historical and Comparative Perspectives on American Employers* (New York: Columbia University Press, 1991). Jeffrey Haydu and J. Zeitlin offer similar assessments. See Haydu, *Between Craft and Class*, p. 215, and Jonathan Zeitlin, "From Labour History to the History of Industrial Relations," *Economic History Review* 40, no. 2, 2d ser. (1987): 175–76.

23. Hobsbawm, *Workers*, p. 161.

24. Alan Fox, *History and Heritage: The Social Origins of the British Industrial Relations System* (London: Allen and Unwin, 1985), pp. 189–90. In the last clause of this sentence Fox is quoting a British union leader.

employees, but they were very slow to organize and tended to initiate weak, low-dues associations once they did combine.[25] Although incomplete, available evidence suggests that American employers were able to organize with less difficulty, and that the associations they established tended to require high dues. This made them more formidable opponents in battles with unions.[26]

One need not try to explain all international differences in the success of labor movements by appealing to variations in employer strength. Indeed, it would be a mistake to open up our discussion of the development of the American labor movement by including employers while forgetting the state. Again, Friedman's work is instructive in this regard.[27] He, too, agrees that employers were better organized in the United States, but he points out that French workers owed their success as much to the French state as to employer weakness or labor's strength. In France, the state feared any unrest that might precipitate yet another constitutional crisis, and, thus, when strike action involved large numbers of workers, the state tended to intervene. Intervention generally resulted in shorter strikes and at least some employer concessions.[28] In the United States, on the other hand, neither the federal nor the state government intervened directly with any frequency, even when strikes were massive. And on the occasions when the government did intervene, it acted—often violently—against the strikers. Thus, in the United States, workers could not count on state action to neutralize intransigent employers. So, even if employers' associations had been equally strong in France and the United States, their impact on the labor movement would have been greater in the United States.[29]

When we consider the possibility that employers' associations were unusually strong and well organized in the United States, together with the existence of a state that set the rules for industrial conflict and then generally absented itself from labor disputes, I think that we

25. Peter N. Stearns, "Against the Strike Threat: Employer Policy toward Labor Agitation in France, 1900–1914," *Journal of Modern History* 40 (1968): 474–500; Gerald Friedman, "The Decline of Paternalism and the Making of the Employer Class, France, 1870–1914," in Jacoby, *Masters to Managers*.

26. Friedman, "Decline"; Bonnett, *Employers' Associations*.

27. Gerald Friedman, "State."

28. See also Shorter and Tilly, *Strikes in France*, pp. 28–45.

29. In New Jersey the only federal intervention in this period occurred in the course of the Knights' 1887 general strike against the coal companies. The courts put the railroads into receivership and then used the receivership as a way of protecting strikebreakers. Workers saw this intervention as merely one more trick of the corrupt, monopolistic railroads; they did not view it as *state* action. Similarly, available evidence suggests that injunctions were sometimes threatened but rarely actually used.

are much closer to understanding the reasons why employers' associations had such a devastating effect on the New Jersey Knights. However, this account leaves a few important aspects of the Knights' demise shrouded in shadows. It tells us little about how the employers were able to mobilize so effectively. Nor does it tell us much about the tactics and rhetoric the Knights used when confronted with organized employers. Finally, it tells us nothing about what the leaders and members of the Knights made of their defeat at the hands of organized employers. Once employers countermobilized, the Knights confronted a whole new set of challenges, and the way they dealt with these challenges shaped not only the fate of the Order, but, to an important extent, the future of the American labor movement.

Looking more closely at a local conflict between the Knights and an employers' association should help illuminate these matters. The case discussed is that of a lockout of leather workers in Newark, New Jersey. I begin by giving some background on Newark's leather industry and labor movement.

The Knights and the Manufacturers: An Exploration of the 1887 Lockout of the Newark Leathermakers

Leather and Labor in Newark

In the 1880s, Newark was a bustling manufacturing center. It was known, as noted in Chapter 4, for the diversity of its products and the varied skills of its labor force. Leather manufacturing stood at the center of this diverse economy, both in terms of the numbers employed and, quite literally, because many other industries depended upon the by-products of leather processing. Trimmings from hides were sold to Newark glue factories; splits found a ready market in the trunk factories; shoe manufacturers bought trimmings and roundings for insoles; and chemical factories purchased hide shavings, which were an essential ingredient for making prussite of potash for Prussian blue. Profits from sales of these waste materials greatly reduced the costs of leather production, thus giving Newark's leather industry an enormous capital advantage. Moreover, leather was adaptable to many uses, and it retained its preeminent place in the city's economy into the twentieth century.[30]

In the 1880s, leather processing, like many other Newark indus-

30. Popper, "Newark," pp. 28–29.

tries, was undergoing the final transition from workshop to factory. As Susan Hirsch has shown, Newark's leather trade had begun the process of industrialization quite early; by 1860 almost three-quarters of all leathermakers worked in factories that had some steam-powered machinery.[31] After the Civil War output expanded rapidly, while at the same time the number of establishments shrank. Average shop size increased steadily (in 1890, average shop size was 66.8) as growing numbers of workers were employed by a shrinking group of employers. This was a nationwide development: by 1890 fewer than one-quarter of the leather establishments in operation twenty years earlier were still left.[32] Task differentiation and new production processes accompanied the industry's consolidation, so that by the 1880s the working of hides into leather was done by growing numbers of unskilled or semi-skilled workers. Only in later operations, such as the splitting of hides and japanning (a finishing process in which a hard gloss was given to patent leather), were large numbers of skilled workers required.[33] But improved production techniques did not moderate the unpleasantness of the labor. Leathermaking had always been odious, dirty work, even when the majority of the employees had been skilled. Industrialization only compounded the situation. Workers were forced to work in foul-smelling, closed rooms, full of vaporous turpentine and benzine, where the temperature routinely reached 90 to 105 degrees in the winter and 105 to 120 degrees in the summer.[34]

The workers who toiled in these unpleasant factories were predominately of Irish and German origin. Nearly one-third (30.7 percent) of the labor force had been born in Ireland, and one-fifth (20 percent) had immigrated from Germany.[35] The remaining group had been born in the United States, often of German or Irish parentage. Many German immigrants arrived in the United States already skilled at leather tanning, and, as a consequence, German workers were found disproportionately in the skilled positions. Irish immigrants, on the other hand, rarely had experience in the industry before leaving Ireland, and most were employed as unskilled laborers.[36]

Diverse ethnic origins had long characterized Newark's leather work force, but neither this nor the industry's early industrialization pre-

31. Hirsch, *Roots*, p. 31.

32. Clark, *History*, 2: 465.

33. Census Bureau, *Special*; U.S. Senate, *Cost of Living in American Towns: Report of an Inquiry by the Board of Trade of London* (62nd Cong., Document 222, 1911), p. 302. Newark had a virtual monopoly over the production of patent leather in the United States.

34. *Newark Evening News* [hereafter *NEN*], May 9, 1887; Hirsch, *Roots*, p. 30.

35. Popper, "Newark," pp. 27–28; figures are for 1880.

36. Ibid., p. 27; Clark, *History*, 2: 465; U.S. Senate, *Immigrants in Industries* (Washington, D.C.: Government Printing Office, 1911), p. 39.

vented the development of craft unions. As in Newark's other artisan-based industries (hatmaking, blacksmithing, trunkmaking, jewelry, etc.), leather journeymen successfully organized a craft union in the 1830s. Such unions were not notably successful in sustaining unity or organization, but they nonetheless were remarkably accomplished at keeping journeymen's wage rates high enough to support families by minimizing female and child labor and by limiting the work week to sixty hours.[37] These gains, however, were wiped out in the depression of the 1870s, along with the craft unions.

With the end of the depression, craft workers again began to organize, although this time many sought to extend organization beyond the skilled trades to the rapidly growing ranks of the less skilled. This desire grew, at least in part, out of a recognition of the changed industrial reality. It may also have reflected the activism of the small group of Newark residents who formed the Socialist Labor Party in 1877, although too little evidence exists to know this with certainty.[38] In any event, it found organizational expression in the founding of LA 1364, a "mixed" Knights of Labor assembly, in 1879.

Despite the predominance of the leather trade in Newark, so far as we know none of LA 1364's early activists were leatherworkers. But like leatherworkers, the early leaders were drawn from trades such as shoemaking and printing that had strong craft traditions.[39] When craft unions themselves were reorganized, LA 1364's leaders became energetically involved in these revitalized craft locals while retaining their allegiance to the Knights. The assembly's members were also active in the creation of the Trades Assembly, an organization initiated in 1879 to encourage the federation of all Newark locals. At least one-half of the delegates to the Trades Assembly in its early years were members of LA 1364.[40] The close relationship between the Knights and the Trades Assembly later led the Trades Assembly to adopt a constitution that incorporated the Order's motto and rhetoric.[41]

Overall, however, Newark's labor movement remained weak in the

37. Hirsch, *Roots*, p. 134.

38. This statement is based on the fact of later socialist participation in LA 1364.

39. For example, the early delegates to the State Labor Congress included a shoemaker, a sawmaker, a cigarmaker, and a printer. Information on the Knights' early years in Newark is drawn from the Kerrison Papers, Rutgers University, Box 1, "Organization"—2nd Draft folder, and Box 4, E-7.

40. They were drawn primarily from three trades: printing, cigarmaking, and hatmaking.

41. Indeed, some scholars such as Ira Kerrison believe that the Knights virtually took over the Trades Assembly. (See the organization files, Kerrison Papers.) But whether or not the Knights actually controlled the Trades Assembly, there is no doubt that they played an important role in it through 1889, when mounting tension between the AFL and the Knights led the Trades Assembly to expel Knights locals.

years following the depression, and the Knights were unable to extend local organization beyond the original assembly until 1881, when they successfully established a second local. Over the next two years, sixteen additional local assemblies and a district assembly (DA 51) were organized, primarily by and for skilled craft workers. One of these, a local assembly of skilled morocco dressers (LA 2932), was the first to be established by leatherworkers.[42]

Then, in April of 1884 the Knights, along with the Trades Assembly and nine craft unions, held a mass meeting to kick off a campaign to "organize the unorganized" (*Newark Evening News* [hereafter *NEN*], Apr. 26, 28, 1884). After this, growth was rapid. By 1886, the majority of Newark's industrial labor force had joined the Knights of Labor (estimates put the number between 12,000 and 15,000).[43] Sixty-one locals were initiated in 1886 alone, which brought the total of active assemblies to ninety. These locals represented most sectors of Newark's diverse industrial economy, including those that employed large numbers of women and immigrant workers. Five were leatherworkers' assemblies; aside from LA 2432, these included LA 4922 (Eureka Assembly), which organized diverse occupations in the leather trade; LA 5080, initiated by skilled Morocco Shavers; LA 5694, established by German tanners; and LA 6975, organized by skilled japanners.[44]

As membership grew, strike activity increased dramatically, drawing new groups of workers into its orbit. In 1886, twice as many strikes took place as had occurred between 1881 and 1885. Indeed, according to the *Newark Evening News*, the number of strikes in May and June alone almost equalled the total for the preceding five years.[45] Along with this heightened conflict came new collective demands and new levels of solidarity. Increasingly, members of Newark's working class claimed that they had the right to redefine the employment relation (by equalizing pay, by preventing the use of boycotted material, by forcing the reinstatement of fired employees), and they engaged in sympathy strikes to reinforce their claims. Almost one-half of the strikes that took place in 1886 involved such issues. In addition, semiskilled and unskilled workers took part in strike activity, most for the first time.[46]

42. Jonathan Garlock and N. C. Builder, "Knights of Labor Data," Inter-University Consortium for Political Research, Ann Arbor, 1973; study data. Morocco leather is a fine, firm, and very flexible leather made from goat skins. Morocco dressers took tanned leather, which was comparatively rough, harsh, and unyielding, and finished it so that it was smooth and pliant.

43. NJBSLI, *Tenth Annual Report, 1887*, p. 170; *NEN*, Nov. 26, 1887.

44. Garlock, *Guide; Newark Daily Advertiser*, Sept. 4, 1886.

45. *NEN*, June 12, 1888; Bureau of Labor, *Third Annual Report*, pp. 332–42.

46. Ibid. Nearly one-half of all strikes in 1886 involved less-skilled workers.

Leatherworkers were among the groups that raised new demands in 1886. As employees of one of the largest and oldest industries in town, their actions were closely watched by others in the labor movement. In May 1886, 300 japanners struck to abolish subcontracting and piece-work and to increase and equalize wages throughout the city (*NEN*, May 10, 1886). At first, the manufacturers refused to meet any of the demands, instead issuing a resolution, stating that they would "sustain each other in running our factories as heretofore" (*NEN*, May 11, 1886). The employers believed they had the strategic advantage, for it was the slow season, and if the strike went on for too long, over 1,000 leatherworkers would be thrown out of work as inventories of unfinished leather piled up. Moreover, they knew that the Knights' district assembly (DA 51) was already attempting to organize community support and financial assistance for the many other workers also out on strike. Despite their confidence, it was the employers, and in particular three small firms, who broke ranks first.[47] Within a week, these small employers had abolished subcontracting and reached a compromise with the Knights on the wage issue. The larger firms held out much longer, but they too began to settle on similar terms after the strike had lasted a month. At the end of the fifth week, the workers won the strike in all firms.

Although the japanners' strike involved only skilled leatherworkers, its success proved advantageous for less-skilled workers as well after wages advanced in a number of shops. In January 1887, an assembly of less-skilled tanners (LA 5694, a German local) and an industrial assembly of leatherworkers (LA 4922, an ethnically diverse local) went on strike to extend higher wages uniformly across the industry.[48] The day after the strike began, the japanners joined the strike, and the following afternoon, the workers were victorious.[49] An agreement was negotiated between DA 51 and the leather manufacturers that not only established a new wage scale but also created a system of shop stewards. These shop stewards would look after the interests of Knights members on the shopfloor and would attempt to settle disputes before strikes were undertaken.

These strikes in the leather industry illustrate a more general pattern. Judging by their actions, between 1879 and the end of 1886, Newark workers asserted a larger, more militant role for the labor movement and learned to cooperate across skill and ethnic

47. NJBSLI, *Ninth Annual Report, 1886*, pp. 200–204.
48. *NEN*, Jan. 5, 1887; NJBSLI, *Tenth Annual Report, 1887*, pp. 258–61.
49. *NEN*, Jan. 6, 1887, and Jan. 7, 1887; *New York Times*, Jan. 7, 1887.

lines. Although important divisions remained (notably, over political strategy), it appears that Newark workers were developing the sense that, as a group, they shared a common fate. In 1884, delegates of the Trades Assembly, still composed largely of craft locals, had to be reminded that it was absolutely necessary that both skilled and un-skilled workers be represented in the Trades Assembly. And again in 1885, when less-skilled buttonmakers undertook a difficult strike, craft workers had to be told that their support was essential for the growth of the labor movement (*NEN*, Aug. 13, 1885). By 1886, how-ever, Newark's workers supported one another across both skill and ethnic lines strike after strike.

In addition to this steadily growing sense of class identity, there is also evidence that Newark workers were beginning to separate their interests more clearly from that of their employers. Through 1885, leaders of both DA 51 and the Trades Assembly went out of their way to emphasize the conservative nature of Newark's labor movement, one even going so far as to declare that "the interests of the working-man and his employer are identical" (*NEN*, Apr. 9, 1885). However, there was a marked shift in attitudes between July 1885 and Septem-ber 1886, as can be seen in a comparison of Labor Day celebrations in each year. Labor Day was not yet a legal holiday, and labor's decision in 1885 to hold the celebration on a workday (rather than on a week-end or an evening) indicates a growing sense of power. But despite the symbolic importance of workers' declaring and enforcing their own day for honoring labor, the 1885 parade included a "miscellaneous display of businessmen" who marched at the end of the procession. A year later, no such display was allowed. As workers prepared for the largest celebration of labor ever seen in Newark or in the state of New Jersey, they extended an invitation to employers to attend the speeches in the park ("so that they would be able to hear the working-man's side of the question explained") but, significantly, did not invite them to march in the parade (*NEN*, June 24, 1885; July 24, 27, 1885; Aug. 9, 1886; Sept. 6–7, 1886).

Workers' increasing sense of distance from their employers is also evident in the resolution, passed in December 1886, that barred em-ployers from serving as delegates to the Knights-dominated Essex County Trades Assembly (a successor organization to the earlier Newark Trades Assembly). What was fueling this growing sense that all employers, not just monopolists, were responsible for workers' op-pression? First, evidence was mounting that employers had begun to define themselves as a group separate from labor. In both Newark and across the nation in 1886, employers initiated associations whose common object was to "eradicate whatever form of organization existed among the wage-earners."[50] In Newark, harness, clothing, brewing, and hat manufacturers all organized in 1886 (*NEN*, May 17, 1886). In addition, Newark's Board of Trade (a citywide organization of Newark's leading manufacturers) petitioned the legislature to reenact the conspiracy laws, which had been repealed in 1883, so that it could prevent workers from using boycotts.[51] As employers began to differentiate themselves more forcefully from labor, it became more difficult for workers to sustain a vision of labor and capital as sharing similar interests. Second, Newark workers lost a devastating 86 percent of all of their strikes in the last six months of 1886. (Compare this with a failure rate of about 50 percent in the first six months of the year.) Surely, employer antagonism had rarely been so obvious to so many Newark workers.

It is impossible to know how widespread this anti-employer view had become by the end of 1886. Certainly, there were those who continued to believe that capital concentration was the true source of increasing inequality. Such workers found it difficult to see how small employers, particularly those who had come up from the bench, could be in the same category as monopolists.[52] Respect lingered for those individuals who had fulfilled the American dream, especially in the minds of skilled workers, whose own radicalization had come in part from the realization that such mobility was no longer possible. Moreover, these workers may have noticed that in several of the strikes ending in victory or compromise in 1886 (the May leatherworkers' strike, the April harnessmakers' strike, the June shoe-industry strike), the small employers had settled first.[53] In the case of the leatherworkers' strike, as already noted, this had been an important reason for workers' eventual victory. Thus, there were strong countervailing influences to the growing anti-employer sentiment. However, given the passage of the resolution barring employers from the Trades Assembly, it seems likely that a majority of the workers represented in that assembly had come to adopt a much firmer definition of workers' opposition by the end of 1886. And it is probable that the majority of Knights and union members in Newark were moving toward a similar

50. Perlman, "Upheaval and Reorganization," p. 414.
51. Bonnett, "Employers' Associations," p. 258. On the Board of Trade, see Popper, "Newark," pp. 79–88, and for a discussion of labor's efforts in getting this law repealed, see Chapter 3.
52. For example, see the speech by Charles Litchman reported in the *NEN*, Aug. 25, 1887.
53. *NEN*, May 17, 1886; NJBSLI, *Ninth Annual Report, 1886*, pp. 193 and 200–208.

view. But clearly, by 1886 the whole issue of who was in the opposition had become much more important, and more politicized, than it had been even a year earlier.

For the first half of 1887, however, the potential for internal dispute over where to draw the line between labor and capital remained latent. But other conflicts did not stay so safely beneath the surface. Disagreements erupted over political action, trade autonomy, and, to a lesser extent, the trial of the Haymarket defendants.[54] Each of these disagreements undermined workers' sense of common identity as well as their willingness to risk activism in the face of growing employers' initiative against the labor movement. Membership fell, certainly in the Knights and probably in the craft unions that had begun to affiliate with the newly formed AFL as well.[55] Moreover, the disagreements undoubtedly exacerbated ethnic and political tensions in the labor movement. German workers, for example, could be found in all camps, but they

54. The arguments over political action followed the campaign of two labor candidates in the 1886 election. With little preparation, the Trades Assembly sponsored two labor candidates–one (a Knights member whose platform was the Order's Declaration of Principles) for a congressional seat, and one for a state assembly seat (NJBSLI, *Tenth Annual Report, 1887; NEN*, Nov. 3, 1886). The assembly candidate lost by a mere six votes, and the congressional candidate (whose opponents included Newark's mayor and the incumbent congressman) came in third with 16 percent of the vote (*NEN*, Nov. 3, 1886). Given the circumstances, both candidates placed respectably, but nonetheless the electoral loss precipitated both acrimonious debates over political action in several meetings of the Trades Assembly and the withdrawal of three craft unions (*NEN*, Nov. 11, 1886). Conflicts over trade autonomy were precipitated, as elsewhere, by the growing hostility between the CMIU and the national leaders of the Knights. There were two local assemblies of cigar workers in Newark (LA 3044 and LA 6040), and many, if not all, of their members were also members of the CMIU. Because of their proximity to New York City, Newark's cigarmakers were parties to the daily ins and outs of the dispute. Nonetheless, Knights and Trade Assembly leaders were able to keep the conflict from spilling over to the local labor movement until February 1887. But when it did spill over, it was a source of bitter debate and tended to pit many German workers (who supported the CMIU) against the Knights. (*NEN*, Feb. 24, 1887; Feb. 26, 1887; Mar. 3, 1887; Mar. 23, 1887; Mar. 31, 1887; Apr. 7, 1887; *John Swinton's Paper*, Feb. 27, 1887 [but local sources contradict this report], Mar. 6, 1887.) Although a face-saving compromise was eventually worked out whereby CMIU members could rejoin the Knights, it came only after the collapse of one local assembly, a loss of membership from many others, and lasting tension in the Trades Assembly over the issue of trade autonomy. The continuing debate over Haymarket, the fairness of the trial, and calls for clemency when the death sentence was imposed also exacerbated tensions among Newark's workers, although not to the extent Oestreicher reports for Detroit. See *Solidarity*, pp. 199–211.

55. There are no reliable membership statistics for late 1886 or early 1887, so it is difficult to document the timing and scope of the membership loss. The NJBSLI reports that there were 7,000 members at the end of 1887. The General Assembly proceedings put the membership of DA 51 (in good standing) at 4,766 in July 1887, but this certainly underestimates Newark's total Knights memberships both because several locals were by then affiliated with NTAs, and because other locals were behind in their dues.

tended to be concentrated in two of them, one composed of staunch craft conservatives and the other of socialists.[56]

By the summer of 1887, an uneasy peace had been negotiated. The open squabbles over political action, which had erupted in the Trades Assembly in late 1886 and early 1887, had quieted with the creation of the Central Labor Club, an organization dedicated to supporting labor candidates. And the spillover of the national conflict between the Knights and the Cigar Makers' International Union had ended in Newark with the Knights losing most of their cigarmaking members but also with a face-saving compromise for DA 51.[57] Certainly, the Knights and their local assemblies had been weakened by the events of the past several months, but at the same time, the Order was much stronger than it had been a short two years before. It undoubtedly had the potential to rebound.

The Lockout of 1887

At the same time, there can be little doubt that it was a propitious moment to launch a counterattack against the Knights, and this the leather manufacturers did in June. Their immediate concern was a provision in their January agreement with the Knights that set a limit on the number of hides a worker could be required to tan each day. More generally, however, they were unhappy about the extent to which the leatherworkers, through contracts negotiated by the Knights, had control over the day-to-day running of the firms.

Manufacturers had coordinated their actions in both the May 1886 and the January 1887 strikes, but no lasting formal association of employers had been created.[58] Owners of the largest leather firms set out to change this state of affairs after the January defeat (*NEN*, Aug. 11, 1887). Many had lost a great deal of money as a result of the dispute, and in the spring they played the activist role in creating a new association, the Leather Manufacturers' Association of New Jersey (LMANJ). A few months later, the association selected one of its members, R. G. Salomon, to violate the 1887 agreement (by ordering his men to complete an additional three hides a day over the agreed-

---

56. As in Detroit, the consequences of each dispute caused dissension within each faction of the labor movement because often they pitted one organization or ethnic group against another. See Oestreicher, *Solidarity*.

57. Some cigar workers stayed with the Knights by becoming members of LA 1364.

58. There may have been an earlier effort to organize the employers, but if so, the result was a weak and unstable association. See Bonnett, *History*, p. 279.

upon limit), assisted him in hiring strikebreakers (when, as expected, all 125 employees struck over the speedup), and turned over to him a large portion of the work of other members to ensure his continued business during the conflict.[59] The Knights were able to induce some of the strikebreakers, recruited from Salem, Massachusetts, to leave, but Salomon successfully obtained others, and the strike was eventually lost. None of the strikers were rehired.[60]

This was the first important strike the employers had won since their defeat to the japanners in May 1886, and it signaled the strength and resolve of the LMANJ not only to the Knights but perhaps more importantly to the manufacturers who did not yet fully support the association. By putting aside their individual short-term interest in gaining a competitive advantage over Salomon to win the strike, the members of the LMANJ demonstrated that they had both the solidarity and the financial resources to potentially drive the Knights out of the leather industry. This undoubtedly led employers outside of the LMANJ to reconsider any conclusions they had drawn about the Knights being a permanent force in Newark's leather industry. Moreover, Salomon's victory demonstrated that the price of breaking ranks could be high. If the members of the LMANJ were willing to forego short-term advantages to defeat their employees, they might also be willing to set them aside to defeat manufacturers who did not join or who defected from the employers' association.[61] Thus, with a single victory, the LMANJ successfully made both the risks of nonmembership and the benefits of solidarity much higher. This probably explains how the LMANJ was able to convince a group of employers who had been unwilling to join the association before the Salomon strike to join in July and to put up bonds of between $2,000 and $5,000 to back their pledge to comply with the association (*NEN*, July 14, 1887).

Buoyed by their victory, the LMANJ announced in mid-July that it was going "to fight the Knights of Labor for control over the shops." Beginning August 1, manufacturers would no longer allow their men to return to work unless they agreed to quit the Order.[62] Charles Dodd, the master workman (or leader) of DA 51, moved im-

59. *NEN*, June 8, 1887; NJBSLI, *Tenth Annual Report, 1887*, pp. 228–29; *Journal of United Labor*, Sept. 24, 1887; Perlman, "Upheaval and Reorganization," p. 415.
60. *NEN*, June 11, 1887, Jul. 25, 1887; NJBSLI, *Tenth Annual Report, 1887*, pp. 258–61.
61. Evidence that the LMANJ was having trouble recruiting employers can be found in the *NEN*, May 9, 1887. J. H. Halsey told the reporter that "the manufacturers also organized a short time ago and wanted us [Halsey and his partner] to join them. . . . We thought we had better paddle our own canoe, and declined to join."
62. *NEN*, July 14, 1887; *John Swinton's Paper*, Jul. 31, 1887; NJBSLI, *Tenth Annual Report, 1887*, pp. 228–29.

mediately to avert trouble by writing to George A. Halsey, the president of the LMANJ, suggesting a meeting between the two men to settle any difficulties between their respective organizations. When Halsey refused to see him, Dodd sent a letter to every leather manufacturer, requesting either a meeting or notification that the manufacturer did "not intend setting aside or annulling" his contract with the Knights (*NEN*, July 26, 1887). Most manufacturers responded to Dodd's request, the majority saying that they would abide by the decision of the Manufacturers' Association. Many declared, however, that "they had no grievance against the Knights of Labor and that the proposed shutdown . . . was solely for the purpose of adjusting trade matters." The Knights seized on this seeming support and attempted to reframe the conflict as one that would hurt the small employers as well as the Knights. As one official said, "we have been expecting this thing for months, and we are fully prepared to meet it. Our different [KOL] associations knew that the formation of the Manufacturers' Association meant an effort to crush out unionism for one thing, *and also to crowd out of the business a few of the smaller firms, in order to give a monopoly of the leather business to the big firms*" [my emphasis] (*NEN*, July 26, 1887).

The LMANJ, however, dismissed the sincerity of members' expressions of friendliness toward the Knights. As one anonymous spokesman for the association told a reporter, "when we passed the resolution to close our beamhouses on [August 1] there was not an employer present who did not know that it meant an attempt to assert our rights as employers and to conduct business for ourselves." He added, "I know that the leather manufacturers, if they hold out together, will eventually crush out of existence the Knights of Labor in this city" (*NEN*, July 28, 1887).

Between mid-July when the manufacturers announced the lockout and August 1, the date the lockout was scheduled to be enforced, the Knights debated whether they should strike before they were shut out. If they struck immediately, some argued, employers would be left with hides midway through the tanning process, which would be ruined if the strike was not settled quickly. But Dodd and the other leaders of DA 51 were anxious to avoid any appearance of responsibility for the trouble; if that happened, it would almost certainly turn public sympathy against them (especially as they had contracts with many of the firms) and would have the added disadvantage of further uniting the manufacturers. In addition, the officers of DA 51 were worried about the high cost of supporting the leatherworkers and wanted to avoid a confrontation for as long as possible. Dodd estimated that to support even a short strike of the 2,000 affected men could cost more than $150,000.[63] Even with the help of the Knights' national leadership (which came to Newark the last week in July), that amount of money would be difficult, if not impossible, to raise (*NEN*, July 27–28, 1887).

The actual conflict began more like a poker game than like the pitched battle between capital and labor that the Knights expected. On August 1, the manufacturers took no immediate action, and the leatherworkers were momentarily jubilant, believing that the inaction signaled internal dissension among the manufacturers. But the events of the next few days played into the employers' hands. When it became obvious that the anticipated shutout was not going to occur, a few leatherworkers attempted to call the bluff of one employer who had heatedly denounced the Knights just a few days earlier. But the shop was not one of the Knights' strongholds, and the other workers, who might have stuck with the Knights in the event of a lockout, resented the minority for trying to precipitate a strike. They refused to follow the militants out of the shop (*NEN*, Aug. 1–3, 1887). Over the next few days, rumors of dissatisfaction with DA 51 appeared in the newspapers, and manufacturers told reporters that they had canvassed their workers and found that most were "willing to give up the order rather than lose their work" (*NEN*, Aug. 4, 1887). The manufacturers added, "in no shop in this city has a hide been put to soak this week. As soon as we are rid of the stock that is liable to spoil we will be prepared for a strike, call-out or lockout . . . We can afford to allow our shops to be kept closed for six months, as there will be no goods on our hands to spoil." Increasingly, it became clear that the Knights were being maneuvered into a position where inaction appeared to be weakness. Only by calling out the leatherworkers could they prove what, just a few days earlier, had been a foregone conclusion: that they had the support of their members. Yet in doing so, they would be the first to break the contracts still in effect between the Knights and the employers. On August 6 the district assembly called out workers in two firms, hoping that a demonstration of their members' loyalty would induce the LMANJ to negotiate. But, although most of the workers heeded the strike call, the LMANJ countered two days later by announcing that it had set a new lockout date.[64] After August 13 all

63. *NEN*, July 26, 1887. This estimate seems high; in the actual course of the strike, nowhere near that amount was raised.

64. It is difficult to get reliable statistics on the number of workers who actually went out in the two shops because this itself became a source of constant dispute in the newspapers. On August 8, the Knights reported that all but 14 of the 250 employees struck at T. P. Howell's shop, and 70 out of 73 men struck at Patrick Reilly & Sons. The employers denied this, Howell claiming that one-half of his men were at work (*NEN*, Aug. 8, 1887). There was probably some exaggeration on both sides, although, at least initially, it ap-

workers who wanted to keep their jobs would have to sign an agreement to quit the Knights, and each member of the LMANJ would have to "conduct his business without any agreement with or recognition of the Knights of Labor" upon penalty of forfeiting his bond (*NEN*, Aug. 8, 1887).

The next several days brought an escalation of rhetoric and action on both sides. Employers whose shops had already been struck began to hire strikebreakers.[65] In one case, policemen were retained to guard the strikebreakers, a move that outraged workers who angrily denounced it as giving the false impression that workers were threatening violence. In addition, the LMANJ announced that it had agents in England, France, and Germany and that they had found skilled leatherworkers "only too willing to come here for bigger wages than they ever could earn at home."[66] At the same time, the manufacturers worked hard to maintain unity. Members visited the employers who were worried that they might suffer crippling production losses should their skilled leatherworkers refuse to quit the Knights. The LMANJ assured these employers that, even though leathermaking was a highly competitive industry, association members would help in every possible way—even going so far as promising to rotate among firms the skilled workers who remained on the job.

For its part, the District Assembly struggled to find an effective strategy for dealing with the much greater resources of the LMANJ. Each day brought increases in the number of employees thrown out of work, as manufacturers rushed to meet the August 13 deadline. An effective communitywide boycott was organized to prevent the sale of food and supplies to strikebreakers, forcing at least one employer to set up both a cafeteria and sleeping quarters inside his factory (*NEN*, Aug. 11, 23, 1887). Workers were also successful in inducing some strikebreakers to leave—eventually, the Knights even paid return passage to England for a few of them (*NEN*, Aug. 29, 1887). But although such tactics helped to maintain day-to-day solidarity, the Knights knew that they had to find a way to break the employers' resolve. It was becoming painfully obvious that some of the employers were willing to do almost anything to break the Knights; not only were they voluntarily giving up months of profit, they were also spending

---

pears that the employers were exaggerating more. After all, they flatly refused to let employees look in their shops despite the fact that if they were telling the truth, they had every reason to have this reported. In addition, it is known that they went to great lengths to obtain strikebreakers. Overall, the NJBSLI, *Tenth Annual Report, 1887*, pp. 260–61, records that 1,255 workers struck or were locked out of a work force of 1,800.

65. *NEN*, Aug. 11, 1887; *New Brunswick Daily Home News*, Aug. 8, 1887; Aug. 11, 1887.
66. *New Brunswick Daily Home News*, Aug. 11, 1887; *NEN*, Aug. 15, 1887.

large sums of money to recruit skilled replacements from as far away as Germany. The Knights talked of a nationwide boycott of all leather made in Newark, but, as one manufacturer soon pointed out, it had little chance of success because the markets for Newark's leather industry were worldwide.[67] Thus the leaders of DA 51 began to believe that their only hope was to undermine employer solidarity.

Both pragmatic and ideological considerations led DA 51 to devote most of its energies to dividing the employers. From a pragmatic point of view they had few choices. Although they assured both the leatherworkers and the press that they had the financial reserves to maintain the strike, at one point even claiming that they could hold out for three months, Dodd and the other district officers must have known from the day the lockout was first announced that they actually had very little money in the treasury. The Order's dues were very low ($3 per year) and the district assembly had no strike fund, so the only way to support strikes once the dues' revenue was gone was to appeal to the local assemblies and trade unions.[68] As noted, Newark workers had lost the majority of their strikes over the past year, which had exhausted the treasury and had sapped the resources of many of the locals in the district as well. Moreover, summer was the slow season for many of Newark's workers, which meant that DA 51 could count on the working-class community for only limited funds (*NEN*, Aug. 16, 1887). The Knights' national executive board promised to help, but despite workers' expectations, its reserves had also been depleted in the many conflicts it had been involved in during 1886 and 1887.

However, pragmatic reasoning alone did not dictate the Knights' strategy. As the officers of DA 51 viewed the forces arrayed against them, the clearest cause of their predicament was indeed concentrated capital. This was shown most clearly by the manufacturers who had initiated the LMANJ and who were now directing the lockout: they were the owners of the three largest leather firms in Newark.[69] It also seemed quite possible that the small employers might yet be persuaded to take a conciliatory stance toward the Knights. Not only, as we have seen, had the smaller manufacturers settled first in the 1886 strike, but the smaller firms disproportionately refused to join the

67. Popper, "Newark," p. 73.
68. NJBSLI, *Tenth Annual Report, 1887*, pp. 42–46.
69. The firms were Geo. A. Halsey, T. P. Howell, and Blanchard Bros. & Lane. See *NEN*, Aug. 11, 1887; *New Brunswick Daily Home News*, Aug. 11, 1887. At the time, T. P. Howell was exporting more patent leather than all other manufacturers in the United States combined, and Blanchard Bros. & Lane's was one of the largest employers in Newark.

employers' association, or, if in the association, delayed posting the lockout notice (*NEN*, Aug. 9–10, 1887). Much of the small employers' reluctance to go along with the LMANJ lay in their greater economic insecurity; because leather manufacturing was a highly competitive industry, they faced bankruptcy when production was disrupted for even a short time. As one smaller employer told a reporter, he "never entertained a thought of fighting the K. of L. when he joined the Manufacturer's Association." But now, given the intensely competitive nature of the leather industry, he was trapped. As he complained to a member of the Knights, "if you call out my men I can not go on with my work, and if I hold out against the order of the association, I will be ruined" (*NEN*, Aug. 10, 1887). Thus, the small employers probably were susceptible to the argument that concentrated capital was as much their enemy as was the Knights of Labor. On August 12, two or three members of the employers' association (we do not know which ones) approached a lawyer to find out whether or not the manufacturers' association could really enforce discipline by keeping their bonds (*NEN*, Aug. 12, 1887). It was also clear that the LMANJ was itself worried about winning and keeping the smaller firms, as they had demonstrated when they assured the small manufacturers that they would lend out skilled workers. Thus, it was not unreasonable for the Knights to believe that, if they could successfully frame the conflict as one of labor and enterprise against monopoly, they might be able to break up the LMANJ and avoid losing the conflict.

But framing the conflict in this way had two significant drawbacks for DA 51: it tended to discourage the Knights from exploiting their ability to disrupt production, and it ran the risk of intensifying internal tension within the labor movement. It discouraged the Knights from walking out during critical periods in the leather-production cycle because workers hoped that if they avoided hurting employers, the latter might be more easily convinced that labor was good and that monopoly was corrupt and unfair. It ran the risk of heightening internal divisions because the view of labor's opposition held by the Knights leaders had by 1887 become the minority position. Indeed, very early in the conflict, it became clear that there were two factions among the leatherworkers, one, a conservative faction that supported DA 51 for the way it was managing the conflict, and another, a radical faction that was unhappy about DA 51's moderation (*NEN*, Aug. 6, 1887). Because these two factions also tended to divide along ethnic lines (the radical faction having more German adherents, and the conservative faction more Yankee, English, and Irish adherents), when DA 51 escalated its attempts to include rhetorically the small employers in labor's camp, the result was increased ethnic conflict along with increased division over labor's vision of itself.

Given the Knights' strategy and their financial constraints, they needed to break the manufacturers' unity fairly early if they were to prevail. The longer the lockout lasted, the more difficult their financial situation would become and the greater the probability of internal division. But this early settlement was not forthcoming. By the eve of the lockout, nearly 800 men were already out, and some of them had been without a job for almost a week, which meant that they would soon need financial support (*NEN*, Aug. 11, 1887). On August 13, the official beginning of the lockout, an additional 455 men were thrown out, bringing the total number of workers to 1,255.[70]

On August 15, DA 51 received more disappointing news: all of the employers who had promised Dodd that they would not participate in the lockout did so. Nonetheless, the Knights kept up their efforts to win over manufacturer support even in the face of this setback— sending some employees back temporarily so that they could take care of hides that might be ruined (*NEN*, Aug. 15, 1887). At the same time, they posted workers at the railroad station in an effort to convince strikebreakers to return home. Eventually, the Knights also sent workers to the immigration headquarters at Castle Rock, New York, where they alerted the commissioner of immigration that leatherworkers might be entering the country illegally as strikebreakers.[71]

By the second week of the lockout, it was becoming increasingly clear that the Knights' appeal to the small manufacturers was not having the desired effect. Although eight of the small manufacturers, who from the beginning had refused to join the employers' association, did not lock out the Knights, the leatherworkers were unable to convince any of the other thirty-three manufacturers to break with the association. Indeed, on August 19, the LMANJ moved to intensify pressure on the eight holdouts. It threatened that if the eight did not join in the lockout, the association would cut off supplies of raw

70. NJBSLI, *Tenth Annual Report, 1887*, pp. 258–61.
71. *NEN*, Aug. 11, 1887; Aug. 15, 1887; Aug. 19, 1887. In 1885, Congress had passed a contract labor law after heavy lobbying by labor. It prevented employers from importing workers under contract to the United States. On August 15 the LMANJ told reporters that it would wait until the European workers it was hiring as strikebreakers were in the United States before it asked them to sign a contract. That way, it would avoid problems with contract labor laws. But on August 19, Knights members were able to convince the commissioner of immigration to prevent six workers from entering the country because of suspected contract labor law violations. On August 24, the manufacturers retaliated against the immigration officers by filing a grievance against them for aiding the Knights (*NEN*, Aug. 24, 1887).

hides and call in all outstanding notes and claims held by members of the LMANJ against these small firms. Of course, such threats also reminded those who belonged to the LMANJ of the possible consequences of breaking ranks. In what was surely an act of desperation, DA 51 responded with a circular addressed to the businessmen of Newark that argued in part: "Gentlemen—The enforced idleness of 1200 men, citizens of this city, who with those dependent upon them for support number about 4000 persons, is a matter which directly affects your interests. Opposition by the manufacturers to a perfectly legal organization of labor, is the cause of this unfortunate state of things, hurtful not only to all those immediately concerned, but to the business community at large; *for what injures one portion in a degree injures all*" (my emphasis; *NEN*, Aug. 20, 1887).

We can only guess at the workers' reaction to this circular because they refused to discuss internal differences in the press. But it is not difficult to imagine what the effect the italicized passage would have had on those workers who had attended the 1886 Labor Day parade or those who had voted in 1886 to exclude all employers from the Trades Assembly. Here were the leaders of the leatherworkers attempting to stretch the Knights' motto, long a clarion call for labor solidarity, into a plea for help from the very men who were daily hiring strikebreakers and waging the strongest assault ever mounted against labor in the city of Newark! Moreover, we can tie the timing of this circular to increasing tension between German and non-German Knights, although, again, we do not have the type of evidence available that would allow us to make an explicit link between DA 51's mounting an effort to win over the small employers and internal dissension within the Knights. Obviously, there were additional reasons why conflict along ethnic lines might have been increased at this time—the growing sense that the lockout would be lost combined with the fact that fewer German leatherworkers were Knights members would by themselves have been enough to aggravate ethnic tensions. But nevertheless, I think that the sentiments expressed in this circular were responsible for some of the divisions among the Knights that the press reported during the third week in August. On August 25, a mixed assembly of German workers (none, so far as we know, were leatherworkers) disbanded and gave the money left in their treasury ($15) to the local assembly of German tanners. One of the reasons given for the disbanding was dissatisfaction over the leadership and management of DA 51 (*NEN*, Aug. 25, 1887).

As the third week of the lockout began, the leatherworkers' position was growing desperate. Local assemblies and trade unions had raised about $1,000 for the leatherworkers since the beginning of the lockout, and more than double that amount had come in from other sources, but this did not go far when divided among 1,200 workers and their families. Complaints about the lack of aid grew bitter, and Dodd was criticized repeatedly for having made promises of aid that DA 51 was unable to keep. He in turn began to attack the trade unions, accusing them of not helping the leatherworkers enough, thus precipitating a round of mutual recriminations. The financial resources were strained further by the continuing need to deal with strikebreakers who now numbered 650.[72] Paying those who decided to return home was costly, a fact the employers exploited. When leatherworkers convinced four British japanners brought over as strikebreakers to return home, a spokesman for the LMANJ responded by saying that he would bankrupt DA 51 by "bring[ing] over japanners until they become tired of paying them to go back" (*NEN*, Aug. 29, 1887).

On August 29, the Knights' national office was at last able to provide some financial aid (the amount was not made public), which temporarily buoyed the spirits of the leatherworkers. But by this time it had become painfully obvious to the workers that the manufacturers were going to be able to hold out longer than the leathermakers. Thanks to the strikebreakers, production in all LMANJ shops was continuing, and, on September 2, the LMANJ called off their daily meetings, saying, "The trouble as far as we are concerned is at an end" (*NEN*, Sept. 2, 1887). The leathermakers refused to give up the fight, however, and in a last hurrah, their fellow workers placed them at the head of the Labor Day parade (held in 1887 on the state's first official labor holiday) and promised them all the proceeds of the celebration. By mid-September, however, it was clear that the leatherworkers had suffered an absolute defeat. Some reapplied for their old jobs, but at least one-half were turned away, and all the shop stewards were blacklisted. Other leathermakers left Newark to find work elsewhere. About 350 still remained out of work at the beginning of November.[73]

The defeat of the leatherworkers in the 1887 lockout ended union organization in Newark's leather industry and had serious repercussions for the city's labor movement. Both organizationally and ideologically, the loss was devastating. Of the three local assemblies directly involved in the lockout, two collapsed when the workers went back to work, and the third disbanded a few months later. Other local

72. NJBSLI, *Tenth Annual Report, 1887*, pp. 258–61.
73. Ibid., pp. 258–61.

assemblies experienced similar failure rates. At the beginning of 1887, there were forty-eight local assemblies of manufacturing workers in Newark, and at the end of 1888 only twelve of these were still active. Moreover, the Knights' inability to prevail over the leather manufacturers severely undermined the influence of those local assemblies that survived, as evidenced in the disarray that accompanied the Knights' strike efforts in 1888 and in the precipitous decline of the Essex County Trades Assembly.[74]

Ideologically, local leaders were unable to offer a convincing argument for how the exercise of working-class solidarity might lead to anything other than another defeat in the future. Indeed, aside from statements in which locals leaders blamed one another for the failure of the strike, no analysis at all was offered. As a result, the Knights' vision was discredited in Newark. When the labor movement rebounded again at the end of the 1890s, it did so by eschewing both the inclusion of less-skilled workers and the Knights' alternative vision of a "workingmen's democracy."

Working-Class Republicanism and Employers' Associations: Some Conclusions from the Newark Case

The Knights' experience with the leather manufacturers in Newark provides further evidence that employers' associations played a key role in the decline of the Order. Once organized, employers had many more resources and a great deal more maneuvering room than workers. Indeed, it is difficult to see how the Knights, no matter what tactics they tried, could have prevailed against the employers so long as the manufacturers were unified and willing to commit so much of their energy and capital to defeating the Order.

The case study also illuminates some of the strategies that allowed American employers to organize so effectively. Employers confronted many of the same types of mobilization obstacles workers faced: they were in a highly competitive environment, were often suspicious of one another's motives, and were divided internally between large and small employers. Their success depended on overcoming their short-term interests in stealing one another's markets and on their ability to maintain solidarity. Certainly, as Offe and Wiesenthal's work on the

---

74. Ibid., p. 231. The decline of the Trades Assembly is chronicled in the *Newark Evening News* throughout 1888 and early 1889; and the disarray of the Knights' strike efforts are evident especially in accounts of the brewers' strike that occurred in April 1888 (see also the April issues of the *New Jersey Unionist*).

logic of collective action suggests, employers' smaller numbers eased mobilization.[75] But small numbers alone were not sufficient to overcome all obstacles, especially not the divisions between small and large employers. Those most committed to the employers' association, the large employers, had to find a way to encourage or coerce the small employers to stay solidary even when it did not seem to be in the latter's interests to do so. Here, the bond, a tactical innovation, provided a sufficient deterrent to breaking ranks, resolving the solidarity problem that had earlier plagued the employers. Once solidarity was ensured, the very monopolization and concentration that the Knights so abhorred was the source of the capital reserves that financed the lockout.

Moreover, the case study helps to clarify the role the Knights' ideology played in the Order's decline. Often, the Knights' producerism is denigrated as backward looking. The implication of this critique is twofold. First, it suggests that the world had so completely changed by the 1880s that any talk of strategic alliances with small employers was a hopeless dream, a throwback to a long-gone era. Second, it implies that the Knights' use of producerist categories prevented them from acting on the basis of working-class interests. Neither of these arguments is supported by the Newark case. In 1886 and early 1887 Newark workers were able to divide the small employers from the large ones and achieved strike victories as a result. Moreover, in Newark, the Knights' ideology did not impede workers from constructing a working class identity. This was demonstrated especially when Knights members offered strike and organizational support across the skill line that had for so long divided the working-class. The fact that Knights spokesmen sometimes expressed sympathy for the plight of the small employer, arguing that he, too, was victimized by large-scale capitalism should not blind us to the distinction workers made between themselves and small employers.[76] Knights members struck small em-

75. Claus Offe and Helmut Wiesenthal, "Two Logics of Collective Action," in *Disorganized Capitalism*, ed. John Keane (Cambridge: MIT Press, 1985).

76. Again, the French case is instructive. In the late nineteenth century, French workers also tried to use divisions between small and large employers to win strikes. In 1901, for example, striking filemakers refused to negotiate with any employer who had not actually worked as a filemaker. As Michael Hanagan notes, workers claimed that other employers wouldn't understand the issues, but this was actually a ploy to appeal to smaller manufacturers. Similarly, Donald Reid notes that workers often sought the support of middle-class employers and shopkeepers in Decazeville. It is useful to remember Joan Scott's remark about Chartism: "political movements develop tactically and not logically, improvising appeals, incorporating and adapting various ideas to their particular cause." Hanagan, *Logic of Solidarity*, p. 188, and personal communication; Donald Reid, *The Miners of Decazeville* (Cambridge: Harvard University Press, 1985); Scott, "On Language," p. 8.

ployers as well as large, and they insisted on the same pay scales and working conditions in both small and large shops.

Producerism, and the Knights' ideology more generally, I am arguing, did not prevent Newark leatherworkers from behaving as a class. Instead, it shaped the Knights' strategic choices and conceptual resources for framing defeat. Strategically, it led Knights leaders in Newark to believe that, once again, they might be able to shatter employer unity by stressing the victimization workers and small employers shared at the hand of large employers. This time, however, the employers' association had destroyed the basis for a strategic alliance between Knights members and small employers. Some workers understood this more quickly than others, and this became a fault line that developed into internal dissension.

As for framing defeat, the Knights' ideology left Newark workers with very pessimistic conclusions about labor's ability to reshape society. Working-class republicanism was a set of beliefs that gave to workers the mission of rescuing the nation while suggesting that they would be able to accomplish this enormous task by organizing thoroughly and by demonstrating their power. If they did this, most Knights believed, they would be able to convince the middle class of the essential truth of their cause. It was not that the Knights did not expect opposition or class conflict: they did. But they also anticipated that once they won workers over to their movement, they would be able to attract the support of others, especially the middle class. When the moment of truth came, and they were unable in reality to convince the small employers of the justice of their cause, they were left, ideologically, with only themselves to blame. As Gregory Kaster has suggested, this has always been the dark side of American labor's language of dissent in the nineteenth century: implicit in its terms was the idea that ultimately workers were responsible if they were unable to take charge of their destiny.[77]

Also important in this regard is the Knights' suspicion of state activism. Although the Knights' ideology accorded a larger role for the government than had most earlier versions of labor republicanism, the Order's suspicion of strong centralized authority tended to blind its leaders to the possibility of calling for state intervention to counter employer power. Again, workers were left with only themselves to blame for the defeat of the Knights.

Thus far I have been analyzing the consequences of the Knights'

---

77. Gregory L. Kaster, "'We Will Not Be Slaves to Avarice': The American Labor Jeremiad, 1827–1877," Ph.D. diss., Boston University, 1990.

ideology for the Order's decline in Newark only. How plausible would it be to generalize more broadly to the nation at large? It is, of course, difficult to know, but the curious silence that followed the defeat of the leatherworkers in Newark can also be found in the labor press outside of Newark, as well as in the biographies of relevant labor leaders.[78] Aside from the inevitable blaming war that went on between a few national officers of the Knights, there are virtually no articles or published speeches assessing the reasons for the Knights' collapse. Neither are there martyrs, nor brave projections of how, next time, the working class would triumph over its enemies. Indeed, there is no sense at all, given the silence, of a next time. It is as if the very opposite of what Doug McAdam terms "cognitive liberation" occurred: instead, what we might call "cognitive encumbrance" took place.[79]

It is instructive in this regard to compare working-class republicanism's implicit doctrine that workers are responsible for any failure to change society and socialism's doctrine that the triumph of the working class is historically inevitable. Ultimately, working-class republicanism simply provided the Knights of Labor with too few ideological resources for explaining what had happened, in Newark or elsewhere. And because the Knights had achieved greater solidarity than had any previous organization, their failure and, hence, responsibility was all the greater.

This chapter offers the beginnings of a new explanation for the failure of the Knights of Labor, one that builds on social movements theory and recognizes the distinction between disposition and action. It suggests that the Knights failed because their rapid growth and early successes resulted in the mobilization of powerful employers' associations. Unlike their counterparts in England and France, these associations had no interventionist state to constrain them, and they had the benefits of rapid economic concentration at their disposal. Employers' disproportionate resources and strategic leverage put the Knights in a nearly hopeless situation, against which they struggled by appealing to small employers. This strategy, which drew upon the ideology

78. This statement is based on a reading of *John Swinton's Paper*, the *National Labor Standard*, the *Trenton Sunday Advertiser*, autobiographies of Terence Powderly and Joseph Buchanan, and every available secondary source on the Knights of Labor.

79. McAdam, *Political Process*, pp. 48–51. McAdam argues that a social-psychological process of "cognitive liberation" must take place before aggrieved social groups will engage in collective action. Cognitive liberation occurs when people "collectively define their situations as unjust and subject to change through group action."

of working-class republicanism, did not work, and it led to internal schisms that rent the organization apart.

This explanation stands in sharp contrast to the standard historical account that attributes the Knights' collapse to a failure of solidarity, particularly to the defection of skilled workers. A statistical analysis of Knights of Labor locals found no support for this scenario. Indeed, it suggested that solidarity between skilled and less-skilled workers played an important role in sustaining locals of less-skilled workers in the difficult years following the Haymarket bombing.

The explanation developed here is also different from that offered by scholars such as Philip Foner. Foner argues that the Knights were destroyed by middle-class members, who, though in the minority, came to dominate the Order, thereby blunting its class appeal. In New Jersey, there is little evidence of domination, at least not in 1887, the one year for which we have enough data to assess the claim. It is true that the Knights tried to win support from small employers when they were confronted by employers' associations, and it is easy to see how Foner and others might conclude that these appeals were the work of middle-class members. But the Newark case study suggests that it was not a middle-class membership that played the decisive role; rather it was the Knights' early success with the same strategy. Moreover, the Knights' experiences in Newark demonstrate that earlier alliances with small employers were tactical; they did not blunt the Knights' working-class appeal or its ability to pursue working-class interests.

The explanation advanced here is more compatible with recent work on the Knights by labor historians such as Richard Oestreicher. Oestreicher argues that the Knights collapsed under the weight of a factionalism that did not correspond in any simple way with the divide between skilled and less-skilled workers or the one between trade unionists and Knights of Labor members. Instead, he traces the divisions to industrial and ethnic diversity. In contrast, this study has placed less emphasis on the direct effects of ethnic and industrial diversity, although it does provide some support for Oestreicher's conclusions. The statistical analysis of assemblies of less-skilled workers suggested that industrial diversity contributed to their failure. And the Knights' attempts to win over the small employers certainly exacerbated tension along ethnic lines. Where Oestreicher and I differ is in our emphasis and in our view of how these internal differences were pushed to the critical point.

Finally, this chapter, and in particular the case study of Newark, also suggests that the lessons workers drew from the Knights' defeat played a significant role in shaping the consequences of the Order's collapse. A process of cognitive encumbrance seems to have occured, in which participants blamed themselves for the failure of local assemblies. This hastened the demise of the Knights of Labor and left workers pessimistic about the future prospects for broad-based unionism in America.

CONCLUSION

Toward a Reinterpretation of
the American Labor Movement

Look for the nul
defeats it all

the N of all
equations

that rock, the blank
that holds them up

which pulled away—
the rock's

their fall. Look
for that nul

that's past all
seeing

the death of all
that's past

all being

—William Carlos Williams, "Paterson"

American labor exceptionalism—that unexpected combination of
weak working-class institutions and unions' political conservatism—
was not foreordained, it was made. The American labor movement
was not born "different," or "more limited," or more "job conscious"
than other labor movements; it became that way in the wake of the collapse of the Knights of Labor.[1] The demise of the Knights foreclosed

1. Quoted terms are from Mike Davis, "Why the U.S. Working Class Is Different,"
New Left Review 123 (1980): 5–44; Everett M. Kassalow, "The More Limited Scope of

important options for the American worker, and labor in the twentieth century was very much shaped by this absence.

Industrial relations and the politics of labor are more favorable to capital in the United States than in Europe, not because American labor failed to organize but because American capital countered the labor movement with effective organization of its own. American exceptionalism is not rooted primarily in workers' consciousness or even in workers' organizational strategy; it does not stem from the absence of class struggle in the United States. Instead, it is the fruit of class struggle waged in the 1880s between *organized* labor and *organized* capital. American industrial relations and labor politics are exceptional because in 1886 and 1887 employers won the class struggle.[2]

Before the defeat of the Knights, American workers had developed union structures and world views that were broadly similar to the labor organizations and self-understandings of workers in Britain and France. In all three countries, the working class appeared on the historical stage at roughly the same moment: the 1830s. Reacting to the bastardization of their trades, journeymen artisans in each nation created organizations that for the first time united journeymen of different crafts. As they built these organizations and went on strike to free themselves from the specter of wage labor, they began to articulate a new language of class. In the United States, as well as in France and England, this new language built on and transformed the traditional discourse of political radicalism. Putting old terms to new uses, artisans began to express a recognition of common identity across trades and a sense of difference between themselves and their employers. Because the traditional discourse used to articulate this new understanding of class categories in each case had been constructed from common intellectual roots, the arguments and terms used to critique the developing capitalist economy were also strikingly similar. French, English, and American workers all claimed that they, the producers, were the "people," that capitalists were a new "aristocracy," that workers' skills were property, and hence, that workers had the right, collectively to control the terms of their labor. Moreover, journeymen in each country envisaged a similar cooperative alternative to the de-

the American Labor Movement," in *National Labor Movements in the Postwar World,* ed. Everett M. Kassalow (Evanston, Ill.: Northwestern University Press, 1963); Perlman, *Theory.*

2. To be sure, there were chinks in labor's armor—Powderly was not the kind of bold, creative leader needed in times of crisis; cleavages between skilled and less-skilled workers had not been permanently overcome, and so on—that made organized capital's task easier. These are discussed later in this chapter.

veloping competitive economy. In sum, there was extensive overlap in journeymen's grievances, language, organizations, and alternative visions in all three countries. At the first moment of working-class formation, the American working class did not differ markedly from the French and English.

In none of these countries was this emergent class consciousness a fully developed proletarianism. Artisans on both sides of the Atlantic generally excluded less-skilled workers from their unions, and, although the language of opposition they used was often inclusive of less-skilled workers, it frequently masked exclusionist assumptions.

For the next several decades, the organizational strategies and class understandings developed in the 1830s continued to dominate the organized labor movement in England, France, and the United States. There were, of course, many differences in the fortunes and trials experienced by the three labor movements: for example, English artisans were more successful in their efforts to stabilize their craft associations, and they retreated the furthest from the most radical aspects of the journeymen's revolt. French and American artisans, in contrast, struggled mightily to maintain any craft unions at all. But there were few ideological or organizational innovations as a result of these varying fortunes and extended struggles. On both sides of the Atlantic the labor movement remained the province of a small number of highly skilled craft workers who made little effort to bridge the great experiential and material gulf that separated them from less-skilled workers.

Toward the end of the nineteenth century, craft unionism and the exclusionist assumptions underlying skilled workers' world views were increasingly called into question. A worldwide depression that began in the 1870s and lingered into the 1890s brought enormous pressure on manufacturers in each country to lower operating expenses. As employers scrambled to reduce labor costs, they experimented with technological innovation, new payment schemes, more systematic management techniques, and factory reorganization, all of which began to alter customary patterns of work and social life for both skilled and less-skilled workers. Rarely did these innovations deskill craft workers overnight or eliminate all of the many differences that divided the work force. However, they increased the number of common grievances and experiences workers shared and also multiplied the number of less-skilled jobs in the industrial economy. These developments made continued exclusionary practices on the part of craft unions a potentially risky strategy.

In reaction to these changed circumstances, labor activists in each of these countries began to construct new inclusive ideologies and union structures. In England, "new unions" were organized, so called because they actively recruited unskilled workers, charged low dues, and were more militant and political than the entrenched craft unions. Ideologically, these unions embraced a moderate socialism that stressed the common oppression of skilled and less-skilled workers, the immorality of capitalist inequality, and parliamentary reform. In France, craft unions began to support the strikes of less-skilled industrial workers, and eventually these efforts led to the founding of industrial unions. Politically, the national union federation (the CGT) supported a policy of revolutionary syndicalism, which called for general strikes to bring about the abolition of the wage system and the distinction between workers and employers. In the United States, the Knights of Labor set out to incorporate workers of all skill levels into the labor movement. It endorsed a set of beliefs and goals I have called "working-class republicanism," that emphasized the power of labor solidarity to abolish social and workplace inequality and to erect a "cooperative commonwealth." In each country, these organizational and ideological efforts led to dramatic increases both in the size of the unionized work force and in the level of industrial militancy.

Beneath this commonality, the three labor movements were more different in the second moment than they had been in the first. Organizationally, the English new union activists did not attempt to incorporate or directly ally with craft unions; instead they organized general unions that were open to workers who were explicitly excluded or implicitly overlooked by the old unions. In France and the United States, in contrast, both industrial unionism and alliances between craft unions and less-skilled workers were encouraged. Ideologically, socialism was embraced by many of the new English and French unions, but working-class republicanism was the doctrine that encouraged egalitarianism and solidarity in the Knights of Labor. Moreover, the relationship between unions and left-wing political parties varied in each case. In France, political activists founded the bulk of the unions; in England, the ILP was created by union activists; and in the United States, local, not national, labor parties were established by members of the Knights.

However, these differences were outweighed by an overriding similarity: all three appeared to be following a common path, as activists in each country built new inclusive unions and endorsed new radical creeds in reaction to similar fundamental transformations in the organization of work and social life. Indeed, because a broad-based and radical oppositional movement was founded first in the United States, socialists in England pointed to the American labor movement as the one to be imitated. In France, labor activists established the French branch of the Knights of Labor.[3] In the mid-1880s it did not look as if the American labor movement would turn out to be the weakest and most politically conservative.

Eventually, however, this is exactly what happened. Although the new unions launched in England and France laid the basis for a permanent broadening of the social base and of the political horizons of the labor movement, efforts by the Knights of Labor to similarly reshape the American labor movement ultimately collapsed. After the Knights of Labor disintegrated, the American labor movement once again became the domain of a small group of skilled workers, organized primarily along craft lines. As such, it was increasingly out of step with labor movements on the other side of the Atlantic. Consequently the failure of the Knights marks the moment when, from a comparative perspective, the American labor movement began to look exceptional.

Once we locate the fall of the Knights as the "moment" at which the American labor movement took the exceptionalist path, many of the reasons that have been given for the weakness of working-class institutions and politics in the United States lose their explanatory power. In particular, those that highlight invariant features of American society become less plausible. It is no longer credible to argue, for example, that the pervasiveness of liberalism and individualism, or the bountiful nature of American capitalism, precluded workers in the United States from acting collectively in ways that rivaled their European counterparts. Before the late 1880s, American workers thought of themselves, organized themselves, and acted together in ways that paralleled the thoughts, organizations, and actions of French and English workers.

Instead, identifying the collapse of the Knights as a critical moment in the making of American exceptionalism prompts us to reframe the question of American labor's distinctiveness. Rather than asking why the American working class is and always has been deviant, the appropriate question is: Why did the American working class *become* different? More specifically, what explains the distinctive history of the Knights of Labor? What were the reasons for the Knights' initial success, and why did it eventually collapse?

This book took a systematic approach to answering these questions. Pursuing statistical analyses and case studies, I examined a number of factors identified in the literature on American exceptionalism, as

---

3. Knights assemblies were also established in Britain, but unlike in France, they appear to have been primarily an effort to control the labor market. See Pelling, *America*.

well as in past studies of the Knights, and I attempted to assess the importance of these factors in accounting for the growth and decline of the Order's local assemblies. Focusing on one important industrial state, New Jersey, I began by examining the emergence of Knights organization among less-skilled workers, the group that had for so long been excluded from the labor movement. Here the effort was to understand the general conditions that encouraged broader unionization and to discover the role existing craft organization had played in helping or hindering the incorporation of less-skilled workers into the Knights. I next turned to the creation of industrial unions, examining whether the kinds of conditions that encouraged less-skilled workers to organize also promoted more formal alliances between skilled and less-skilled workers. Finally, the demise of the Knights' local assemblies was examined to determine the extent to which a failure of solidarity between skilled and less-skilled workers might account for the Knights' collapse.

The statistical analyses and case studies revealed that alliances and solidarity played a prominent role in the rapid mobilization of the Knights. No confirmation was found for the oft-repeated argument that American craft workers were unusually "job conscious" or unresponsive to solidaristic appeals. Instead, skilled workers in New Jersey, like skilled workers in other nations, were both craft and class conscious. The Knights were able to mobilize rapidly because they provided an organizational structure that allowed workers to forge solidarity by mobilizing community ties. In late-nineteenth-century America, community—not industry—provided the sturdiest foundation for building an inclusive labor movement, and within that arena skilled craft workers provided the organizers, resources, and moral support that were necessary for less-skilled workers to unionize. As noted in the Introduction, community was also the underlying basis for alliances across the skill divide in France, the one other country where we have enough detailed knowledge about alliance dynamics to make a comparative assessment.

I found that factors frequently highlighted in standard accounts of American exceptionalism to explain the weakness of the American labor movement had no significant inhibiting effect on the organization of less-skilled workers in the New Jersey Knights. Ethnic diversity did not impede the organization of the less skilled or industrial unionism. Nor did competition and conflict between Knights local assemblies and non-Knights locals hinder the growth of Knights organization among less-skilled workers.

Instead, the picture that emerges from the statistical analyses of the creation of assemblies of less-skilled workers, and from the case studies of Trenton and Newark is one in which the Order was growing and doing well through 1886. Organizational growth was especially rapid in the kinds of communities and industries where a majority of New Jersey wage earners lived and worked: larger urban areas and industries characterized by large factories and rapid mechanization.

Why, then, did the Knights collapse? The evidence gathered here suggests that it was because of neither failed solidarity nor rivalry between the Knights and the trade unions. Instead, a number of factors were correlated with the demise of the Knights' local assemblies: rapid proliferation of less-skilled locals, which sapped the Knights' resources; differences in the social and economic foundations that best sustained locals of skilled and less-skilled workers, which multiplied the Order's strategic problems; high wage differentials and industrial diversity, which had little effect on skilled assemblies but accelerated the disintegration of assemblies of less-skilled workers; and, eventually, the declining fortunes of the national organization, which rebounded to the detriment of all New Jersey assemblies. In addition, one other factor was especially devastating to the longevity of both types of local assemblies: the presence of employers' associations. Skilled-workers craft assemblies collapsed 250 percent faster when employers organized, and less-skilled-workers' assemblies disappeared 70 percent faster when employers organized than when they did not.[4] As the case study of Newark's leather industry in Chapter 7 made clear, employers' associations proved to be so damaging in large part because the very economic concentration the Knights deplored provided organized employers with the resources to wage a knock-down, drag-out fight with the Knights. In addition, local, state, and federal officials stayed conspicuously on the sidelines during the conflict, and this worked to the advantage of the employers.

Many of the claims made in this book will prove less controversial than the role I have attributed to employers' associations.[5] Scholars have usually looked to weaknesses within the labor movement itself to explain the collapse of the Knights, just as, more generally, they have focused most commonly on only one of the relevant actors—workers —when trying to explain the development of the labor movement.

However, comparative history provides supporting evidence for my

---

4. The statistic for less-skilled assemblies applies only to the post-1886 period.

5. As noted in the Introduction, note 19, Leon Fink has recently highlighted the importance of employer power in the demise of the Knights. Unlike this study, however, his does not emphasize employers' associations, but focuses instead on the actions of large, dominant employers such as Andrew Carnegie. I agree that the actions of these giant employers were highly significant but would add that their actions reflected a more widespread tendency.

claim that employers' associations played a significant role in the defeat of the Knights. As noted in Chapter 7, many British historians have argued that British employers made few attempts to eliminate the new unions totally, even when these unions began to experience setbacks and large membership losses. Comparativists have suggested that this provides but one example of a larger pattern of greater acceptance of unions by British employers than by American employers. Three reasons are generally given for the comparative openness of British employers: First, the British economy was dominated by much smaller firms, which had fewer resources to resist unionism than their American counterparts. Second, although the British state generally maintained a "studied appearance of neutrality" in labor disputes, it generally worked behind the scenes to encourage mediation and conciliation. Third, many British employers seem to have longed for upper-class respectability, where "proper relations of mutual support and respect between the ranks" was expected.[6]

French employers, in contrast to the British, were probably as intransigent and hostile as American employers toward their employees.[7] However, as we saw in Chapter 7, the French economy, like the British, was more dominated by small firms than the American; thus, French employers had fewer financial resources than American employers. French employers also seem to have been much less able to organize collectively than their American counterparts. Even more important, they were unable to act vigorously on their hostility because the French state tended to intervene in industrial disputes, especially when strikes were large, to force employers to compromise.

Thus, when the experiences of New Jersey workers in the Knights of Labor are considered side by side with the experiences of workers involved in efforts to build broad-based unions in France and England, the role employers and the state played in shaping the ultimate fate of the labor movement stands in sharp relief. In New Jersey, workers who fought to build stable unions across the skill divide squared off against organized, intransigent employers and a laissez-faire state that refused to intervene, even informally, to encourage compromise and mediation. In France, those who struggled to create a broader labor movement confronted the same kind of anti-union attitudes on the part of employers, but this was combined with less employer organization and a state that was willing to step into the fray when conflicts involved large numbers of workers. In Britain, new unionists encoun-

6. Holt, "Trade Unionism"; Jacoby, *Masters to Managers*; Fox, *History*; Zeitlin, "From Labor History."
7. Stearns, "Against the Strike Threat."

tered less employer intransigence, less employer organization, and a state that was willing to work behind the scenes to encourage employers to compromise. In short, American employers and the American state were more anomalous than were American workers.

It would be going too far, however, to argue that the kind of events and forces stressed in traditional accounts of the Knights played no role at all in the Knights' demise. Certainly, Terence Powderly was a vacillating, often ineffectual leader, who was more timid and less militant than many of his members. At the local level, too, leaders such as those who ran Newark's District Assembly 51 were often indecisive or full of false bravado when confronted by organized employers.[8] Certainly, too, the red scare that followed in the wake of Haymarket played a role in the Knights' collapse. It caused internal dissension and turned the opinions of the middle class against the Knights, thus allowing employers greater latitude in their efforts to defeat the Order. Finally, the conflict with the AFL, coming on top of Haymarket, surely weakened the Knights and made it more difficult for locals to fight the employers' assault effectively.

These factors have been underemphasized here, obscured in part by my focus on the Knights' local assemblies. Undoubtedly, even without employers' superior resources, the Knights would have suffered membership losses after Haymarket and after the creation of the AFL. However, had the Knights met less tenacious and organized resistance on the part of employers, the chances of survival and regeneration unquestionably would have been much greater. Again the comparison with Britain's new unions is instructive. These new unions, like the Knights of Labor, experienced a big fall in membership after the first dramatic membership gains, and they also encountered often bitter conflicts with the craft unions. However, as we have seen, employers did not go all out to eradicate the new unions. Thus, they survived, if in weakened form, to provide an organizational base when there was a new wave of industrial unrest in 1911–13. This time around, new union activists were able to extend permanently the labor movement's organizational reach and political power. Moreover, because the new unions survived, there was a gradual movement of the old craft unions to the political left. This occurred for two reasons. First, the initial success and continued survival of the new unions inspired and strengthened the radical element within

8. One probable reason we see much the same pattern in other communities is that this false bravado was the outgrowth of the leader's certainty that public opinion would be on the Knights' side once workers had demonstrated their numbers, their fervor, and their power.

the old unions. Second, even after the industrial retreat, activists in the new unions continued to encourage electoral action and political organization, and, at the municipal level, this activity resulted in political gains such as minimum wage and maximum hour laws. These gains were sufficient to convince many in the old unions to look more favorably on left-wing politics and general unionism.[9] In the United States, in contrast, the Knights as a national organization did not survive the depression of the 1890s and was not around when there was again an upsurge of industrial unrest beginning in 1909.[10]

The Consequences of the Knights' Collapse

Why, one might still inquire, was the defeat of the Knights so critical in setting the American working class on the path to exceptionalism? Why did its collapse foreclose the possibility of a successful broad-based labor movement for nearly forty years? Here I would point to the importance of ideological, organizational, and structural changes that took place in the wake of the Knights' defeat.

Ideologically, the Knights' defeat demoralized those who championed radical reform and classwide organization while empowering those who promoted pragmatic politics and sectional labor unions. Both the demoralized and the empowered drew lessons from the defeat of the Order, and these lessons made it much more difficult for radical activists to persuade workers that inclusive unionism was possible or desirable.

Consider, first, the demoralized. Defeats in battle almost always prove debilitating in the short run, but their long-term consequences depend on how they are framed and how responsibility is apportioned. Working-class republicanism provided few conceptual resources for interpreting the Knights' defeat in any but the bleakest of terms. If workers organized thoroughly and demonstrated their power, the ideology advised, the Order would be able to persuade the larger society of the importance and justice of their cause. When the moment of truth came, and the Knights were in reality defeated by organized employers, they were left, ideologically, with only themselves to blame. Thus, many workers drew the lesson that broad orga-

9. Hunt, *British Labour*, pp. 309–15. See also Gary Marks, *Unions in Politics: Britain, Germany, and the United States in the Nineteenth and Early Twentieth Centuries* (Princeton: Princeton University Press, 1989), pp. 210–11.

10. The dating is adapted from Montgomery's discussion of the strike decade that began in 1909. Montgomery, *Workers' Control*, pp. 91–112.

nization and radical goals were doomed to failure. A process I have termed "cognitive encumbrance" occurred, in which defenders of broad-based unionism were plunged into a gloomy despair that made it tough for them to convince workers to try again to build an inclusive labor movement. This despair also made it difficult to recognize new political opportunities when they arose.

The empowered also drew lessons from the Knights' failure. Samuel Gompers, president of the AFL, justified his moderate, conservative policies by noting that he had seen "how professions of radicalism and sensationalism concentrated all the forces of organized society against a labor movement and nullified in advance normal, necessary activity." [11] Along with other AFL leaders, Gompers interpreted the destruction of the Knights as a warning. The majority of unions affiliated with the AFL heeded this warning by reconfirming their commitment to sectional unionism and pragmatic, nonradical politics.

Ideologically, then, the Knights' defeat left a bitter legacy for the American labor movement. Working-class republicanism and open unions were discredited, and the case for "pure and simple" trade unionism was strengthened.

Organizational dynamics stemming from the Knights' demise also made it difficult for defenders of inclusive union strategies to rebuild an effective, broad-based movement. Once the national craft unions affiliated with the AFL became firmly established, institutional and competitive pressures made it much more difficult to create industrial and general unions. As sociologists know from the work of organizational ecologists and institutionalists, established organizations tend to constrain the form of new organizations: first, because established organizations favor conforming organizations when providing sponsorship, forming coalitions, or negotiating agreements; second, because established organizations provide clear models; and third, because once people belong to dominant organizations, it becomes more difficult to recruit them for a competitive form.[12]

11. Samuel Gompers, *Seventy Years of Life and Labor* (New York: E. P. Dutton, 1925), p. 97. Gompers made the remark when discussing the role of radicals in the Tompkins Square riot of 1873, but it is clear that he meant the remark to be more general.

12. This paragraph and the next draw on arguments that Carol Conell and I developed in our article, "Formal Organization." For the research of organizational ecologists, see Michael T. Hannan and John Freeman, "The Ecology of Organizational Foundings: American Labor Unions, 1836–1985," *American Journal of Sociology* 92 (1987): 910–43; Michael T. Hannan and John Freeman, *Organizational Ecology* (Cambridge: Harvard University Press, 1989), pp. 55–61 and 97–105. For the research of the institutionalists, see Paul J. DiMaggio and Walter W. Powell, "The Iron Cage Revisited: Institutional Isomorphism and Collective Rationality in Organizational Fields," *American Sociological Review* 48 (1983): 147–60.

Certainly, in the American labor movement, all these institutional and competitive forces made it more difficult to establish industrial or general unions after the AFL achieved dominance in the late 1890s. Exclusive jurisdiction was a guiding principle of the AFL; it held that only one union could hold rights to organize any particular group of workers. Unions that attempted to challenge the jurisdiction of any other union were simply not admitted to the federation. This effectively prevented most industrial unions from membership as they unavoidably challenged the monopoly of craft unions in many industries. Moreover, sponsorship was provided much more readily (and in many cases, exclusively) to workers who were willing to adopt sectional organizing strategies. Organizers were generally hired by national craft unions, and they initiated only craft locals. Over time, it became more and more difficult to establish alternative union structures. As a result, attempts to do so were few, and these efforts met with much less success than had those of the Knights of Labor.[13]

Finally, economic and social changes made working-class unity more difficult to achieve after the late 1890s. First, the labor force grew even more diverse than it had been in the 1870s and 1880s. Beginning in 1895, the pace of immigration accelerated, and the national origin of those who arrived on American shores shifted dramatically. In the first decade of the twentieth century, more immigrants came to the United States than had ever arrived in any other decade of American history.[14] The great majority came from southern and eastern Europe, which meant that their linguistic and cultural background was very different from that of both native-born Americans and earlier immi-

13. For example, the Industrial Workers of the World (IWW), founded in 1905, was much less successful at organizing than the Knights. The organization never organized more than 120,000 workers and for most of its existence probably had a membership closer to 15,000, this at a time when the working class was much larger than it had been when the Knights counted at least 750,000 members. (Figures given in Henry Pelling, *American Labor* [Chicago: University of Chicago Press, 1960], p. 114; and Melvyn Dubofsky, *We Shall Be All: A History of the Industrial Workers of the World* [New York: Quadrangle, 1969].) One member of the IWW, J. S. Biscay, enumerated some of the problems with trying to convert craft workers to the IWW and to new union forms. Responding to those who advocated the European strategy of "boring from within" to win over adherents in the AFL to syndicalism, he argued, "To start boring from within with all the craft unionists prejudiced already would mean the disbanding of the I.W.W, and hardly causing a ripple in the crafts. Their overwhelming membership would soon dispose of the few capable men who would begin their 'boring.' The rest of the rank and file of the I.W.W. being of the floating element to a large extent, can't get into the crafts to 'bore.' " Quoted in Dubofsky, *We Shall Be All*, p. 224.

14. Easterlin et al., *Immigration*, p. 2, Table 1.1. See also John Higham, *Send These to Me: Immigrants in Urban America* (Baltimore: Johns Hopkins University Press, 1984), chaps. 1–2.

grants. The British, Irish, and German workers who immigrated in the 1870s and 1880s found an earlier generation of their compatriots already employed in the industrial economy, but these new immigrants did not. Thus, they had fewer ties to the already established working class than the "old-stock" immigrants. Moreover, employers increasingly organized factory work on the basis of ethnicity and language. When the U.S. Immigration Commission concluded its report on immigrants in industry in 1911, it observed that immigrants were often separated from native workers and also "subdivided into smaller groups . . . in order to ensure more ease of handling." [15] The commission noted that there had been "a sharp segregation . . . into distinct occupations" within a short space of time. Available evidence suggests that this was a more systematic policy after the turn of the century than it had been before.[16] The upshot of this increasing diversity and occupational segmentation was heightened racism and nativism in the AFL and in the labor press. This stood in poignant contrast to the relative tolerance and egalitarianism of the Knights.

Second, after the end of the long depression, evidence suggests that there were widening wage differentials for skilled and less-skilled work. Andrew Dawson has estimated that the wages of most highly skilled workers increased an average of 74 percent between 1890 and 1914 but that those of unskilled workers rose only 31 percent.[17] Similarly, Peter Shergold's study of workers in Pittsburgh documents a rapid increase in skilled-workers' real wages after the depression of the 1890s that was not shared by unskilled workers.[18] As this study of Knights locals has indicated, wage differentials tended to encourage workers to organize sectionally rather than broadly and to undermine the viability of locals of less-skilled workers. Widening wage differentials, therefore, could be expected to decrease the likelihood of alliances between skilled and less-skilled workers and to have made broad-based unionism more difficult.

Third, there was increased spatial segregation of the working class. In metropolitan areas such as Boston, Philadelphia, and Detroit, the development of urban transportation networks resulted in "street-car" suburbs that were inhabited largely by skilled workers, both native-

15. Quoted in Gordon, Edwards, and Reich, *Segmented Work*, pp. 141–42.
16. Gordon, Edwards, and Reich, *Segmented Work*, pp. 142–43, summarize this evidence. See also Montgomery, *Beyond Equality*, pp. 35–36; Hershberg, *Philadelphia*.
17. Andrew Dawson, "The Paradox of Dynamic Technological Change and the Labor Aristocracy in the United States, 1880–1914," *Labor History* 20 (1979), p. 332.
18. Peter R. Shergold, *Working-Class Life: The "American Standard" in Comparative Perspective, 1899–1913* (Pittsburgh: University of Pittsburgh Press, 1982).

born and those of "old" immigrant groups.[19] Thus, skilled workers began to live at greater distances from their place of employment and from the neighborhoods occupied by new immigrant groups. These residential patterns deepened the growing social distance between skilled, native-born, and old immigrant groups on the one hand, and less-skilled, new immigrant groups on the other. This growing spacial segregation, according to my findings, would undermine the community ties that played such an important role in the mobilization of the Knights.

One might reasonably ask whether these economic and social changes might have undermined working-class unity even if the Knights had survived. To answer this question with any degree of certainty is, of course, impossible, but some hints along these lines are offered in John Cumbler's study of Fall River and Lynn, Massachusetts.[20] Lynn was an early stronghold of industrial unionism; by the time new immigrant groups began to arrive, its working class had built strong and inclusive working-class institutions. As a result, the new immigrants were assimilated into working-class institutions and understandings of American society. Workers in Fall River, on the other hand, were unable to build the same integrating working-class institutions; consequently the pressures of Portuguese and Polish immigration at the turn of the century fragmented the community into ethnic enclaves, undermining collective action and community cohesion. Had the Knights survived, more communities would have been like Lynn and fewer like Fall River.

Thus, for ideological, organizational, and structural reasons, the 1870s and 1880s proved to be a critical period for the establishment of an inclusive labor movement. A decade later, the promise of working-class solidarity had been discredited along with the Knights' alternative vision of the future, the AFL had become the dominant organization in the labor movement, and the working class itself had grown more diverse and divided. Efforts to incorporate less-skilled workers into the labor movement were effectively doomed for two generations. Only after the social and economic crisis that spurred the New Deal

19. Sam Bass Warner, *Streetcar Suburbs: The Process of Growth in Boston, 1870–1900,* 2d ed. (Cambridge: Harvard University Press, 1978); Theodore Hershberg, Alan N. Burstein, Eugene P. Ericksen, Stephanie W. Greenberg, William L. Yancey, "A Tale of Three Cities: Blacks, Immigrants, and Opportunity in Philadelphia, 1850, 1930, 1970," in Hershberg, *Philadelphia,* pp. 461–91; Olivier Zunz, *The Changing Face of Inequality: Urbanization, Industrial Development and Immigrants in Detroit, 1880–1920* (Chicago: University of Chicago Press, 1982).

20. Cumbler, *Working-Class Community.*

had severely weakened the AFL, undermined public support for business dominance, and encouraged government intervention on the side of labor were less-skilled workers successfully incorporated into the labor movement.

Political Institutions and American Exceptionalism

I have been elaborating an argument for the last several pages about why the 1880s were a critical moment in the development of the labor movement in the United States. I have implied that if the Knights of Labor had survived, the United States would have had a very different—and less exceptional—labor history. The comparative case I have had most in mind is the British: there, as we have seen, the new unions survived a less ruthless employers' assault and were able to provide an organizational basis for rapidly and permanently expanding the labor movement when a new strike wave took place in 1911–13. Because a similar upsurge in unrest took place in the United States beginning in 1909, I believe that this comparative case offers an alternative path of development that the American labor movement might plausibly have taken.

Some readers will no doubt object that American party structures and political institutions would have precluded the Knights of Labor from following the path of the British new unionists even had it not been subjected to greater employer hostility. Ira Katznelson, for example, has argued that structural obstacles to working-class political mobilization were already in place by 1860 that made the American political arena more resistant to class-based appeals than the British.[21] Most important, he points to party and patronage systems that organized voters into ethnic and community blocks that cut across class and occupational identities. The organization of politics in America, he believes, created a radical division between the politics of work and the politics of community, which made it extremely difficult to appeal to workers by mobilizing class solidarities. By extension, Katznelson's argument would suggest that even if the Knights had survived, the American party and patronage system would have made it much more difficult for the Knights to have achieved the kinds of political gains that nourished and legitimated the British new unions after they experienced repeated strike losses in the industrial arena.

Other scholars have argued in a similar vein that key constitutional

21. Katznelson, *City Trenches;* "Working-Class Formation and the State," pp. 257–84.

features of American politics discriminate against independent labor campaigns.[22] Three features are mentioned most frequently: America's winner-take-all-electoral system, its constitutional focus on the presidency, and the presidential selection method that in practice constructs the whole country as a single constituency through the electoral college. Both Britain and the United States have winner-take-all systems, so that would not necessarily have precluded an undefeated Knights of Labor from pursuing the path of the British new unionists. However, America's presidential system differs from England's parliamentary arrangement and this difference certainly would have made it more difficult for the Knights to exploit local and regional successes as a way to build political support for later advances, as did the British new unionists.

This book has itself demonstrated that these arguments have a great deal of merit. As detailed in Chapter 4, New Jersey activists who attempted to pursue a working-class agenda in the political realm confronted very difficult political obstacles. Certainly, the American electoral and party system would have made the Knights' task even more difficult than that faced by the British new unionists.

However, it would be overstating the evidence to conclude that something analogous to the British path was out of the question in the United States. We simply do not know whether the Knights would have been able to overcome the substantial political obstacles they would have faced. The critical historical contest that would allow us to assess the absolute impermeability of the political arena posited by Katznelson and others never took place. To the contrary, the Knights experienced overwhelming opposition from employers, rapid, destablizing growth, and demoralization long before they could be undone by the nature of American electoral politics.

Two additional observations are worth making in this regard. First, the empirical findings I report in this book call into question at least one aspect of Katznelson's version of the political institutional argument for American exceptionalism. As demonstrated in Chapter 5, community was a basis for working-class action in the 1880s; the nature of American politics did not fully undermine its importance as a mobilizing nexus until after the collapse of the Knights.[23] Thus, it is likely

22. See, for example, E. E. Schattschneider, *Party Government* (New York: Holt, 1942), pp. 65–98; Seymour Martin Lipset, *The First New Nation* (Garden City, N.Y.: Anchor Books, 1967), pp. 327–65; Marks, *Unions in Politics*, pp. 217–20; and Steven J. Rosenstone, Roy L. Behr, and Edward H. Lazarus, *Third Parties in America: Citizen Response to Major Party Failure* (Princeton: Princeton University Press, 1984), chap. 2.

23. Moreover, as noted in Chapter 7, when Knight members did participate in third-

that the separation between work and community life was less impermeable in the 1880s than Katznelson believes.

Second, as Gary Marks has recently shown in his book of unions in Britain and in the United States in the late nineteenth and early twentieth centuries, it would have been from the ranks of inclusive unions such as the Knights that one would expect to have seen efforts mounted to overcome the political obstacles that were thrown up by the American electoral system.[24] The weak labor-market position of inclusive unions, Marks demonstrates, almost always led them to pursue a strategy of extensive political regulation of labor-markets. Unlike the exclusionary craft unions, inclusive unions could not hope to improve their working conditions by controlling the supply of labor in a particular occupation. Instead, their best bet for improving working conditions was to seek political regulation of minimum wages and maximum hours. Moreover, inclusive unions had political resources in their broader membership constituency that craft unions lacked. In short, both their labor-market positions and their political resources prompted inclusive unions to press for the establishment of labor

---

party campaigns, this participation did not significantly contribute to the decline of the local assemblies.

Martin Shefter, one of Katznelson's collaborators in *Working-Class Formation*, offers a chronology similar to mine when he suggests that 1886 was a critical turning point in the history of the American working class. In 1886, he argues, one of the most distinctive features of American working-class development—workers' orientation toward the political mainstream—was very nearly undermined as increasing numbers of workers abandoned the major parties for local labor and "fusion" parties. Only the launching of a concerted antilabor crusade and the resulting divisions within the labor movement over how to respond prevented a realignment of the labor movement toward more independent politics.

I obviously agree with Shefter's chronology. Our only disagreement is over the relative role of employers and of the state in the counteroffensive. Shefter emphasizes the role of courts and state legislatures, and I underscore the role of employers. To be sure, as I have tried to make clear, the state's hand can be discerned in the latitude given to employers to hire strikebreakers and Pinkertons and in the general expansion of property rights in this era. But I think that these kinds of state actions were more important than direct deeds such as the new laws and court convictions cited by Shefter. Eventually, with the innovation of the labor injunction, the courts would begin to act in a very direct manner. But labor injunctions were not widely used until after the Debs decision in 1894.

Experientially, as Shefter points out elsewhere in his essay, it mattered for workers' image of the state whether government officials acted in a publicly interventionist manner through obviously repressive laws, police action, and court convictions or in a less intrusive fashion by allowing the use of private police like the Pinkertons. Because workers generally experienced repression at the hands of employers rather than of the state, they were less likely to see the state itself as a target of change.

See Martin Shefter, "Trade Unions and Political Machines: The Organization and Disorganization of the American Working Class in the Late Nineteenth Century," in *Working-Class Formation*, ed. Katznelson and Zolberg, esp. pp. 211–12 and 252.

24. Marks, *Unions in Politics*.

parties. That is why, Marks argues, the core support for both socialist and independent labor activity in the late nineteenth and early twentieth century in both Britain and the United States came from inclusive unions.

Once the Knights were defeated, however, only a small minority of all labor unions in the United States were inclusive unions. As a result, few union leaders made any effort to surmount the political obstacles put in the way of third-party success by American political institutions. Comparatively, as Marks points out, the American labor movement looks exceptional in the years after the Knights' collapse not only because there was no labor party and no broad-based union movement but also because the majority of established union leaders made no attempt to build a labor party or to pursue the types of political goals that might have stimulated working-class support for a labor party. Surely, this lack of effort is at least part of the reason no labor party was ever established in the United States.

In sum, the American constitutional and electoral system would have made it more difficult for an undefeated Knights of Labor to have accrued the kinds of political successes that helped the British new unionists to survive into the twentieth century. However, it would be going further than the evidence will allow to conclude that electoral impediments would have indubitably prevented the Knights from following a path similar to that taken by the new unionists. Had there been more inclusive unions in the United States at the beginning of the twentieth century, there would have been more union leaders attempting to surmount the political obstacles thrown up by American political institutions.

Long-Term Reverberations of the Knights' Collapse

In the past few years historical sociologists have begun to alert us to the ways in which contingent events can have enormous consequences because of the timing of their occurrence and the path-dependent nature of social processes.[25] The Knights' efforts to change history mattered, although certainly not in the way its members wanted. Rather

25. Andrew Abbott, "Transcending General Linear Reality," *Sociological Theory* 6 (Fall 1988): 169–86, and "Conceptions of Time and Events in Social Science Methods: Causal and Narrative Approaches," *Historical Methods* 23, no. 4 (1990): 140–50; William H. Sewell, Jr., "Three Temporalities: Toward an Eventful Sociology," in *The Historic Turn in the Human Sciences,* ed. Terrence J. McDonald (Ann Arbor: University of Michigan Press, Forthcoming).

than democratizing industry and creating the regulated market economy they sought, the Knights' actions led to the countermobilization of employers and the delegitimation of inclusive strategies of labor organization.

The repercussions of this countermobilization and delegitimation lingered for a very long time. I have already argued that the weakness and political conservatism of the American labor movement from the mid-1890s through the mid-1930s owes much to the defeat of the Knights. I think that one additional consequence can be tied, at least partially, to the Knights' collapse as well. By international standards, American industry is characterized by an unusual amount of job simplification and occupational specialization.[26] To borrow Alan Fox's highly evocative terms, it is an example of a low-trust, low-discretion system.[27] This can be connected directly, I submit, to the tardiness with which successful broad-based unionism developed in the United States. By the time the CIO began to organize America's mass-production industries in the 1930s, job structures were already highly differentiated, and, after some initial efforts to increase the amount of worker discretion on the job, unions adopted an approach to collective bargaining that conformed to the kinds of job structures that had become institutionalized in America's mass-production industries. Both unions and employers soon engaged in a negotiating process in which each tried to use job definitions and bureaucratic rules to their own advantage. Over time, this led to ever more narrowly defined and simplified jobs, a reality that commentators on both the left and right regularly bemoan and that, many argue, seriously undermines the ability of American business to manufacture quality products. Again, it is impossible to know what would have happened had the Order survived, renewed its organizational efforts, and unionized a substantial proportion of the less-skilled work force. However, had this occurred, it is likely that job structures might look less fragmented and simplified today. The lateness of broad-based unionism, therefore, affects us all.

26. Robert Cole's comparative work on Japan and the United States has stimulated my thinking about these matters. See Robert E. Cole, *Work, Mobility, and Participation* (Berkeley: University of California Press, 1979), esp. pp. 101–7.

27. Alan Fox, *Beyond Contract: Work, Power, and Trust Relations* (London: Faber, 1974).

1

Communities

With one exception, all towns with populations exceeding 2,500 were included in the study. The exception was Atlantic City, which was omitted because of excessive missing data.

Bergen County
  Englewood
  Hackensack
Burlington County
  Bordentown
  Burlington
  Mt. Holly
Camden County
  Camden
  Gloucester
Cumberland County
  Bridgeton
  Millville
  Vineland
Essex County
  Belleville
  Bloomfield
  Montclair
  Newark

The Oranges
Gloucester County
 Glassboro
 Woodbury
Hudson County
 Bayonne
 Harrison
 Hoboken
 Jersey City
 Union
 West Hoboken
Hunterton County
 Lambertville
Mercer County
 Princeton
 Trenton
Middlesex County
 New Brunswick
 Perth Amboy
 South Amboy
Monmouth County
 Asbury Park and Ocean Grove
 Freehold
 Keyport
 Long Branch
 Redbank
Morris County
 Boonton
 Dover
 Morristown
Passaic County
 Passaic
 Paterson
Salem County
 Salem
Somerset County
 Somerville
Union County
 Elizabeth
 Plainfield
 Rahway

Warren County
  Belvidere
  Hackettstown
  Oxford
  Phillipsburg
  Washington

Industry Classification

The following industry groups are based on the classification system devised by the Massachussetts Bureau of Statistics of Labor in its Thirty-Eighth Report (Boston: State Printers, 1907). I modified it only in cases where it was impossible to unambiguously assign labor organizations to an appropriate industry. In those cases, I combined categories.

1B Stone and earthenware
2A Boots and shoes
2C Hats
2D Garments
3A Food products
3B Liquors
3C Tobacco
4A Leather goods
4B Rubber goods
5A Iron, steel, and machinery
5B Nonferrous metal manufacturing
5C Shipbuilding
5X Jewelry
5Z Carriages, wagons, and agricultural implements
6A Paper and paper goods
7A Printing and allied trades

10A   Bleaching, dyeing, and printing textiles
10B   Cotton goods and mixed textiles
10C   Flax and jute goods
10E   Woolen and worsted goods
10F   Silk
12A   Saw-mill products and planing-mill products
12D   Wood turning and carving
      Furniture
      Musical instruments
13A   Drugs and chemicals
      Paints and dyes
      Soap and candles
      Animal and mineral oil products
      Petroleum refining
13B   Glass and glassware
13C   Light and power

3

Event-History Analysis

The methodological problem in Chapters 5–7 is to model dynamic processes: the emergence and disappearance of Knights of Labor assemblies. Having constructed organizational histories for every local industry and every town in New Jersey, I wanted to analyze statistically two portions of this sequence—the development of organization among less-skilled workers and the demise of all types of Knights local assemblies.

Event-history analysis provides a way of analyzing a longitudinal record of when events happened to a sample of individuals or collectivities.[1] For the sake of illustration, consider first the "event" modeled in Chapter 5: the founding of a new Knights of Labor local that incorporates less-skilled workers.

Formally, let $P_{jk}(t, t + \Delta t)$ be the probability that an individual (or collectivity) in state j at time t is in some other state k at time $t + \Delta t$,

---

1. For an introduction to event-history analysis, see Glenn R. Carroll, "Dynamic Analysis of Discrete Dependent Variables: A Didactic Essay," *Quality and Quantity* 19 (1983): 425–60; Paul D. Allison, *Event History Analysis*, Sage University Paper Series on Quantitative Applications in the Social Sciences (Beverly Hills, Calif.: Sage Publications, 1984); and Lawrence E. Raffalovich and David Knoke, "Quantitative Methods for the Analysis of Historical Change," *Historical Methods* 16 (1983): 149–54. My discussion draws especially from these sources. A more technical exposition can be found in Tuma and Hannan, *Social Dynamics*. A nontechnical, more philosophical discussion is presented in Andrew Abbott, "Sequences of Social Events: Concepts and Methods for the Analysis of Order in Social Processes," *Historical Methods* 16 (1983): 129–47.

that is, the probability of a change in state in the interval between t and $t + \Delta t$. Then, the instantaneous rate of transition from state j to state k is defined as the probability of change of state per unit of time as the time unit becomes infinitesimally small:

$$r(t) = \lim_{t \to 0}[P_{jk}(t, t + \Delta t)/\Delta t]. \tag{1}$$

In the analysis presented in Chapter 5, the collectivity is the local industry; state j is defined as the absence of Knights of Labor organization among less-skilled workers, and state k is the existence of Knights of Labor organization among less-skilled workers. Time is measured in years.[2] The dependent variable, $r(t)$, is the rate at which Knights of Labor organization develops among less-skilled workers.

Equation (1) expresses the rate of founding as a function of time. But the rate of any event may depend not only on time but also on exogenous variables. Indeed, the main empirical interest in Chapter 5 is not to estimate the rate at which new less-skilled labor organizations are founded but to determine how the rate of founding is affected by such factors as average establishment size and the presence of craft organization. Causal effects are built into the model by expressing the relationship between the rate and the exogenous variables as follows:

$$\ln r(t) = a_0 + b_1 X_1 + b_2 X_2 + \cdots c_1 Y_1(t) + c_2 Y_2(t) + \cdots, \tag{2}$$

where the X's are independent variables that, although varying across local industries, do not change over time; the $Y(t)$'s are independent variables that do vary over time; and a_0, the b's, and the c's are parameters to be estimated. I chose a log-linear specification because it ensures that the predicted rate will be positive and because all effects are expressed as proportional to the rate. Thus a positive value on a parameter indicates the amount by which a marginal change in the in-

2. Although in practice a local assembly of less-skilled workers could develop at any point in time, I have information only about the year such a local was established. Hence, one might argue that discrete-time models would be more appropriate. (This would offer an additional advantage: discrete-time hazard rates translate directly into probabilities, and probabilities are easier for many people to grasp concretely.) However, methodologists are generally unsympathetic to such reasoning because it allows the data to dictate the form of the model. As Carroll points out in his didactic essay on event-history analysis, it is preferable to motivate the model substantively and estimate the parameters from available data, whatever the form. I took this advice to heart; nonetheless, it should be noted that results from at least one family of discrete-time methods are generally quite similar to the continuous-time methods used here. See Allison, *Event History Analysis*, p. 22, for a discussion of this issue. Tuma and Hannan also discuss the advantages of continuous-time methods in *Social Dynamics*, pp. 82–88.

dependent variable increases the (logged) rate at which labor organizations of less-skilled workers are founded. Correspondingly, a negative value shows that the exogenous variable reduces the rate of founding. For those readers unfamiliar with event-history methodology, it should be noted that a rate equation in its log-linear specification bears a strong resemblance to the more familiar linear-regression equation.

Equation (2) assumes that the rate at which labor organizations are founded is time independent; that is, that the rate does not vary with historical time. Chapter 5 also reports models that include period effects. The Knights grew much more rapidly before 1887 than they did afterward. The way I model this is to include two time periods (1880–86 and 1887–95) during which I estimate the rate of founding of Knights locals:

$$
\begin{aligned}
\ln r(t_{1880-86} &= a_0 + b_1X_1 + b_2X_2 + \cdots c_1Y_1(t) + c_2Y_2(t) + \cdots, \\
\ln r(t_{1887-95} &= a_0 + b_1X_1 + b_2X_2 + \cdots c_1Y_1(t) + c_2Y_2(t) + \cdots,
\end{aligned}
\tag{3}
$$

where all terms are defined as in Equation (2). These models allow independent-variable effects to differ between time periods.

All parameters were estimated using a maximum-likelihood procedure, implemented in the computer program, RATE, developed by Nancy Tuma.[3] Estimators from this procedure have been found to remain quite good even when the sample size is small and the degree of (right) censoring is high; that is, when the mean number of events is low as in these data.[4] In addition, the RATE program provides estimates of a maximum-likelihood Chi-square statistic (χ^2); these are used here to select the best fitting model from a set of hierarchical models.

The models estimated in Chapter 6 are very similar to those esti-

3. Nancy Tuma, *Invoking RATE* (Menlo Park, Calif.: SRI International, 1980).
4. Nancy B. Tuma and Michael T. Hannan, "Approaches to the Censoring Problem in Analysis of Event Histories," in *Sociological Methodology*, ed. Karl F. Schuessler (San Francisco: Jossey-Bass), pp. 209–40. It should be noted that my data also suffered from left censoring problems. The observation period for the analysis of emergence is 1880–95. In actuality, however, some locals of less-skilled workers were founded before 1880. Unfortunately, I was unable to make use of the information I had about these early assemblies because I had incomplete information about the trade unions in existence before 1880. It was impossible to know, for instance, whether or not a craft union was in existence when a local assembly of less-skilled workers was founded prior to 1880. Consequently, it was necessary to limit the analysis to the period for which complete information was available, in spite of the fact that some observations were then left censored. In order to avoid estimation problems because of this, I discarded the censored observations and analyzed only those episodes that started after 1880. Although this represented a loss of information, it avoided bias in the parameter estimates.

mated in Chapter 5. The primary difference is that two "events" are modeled in Chapter 6: the founding of new quasi-industrial locals and the founding of new sectional locals.

In addition, the analysis in Chapter 6 does not distinguish the initial organization of less-skilled workers from subsequent organization; all locals of less-skilled workers are included in the analysis. In event-history parlance, the models in Chapter 6 incorporate both repeated events (i.e., the founding of all locals of less-skilled workers are included) and multiple kinds of events (i.e., quasi-industrial locals are distinguished from sectional locals). This makes the models more complicated to estimate than the ones in Chapter 5, but it does not change the way the parameters are interpreted.

The models reported in Chapter 7 are also quite similar to those presented in Chapter 5, except that the event of interest is the dissolution of a local assembly rather than the emergence of one. Thus, in that chapter, the "collectivity" represented in Equation (1) is the local assembly rather than the local industry.

Normally failure-rate models include an estimate of the rate of declining age dependence over time, and I initially estimated both models in Chapter 7 by using a Makeham law specification. However, the data on the local assemblies do not display the usual form of age dependence—or, for that matter, any perceptible form of monotonic age dependence—and the more sophisticated models do not significantly improve on the constant-rate models used here. When Carroll and Huo estimated failure-rate models for all the local assemblies in the United States, they found a similar lack of monotonic age dependence.[5] They went on to estimate models that included time-period effects, but their time periods were defined on the basis of age, not historical time. When I estimated models for assemblies of less-skilled workers, I included historical time periods rather than age time periods because my reading of the Knights' history suggests that this is the more important type of time dependence. In addition, I wanted to have models that were comparable to those I had used in the earlier chapters on the formation of Knights local assemblies.

5. Glenn R. Carroll and Paul Yangchung Huo, "Organizational and Electoral Paradoxes of the Knights of Labor," in *Ecological Models of Organizations*, ed. Glenn R. Carroll (Cambridge: Ballinger, 1988).

Bibliography

Manuscript Sources

Herbert Gutman Papers. New York Public Library.

Ira Kerrison Papers. Rutgers University Library, New Brunswick, N.J.

John Hayes Papers. Catholic University of America, Washington, D.C. Available in a microfilm edition at the University of California, Berkeley. John A. Turcheneske, Jr., ed., *A Guide to the Microfilm Edition*. Glen Rock, N.J.: Microfilming Corporation of America, 1975.

Knights of Labor Data Bank. Inter-University Consortium for Political and Social Research, Ann Arbor. A guide to the use of this computer data bank is Garlock, Jonathan, and N. C. Builder, *The Knights of Labor Data Bank: User's Manual and Index to Local Assemblies*. Ann Arbor, Mich.: Inter-University Consortium for Political and Social Research (ICPSR 0029), 1973.

Terence Vincent Powderly Papers. Catholic University of America, Washington, D.C. Available in a microfilm edition at the University of California, Berkeley. John A. Turcheneske, Jr., ed., *A Guide to the Microfilm Edition*. Glen Rock, N.J.: Microfilming Corporation of America, 1975.

Trenton, New Jersey, Pottery Assemblies. Proceedings, District Assembly 160, and Local Assembly 1962, 1890–1892. Available on microfilm from the Trenton Public Library.

U.S. Department of the Interior Census Bureau. Manufacturing Schedules. New Jersey, 1880. Available on microfilm from the National Archives, Washington, D.C.

Works Progress Administration Papers. New Jersey State Archives, Trenton, N.J.

Government Documents

Massachusetts Bureau of Statistics of Labor. *Thirty-Eighth Annual Report.* Boston: State Printers, 1907.

New Jersey. *Census of the State of New Jersey for 1875.* Paterson: Chiswell and Wurts, 1876.

——. "Census of 1885," in *Acts of the 110th Legislature of New Jersey.* Trenton: MacCrellish & Quiqley, 1886.

New Jersey Bureau of Statistics of Labor and Industries. *Fourth Annual Report of the Bureau of Statistics of Labor and Industries of New Jersey for the Year Ending October 31, 1881.* Somerville, New Jersey: State of New Jersey, 1881.

——. *Fifth Annual Report of the Bureau of Statistics of Labor and Industries for the Year Ending October 31, 1882.* Trenton: State of New Jersey, 1882.

——. *Sixth Annual Report of the Bureau of Statistics of Labor and Industries for the Year Ending October 31, 1883.* Trenton: State of New Jersey, 1883.

——. *Seventh Annual Report of the Bureau of Statistics of Labor and Industries for the Year Ending October 31, 1884.* Trenton: State of New Jersey, 1885.

——. *Eighth Annual Report of the Bureau of Statistics of Labor and Industries for the Year Ending October 31, 1885.* Trenton: State of New Jersey, 1885.

——. *Ninth Annual Report of the Bureau of Statistics of Labor and Industries for the Year Ending October 31, 1886.* Trenton: State of New Jersey, 1886.

——. *Tenth Annual Report of the Bureau of Statistics of Labor and Industries for the Year Ending October 31, 1887.* Somerville: State of New Jersey, 1888.

——. *Thirteenth Annual Report of the Bureau of Statistics of Labor and Industries for the Year Ending October 31, 1890.* Trenton: State of New Jersey, 1891.

——. *Fifteenth Annual Report of the New Jersey Bureau of Statistics of Labor and Industries for the Year Ending October 31, 1892.* Trenton: State of New Jersey, 1893.

——. *Sixteenth Annual Report of the Bureau of Statistics of Labor and Industries for the Year Ending October 31, 1893.* Trenton: State of New Jersey, 1894.

——. *Seventeenth Annual Report of the New Jersey Bureau of Statistics of Labor and Industries for the Year Ending October 31, 1894.* Trenton: State of New Jersey, 1895.

——. *Eighteenth Annual Report of the New Jersey Bureau of Statistics of Labor and Industries for the Year Ending 1895.* Trenton: State of New Jersey, 1896.

——. *Twenty-second Annual Report of the Bureau of Statistics of Labor and Industries for the Year Ending October 31, 1899.* Trenton: State of New Jersey, 1899.

——. *Twenty-third Annual Report of the Bureau of Statistics of Labor and Industries for the Year Ending October 31, 1900.* Camden: State of New Jersey, 1901.

New York Bureau of Statistics of Labor. *Fifth Annual Report for the Year 1887.* Albany: Troy Press Co., 1888.

United States. Commissioner of Labor. *Third Annual Report, 1887: Strikes and Lockouts.* Washington, D.C.: Government Printing Office, 1888.

——. *Tenth Annual Report, 1894: Strikes and Lockouts.* Vols. 1 and 2. Washington, D.C.: Government Printing Office, 1896.

United States. Department of Commerce. *Historical Statistics of the United States, Colonial Times to 1970.* Part 1. Washington, D.C.: Government Printing Office, 1975.

United States. Department of the Interior. *Report on the Social Statistics of Cities.* Washington, D.C.: Government Printing Office, 1886.

——. *Statistics of Manufactures of the United States at the Tenth Census, 1880.* Washington, D.C.: Government Printing Office, 1883.

——. *Abstract of the Eleventh Census.* Washington, D.C.: Government Printing Office, 1894.

——. *Report on Manufacturing Industries at the Eleventh Census: 1890.* Washington, D.C.: Government Printing Office, 1895.

——. *Report on the Population of the United States at the Eleventh Census: 1890,* Part 2. Washington, D.C.: Government Printing Office, 1892.

——. *Twelfth Census of the United States, taken in the year 1900. Manufactures.* Washington, D.C.: Government Printing Office, 1902.

——. *Special Report on Employees and Wages, 1890–1900.* Washington, D.C.: Government Printing Office, 1903.

United States Senate. *Testimony Taken by the Committee upon the Relations between Labor and Capital.* Washington, D.C.: Government Printing Office, 1885.

——. *Cost of Living in American Towns: Report of an Inquiry by the Board of Trade of London.* 62nd Cong., Document 222, 1911.

——. *Immigrants in Industries.* Washington, D.C.: Government Printing Office, 1911.

Books and Articles

Abbott, Andrew. "Transcending General Linear Reality." *Sociological Theory* 6 (Fall 1988): 169–86.

——. "Conceptions of Time and Events in Social Science Methods: Causal and Narrative Approaches." *Historical Methods* 23, no. 4 (1990): 140–50.

Abbott, Edith. *Women in Industry: A Study in American Economic History.* Reprint edition, New York: Arno Press, 1969. New York: D. Appleton, 1910.

Allen, Ruth A. *The Great Southwest Strike.* Austin: University of Texas Press, 1942.

Aminzade, Ronald. "Revolution and Collective Political Violence: The Case of the Working Class of Marseille, France, 1830–1871." Working Paper 86. Center for Research on Social Organization, University of Michigan, Ann Arbor, 1973.

——. *Class, Politics, and Early Industrial Capitalism: A Study of Mid-Nineteenth-Century Toulouse, France.* Albany: State University of New York Press, 1981.

——. "Reinterpreting Capitalist Industrialization: A Study of Nineteenth-Century France." In *Work in France: Representations, Meaning, Organization, and Practice,* edited by Steven L. Kaplan and Cynthia J. Koepp, 393–417. Ithaca: Cornell University Press, 1986.

Anderson, Gregory. "Some Aspects of the Labour Market in Britain, c. 1870–1914." In *A History of British Industrial Relations, 1875–1914*, edited by Chris Wrigley. Brighton, Eng.: Harvester Press, 1982.

Appleby, Joyce. "What Is Still American in the Political Philosophy of Thomas Jefferson?" *William and Mary Quarterly* 39 (1982): 287–309.

Aronowitz, Stanley. *False Promises: The Shaping of American Working-Class Consciousness*. New York: McGraw-Hill, 1973.

Ashenfelter, Orley, and John H. Pencavel. "American Trade Union Growth: 1900–1960." *Quarterly Journal of Economics* 83 (1969): 434–48.

Aveling, Edward, and Eleanor Marx Aveling. *The Working-Class Movement in America*. Reprint edition, Arno Press, 1969. London: Swan Sonnenschein & Co., 1891.

Bagwell, Philip S., and G. E. Mingay. *Britain and America: A Study of Economic Change*. New York: Praeger, 1970.

Bailyn, Bernard. *The Ideological Origins of the American Revolution*. Cambridge: Harvard University Press, 1967.

Bender, Thomas. *Community and Social Change in America*. Baltimore: Johns Hopkins University Press, 1978.

Bensman, David. *The Practice of Solidarity: American Hat Finishers in the Nineteenth Century*. Urbana: University of Illinois Press, 1985.

Berenson, Edward. *Populist Religion and Left-Wing Politics in France, 1830–1852*. Princeton: Princeton University Press, 1984.

Berlanstein, Lenard R. *The Working People of Paris, 1871–1914*. Baltimore: Johns Hopkins University Press, 1984.

Berthoff, Rowland. "Independence and Attachment, Virtue and Interest: From Republican Citizen to Free Enterpriser." In *Uprooted Americans: Essays to Honor Oscar Handlin*, edited by Richard Bushman, Neil Harris, David Rothman, Barbara Solomon, and Stephen Thernstrom, 97–124. Boston: Little Brown, 1979.

——. "Peasants and Artisans, Puritans and Republicans: Personal Liberty and Communal Equality in American History." *Journal of American History* 69, no. 3 (1982): 579–98.

Birdsall, William C. "The Problem of Structure in the Knights of Labor." *Industrial and Labor Relations Review* 6 (1953): 532–46.

Blewett, Neal. "The Franchise in the United Kingdom, 1885–1918." *Past and Present* 32 (December 1965): 27–56.

Blodgett, Julie. "Fountain of Power: The Origins of the Knights of Labor in Philadelphia, 1869–1874." Paper presented at the Knights of Labor Centennial Symposium, Chicago, May 17–19, 1979.

Blumin, Stuart M. *The Emergence of the Middle Class*. Cambridge: Cambridge University Press, 1989.

Bole, Robert D., and Edward H. Walton. *The Glassboro Story*. York, Penn.: Maple Press Company, 1964.

Bonnell, Victoria E. *Roots of Rebellion: Workers, Politics, and Organizations in St. Petersburg and Moscow, 1900–1914*. Berkeley: University of California Press, 1983.

Bonnett, Clarence. *Employers' Associations in the United States.* New York: Vantage, 1956.

Boxer, Marilyn J. "Protective Legislation and Home Industry: The Marginalization of Women Workers in Late Nineteenth-Early Twentieth Century France." *Journal of Social History* 20, no. 1 (1986): 45–65.

Brecher, Jeremy. *Strike!* Boston: South End Press, 1972.

———. "The Knights of Labor and Strikes, 1885–86." Paper presented at Knights of Labor Centennial Symposium, Chicago, May 17–19, 1979.

Brenner, Johanna, and Maria Ramas. "Rethinking Women's Oppression." *New Left Review* 144 (May–June 1984): pp. 33–71.

Bridges, Amy. "Becoming American: The Working Classes in the United States before the Civil War." In *Working-Class Formation*, edited by Ira Katznelson and Aristide R. Zolberg, 157–96. Princeton: Princeton University Press, 1986.

———. *A City in the Republic.* Ithaca: Cornell University Press, 1987.

Briggs, Asa. *The Collected Essays of Asa Briggs.* Vol. 1. Urbana: University of Illinois Press, 1985.

Britt, David, and Omer Galle. "Industrial Conflict and Unionization." *American Sociological Review* 37 (1972): 46–57.

Brody, David. *Steelworkers in America: The Nonunion Era.* Cambridge: Harvard University Press, 1960.

———. "Labor Movement." In *Encyclopedia of American Political History*, edited by Jack P. Greene, 709–27. New York: Scribner's, 1984.

Brown, E. H. Phelps, and Margaret Browne. *A Century of Pay.* London: Macmillan, 1968.

Buchanan, Joseph Ray. *The Story of a Labor Agitator.* New York: The Outlook Company, 1903.

Bucki, Cecelia. "Dilution and Craft Tradition: Bridgeport, Connecticut, Munitions Workers, 1915–1919." *Social Science History* 4 (1980): 105–24.

Burawoy, Michael. *Manufacturing Consent.* Chicago: University of Chicago Press, 1979.

Butler, John L. "History of Knights of Labor Organization in Pennsylvania." In *Fifteenth Annual Report of the Secretary of Internal Affairs of the Commonwealth of Pennsylvania.* Part III: *Industrial Statistics.* Harrisburg, Penn.: E. K. Meyers, 1888.

Cadman, John W., Jr. *The Corporation in New Jersey.* Cambridge: Harvard University Press, 1949.

Calhoun, Craig. "Transition in Social Foundations for Collective Action." *Social Science History* 4 (1980): 419–51.

Cameron, R. E. "Economic Growth and Stagnation in Modern France, 1815–1914." *Journal of Modern History* 20 (1958): 1–13.

Carroll, Glenn R., and Paul Yangchung Huo. "Organizational and Electoral Paradoxes of the Knights of Labor." In *Ecological Models of Organizations*, edited by Glenn R. Carroll. Cambridge: Ballinger, 1988.

Catling, Harold. *The Spinning Mule.* Newton Abbott, London: David and Charles, 1970.

Chandler, Alfred D. *The Visible Hand*. Cambridge: Harvard University Press, 1977.

Cherrington, W. P. *Exposition and Defense of the Principles, Demands, and Purposes of the Noble Order of the Knights of Labor*. Boston: Co-operative Printing and Publishing Co., 1886.

Clark, Victor S. *History of Manufactures in the United States*. Vols. 1 and 2. Washington, D.C.: Carnegie Institution, 1929. Reprint. New York: Peter Smith, 1949.

Clawson, Dan. *Bureaucracy and the Labor Process*. New York: Monthly Review Press, 1980.

Clegg, H. A., Alan Fox, and A. F. Thompson. *A History of British Trade Unions since 1889*. Vol. 1. Oxford: Clarendon Press, 1964.

Clews, Henry. "Shall Capital or Labor Rule?" *North American Review* 142 (1886): 598–602.

Clough, S. B. "Retardative Factors in French Economic Development in the Nineteenth and Twentieth Centuries." *Journal of Economic History* 6, Suppl. (1946): 91–210.

Cohen, Lizabeth. *Making a New Deal*. Cambridge: Cambridge University Press, 1990.

Cole, G. D. H.. *A Short History of the British Working-Class Movement, 1789–1947*. London: George Allen and Unwin, 1948.

Cole, G. D. H., and Raymond Postgate. *The Common People, 1746–1946*. London: Methuen, 1961.

Cole, Robert E. *Work, Mobility, and Participation*. Berkeley: University of California Press, 1979.

Commons, John R. "Is Class Conflict in America Growing and Is It Inevitable?" *American Journal of Sociology* 13 (1908): 761–62.

Commons, John R., U. B. Phillips, E. A. Gilmore, H. L. Sumner, and J. B. Andrews, eds. *Documentary History of American Industrial Society*. Vol. 5. New York: Russell and Russell, 1958.

———. *Documentary History of American Industrial Society*. Vol. 6. New York: Russell and Russell, 1958.

Commons, John R., D. J. Saposs, H. L. Sumner, E. B. Mittelman, H. E. Hoagland, J. B. Andrews, and S. Perlman, eds. *History of Labour in the United States*. New York: Macmillan, 1918.

Conell, Carol, and Kim Voss. "Formal Organization and the Fate of Social Movements." *American Sociological Review* 55 (1990): 255–69.

Conk, Margo A. *The United States Census and New Jersey Urban Occupational Structure, 1870–1940*. Ann Arbor: UMI Research Press, 1978.

Cook, Ezra. *Knights of Labor Illustrated*. Chicago: Ezra A. Cook, 1886.

Cooper, Patricia A. *Once a Cigar Maker*. Urbana: University of Illinois Press, 1987.

Cross, Gary S. *Immigrant Workers in Industrial France*. Philadelphia: Temple University Press, 1983.

Cumbler, John T. *Working-Class Community in Industrial America*. Westport, Conn.: Greenwood, 1979.

Currie, R., and R. M. Hartwell, "The Making of the English Working Class?" *Economic History Review* 18, 2d ser. (December 1965): 633–42.

David, Henry. *The History of the Haymarket Affair*. New York: Farrar and Rinehart, 1936.

Davis, Mike. "Why the U.S. Working Class Is Different." *New Left Review* 123 (1980): 5–44.

Davis, Philip Curtis. "The Persistence of Partisan Alignment: Issues, Leaders, and Votes in New Jersey, 1840–1860." Ph.D. diss., Washington University, 1978.

Dawley, Alan. *Class and Community*. Cambridge: Harvard University Press, 1976.

Dawson, Andrew. "The Paradox of Dynamic Technological Change and the Labor Aristocracy in the United States, 1880–1914." *Labor History* 20 (1979): 325–51.

Debouzy, Marianne. *In the Shadow of the Statue of Liberty: Immigrants, Workers, and Citizens in the American Republic*. Saint-Denis, France: Presses Universitaires de Vincennes, 1988.

Degler, Carl. *Out of Our Past*. 3d ed. New York: Harper Colophon, 1984.

de Vyver, Frank T. "The Organization of Labor in New Jersey before 1860." Ph.D. diss., Princeton University, 1934.

Diggins, John Patrick. "Comrades and Citizens: New Mythologies in American Historiography." *American Historical Review* 90 (1985): 614–38.

DiMaggio, Paul J., and Walter W. Powell. "The Iron Cage Revisited: Institutional Isomorphism and Collective Rationality in Organizational Fields." *American Sociological Review* 48 (1983): 147–60.

Dublin, Thomas. *Women at Work*. New York: Columbia University Press, 1979.

Dubofsky, Melvyn. *We Shall Be All: A History of the Industrial Workers of the World*. New York: Quadrangle, 1969.

Durkheim, Emile. *The Division of Labor in Society*. Translated by George Simpson. New York: Macmillan, 1933.

Easterlin, Richard A., David Ward, William S. Bernard, and Reed Ueda. *Immigration: Dimensions of Ethnicity*. Cambridge: Belnap Press of Harvard University Press, 1982.

Ebner, Michael Howard. "Passaic, New Jersey, 1855–1912: City-Building in Post–Civil War America." Ph.D. diss., University of Virginia, 1974.

Edwards, P. K. *Strikes in the United States*. New York: St. Martin's Press, 1981.

Elbaum, Bernard, and Frank Wilkinson. "Industrial Relations and Uneven Development: A Comparative Study of the American and British Steel Industries." *Cambridge Journal of Economics* 3 (1979): 275–303.

Elster, Jon. *Making Sense of Marx*. Cambridge: Cambridge University Press, 1985.

Essex County Trades Council. *Illustrated History of the Essex Trades Council and Affiliated Unions*. Newark, N.J.: Essex Trades Council, 1899.

Feldman, David, and Gareth Stedman Jones. *Metropolis London*. London: Routledge, 1989.

Field, John. "British Historians and the Concept of the Labor Aristocracy." *Radical History Review* 19 (1978): 61–85.

Fink, Leon. "Class Conflict in the Gilded Age." *Radical History Review* 3, nos. 1–2 (1975): 56–72.

———. *Workingmen's Democracy: The Knights of Labor and American Politics.* Urbana: University of Illinois Press, 1983.

———. "Labor, Liberty, and the Law: Trade Unionism and the Problem of American Constitutional Order." *Journal of American History* 74 (1987): 904–25.

———. "The New Labor History and the Powers of Historical Pessimism: Consensus, Hegemony, and the Case of the Knights of Labor." *Journal of American History* 75 (June 1988): 115–36.

———. "Looking Backward: Reflections on Workers' Culture and Certain Conceptual Dilemmas within Labor History." In *Perspectives on American Labor History: The Problem of Synthesis,* edited by J. Carroll Moody and Alice Kessler-Harris, 5–29. DeKalb: Northern Illinois University Press, 1989.

Fischer, Claude. *The Urban Experience.* San Diego: Harcourt, Brace, Jovanovich, 1984.

Flora, Peter, Jens Alber, Richard Eichenberg, Jürgen Kohl, Franz Kraus, Winfried Pfenning, and Kurt Seebohm. *State, Economy, and Society in Western Europe, 1815–1975.* Frankfurt: Campus Verlag, 1983.

Foner, Eric. *Tom Paine and Revolutionary America.* London: Oxford University Press, 1976.

———. *Politics and Ideology in the Age of the Civil War.* New York: Oxford University Press, 1980.

———. "Why Is There No Socialism in America?" *History Workshop* 17 (1984): 57–80.

Foner, Philip S. *History of the Labor Movement in the United States.* Vol. 2. 2d ed. New York: International Publishers, 1975.

———. *History of the Labor Movement in the United States.* Vol. 3. New York: International Publishers, 1964.

Forbath, William E. "In 'The Mother Country' Law Is Protected from the 'Gusty and Unthinking Passions' of Politics: Courts and the Making of Modern Politics in the United States and England." Manuscript, UCLA, 1990.

———. "The Ambiguities of Free Labor: Labor and the Law in the Gilded Age." *Wisconsin Law Review* (1985): 767–817.

———. "The Shaping of the American Labor Movement." *Harvard Law Review* 102 (1989): 1109–256.

Form, William. "On the Degradation of Skills." *Annual Review of Sociology* 13 (1987): 29–47.

Foster, John. *Class Struggle and the Industrial Revolution.* London: Weidenfeld and Nicolson, 1974.

Fox, Alan. *Beyond Contract: Work, Power, and Trust Relations.* London: Faber, 1974.

———. *History and Heritage: The Social Origins of the British Industrial Relations System.* London: Allen and Unwin, 1985.

Friedman, Gerald. "Politics and Unions: Government, Ideology, and the Labor Movement in the United States and France, 1880–1914." Ph.D. diss., Harvard University, 1985.

———. "The State and the Making of the Working Class: France and the United States, 1880–1914." *Theory and Society* 17 (1988): 403–30.

———. "The Decline of Paternalism and the Making of the Employer Class, France, 1870–1914." In *Masters to Managers: Historical and Comparative Perspectives on American Employers,* edited by Sanford Jacoby, 153–72. New York: Columbia University Press, 1991.

Friedman, Lawrence M. *A History of American Law,* 2d ed. New York: Simon and Schuster/Touchstone Books, 1985.

Garlock, Jonathan. "A Structural Analysis of the Knights of Labor." Ph.D. diss., University of Rochester, 1974.

———. "The Knights of Labor: A 19th-Century American Experiment with Popular Justice." Paper presented to the Social Science History Association, Columbus, Ohio, Nov. 1978.

———, comp. *Guide to the Local Assemblies of the Knights of Labor.* Westport, Conn.: Greenwood, 1982.

Geary, Dick. *European Labour Protest, 1848–1939.* London: Croom Helm, 1981.

Gerth, H. J., and C. W. Mills. *From Max Weber: Essays in Sociology.* New York: Oxford University Press, 1946.

Giddings, Frank. "Cooperation." In *The Labor Movement: The Problem of Today,* edited by George E. McNeill, 508–31. Boston: A. M. Bridgeman, 1887.

Gitelman, Howard M. "The Waltham System and the Coming of the Irish." *Labor History* 8 (1967): 227–53.

Goldin, Claudia. *Understanding the Gender Gap: An Economic History of American Women.* New York: Oxford University Press, 1990.

Gompers, Samuel. *Seventy Years of Life and Labor.* New York: E. P. Dutton, 1925.

Gordon, David M. "Capitalist Development and the History of American Cities." In *Marxism and the Metropolis,* edited by William K. Tabb and Larry Sawers, 25–63. New York: Oxford University Press, 1978.

Gordon, David M., Richard Edwards, and Michael Reich. *Segmented Work, Divided Workers.* Cambridge: Cambridge University Press, 1982.

Griffen, Clyde, and Sally Griffen. *Natives and Newcomers.* Cambridge: Harvard University Press, 1978.

Grob, Gerald N. *Workers and Utopia.* Chicago: Quadrangle, 1969.

Gutman, Herbert. "The Worker's Search for Power: Labor in the Gilded Age." In *The Gilded Age: A Reappraisal,* edited by H. Wayne Morgan, 38–68. Syracuse: Syracuse University Press, 1963.

———. *Work, Culture, and Society in Industrializing America.* New York: Vintage, 1977.

———. *Power and Culture: Essays on the American Working Class.* New York: Pantheon, 1987.

Gutman, Herbert, and Ira Berlin. "Class Composition and the Development of the American Working Class, 1840–1890." In *Power and Culture,* edited by Ira Berlin, 380–95. New York: Pantheon, 1987.

Hanagan, Michael P. "Artisan and Skilled Worker: The Problem of Definition." *International Labor and Working Class History* 12 (Nov. 1977): 23–31.
——. *The Logic of Solidarity*. Urbana: University of Illinois Press, 1980.
——. "Response." *International Labor and Working-Class History* 24 (1984): 31–36.
——. "Solidarity Logics: Introduction." *Theory and Society* 17 (1988) 309–27.
——. *Nascent Proletarians*. Oxford: Basil Blackwell, 1989.
Hanagan, Michael P., and Charles Stephenson. "The Skilled Worker and Working-Class Protest." *Social Science History* 4 (1980): 5–13.
Handlin, Oscar. *The Uprooted*. Boston: Little Brown, 1951.
Hannan, Michael T., and John Freeman. "The Ecology of Organizational Foundings: American Labor Unions, 1836–1985." *American Journal of Sociology* 92 (1987): 910–43.
——. *Organizational Ecology*. Cambridge: Harvard University Press, 1989.
Hanson, Russell L. *The Democratic Imagination in America*. Princeton: Princeton University Press, 1985.
Hareven, Tamara, and Randolph Langenbach. *Amoskeag*. New York: Pantheon, 1978.
Harley, C. K. "Skilled Labour and the Choice of Technique in Edwardian Industry." *Explorations in Economic History* 11 (1974): 391–414.
Harrison, Royden. *Before the Socialists*. London: Routledge and Kegan Paul, 1965.
Hartwell, R. M., and R. Currie. "The Making of the English Working Class?" *Economic History Review* 18, no. 3 (1965).
Hattam, Victoria. "Economic Visions and Political Strategies: American Labor and the State, 1865–1896." *Studies in American Political Development* 4 (1990): 82–129.
Haupt, Heinz-Gerhard. "The Petite Bourgeoisie in France, 1850–1914: In Search of the Juste Milieu?" In *Shopkeepers and Master Artisans in Nineteenth-Century Europe*, edited by Geoffrey Crossick and Heinz-Gerhard Haupt. London: Methuen, 1984.
Haydu, Jeffrey. *Between Craft and Class*. Berkeley: University of California Press, 1988.
Hays, Samuel P. *The Response to Industrialism, 1885–1914*. Chicago: University of Chicago Press, 1957.
Hechter, Michael. *Internal Colonialism*. Berkeley: University of California Press, 1975.
Hershberg, Theodore, ed. *Philadelphia: Work, Space, Family, and Group Experience in the 19th Century*. Oxford: Oxford University Press, 1981.
Hershberg, Theodore, Alan N. Burstein, Eugene P. Ericksen, Stephanie W. Greenberg, and William L. Yancey. "A Tale of Three Cities: Blacks, Immigrants, and Opportunity in Philadelphia, 1850, 1930, 1970." In *Philadelphia: Work, Space, Family, and Group Experience in the Nineteenth Century*, edited by Theodore Hershberg, 461–91. New York: Oxford University Press, 1981.
Higham, John. *Send These to Me: Immigrants in Urban America*. Baltimore: Johns Hopkins University Press, 1984.

Higonnet, Patrice. *Sister Republics*. Cambridge: Harvard University Press, 1988.

Hilbert, F. W. "Employers' Associations in the United States." In *Studies in American Trade Unionism*, edited by Jacob H. Hollander and George Barnett. New York: Henry Holt, 1906.

Hinton, James. "The Rise of a Mass Labour Movement: Growth and Limits." In *A History of British Industrial Relations, 1875–1914*, edited by Chris Wrigley. Brighton, Eng.: Harvester Press, 1982.

Hirsch, Susan E. *The Roots of the American Working Class*. Philadelphia: University of Pennsylvania Press, 1978.

Hobsbawm, Eric J. *Labouring Men*. London: Weidenfeld and Nicolson, 1964.

——. *Industry and Empire*. Harmondsworth, Middlesex: Penguin, 1969.

——. *Workers: Worlds of Labor*. New York: Pantheon, 1984.

Hoerder, Dirk, ed. *"Struggle a Hard Battle."* DeKalb: Northern Illinois University Press, 1986.

Hofstader, Eric. *Age of Reform*. New York: Knopf, 1955.

Hohenberg, Paul M., and Lynn H. Lees. *The Making of Urban Europe, 1000–1950*. Cambridge: Harvard University Press, 1985.

Hollis, Patricia. *Class and Conflict in Nineteenth-Century England, 1815–1850*. London: Routledge and Kegan Paul, 1973.

Holt, James. "Trade Unionism in the British and U.S. Steel Industries, 1880–1914: A Comparative Study." In *The Labor History Reader*, edited by Daniel Leab, 166–96. Urbana: University of Illinois Press, 1977.

Horwitz, Morton J. *The Transformation of American Law, 1780–1860*. Cambridge: Harvard University Press, 1977.

Hunt, Edward H. *British Labour History, 1815–1914*. Atlantic Highlands, N.J.: Humanities Press, 1981.

Ingham, Geoffrey K. "Organizational Size, Orientation to Work, and Industrial Behavior." *Sociology* 1 (1967): 239–58.

Jackson, Robert M. *The Formation of Craft Labor Markets*. Orlando: Academic Press, 1984.

Jacoby, Sanford, ed. *Masters to Managers: Historical and Comparative Perspectives on American Employers*. New York: Columbia University Press, 1991.

James, Edward T. *American Labor and Political Action, 1865–1896*. Ph.D. diss., Harvard University, 1954.

Jennings, Jeremy. *Syndicalism in France: A Study of Ideas*. Houndsmills, England: St. Anthony's/Macmillan Series, 1990.

Johnson, Christopher. "Patterns of Proletarianization: Parisian Tailors and Lodeve Woolens Workers." In *Class Consciousness and Class Experience in Nineteenth-Century Europe*, edited by John M. Merriman, 57–114. New York: Holmes and Meier, 1979.

Jones, Gareth Stedman. "Class Struggle and the Industrial Revolution." *New Left Review* 90 (1975): 35–69.

——. *Languages of Class*. Cambridge: Cambridge University Press, 1983.

Joyce, Patrick. "Work." In *The Cambridge Social History of Britain, 1750–1950*, edited by F. M. L. Thompson, vol. 2, 131–94. Cambridge: Cambridge University Press, 1990.

———. *Visions of the People*. Cambridge: Cambridge University Press, 1991.

Karabel, Jerome. "The Failure of American Socialism Reconsidered." *The Socialist Register* 18 (1979): 204–27.

Kaster, Gregory L. " 'We Will Not Be Slaves to Avarice': The American Labor Jeremiad, 1827–1877." Ph.D. diss., Boston University, 1990.

Katznelson, Ira. *City Trenches: Urban Politics and the Patterning of Class in the United States*. Chicago: University of Chicago Press, 1982.

———. "Working-Class Formation and the State: Nineteenth-Century England in American Perspective." In *Bringing the State Back In*, edited by Peter Evans, Dietrich Rueschemeyer, and Theda Skocpol. Cambridge: Cambridge University Press, 1985.

Katznelson, Ira, and Aristide R. Zolberg, eds. *Working-Class Formation*. Princeton: Princeton University Press, 1986.

Kelley, Robert. "Ideology and Political Culture from Jefferson to Nixon." *American Historical Review* 82, no. 3 (1977): 531–62.

Kerr, Clark, and Abraham Siegel. "The Interindustry Propensity to Strike—An International Comparison." In *Industrial Conflict*, edited by Arthur Kornhauser, Robert Dubin, and Arthur M. Ross. New York: McGraw-Hill, 1954.

Kessler-Harris, Alice. "Where Are the Organized Women Workers?" In *A Heritage of Her Own: Toward a New Social History of American Women*, edited by Nancy Cott and Elizabeth Pleck. New York: Simon and Schuster, 1979.

———. *Out to Work*. Oxford: Oxford University Press, 1982.

Kindleberger, C. P. *The Economic Growth of France and Britain, 1851–1950*. Cambridge: Harvard University Press, 1964.

Kloppenberg, James T. "The Virtues of Liberalism: Christianity, Republicanism, and Ethics in Early American Political Discourse." *Journal of American History* 74 (1987): 9–33.

Koditschek, Theodore. *Class Formation and Urban-Industrial Society: Bradford, 1750–1850*. New York: Cambridge University Press, 1990.

Kolko, Gabriel. *Main Currents in American History*. New York: Harper and Row, 1976.

Landes, David. "French Entrepreneurship and Industrial Growth in the Nineteenth Century." *Journal of Economic History* 9 (1949): 45–61.

Laslett, John M., and Seymour M. Lipset, eds. *Failure of a Dream: Essays in the History of American Socialism*. Garden City, N.Y.: Anchor, 1974.

Laurie, Bruce. *Working People of Philadelphia, 1800–1850*. Philadelphia: Temple University Press, 1980.

———. *Artisans into Workers*. New York: Noonday Press, 1989.

Laurie, Bruce, and Mark Schmitz. "Manufacture and Productivity: The Making of an Industrial Base, Philadelphia, 1850–1880." In *Philadelphia: Work, Space, Family, and Group Experience in the Nineteenth Century*, edited by Theodore Hershberg, 43–92. New York: Oxford University Press, 1981.

Lazerow, Jama. "The Knights of Labor: Boston as a Case Study." Paper presented at the Knights of Labor Centennial Symposium, Chicago, May 17–19, 1979.

Lazonick, William H. "Industrial Relations and Technical Change: The Case of the Self-Acting Mule." *Cambridge Journal of Economics* 3 (1979): 226–62.

——. "Production Relations, Labor Productivity, and Choice of Technique: British and U.S. Cotton Spinning." *Journal of Economic History* 41 (1981): 491–516.

Lebergott, Stanley. *Manpower in Economic Growth.* New York: McGraw-Hill, 1964.

Lees, Lynn H. *Exiles of Erin.* Manchester: Manchester University Press, 1979.

Leikin, Steve. "The Practical Utopians: Cooperation and the American Labor Movement, 1860–1890." Ph.D. diss., University of California, Berkeley, 1992.

Lequin, Yves. "Labour in the French Economy since the Revolution." In *The Cambridge Economic History of Europe,* edited by Peter Mathias and M. M. Postan, vol. 7, 296–346. Cambridge: Cambridge University Press, 1978.

Levine, Bruce, Stephen Brier, David Brundage, Edward Countryman, Dorothy Fennell, and Marcus Rediker. *Who Built America?* Vol. 1. New York: Pantheon, 1989.

Levine, Susan. "Labor's True Woman: Domesticity and Equal Rights in the Knights of Labor." *Journal of American History* 70 (1983): 323–33.

——. *Labor's True Woman: Carpet Weavers, Industrialization, and Labor Reform in the Gilded Age.* Philadelphia: Temple University Press, 1984.

Lewis, Steven. "Reassessing Syndicalism: The *Bourses du Travail* and the Origins of French Labor Politics." Paper presented at the Shifting Boundaries of Labor Politics conference, Cambridge, Mass., March 12–14, 1993.

Lieberson, Stanley. "Measuring Population Diversity." *American Sociological Review* 34 (1969): 850–62.

Lincoln, James R. "Community Structure and Industrial Conflict: An Analysis of Strike Activity in SMSAs." *American Sociological Review* 43 (1978): 199–220.

Lipset, Seymour Martin. *The First New Nation.* Garden City, N.Y.: Anchor Books, 1967.

Lipset, Seymour Martin, Martin A. Trow, and James S. Coleman. *Union Democracy.* Garden City, N.Y.: Anchor Books, 1962.

Lockwood, D. "Sources of Variation in Working-Class Images of Society." *Sociological Review* 14 (1966): 249–67.

Lorwin, Val R. "France." In *Comparative Labor Movements,* edited by Walter Galenson, 313–409. New York: Prentice-Hall, 1952.

McAdam, Doug. *Political Process and the Development of Black Insurgency.* Chicago: University of Chicago Press, 1982.

——. "The Decline of the Civil Rights Movement." In *Social Movements of the Sixties and Seventies,* edited by Jo Freeman, 298–319. White Plains, N.Y.: Longman, 1983.

McCloskey, D. N. "Did Victorian Britain Fail?" *Economic History Review* 23, 2d ser. (1970): 446–59.

McCormick, Richard P. "An Historical Overview." In *Politics in New Jersey*, edited by Alan Rosenthal and John Blydenburgh, 1–30. Rutgers, N.J.: Eagleton Institute of Politics, 1975.

McDougall, Mary Lynn. "Consciousness and Community: The Workers of Lyon, 1830–1850." *Journal of Social History* 12, no. 1 (1978): 129–45.

McGaw, Judith A. "'A Good Place to Work.' Industrial Workers and Occupational Choice: The Case of Berkshire Women." *Journal of Interdisciplinary History* 10 (1979): 227–48.

McGerr, Michael E. *The Decline of Popular Politics*. New York: Oxford University Press, 1986.

McKibbin, Ross. *The Ideologies of Class*. Oxford: Clarendon, 1990.

McNall, Scott. *The Road to Rebellion*. Chicago: University of Chicago Press, 1988.

McNeill, George E. *The Labor Movement: The Problem of Today.* Boston: A. M. Bridgman and Co., 1887.

Mann, Michael. *The Sources of Power*. Vol. 2. New York: Cambridge University Press, forthcoming.

Marks, Gary. *Unions in Politics: Britain, Germany, and the United States in the Nineteenth and Early Twentieth Centuries*. Princeton: Princeton University Press, 1989.

Marx, Karl. "Germany: Revolution and Counter-Revolution." In *Selected Writings of Karl Marx*, edited by V. Adoratsky. New York: International Publishers, 1936.

——. *Economic and Philosophic Manuscripts of 1844*. Moscow: International Publishers, 1961.

——. *Karl Marx: Selected Writings*. Edited by David McLellen. Oxford: Oxford University Press, 1977.

Marx, Karl, and Frederick Engels. *The German Ideology: Part One with Selections from Parts Two and Three and Supplementary Texts*. Edited by C. J. Arthur. New York: International Publishers, 1970.

——. *Letters to Americans, 1848–1895*. New York: International Publishers, 1953.

Mendels, Franklin F. "Proto-Industrialization: The First Phase of the Industrialization Process." *Journal of Economic History* 32 (1972): 241–61.

Merriman, John. *The Red City: Limoges and the French Nineteenth Century*. New York: Oxford University Press, 1985.

Michels, Roberto. *Political Parties*. Glencoe, Ill.: The Free Press, 1949.

Mink, Gwendolyn. *Old Labor and New Immigrants in American Political Development*. Ithaca: Cornell University Press, 1986.

Mitchell, Brian R. *European Historical Statistics, 1750–1900*. New York: Columbia University Press, 1975.

Modell, John. "The Peopling of a Working-Class Ward: Reading, Pennsylvania, 1850." *Journal of Social History* 5 (1971): 71–95.

Monds, Jean. "Workers' Control and the Historians: A New Economism." *New Left Review* 97 (1976): 81–100.

Montgomery, David. "The Working Classes of the Pre-Industrial American City, 1780–1830." *Labor History* 9, no. 1 (1968): 3–22.

———. *Workers' Control in America*. Cambridge: Cambridge University Press, 1979.

———. *Beyond Equality*. Urbana: University of Illinois Press, 1981.

———. "Labor in the Industrial Era." In *A History of the American Worker*, edited by Richard B. Morris, 79–113. Princeton: Princeton University Press, 1983.

———. *The Fall of the House of Labor*. Cambridge: Cambridge University Press, 1987.

———. "William H. Sylvis and the Search for Working-Class Citizenship." In *Labor Leaders in America*, edited by Melvyn Dubofsky and Warren Van Tine, 3–29. Urbana: University of Illinois, 1987.

Moorhouse, H. F. "The Marxist Theory of the Labor Aristocracy." *Social History* 3 (1978): 61–82.

———. "The Significance of the Labor Aristocracy." *Social History* 6 (1981): 229–35.

More, Charles. *Skill and the English Working Class*. New York: St. Martin's Press, 1980.

Morris, R. J. *Class and Class Consciousness in the Industrial Revolution, 1780–1850*. Macmillan, 1979.

Moss, Bernard H. *The Origins of the French Labor Movement, 1830–1914: The Socialism of Skilled Workers, 1830–1914*. Berkeley: University of California Press, 1976.

Nash, Gary. *The Urban Crucible*. Cambridge: Harvard University Press, 1979.

Nelson, Daniel. *Managers and Workers*. Madison: University of Wisconsin Press, 1975.

Newman, Philip Charles. *The Labor Legislation of New Jersey*. Washington, D.C.: American Council on Public Affairs, 1943.

Nichols, Jeannette Paddock. "The Industrial History of New Jersey in the Middle Period." In *New Jersey: A History*, edited by Irving S. Kull, vol. 2, 583–615. New York: The American Historical Society, 1930.

———. "The Industrial History of New Jersey since 1861." In *New Jersey: A History*, edited by Irving S. Kull, vol. 3, 892–940. New York: The American Historical Society, 1930.

Noiriel, Gérard. *Workers in French Society in the 19th and 20th Centuries*. New York: Berg, 1990.

Oberschall, Anthony. *Social Conflict and Social Movements*. Englewood Cliffs, N.J.: Prentice-Hall, 1973.

O'Brien, Patrick, and Caglar Keyder. *Economic Growth in Britain and France, 1780–1914*. London: Allen and Unwin, 1978.

Oestreicher, Richard J. "A Note on Knights of Labor Membership Statistics." *Labor History* 25, no. 1 (Winter 1984): 102–8.

———. *Solidarity and Fragmentation: Working People and Class Consciousness in Detroit, 1875–1900*. Urbana: University of Illinois Press, 1986.

———. "Terence V. Powderly, the Knights of Labor, and Artisanal Republicanism." In *Labor Leaders in America*, edited by Melvyn Van Tine and Warren Dubofsky. Urbana: University of Illinois Press, 1987.

———. "Urban Working-Class Political Behavior and Theories of American

Electoral Politics, 1870–1940." *Journal of American History* 74, no. 4 (1988): 1257–86.

Offe, Claus, and Helmut Wiesenthal. "Two Logics of Collective Action." In *Disorganized Capitalism*, edited by John Keane. Cambridge: MIT Press, 1985.

Olson, Mancur. *The Logic of Collective Action*. Cambridge: Cambridge University Press, 1965.

Payne, P. L. "The Emergence of the Large-Scale Company in Great Britain, 1870–1914." *The Economic History Review* 20 3, 2d ser. (1967): 519–42.

Pelling, Henry. *America and the British Left*. London: Adam and Charles Black, 1956.

——. *The Origins of the Labour Party, 1880–1900*. 2d ed. Oxford: Oxford University Press, 1965.

——. *A History of British Trade Unionism*. 3d ed. London: Macmillan, 1976.

Perlman, Selig. "Upheaval and Reorganization (since 1876)." In *History of Labour in the United States*, edited by John R. Commons, vol. 2, 195–587. New York: Macmillan, 1918.

——. *A Theory of the Labor Movement*. New York: Macmillan, 1928.

Perrot, Michelle. *Les Ouvriers en grève, 1871–1890*. The Hague: Mouton de Gruyter, 1974. (Translated as *Workers on Strike*. Leamington Spa: Berg, 1987.)

——. "On the Formation of the French Working Class." In *Working-Class Formation*, edited by Ira Katznelson and Aristide R. Zolberg. Princeton: Princeton University Press, 1986.

Pessen, Edward. *Riches, Class, and Power before the Civil War*. Lexington, Mass.: D. C. Heath, 1973.

——. *Jacksonian America*. Rev. ed. Urbana: University of Illinois Press, 1985.

Pocock, J. G. A. "Virtue and Commerce in the Eighteenth Century." *Journal of Interdisciplinary History* 3 (1972): 119–34.

Popper, Samuel H. "Newark, N.J., 1870–1910: Chapters in the Evolution of an American Metropolis." Ph.D. diss., New York University, 1951.

Powderly, Terence V. *The Path I Trod: The Autobiography of Terence V. Powderly*. Edited by Harry J. Carman, Henry David, and Paul N. Gutherie. New York: AMS Press, 1968.

Price, Richard. *Labour in British Society*. London: Croom Helm, 1986.

——. "Britain." In *The Formation of Labour Movements, 1870–1914: An International Perspective*, edited by Marcel Van Der Linden and Jürgen Rojahn, vol. 1, 3–24. Leiden: E. J. Brill, 1990.

Price, Roger. *A Social History of Nineteenth-Century France*. New York: Holmes and Meier, 1987.

Prothero, Iorwerth. "William Benbow and the Concept of the 'General Strike.'" *Past and Present* 63 (1974): 132–71.

Prude, Jonathan. "The Social System of Early New England Textile Mills: A Case Study, 1812–1840." In *Working-Class America*, edited by Michael H. Frisch and Daniel J. Walkowitz. Urbana: University of Illinois Press, 1983.

Raffalovich, Lawrence E., and David Knoke, "Quantitative Methods for the Analysis of Historical Change," *Historical Methods* 16 (1983): 149–54.

Reardon, Judy A. "Belgian and French Workers in Nineteenth-Century Roubaix." In *Class Conflict and Collective Action,* edited by Louise A. Tilly and Charles Tilly. Beverly Hills: Sage, 1981.

Reid, Donald. *The Miners of Decazeville.* Cambridge: Harvard University Press, 1985.

Reynolds, John F. *Testing Democracy.* Chapel Hill: University of North Carolina Press, 1988.

Rock, Howard. *Artisans of the New Republic.* New York: New York University Press, 1984.

Rodgers, Daniel T. *Contested Truths: Keywords in American Politics since Independence.* New York: Basic Books, 1987.

Rose, M. E. "Social Change and the Industrial Revolution." In *The Economic History of Britain since 1700,* edited by Roderick Floud and Donald McCloskey, vol. 1, 253–76. Cambridge: Cambridge University Press, 1981.

Rosenblum, Gerald. *Immigrant Workers: Their Impact on American Labor Radicalism.* New York: Basic Books, 1973.

Rosenstone, Steven J., Roy L. Behr, and Edward H. Lazarus. *Third Parties in America: Citizen Response to Major Party Failure.* Princeton: Princeton University Press, 1984.

Ross, Steven J. *Workers on the Edge.* New York: Columbia University Press, 1985.

Rothbart, Ronald. "Work, Family, and Protest: Immigrant Labor in the Steel, Meatpacking, and Anthracite Industries, 1880–1920." Ph.D. diss., University of California, Berkeley, 1988.

Rubery, Jill. "Structured Labour Markets, Worker Organization, and Low Pay." *Cambridge Journal of Economics* 2 (1978): 17–36.

Rule, John. "Artisan Attitudes: A Comparative Survey of Skilled Labour and Proletarianization before 1848." *Bulletin of the Society for the Study of Labour History* 50 (1985): 22–31.

——. *The Labouring Classes in Early Industrial England, 1750–1850.* London: Longman, 1986.

——. "The Property of Skill in the Period of Manufacture." In *The Historical Meanings of Work,* edited by Patrick Joyce, 99–118. Cambridge: Cambridge University Press, 1987.

Salvatore, Nick. *Eugene V. Debs: Citizen and Socialist.* Urbana: University of Illinois Press, 1982.

——. Introduction to *Seventy Years of Life and Labor: An Autobiography by Samuel Gompers,* edited by Nick Salvatore, xi–xli. New York: ILR Press, 1984.

——. "Response." *International Labor and Working-Class History* 24 (1984): 25–30.

——. "Some Thoughts on Class and Citizenship in the Late Nineteenth Century." In *In the Shadow of the Statue of Liberty: Immigrants, Workers, and Citizens in the American Republic, 1880–1920,* edited by Marianne Debouzy, 215–30. Saint-Denis, France: Presses Universitaires de Vincennes, 1988.

Samuel, Raphael. "The Workshop of the World: Steam Power and Hand Technology in Mid-Victorian Britain." *History Workshop* 3 (1977): 6–72.

Saxton, Alexander. *The Rise and Fall of the White Republic.* London: Verso, 1990.

Schattschneider, E. E. *Party Government.* New York: Holt, 1942.

Schindehutte, Richard. "Organized Labor and Class Struggle: The Knights and 'All of Labor,' 1870–1890." Paper presented at the Knights of Labor Centennial Symposium, Chicago, May 17–19, 1979.

Schneider, Linda. "The Citizen Striker: Workers' Ideology in the Homestead Strike of 1892." *Labor History* 21, no. 1 (Winter 1982): 1–13.

Scott, Joan W. *The Glassworkers of Carmaux.* Cambridge: Harvard University Press, 1974.

——. "On Language, Gender, and Working-Class History." *International Labor and Working-Class History* 21 (1987): 1–13.

——. *Gender and the Politics of History.* New York: Columbia University Press, 1988.

Sewell, William H., Jr. "Social Change and the Rise of Working-Class Politics in Nineteenth-Century Marseille." *Past and Present* 65 (1974): 75–109.

——. "The Working Class of Marseille under the Second Republic: Social Structure and Political Behavior." In *Workers and the Industrial Revolution,* edited by Peter N. Stearns and Daniel J. Walkowitz, 75–116. New Brunswick, N.J.: Transaction Books, 1974.

——. *Work and Revolution in France: The Language of Labor from the Old Regime to 1848.* Cambridge: Cambridge University Press, 1980.

——. *Structure and Mobility.* Cambridge: Cambridge University Press, 1985.

——. "Artisans, Factory Workers, and the Formation of the French Working Class, 1789–1848," in *Working-Class Formation,* edited by Ira Katznelson and Aristide R. Zolberg, 45–71. Princeton: Princeton University Press, 1986.

——. "How Classes Are Made: Critical Reflections on E. P. Thompson's Theory of Working-Class Formation." In *E. P. Thompson: Critical Perspectives,* edited by Harvey J. Kaye and Keith McClelland, 50–77. Philadelphia: Temple University Press, 1990.

——. "Three Temporalities: Toward an Eventful Sociology," in *The Historic Turn in the Human Sciences,* ed. Terrence J. McDonald. Ann Arbor, Mich.: University of Michigan Press, Forthcoming.

Shafer, Byron E., ed. *Is America Different? A New Look at American Exceptionalism.* Oxford: Clarendon Press, 1991.

Shalev, Michael, and Walter Korpi. "Working-Class Mobilization and American Exceptionalism." *Economic and Industrial Democracy* 1 (1980): 31–61.

Shalhope, Robert E. "Toward a Republican Synthesis: The Emergence of an Understanding of Republicanism in American Historiography." *William and Mary Quarterly* 29 (1972): 49–80.

——. "Republicanism and Early American Historiography." *William and Mary Quarteerly* 39 (1982): 334–56.

Shefter, Martin. "Trade Unions and Political Machines: The Organization and Disorganization of the American Working Class in the Late Nineteenth Century," in *Working-Class Formation,* ed. Ira Katznelson and Aristide R. Zolberg, 197–278. Princeton: Princeton University Press, 1986.

Shergold, Peter R. *Working-Class Life: The "American Standard" in Comparative Perspective, 1899–1913.* Pittsburgh: University of Pittsburgh Press, 1982.

Sheridan, George J., Jr. "Household and Craft in an Industrializing Economy: The Case of the Silk Weavers of Lyon." In *Consciousness and Class Experience* in *Nineteenth-Century Europe,* edited by John M. Merriman, 107–28. New York: Holmes and Meier, 1979.

Shorter, Edward, and Charles Tilly. *Strikes in France, 1830–1968.* Cambridge: Cambridge University Press, 1974.

Skowronek, Stephen. *Building a New American State.* Cambridge: Cambridge University Press, 1982.

Sombart, Werner. *Why is There No Socialism in the United States?* trans. Patricia M. Hocking and C. T. Husbands, 1906. Reprint edition, White Plains, N.Y.: International Arts and Science Press, 1976.

Stansell, Christine. *City of Women.* Urbana: University of Illinois Press, 1987.

Stearns, Peter N. "Against the Strike Threat: Employer Policy toward Labor Agitation in France, 1900–1914." *Journal of Modern History* 40 (1968): 474–500.

——. *Revolutionary Syndicalism and French Labor: A Cause without Rebels.* New Brunswick: Rutgers University Press, 1971.

——. *Lives of Labor.* New York: Holmes and Meier, 1975.

Stephenson, Charles. "The Process of Community, Class, Culture, and Ethnicity in Nineteenth-Century Newark." In *New Jersey's Ethnic Heritage,* edited by Paul A. Stellhorn. Trenton: New Jersey Historical Commission, 1978.

Stern, Marc. "The Potters of Trenton, New Jersey, 1850–1902: A Study in the Industrialization of Skilled Trades." Ph.D. diss., State University of New York at Stony Brook, 1986.

Stinchcombe, Arthur L. *Information and Organizations.* Berkeley: University of California Press, 1990.

Stone, Katharine. "The Origins of Job Structures in the Steel Industry." *Review of Radical Political Economy* 6 (1974): 115–70.

Stovall, Tyler. *The Rise of the Paris Red Belt.* Berkeley: University of California Press, 1990.

Stromquist, Shelton. "United States of America." In *The Formation of Labour Movements, 1870–1914: An International Perspective,* edited by Marcel Van Der Linden and Jürgen Rojahn, vol. II, 543–78. Leiden, The Netherlands: E. J. Brill, 1990.

Taagepera, Rein, and James Lee Ray. "A Generalized Index of Concentration." *Sociological Methods and Research* 5 (1977): 367–83.

Thane, P. "Social History, 1860–1914." In *The Economic History of Britain since 1700,* edited by Roderick Floud and Donald McCloskey, vol. II, 198–238. Cambridge: Cambridge University Press, 1981.

Thernstrom, Stephan. *The Other Bostonians: Poverty and Progress in the American Metropolis, 1880–1970.* Cambridge: Harvard University Press, 1973.

Tholfsen, Trygve R. *Working-Class Radicalism in Mid-Victorian England.* New York: Columbia University Press, 1977.

Thomis, Malcom I. *The Town Labouror and the Industrial Revolution.* New York: Harper and Row, 1974.

Thompson, Dorothy. *The Chartists.* New York: Pantheon, 1984.

Thompson, Edward P. *The Making of the English Working Class.* New York: Vintage, 1966.

Tilly, Charles. *From Mobilization to Revolution.* Reading, Mass.: Addison-Wesley, 1978.

————. "Solidarity Logics: Conclusions." *Theory and Society* 17 (1988): 451–58.

Tilly, Charles, and Lynn H. Lees. "The People of June, 1848." In *Revolution and Reaction*, edited by Roger Price, 170–209. London: Croom Helm, 1975.

Tilly, Louise. "Paths of Proletarianization: Organization or Production, Sexual Division of Labor, and Women's Collective Action." *Signs* 7, no. 2 (1981): 400–417.

Tilly, Louise A., and Joan W. Scott. *Women, Work, and Family*. New York: Methuen, 1987.

Tomlins, Christopher L. *The State and the Unions*. Cambridge: Cambridge University Press, 1985.

Tranter, N. L. "The Labour Supply, 1780–1860." In *The Economic History of Britain since 1700*, edited by Roderick Floud and Donald McCloskey, vol. I, 204–26. Cambridge: Cambridge University Press, 1981.

Troy, Leo. *Organized Labor in New Jersey*. Princeton: Van Nostrand, 1965.

Tuma, Nancy B., and Michael T. Hannan. *Social Dynamics: Models and Methods*. Orlando: Academic Press, 1984.

Turbin, Carole. "Beyond Conventional Wisdom: Women's Wage Work, Household Economic Contribution, and Labor Activism in a Mid-Nineteenth Century Working-Class Community." In *To Toil the Livelong Day*, edited by Carol Groneman and Mary Beth Norton, 47–67. Ithaca: Cornell University Press, 1987.

Turk, Jessie Rose. "Trenton, New Jersey, in the Nineteenth Century: The Significance of Location in the Historical Geography of a City." Ph.D. diss., Columbia University, 1964.

Tyrrell, Ian. "American Exceptionalism in an Age of International History." *American Historical Review* 96 (1991): 1031–55.

Ulman, Lloyd. *The Rise of the National Trade Union*. Cambridge: Harvard University Press, 1955.

Vecoli, Rudolph J. *The People of New Jersey*. Princeton: Van Nostrand, 1965.

Voss, Kim. "Working-Class Formation and the Knights of Labor." Ph.D. diss., Stanford University, 1986.

————. "Labor Organization and Class Alliance: Industries, Communities, and the Knights of Labor." *Theory and Society* 17 (1988): 329–64.

Walkowitz, Daniel J. *Worker City, Company Town: Iron and Cotton-Worker Protest in Troy and Cohoes, New York*. Urbana: University of Illinois Press, 1978.

————. *Worker City, Company Town*. Urbana: University of Illinois Press, 1981.

Ware, Norman J. *The Labor Movement in the United States, 1860–1895: A Study in Democracy*. New York: D. Appleton and Company, 1929.

Warner, Sam Bass. *Streetcar Suburbs: The Process of Growth in Boston, 1870–1900*. 2d ed. Cambridge: Harvard University Press, 1978.

Weber, Eugen Joseph. *Peasants into Frenchmen*. Stanford, Calif.: Stanford University Press, 1976.

Weibe, Robert H. *The Search for Order, 1877–1920*. New York: Hill and Wang, 1967.

Whipp, Richard. "The Stamp of Futility: The Staffordshire Potters, 1880–1905." In *Divisions of Labour*, edited by Royden Harrison and Jonathan Zeitlin, 87–113. Brighton, Eng.: Harvester Press, 1985.

Wilentz, Sean. "Artisan Republican Festivals and the Rise of Class Conflict in New York City, 1788–1837." In *Working-Class America*, edited by Michael Frisch and Daniel J. Walkowitz. Urbana: University of Illinois Press, 1983.

———. "Against Exceptionalism: Class Consciousness and the American Labor Movement, 1790–1920." *International Labor and Working Class History* 26 (1984): 1–24.

———. *Chants Democratic: New York City and the Rise of the American Working Class, 1788–1850*. New York: Oxford University Press, 1984.

———. "Society, Politics, and the Market Revolution, 1815–1848." In *The New American History*, edited by Eric Foner. Philadelphia: Temple University Press, 1990.

Williams, Raymond. *Keywords*. New York: Oxford University Press, 1983.

Williamson, Jeffrey G., and Peter H. Lindert. *American Inequality: A Macroeconomic History*. New York: Academic Press, 1980.

Wood, Gordon. *The Creation of the American Republic: 1776–1787*. New York: Norton, 1972.

Wright, Carroll D. "An Historical Sketch of the Knights of Labor." *The Quarterly Journal of Economics* 1 (1887): 137–68.

Wright, D. G. *Popular Radicalism: The Working-Class Experience, 1780–1880*. London: Longman, 1988.

Yellowitz, Irwin. *Industrialization and the American Labor Movement, 1850–1900*. Port Washington, N.Y.: Kennikat Press, 1977.

Young, Alfred F., ed. *The American Revolution: Explorations in the History of American Radicalism*. DeKalb: Northern Illinois University Press, 1976.

Young, James D. *Socialism and the English Working Class: A History of English Labour, 1883–1939*. New York: Harvester Wheatsheaf, 1989.

Zald, Mayer N., and Roberta Ash. "Social Movement Organizations: Growth, Decay, and Change." In *Studies in Social Movements: A Social Psychological Perspective*, edited by Barry McLaughlin. New York: The Free Press, 1969.

Zeitlin, Jonathan. "Engineers and Compositors: A Comparison." In *Divisions of Labour*, edited by Royden Harrison and Jonathan Zeitlin, 185–250. Brighton, Eng.: Harvester Press, 1985.

———. "From Labor History to the History of Industrial Relations." *Economic History Review* 40, no. 2, 2d ser. (1987): 159–84.

Zembala, Dennis. "Glassworkers in the Knights of Labor: Technology, Labor, and the Roots of Modernism." Paper presented at the Knights of Labor Centennial Symposium, Chicago, May 17–19, 1979.

Zolberg, Aristide R. "How Many Exceptionalisms?" In *Working-Class Formation: Nineteenth-Century Patterns in Western Europe and the United States*, edited by Ira Katznelson and Aristide R. Zolberg, 397–455. Princeton: Princeton University Press, 1986.

Zunz, Olivier. *The Changing Face of Inequality: Urbanization, Industrial Development and Immigrants in Detroit, 1880–1920*. Chicago: University of Chicago Press, 1982.

Index

AFL. *See* American Federation of Labor

Agriculture, cross-national comparisons of, 50–51, 68

American economy, 53–54

American exceptionalism, 1, 45, 231, 235; challenged, 17, 235; political institutions and, 245–49

American Federation of Labor (AFL), 2, 13, 75, 79, 241–42; Knights' relationship to, 187, 239

American labor movement: discriminatory practices in, 82; "the great upheaval" in, 77–79; history of, 22, 72–74. *See also* Knights of Labor

American state: labor movement and, 225, 226, 245–49; political institutions of, 115, 116–17, 121–23, 248. *See also* Legal system

Analytical methods. *See* Research methods

Anticapitalism, 32, 44

Anti-employer views, 210–12

Antitrust legislation, 119

Anti-union sentiment, 30–31, 133. *See also* Employer countermobilization

Artisans. *See* Journeymen artisans; Master artisans; Radical artisans

Artisan system, changes in, 27–28

Aveling, Edward, 87

Aveling, Eleanor Marx, 87, 90

Black workers, 81

"Bloc recruitment" practices, 76

Board of Trade, Newark, 211

Bourse du Travail, 95–96

Boycotts, 127, 171

Britain. *See* England

Brody, David, 122

Brown, E. H. Phelps, 68

Browne, Margaret, 68

Capitalism, 218, 232, 235. *See also* National economies; National markets

Capitalist ideology, 86–87, 115, 118–19; anti-union sentiment, 30–31, 133. *See also* Republican ideology

Capital-to-labor ratio, 151; effect of, on organizing broad-based union locals, 179; effect of, on organizing less-skilled workers, 156t, 200t; effect of, on survival rate of union locals, 192t, 200t

Carpenters' strike of 1833, 29

Central Labor Club, 213

Ceremony, Knights' initiation, 87

CGT (*Confédération Générale du Travail*), 96–100, 234

Champion, H. H., 90

Cherrington, W. P., 88

Chevalerie du Travail Française, 99

Child labor, 113, 114; laws against, 117, 125–26

283